Confiscation Law Handbook

Confiscation Law Handbook

Ruth Barber

Solicitor Advocate and Director of Frisby & Co Solicitors

Adrian Eissa

Barrister at Garden Court Chambers

Bloomsbury Professional

Bloomsbury Professional Ltd, Maxwelton House, 41–43 Boltro Road, Haywards Heath, West Sussex, RH16 1BJ

ISBN: 978 1 84766 707 6

Typeset by Kerrypress Ltd, Luton, Beds
Printed and bound in Great Britain by Hobbs the Printers Ltd, Totton, Hampshire

Preface

The idea for this handbook was conceived during our efforts as busy practitioners to grasp a quick understanding of confiscation law and its constant developments.

This book is written for those practitioners dealing with confiscation law for the first time, experienced criminal practitioners struggling to keep up with the plethora of case law on the subject, and experienced confiscation practitioners who simply want an aide memoir available at court.

It does not attempt an academic analysis of the law, nor attempt to cover every conceivable aspect of the subject. This volume aims to complement, not substitute other detailed textbooks available.

We have written a book that we want to use: straightforward and clearly indexed. We hope you find it useful. We are nonetheless grateful for any feedback that might improve subsequent editions.

Ruth Barber

Adrian Eissa

August 2011

Foreword

Confiscation law continually evolves. One only has to look at the daily law reports and the number of proceeds of crime related matters reaching the higher courts to appreciate how these cases mould and shape the bedrock of existing legislation which defines this area of the law. That becomes the value of a book such as this. It gives to the reader an instant source of reference in this often complicated field of practice. It fills a hole on the bookshelf by providing the type of introductory guide that many of us who have practised full-time in this area would have wished for when we began our careers.

This book's publication comes at an interesting time. The confiscation scheme is currently subject to the restraints of a challenging economic climate. Legal aid and LSC funding in the UK have suffered a sustained attack, inhibiting many defence practitioners from being able to prepare properly for confiscation and forfeiture related hearings. Conversely, there is more than anecdotal evidence that those responsible for the prosecution and enforcement of restraint and confiscation cases are affording this area fewer resources, with lawyers within government departments often compromising on the quality of the arguments they advance, in the name of austerity.

Of course, any perceived failings in the system should not lead to despondency nor detract from the importance of getting this area of the law right. In time, new legislation will be introduced and recovery of the proceeds of crime will return to the centre stage. That is because confiscation law matters. The general public do not want to see their neighbours or associates 'getting away with it'. The delicious irony is that, when run properly, this area of the law should pay for itself; not only stripping wrongdoers of their ill-gotten gains, but ensuring that monies recovered are re-invested back into central funds for the benefit of society as a whole.

Ruth Barber and Adrian Eissa, both practitioners of considerable experience, are to be congratulated on drawing together in one concise volume the essential elements of asset recovery. Clear and practical, this book will be a valuable resource to judges, barristers, solicitors, legal executives, financial investigators and the like.

Mark Sutherland Williams

3 Paper Buildings,
Temple
August 2011

Contents

Contents

Contents

Table of statutes

Table of statutory instruments

Table of cases

Chapter 1   A brief history and overview of confiscation law

'… when he thus sins and becomes guilty, he must return what he has stolen or taken by extortion … he must make restitution in full, add a fifth of the value to it and give it all to the owner on the day he presents his guilty offering.'
Lev 5:17

Contents summary

History of confiscation law – legislation – the confiscation objective – civil proceedings – international proceedings – restraint – POCA procedure – the assumptions – pecuniary advantage – apportionment – recoverable amount – tainted gifts – time to pay – appeals – funding – compensation – defendants who abscond – variation of the order – case law – the future

History of confiscation law

1.1   The notion of restitution is as old as written history, as the above example from Leviticus illustrates. Curious then that confiscation as a form of restitution was only first established in English law in 1987 with the introduction of the Drug Trafficking Offences Act 1986. Prior to this Act, the only avenue of restitution available to the criminal courts was forfeiture, and then only for those offences where the power was specifically prescribed.

1.2   The limits of forfeiture were established in 1980[1] when the House of Lords ruled that the power of forfeiture was limited to the physical items used to commit the offence and could not be extended to include the defendant's unlawfully gained profit.

1.3   The profits available from drug trafficking were such that for some criminals, custody simply became a professional hazard. Since the law allowed them to retain their unlawfully gained profits, upon release they could abandon the perils of a criminal lifestyle and simply enjoy the proceeds. This position was clearly unsustainable.

Legislation

1.4   Parliament enacted the Drug Trafficking Offences Act 1986 on 10 January 1987. This legislation was found to be inadequate as it only allowed for the

---

[1]   *R v Cuthbertson* [1980] 2 All ER 401.

confiscation of the proceeds of drug trafficking. The Criminal Justice Act 1988 swiftly followed which allowed the courts to confiscate the proceeds of any indictable offence.

1.5   The Criminal Justice (International Co-operation) Act 1990 allowed prosecutors to apply to the court to amend confiscation orders where hidden assets were discovered. The Drug Trafficking Act 1994 consolidated the two former Acts.

1.6   Yet by 1998 the legislation remained ineffective. A report commissioned by the Cabinet Office[2] found that less than 20% of drug trafficking convictions, and an even smaller percentage of other convictions, resulted in confiscation orders. Worse, of the orders made, less than 50% were realised annually.

1.7   On 24 March 2003 the Proceeds of Crime Act (POCA) 2002 came into force. This Act is intended to establish a comprehensive framework for confiscation proceedings. The Criminal Justice Act 1988 and the Drug Trafficking Act 1994 apply to all offences committed before 24 March 2003 or which overlap that date.

The confiscation objective

1.8   The use of the word 'confiscation' tends to imply a simple taking back of property or proceeds unlawfully gained. Unfortunately the legislation is not so simple: it aims to recover the value of the defendant's unlawful proceeds, defined as the 'defendant's benefit'. The statutory provisions governing the calculation of the defendant's benefit are highly complex, and are continually being defined by a plethora of case law. As such the defendant's benefit often bears little relation to the actual profit obtained.

1.9   A confiscation order will be made in the sum of the benefit figure unless the defendant can prove, on a balance of probabilities, that his realisable assets are less. In practice it is extremely difficult for a convicted criminal, in the absence of independent corroboration, to provide convincing testimony. Often a defendant's best route to reduce the order is to mount a legal or expert challenge to the basis of the calculation of the benefit figure. In cases of complexity a forensic accountant may assist in that regard.

1.10   Whilst confiscation proceedings usually follow a criminal conviction (although there is power to obtain civil recovery in the absence of conviction) the procedure is a criminal and civil hybrid. In particular, both prosecution and defence discharge their burden of proof on the balance of probabilities and a contested hearing is determined by a judge alone.

1.11   The effect is draconian. However since the order is not regarded as a penalty, the safeguards surrounding the trial process do not apply.

---

[2]   'Recovering the Proceeds of Crime' (PIU, June 2000).

1.12   The Crown Court must proceed with a POCA confiscation hearing if a defendant is convicted of an acquisitive crime, and either the prosecutor has asked the court to proceed[3] or the court believes it is appropriate to do so.[4]

Civil proceedings

1.13   POCA[5] permits civil recovery proceedings to be brought via the civil courts even when no criminal proceedings have commenced or where the defendant has been acquitted. In such proceedings, the court need only find on a balance of probabilities that any matters alleged to constitute unlawful conduct have occurred, or that any person intended to use any cash in unlawful conduct.[6]

International proceedings

1.14   High value crime frequently involves activity overseas. The jurisdictional scope of the Acts is, therefore, not limited to assets within the UK. The Acts contain reciprocal arrangements to allow for both the UK assets of persons prosecuted overseas and the overseas assets of UK defendants to be restrained. Any overseas assets held by a UK defendant can be used to satisfy a confiscation order.

Restraint

1.15   Under POCA, a restraint order may be sought and made as soon as a criminal investigation is commenced in England and Wales. The purpose of the restraint order is to preserve assets to satisfy a potential confiscation order that might otherwise be dissipated.

1.16   There are five conditions for obtaining restraint orders under POCA and satisfaction of any one of them will allow a restraint order to be made. Each of the five conditions requires the prosecutor to prove that the defendant has benefited from his criminal conduct. The conditions are as follows:

1   A criminal investigation has been started.

2   Criminal proceedings have commenced and not concluded.

3   An application by the prosecutor has been made to reconsider a case in the light of fresh evidence where no confiscation order was made.

4   An application by the prosecutor has been made to make a new calculation of the benefit figure based on fresh evidence.

---

[3]   The prosecutor has a discretion to instigate proceedings. Guidance on the exercise of the discretion was issued to the CPS in May 2009.
[4]   POCA, s 6(1).
[5]   POCA, s 240(2).
[6]   POCA, s 241(3).

5   An application by the prosecutor (or an enforcement receiver) has been made to increase a confiscation order when it appears that the value of defendant's assets exceeds that found to be available at the time the confiscation order was made.

1.17   Restraint orders can be applied to any person or body holding assets in which the defendant has an interest.

1.18   A restraint order may be varied to allow for reasonable living expenses, and to make provision for a person to carry on a trade, business, profession or occupation. Whilst there is provision for reasonable legal expenses, they cannot be legal expenses incurred in relation to the offences in relation to which the restraint order has been sought.

1.19   Whilst the prosecutor will have information about the defendant's assets, it is not uncommon upon making the request for a restraint order to include a provision requiring the defendant to disclose the full extent of his realisable property. This is called a disclosure order.

1.20   In order to manage, control and preserve the value of the defendant's restrained assets there is power for the court to appoint a management receiver.

1.21   Failing to comply with orders made by the court in relation to restraint, receivership or disclosure is treated as contempt.

POCA procedure

1.22   The standard steps of the POCA confiscation procedure are as follows:

1   Conviction.

2   Request by the prosecutor for confiscation proceedings.[7]

3   Defendant required to disclose details of assets.[8]

4   Prosecutor provides statement of information.[9]

5   Defendant required to respond to the prosecutor's statement.[10]

6   Value of the order to be made agreed between the parties, or case set down for hearing and value of the order determined by the court at the conclusion of the hearing.

The assumptions

1.23   POCA proceedings are unlike the criminal trial that usually precedes them. During the trial it is for the prosecution to prove the defendant's guilt beyond

---

[7]   POCA, s 6.
[8]   POCA, s 18.
[9]   POCA, s 16.
[10]   POCA, s 17.

reasonable doubt. Any burden borne by the defendant is on the balance of probabilities. Post-conviction each side bears the burden of proof only on the balance of probabilities. The prosecution is required to prove the benefit and value of the defendant's proceeds from criminal conduct.

1.24 If the defendant has a criminal lifestyle the court must make four assumptions.[11] A criminal lifestyle is identified if the specific offence is listed in Sch 2 to the Act, if it constitutes conduct forming part of a course of criminal activity or if it is an offence committed over a period of at least six months and the defendant has benefited from the conduct.[12] The assumptions are summarised as:

1   that any property transferred to the defendant at any time after the relevant day was obtained as a result of his general criminal conduct and at the earliest time he appears to have held it;

2   that any property held by the defendant at any time after the date of conviction was obtained by him as a result of his general criminal conduct and at the earliest time he appears to have held it;

3   that any expenditure incurred by the defendant at any time after the relevant day was met from property obtained by him as a result of his general criminal conduct;

4   for the purpose of valuing any property obtained (or assumed to have been obtained) by the defendant, he obtained it free from any other interest in it.

1.25 The 'relevant day' is the first day in the period of six years ending with:

1   the day when proceedings in the offence concerned were started against the defendant; or

2   if there are two or more offences and proceedings for them were started on different days, the earliest of those days.

1.26 Once the assumptions have been applied the burden is on the defendant to rebut the assumptions on the balance of probabilities. Having been convicted, usually of offences involving dishonesty or otherwise disreputable conduct, this may be a difficult burden to discharge. 'The fact that his credibility may already have been badly damaged is not a shield behind which he can hide.'[13] Giving evidence opens the defendant up to cross examination. In an effort to discharge the burden by giving evidence the defendant is at risk of worsening his position. The defendant wishing to succeed in showing the assumptions are incorrect must produce clear and cogent evidence. Vague and generalised assertions unsupported by evidence would rarely, if ever, be sufficient to discharge the burden on the defendant.[14]

---

11   POCA s 10.
12   POCA, s 75.
13   *R v Siddique* [2005] EWCA Crim 1812 at [27] per Bennett J.
14   *R v Walbrook and Glasgow* [1994] Crim LR 613.

1.27   The court must apply the assumptions except to the extent that they are shown to be incorrect in the defendant's case or where there would be a serious risk of injustice if the assumptions were made.[15]

Pecuniary advantage

1.28   In some offences, the defendant does not obtain the property as a result of the offence, but rather as a pecuniary advantage. This is particularly the case in tax or VAT evasion cases. The defendant is liable to have a confiscation order made against him in the amount of the pecuniary advantage.[16] In this regard s 76(5) provides that 'if a person obtains a pecuniary advantage as a result of or in connection with conduct, he is to be taken to obtain as a result of or in connection with the conduct a sum of money equal to the value of the pecuniary advantage'. The words 'taken to obtain' do not create a mere rebuttable presumption; the section is mandatory in its application.[17]

Apportionment

1.29   The basic principle is that each of the participants in a joint criminal enterprise is liable to obtain a benefit order for the value of the whole enterprise. The benefit is not apportioned between the participants.[18] In deciding whether or not to apportion the benefit figure the court will have regard to the respective roles of the defendants.[19] In appropriate cases where the role of the respective defendants is not clear the judge may equally apportion the benefit figure between the accused.[20]

Recoverable amount

1.30   The amount ultimately recoverable from the defendant is an amount equal to the defendant's benefit from the criminal conduct, unless the defendant shows that the available amount is less.[21]

1.31   The amount recoverable[22] is the total value of all the free property held by the defendant minus the total amount payable in pursuance of obligations in relation to that property[23] and the total of all tainted gifts.

---

[15]   POCA, s 10(6).
[16]   POCA, s 76(5) and (6) and *R v Dimsey and Allen* 2000 1 Cr App R (S) 497.
[17]   *R v Takkar* [2011] EWCA Crim 646.
[18]   *R v May* [2008] UKHL 28.
[19]   *R v Sivaraman* [2008] EWCA Crim 1736.
[20]   *R v Gibbons* [2003] 2 Cr App R (S) 169, CA.
[21]   POCA, s 7.
[22]   POCA, s 9(1).
[23]   Priority obligations are fines made by the court on conviction, or sums which would be included amongst preferential debts if the defendant's bankruptcy commenced on the date the confiscation order. See POCA, s 9(2).

1.32 It is for the defendant to show, on the balance of probabilities that the value of his realisable assets is less than the amount of his benefit.[24]

Hidden assets

1.33 The confiscation order need not be limited to the amount which the prosecution can prove to be the value of the defendant's assets. The court can conclude that the defendant has hidden assets. Once the prosecution has established the existence of benefit, there is no requirement that the Crown establish a prima facie case in relation to realisable hidden assets; the burden shifts to the defendant to establish, if he can, his realisable assets to the satisfaction of the court.[25]

Tainted gifts

1.34 If the defendant transfers property to another person for consideration, his value is significantly less than the value of the property at the time the transfer is to be treated as making gift. Such gifts are known as tainted gifts, and regarded as simply an attempt to disperse assets by placing them in the names of other people. The gift is tainted if it is made by the defendant to any person during the period beginning six years before the commencement of proceedings or made by the defendant at any time and the gift was from the proceeds of crime.[26]

Time to pay

1.35 The amount of the order is liable to be paid immediately[27] and the court should allow the defendant time to pay. This time must not exceed six months. The defendant can apply to the court within this period for the time to pay to be extended and court will do so if there are exceptional circumstances.[28]

1.36 If the order is not paid, the defendant must serve a period of imprisonment in default. Serving the sentence, however, does not extinguish the debt.[29]

Appeals

1.37 A defendant may appeal against a confiscation order to the Court of Appeal (Criminal Division) where there is a basis for a legal challenge to the court's decision in relation to the order.

1.38 An application to vary the order can be made to the court when the assets, when realised, raise a lesser amount than anticipated.

---

[24] *R v Comiskey* [1991] 93 Cr App R 227.
[25] *R v Barnham* [2005] EWCA Crim 1049.
[26] POCA, s 77(2) and (3).
[27] POCA, s 11(1).
[28] POCA, s 11(4).
[29] POCA, s 38(5).

1.39   Confiscation orders are enforced as though they are fines. The business of enforcing the order is therefore undertaken in the magistrates' court, and it is the magistrates' court that has the power to activate the default sentence imposed by the Crown Court if the order is not paid.

1.40   After a confiscation order has been made, the only further role of the Crown Court is to consider applications for the appointment of enforcement receivers.

1.41   It is in the defendant's interest to voluntarily satisfy the order; however, if the defendant is unwilling or unable to do so the Crown Court may appoint an enforcement receiver.[30] The role of the enforcement receiver is to realise the assets to discharge the confiscation order. The court can appoint a receiver if the order is not satisfied and is not subject to appeal. The court is not bound to appoint a receiver; the effect of appointing a receiver is that the defendant's assets would defray the fees and disbursements of the receiver. The receiver's costs typically make a large dent in the funds available to discharge the order; therefore the courts generally consider the appointment of receiver as a last resort.[31]

Funding

1.42   The scope for a defendant to fund private legal representation in confiscation proceedings is very limited. A restraint order may be subject to an exception to allow for reasonable legal expenses;[32] however, such an exception must not include any legal expenses that relate to an offence where the defendant has benefited from his criminal conduct or the recipient of a tainted gift.[33] In effect in criminal proceedings, restrained assets may not be released for the purposes of funding the defence.

1.43   If the defendant has been in receipt of public funding for the substantive criminal proceedings, funding will continue for the confiscation proceedings, albeit still subject to the normal criteria for scope, merit and means. Since the vast majority of defendants subject to confiscation proceedings are in custody, the availability of public funding is rarely problematic, and since the scope for funding the proceedings from private means is so limited it is in the interests of justice that public funding be made available.

1.44   Whilst the court can make money for ordinary living expenses available from restrained assets, this money cannot be used to defray legal expenses.[34]

Compensation

1.45   Compensation is available for an acquitted defendant under POCA; however, the amount that the Crown Court will order to be paid is simply the amount the court

---

[30]   POCA, s 50.
[31]   *Re HN* [2005] EWHC Admin 2982.
[32]   POCA, s 41(3).
[33]   POCA, s 41(5).
[34]   *Michael Joseph McInerney v Financial Services Authority* [2009] EWCA Crim 997.

believes to be just. The defendant must show loss in consequence of something done in relation to the property by or in pursuance of an order under POCA.

Defendants who abscond

1.46 Confiscation orders can be made against defendants who abscond either pre[35] or post[36] conviction. Appropriate safeguards are incorporated into the legislation to prevent unfairness to the defendant or any affected third parties. The discretion to proceed in the absence of a defendant should never be exercised where the actions of the state have caused the absence of the defendant.[37]

Variation of the order

1.47 Where the defendant's circumstances change after the order has been made there is power to amend the order to:

(a)   impose an order when one was not previously made;[38]

(b)   consider benefit;[39]

(c)   increase the benefit figure;[40]

(d)   increase the available amount;[41]

(e)   decrease the available amount; or[42]

(f)   discharge the order.[43]

Case law

1.48 Despite the courts constantly referring defendants back to the wording of the statute and urging them to resist reliance on judicial exegesis,[44] this topic has spawned a plethora of, sometimes contradictory, case law. It is therefore wise to check the latest position prior to finalising an argument.

The future

1.49 Confiscation is one of the few criminal justice policies which is almost universally popular amongst everyone apart from those who find themselves subject

---

[35] POCA, s 28.

[36] POCA, s 27.

[37] *R v Gavin* [2010] EWCA Crim 2727 in which the defendant was deported against his will and confiscation proceedings conducted in his absence

[38] POCA, s 19(1).

[39] POCA, s 20.

[40] POCA, s 21.

[41] POCA, s 22.

[42] POCA, s 23.

[43] POCA, s 30.

[44] *R v May* [2008] UKHL 28 at [48].

to its provisions. Less well-known is that the money recovered goes to the Treasury and is used, at least in part, to fund crime fighting initiatives. Many of the agencies recovering the money have targets to reach and the attrition rate between the amount of money assessed as benefit by financial investigators as against the amount of money recovered is 95%.[45] Expect further legislative efforts to streamline the system, which may further erode the opportunities for defendants to contest and challenge orders.

---

[45] See http://www.homeoffice.gov.uk/publications/science-research-statistics/research-statistics/crime-research/horr17/horr17-report?view=Binary

Chapter 2   Basic principles of confiscation law

'Life is not fair. Get used to it.'
Bill Gates

Contents Summary

Breakdown of POCA 2002, ss 6–14 of POCA 2002 – the making of the order – the recoverable amount – the defendant's benefit – the available amount – assumptions to be made in case of a criminal lifestyle – time for payment – interest – effect on sentencing – postponement of proceedings

---

The basic provisions

Section	Title	Provision
6	The making of the order	Sets out the steps that must be taken for the order to be made.
7	The recoverable amount	The amount that the defendant will be ordered to pay.
8	Defendant's benefit	What constitutes benefit.
9	The available amount	Those assets that can be considered by the court as recoverable – some obligations have priority over a confiscation order.
10	Assumptions to be made in case of a criminal lifestyle	These are assumptions that will made by the court about the defendant's assets and transactions in the event he is found to have a criminal lifestyle. The assumptions are potentially rebuttable by the defendant.
11	Time for payment	Payment is due upon the making of the order but can be deferred in certain circumstances.
12	Interest on unpaid sums	Interest is due on sums unpaid when the order is due for payment.
13	Effect on the court's other powers	The court must deal with confiscation before imposing a fine or certain other orders involving the defendant's assets.

| 14 | **Postponement of proceedings** | Proceedings may be postponed for up to 2 years. If there are 'exceptional circumstances' this period may be extended. |

What are the requirements for a confiscation order to be made?

2.1 POCA 2002, s 6 can be broken down into the following elements:

1 A mandatory requirement for the Crown Court to proceed if the elements are satisfied.

2 Proceedings must be in the Crown Court, either as a result of conviction, sentence or committal to the Crown Court for the purpose of confiscation proceedings.

3 The prosecutor must ask the Court to proceed, or the court can proceed of its own motion.

4 The court must decide whether the defendant has a **criminal lifestyle**, and if so whether he has **benefited** from his **general criminal conduct**. If he does not have a criminal lifestyle the court must decide whether he has **benefited** from his **particular criminal conduct**.

5 If the court decides that the defendant has **benefited** from either his general or particular criminal conduct it must decide the **recoverable amount** and make an order requiring him to pay that amount.

6 If the victim of the conduct intends to start proceedings against the defendant in respect of loss, injury or damage sustained in connection with the conduct, 5 above is not a duty but a power of the court.

7 The court decides the defendant's **benefit** and whether he has a **criminal lifestyle** on the balance of probabilities.

8 An order cannot be made if the defendant absconds.[1]

(*The words in bold are defined below.*)

Criminal lifestyle

2.2 'Criminal lifestyle' is defined in POCA, s 75.

The defendant has a criminal lifestyle if the relevant offence(s) is:

(a) specified in Sch 2 to POCA ('lifestyle' offences);

(b) part of a course of criminal activity; or

---

[1] Except in accordance with the powers granted under POCA, ss 27 and 28.

(c)   committed over a period of at least six months and the defendant has benefited from the conduct which constitutes the offence.

BUT – in order to be found to have a criminal lifestyle through either (b) or (c), the defendant must have obtained a relevant benefit of at least £5,000.

The defendant's benefit

2.3   Under POCA s 8, if the court is proceeding under s 6 this section applies for the purpose of:

(a)   deciding whether the defendant has **benefited** from **conduct**; and

(b)   deciding his **benefit** from the **conduct**.

The court must:

(a)   take account of **conduct** occurring up to the time it makes its decision;

(b)   take account of **property obtained** up to that time.

Relevant benefit

2.4   There are two definitions of **relevant benefit** under s 75(5) and s 75(6). These depend on whether the offence constitutes conduct forming a **course of criminal activity** or whether the offence has been committed over a period of at least six months.

2.5   If the offence constitutes **conduct** forming a **course of criminal activity** then relevant benefit is:

(a)   benefit from **conduct** which constitutes the offence;

(b)   benefit from any other **conduct** which forms part of course of criminal activity and which constitutes an offence of which the defendant has been convicted;

(c)   benefit from **conduct** which constitutes an offence which has or will be taken into consideration by the court in sentencing a defendant for an offence in (a) or (b).

2.6   If the offence has been committed over a period of a least six months and the defendant has benefited from conduct which constitutes the offence then relevant benefit is:

(a)   benefit from conduct which constitutes the offence; or

(b)   benefit from conduct which constitutes an offence which has been or will be taken into account by the court in sentencing the defendant for the offence mentioned in (a).

Criminal conduct

2.7   Criminal conduct is defined in POCA, s 76(1) as:

'Conduct which constitutes an offence in England and Wales or would constitute such an offence if it occurred in England and Wales'

When does a person benefit from criminal conduct?

2.8   Under POCA s 76(4), a person benefits from conduct if he obtains property as a result of or in connection with the conduct.

Pecuniary advantage and conduct

2.9   POCA, s 76(5), (6) provide that if a person obtains a **pecuniary advantage** as a result of or in connection with the conduct, he is to be taken to **obtain** as a result of or in connection with the conduct a sum of money equal to the value of the **pecuniary advantage**.

References to property or a **pecuniary advantage obtained** in connection with conduct include references to property or a **pecuniary advantage obtained** both in that connection and some other.

Pecuniary advantage

2.10   Pecuniary advantage is the evasion of a debt that the defendant would otherwise be liable to pay, typically evasion of excise duty or underpayment of income tax.[2]

Value of the benefit

2.11   POCA, s 76(7) provides that if a person benefits from conduct his benefit is the value of the property obtained. Under POCA, s 84(2)(b), property is obtained by a person if he obtains an interest in it, and its value is defined by ss 79 and 80.

The material time for valuing property is the time when the court makes its decision.

Value of property obtained from criminal conduct

2.12   Under POCA, s 80(2), the value of the property at the material time is the greater of the following:

(a)   the value of the property (at the time the person obtained it), adjusted to take account of later changes in the value of money;

(b)   the value (at the material time) of the property found under s 80(3).

---

[2]   *R v Dimsey and Allen* [2000] 1 Cr App R (S) 497: deferring payment of tax is a 'pecuniary advantage'.

Value of the property obtained by the defendant

2.13   POCA, s 80(3) provides that:

'(a)   if the person holds the property obtained, the property found under this subsection is that property;

(b)   if he holds no part of the property obtained, the property found under this subsection is any property which directly or indirectly represents it in his hands;

(c)   if he holds part of the property given, the property found under this subsection is that part and any property which directly or indirectly represents the other part in his hands.'

General criminal conduct

2.14   Under POCA, s 76(2), general criminal conduct of the defendant is all his criminal conduct, and it is immaterial:

(a)   whether conduct occurred before or after the passing of POCA;

(b)   whether property constituting a benefit from conduct was obtained before or after the passing of POCA.

General criminal conduct is inclusive of particular criminal conduct.

Particular criminal conduct

2.15   Under POCA, s 76(3), particular criminal conduct is conduct which:

(a)   constitutes the offence or offences concerned;

(b)   constitutes offences of which he was convicted in the same proceedings as those in which he was convicted of the offences(s) concerned;

(c)   conduct which constitutes offences which the court will be taking into consideration in deciding his sentence for the offence or offences concerned.

When does conduct form a part of a course of criminal activity?

2.16   POCA, s 75(3) provides that:

'Conduct forms part of a course of criminal activity if the defendant has benefited from the conduct and—

(a)   in the proceedings in which he was convicted, he was convicted of three or more other offences, each of three or more of them constituting conduct from which he has benefited, or

(b)   in the period of six years ending with the day the proceedings were

15

started, (or if there is more than one such day, the earliest day) he was convicted on two separate occasions of an offence constituting conduct from which he has benefited.'

Offences committed before 24 March 2003

2.17

- Conduct will not form part of a course of criminal activity where any of the three trigger offences under POCA, s 75(3)(a) was committed before 24 March 2003.[3]

- The court must not take into account benefit from any offence being taken into consideration under s 75(5)(c) committed before 24 March 2003 as conduct forming part of his criminal activity when assessing whether the defendant has a criminal lifestyle.

- Conduct shall form part of a course of criminal activity under s 75(3)(b) if the two trigger offences were committed before 24 March 2003. Equally benefit from those offences can be taken into account in determining whether the defendant has a criminal lifestyle.

- Where criminal lifestyle is being considered as a result of an offence committed over a period of at least six months, benefit from offences being taken into consideration committed before 24 March 2003 under s 75(6)(b) must not be taken into account.

The assumptions

2.18   When the defendant has a **criminal lifestyle**, POCA, s 10 provides that the court must make four assumptions for the purpose of deciding whether he has benefited from his **general criminal conduct** and deciding his **benefit** from the conduct. Although the assumptions are mandatory the court must not make the assumptions if they are shown to be incorrect or there would be a serious risk of injustice if the assumption were made.[4] The defendant, if he is able to do so, can rebut these assumptions on the balance of probabilities.

2.19   There are four assumptions:

1   That any property transferred to the defendant at any time after the **relevant day**[5] was obtained by him:

   (a)   as a result of his general criminal conduct;

   (b)   at the earliest time he appears to have held it.

---

3   See Proceeds of Crime Act 2002 (Commencement No 5) (Amendment of Transitional Provisions) Order 2003, SI 2003/531; *CPS v Moulden* [2009] 2 All ER 912.
4   POCA, s 10(6).
5   Defined at 2.26 below.

2   That any property held by the defendant at any time after the **date of conviction**[6] was obtained by him:

(a)   as a result of his general criminal conduct;

(b)   at the earliest time he appears to have held it.

3   That any expenditure incurred by the defendant at any time after the relevant day was met from property obtained by him as a result of his general criminal conduct.

4   For the purpose of valuing any property obtained (or assumed to have been obtained) by the defendant, he obtained it free from any other interest in it.

Date of conviction

2.20   The date of conviction is either the date on which the defendant was convicted of the offence concerned, or if there are two or more offences and the convictions were on different dates, the date of the latest.

What is the recoverable amount?

2.21   Under POCA, s 7, the basic principle is that the recoverable amount is an amount equal to the defendant's benefit.

It is for the defendant to show on the balance of probabilities[7] that the available amount is less than the benefit.

If the amount available is nil, an order will be made in a nominal amount, usually £1.

What is the available amount?

2.22   The available amount as defined in POCA, s 9 is the value of all the defendant's free property minus the total amount payable in pursuance of obligations which then have priority plus the value of any **tainted gifts** made.

Priority obligations

2.23   Obligations which take priority are:

●   a fine or other order made by the court at any time before the confiscation order is made;

●   a sum which would be included amongst the preferential debts if the defendant's bankruptcy had commenced on the date of the confiscation order, or his winding up had been ordered on that date.

---

6   POCA, s 10(10).
7   *R v Cominskey* [1991] 93 Cr App R 227.

Tainted gifts

2.24 Tainted gifts are suspicious disposals of the defendant's assets.

The issue of whether a gift is tainted can only be considered if the court has decided that the defendant has a criminal lifestyle, or no decision has been made as to whether the defendant has a criminal lifestyle.[8]

However, if the court finds that the defendant does not have a criminal lifestyle a gift will be tainted if it was made by the defendant at any time after the offence was committed or, if his particular criminal conduct consists of two or more offences and they were committed on different dates, the date of the earliest.[9]

When is a gift tainted?

2.25 Under POCA, s 77(2), (3), a gift is tainted if it was made by the defendant at any time after the **relevant day** and was of property which:

(a)   was obtained by the defendant as a result of or in connection with his general criminal conduct; or

(b)   (in whole or in part and whether directly or indirectly) represented in the defendant's hands property obtained by him as a result of or in connection with his general criminal conduct.

Relevant day

2.26 Section 77(9) of POCA defines the relevant day as the first day of the period of six years ending with:

(a)   the day when proceedings for the offence were started against the defendant; or

(b)   if there are two or more offences and proceedings were started on different days, the earliest of those days.

Transfers at an undervalue

2.27 Under POCA, s 78(1), if the defendant transfers property to another person for a consideration whose value is significantly less than the value of the property at the time of the transfer he is to be treated as making a gift.

Value of tainted gifts

2.28 POCA, s 81(1) provides:

'The value at any time (the material time) of a tainted gift is the greater of the following:

---

8   POCA, s 77(1).
9   POCA, s 77(5).

(a)   the value (at the time the gift) of the property given, adjusted to take account of later changes in the value of money

(b)   The value (at the material time) of the property found under subsection (2).'

The value of property held by the recipient (tainted gifts)

2.29   POCA, s 81(2) provides that:

'(a)   if the recipient holds the property given, the property found under this subsection is that property;

(b)   if the recipient holds no part of the property given, the property found under this subsection is any property which directly or indirectly represents it in his hands;

(c)   if the recipient holds part of the property given, the property found under this subsection is that part and any property which directly or indirectly represents the other part in his hands.'

Hidden assets

2.30   The defendant should, however, be aware that the value of the confiscation order is not limited to the amount which the prosecution can prove is that value of the defendant's assets. The recoverable amount is an amount equal to the defendant's benefit from the conduct concerned unless the defendant shows that the available amount is less than that benefit.[10] It is for the defendant to satisfy the court as to the amount which is realisable.[11] A judge can simply conclude from the facts that hidden assets are available;[12] the prosecution is not required to establish a prima facie case of hidden assets before the defendant is required to address the issue.[13] The prosecutor's section 16 statement should make clear the basis of the prosecution assessment of benefit. The court is entitled to draw reasonable inferences as to the existence of realisable assets from evidence satisfying it to the requisite standard of proof.[14]

Any assets whether legitimately acquired or not are vulnerable in confiscation to satisfy an order.[15]

Time for payment

2.31   Under POCA, s 11, the amount due is payable upon the making of the order, but the defendant may show that he needs time to pay. The court may then make an

---

10   POCA, s 7(1) and (2).
11   *R v Ilsemann* [1991] Crim LR 141
12   *R v Wright* [2006] EWCA Crim 1257.
13   *R v Barnham* [2005] EWCA Crim 1049.
14   *R v Peacock and Gillett* [2009] EWCA Crim 645.
15   *R v Currey* [1995] 16 Cr App R(S) 421.

order for payment to be made in a specified period which starts on the day the order is made and must not exceed six months. If within the period the defendant applies to the Crown Court for the order to be extended and the court believes there are exceptional circumstances, the period can be extended, but must not exceed 12 months from the date the order was made. The court can direct payments of the order by instalments. Any appeal against the order does not affect the time for payment.

Imprisonment in default

2.32 If the defendant does not pay, the periods of imprisonment in default as shown in the table below may be ordered. These are maximum periods and the court may order a lesser period if it is minded to do so.

An amount not exceeding £200	7 days
An amount exceeding £200 but not exceeding £500	14 days
An amount exceeding £500 but not exceeding £1,000	28 days
An amount exceeding £1,000 but not exceeding £2,500	45 days
An amount exceeding £2,500 but not exceeding £5,000	3 months
An amount exceeding £5,000 but not exceeding £10,000	6 months
An amount exceeding £10,000 but not exceeding £20,000	12 months
An amount exceeding £20,000 but not exceeding £50,000	18 months
An amount exceeding £50,000 but not exceeding £100,000	2 years
An amount exceeding £100,000 but not exceeding £250,000	3 years
An amount exceeding £250,000 but not exceeding £1,000,000	5 years
An amount exceeding £1,000,000	10 years

Under s 38(2) and (5) of POCA, the provisions of the Powers of Criminal Courts (Sentencing) Act 2000 apply to the enforcement of a confiscation order in the same way as they do to the enforcement of a fine in the Crown Court. The court therefore must impose a term to be served in default at the time of making the order. Serving the default sentence does not extinguish the debt. Other forms of enforcement can be employed.

Only half of the period in default will be served, and the defendant will be unconditionally released after this period.[16]

Interest

2.33 Under POCA, s 12, if the amount to be paid under the order is not paid on time interest will be paid[17] on the sum outstanding and forms part of the order.

---

[16] Criminal Justice Act 2003, s 258.
[17] At the rate of civil judgement debts, currently 8%.

Effect of the confiscation order on the court's other powers

2.34 POCA, s 13(2) and (4) provide as follows:

'(2) The court must take account of the confiscation order before

(a)it imposes a fine on the defendant or

(b)it makes making an order falling within subsection 3.'

'(4)Subject to subsection 2 the court must leave the confiscation order out of account in deciding the appropriate sentence for the defendant.'

Compensation orders and orders under ss 130 and 143 of the Powers of Criminal Courts (Sentencing) Act 2000 are orders made under subs (3). Under POCA, s 13(5) where the court makes both a confiscation and a compensation order under s 130 of the Powers of Criminal Courts (Sentencing) Act 2000, if the court believes the defendant does not have sufficient means to satisfy both orders, the court must specify the amount of compensation which is to be paid from the amount recovered in the confiscation order. This will be the amount the court believes will not be recoverable because of the defendant's insufficiency of means.

Orders for prosecution costs should only be made where the defendant has funds available after payment of the confiscation order.[18]

Postponement of confiscation proceedings

2.35 Under POCA, s 14, the court may either proceed under s 6 before it sentences the defendant for the offence(s) or postpone proceedings for a specified period.

The court may order more than one postponement and the period of postponement may be extended, but any period of postponement must not end after the permitted period had finished.

The permitted period is a period of two years starting with the date of conviction. Postponements can be granted beyond two years as long as the application for further postponement is made before the previous period of postponement ends and the court finds that there are 'exceptional circumstances' which justify further postponements.

The judge is entitled to find there are exceptional circumstances, if there was a prospect that an earlier hearing would be wasted and an unjust order made.[19]

---

[18] *R v Szrajber* [1994] Crim LR 543.
[19] *R v Jagdev* [2002] 1 WLR 3017.

Postponement pending appeal against conviction

2.36 Under POCA, s 14(6) unless there are 'exceptional circumstances', proceedings cannot be postponed for more than three months after the determination of any appeal against conviction.

Abuse of process

2.37 Following a request by a prosecutor, the court has no discretion whether or not to make a confiscation order against a defendant who falls within the statutory regime. The court does retain a power to stay proceedings as an abuse of process in those limited and exceptional cases where seeking a confiscation order might be considered oppressive.[20]

In May 2009, guidance was published by the CPS to inform the exercise of the prosecutor's discretion to instigate confiscation proceedings.[21] The guidance identifies four particular heads of potential abuse, although applications can be argued under other heads.

1   Where the crown has previously agreed not to proceed.

2   Where the defendant has voluntarily paid full compensation to the victim(s) and has not otherwise profited.

3   When the property obtained by the defendant was in the most part obtained legitimately.[22]

4   Where employment has been obtained as a consequence of lies. Strictly wages would then constitute benefit, but the link may be regarded as too remote.[23]

On 5 November 2009 guidance was issued by the Attorney General[24] on the use of asset recovery powers in cases where there has been no conviction. This guidance provides a non-exhaustive list of circumstances in which use of the non-conviction based powers might be appropriate because it is not feasible to secure a conviction (in summary):

1   The only known criminality is overseas, and proceedings cannot be instigated in the Courts of England and Wales or Northern Ireland.

2   No identifiable living suspect is within the jurisdiction or capable of being brought within the jurisdiction.

3   Proceeds of crime can be identified but not linked to any individual suspect or offence.

---

[20]   *R v Paulet* [2009] EWCA Crim 288.
[21]   *Guidance for Prosecutors on the Discretion to Instigate Confiscation Proceedings* (available at http://www.cps.gov.uk/ news/assets/uploads/files/prosecutors_discretion_280509.pdf).
[22]   *R v Shabbir* [2009] 1 Cr App (S) 84.
[23]   *R v Carter* [2006] EWCA Crim 416.
[24]   *Attorney General's Guidance to Prosecuting Bodies on their Asset Recovery Powers under the Proceeds of Crime Act 2002* (reproduced at APPENDIX 4).

4   A criminal investigation is unlikely to generate enough evidence to create a realistic prospect of conviction.

5   A criminal investigation has been conducted and insufficient evidence has been found to create a realistic prospect of conviction.

6   A prosecution has not resulted in a conviction.

Summary

Will an order be made?

2.38

1   Are the proceedings in the Crown Court? If not, have the magistrates committed the case to the Crown Court for the purposes of confiscation proceedings?

2   Has the prosecutor asked the court to proceed to confiscation? If not, has the court proceeded of its own motion?

3   Does the defendant have a criminal lifestyle? If not, has he benefited from his particular criminal conduct?

4   Has he benefited to at least the value of £5,000?

6   If the above requirements are fulfilled the court will now decide the recoverable amount and make an order in that sum.

Burden and standard of proof?

2.39

1   Standard of proof for both the prosecution and the defence is the balance of probabilities.

2   The prosecution are required to prove the defendant's benefit and the value of the defendant's proceeds from criminal conduct. They are assisted by the four mandatory assumptions.

3   The order will be made in the sum of the defendant's benefit unless the defendant proves that the available amount is less than the benefit.

Postponement

2.40

1   Confiscation proceedings can be delayed beyond two years if there are exceptional circumstances.

2   Proceedings may be delayed pending appeal against conviction, but not longer than three months after the appeal is determined.

3   An appeal against the confiscation order will not extend the time allowed for payment which is a maximum of 12 months.

4   If the order is not paid when due a period of imprisonment in default will be imposed.

5   Interest is payable on unpaid sums.

Table of definitions

2.41

Phrase	Section of POCA where phrase is defined
benefit	8
available amount	9
recoverable amount	7
criminal lifestyle	75
general criminal conduct	76(2)
course of criminal conduct	75(3)
criminal conduct	76(1)
pecuniary advantage	*R v Chambers* [2008] EWCA Crim 2467 76(5)
obtain	*R v Jennings* [2008] UKHL 29
value of benefit obtained	76(7)
particular criminal conduct	76(3)
relevant day	77(9)
date of conviction	10(10)
tainted gifts	77(2) and (3)
transfers at an undervalue	78(1)
hidden assets	*R v Wright* [2006] EWCA Crim 1257
time for payment	11
interest	12
assumptions	10
relevant benefit	75(5) and 75(6)
criminal conduct	76(1)
value of property	79, 80 and 81

Chapter 3   Restraint

'Money is not the most important thing in the world. Love is. Fortunately I love money.'
Jackie Mason

Contents Summary

Purpose of restraint orders – obtaining restraint orders – scope and duration of restraint orders – property restrained by the order – money that can be released from restraint (reasonable living expenses – business expenses – legal expenses) – applications to vary and discharge restraint orders – principles under which the court is required to act – seizure of assets-disclosure orders – repatriation orders – enforcement-management receivers – discharge of receivers – Capewell guidelines

POCA, s 40	The five considerations for the making of a restraint order
40(1)	A restraint order may be made if any of the five conditions are fulfilled.
40(2)	A criminal investigation has been started and the offender has benefited from his criminal conduct.
40(3)	Proceedings for an offence have been started and not concluded, and the defendant has benefited from his criminal conduct.
40(4)	An application for reconsideration in the Crown Court in a case where no confiscation order was made – in the light of fresh evidence or because the defendant has absconded.
40(5)	Reconsideration of benefit.
40(6)	Reconsideration of the available amount.

Purpose of restraint orders

3.1   Restraint orders are sought by the prosecutor to preserve assets for the purpose of contemplated confiscation proceedings.

The orders are therefore normally sought just before or just after criminal proceedings have commenced, but they may be sought at any stage.

POCA applies to offences committed after 24 March 2003. Therefore the prosecutor must consider at the outset of the investigation whether any charges are likely to be preferred relating to offences prior to this date. If restraint proceedings are brought under POCA, and it transpires that charges will be preferred under the earlier legislation, the prosecutor must apply to the High Court for a restraint order under the appropriate legislation and seek the discharge of the POCA order.

Obtaining restraint orders under POCA

3.2 There are five separate conditions under which the Crown Court can make a restraint order.

These conditions are set out in POCA, s 40(2)–(6).

1   *Criminal investigations*

POCA, *s 40(2)* A criminal investigation has started in England Wales with regard to an offence and there is reasonable cause to believe that the alleged offender has benefited from his criminal conduct.

'Criminal investigation' is defined as an investigation which police officers or other persons have a duty to conduct with a view to it being ascertained whether a person should be charged with an offence.[1]

2   *Criminal proceedings have already started*

POCA *s 40(3)* Proceedings for an offence have been started in England and Wales and not concluded, and there is reasonable cause to believe that the defendant has benefited from his criminal conduct.

Proceedings are concluded against the defendant if he is acquitted on all counts, if the conviction is quashed or the defendant pardoned before the order is made. If a confiscation order is made proceedings are concluded when the order is satisfied or discharged or when the order is quashed and there is no further possibility of an appeal against the decision to quash the order.[2]

A right of appeal by the prosecutor exists when the defendant has been convicted of an offence, but the Crown Court decides not to make a confiscation order against him. Whilst the appeal is being considered the restraint order can remain in force.[3]

3   *Application for reconsideration to be made*

POCA, *s 40(4)* This condition applies when the prosecutor has invited the Crown Court to reconsider a case in the light of fresh evidence where no confiscation order was made, or to make a confiscation order against a defendant that has absconded.[4]

Such applications are concluded where the court decides not to make a confiscation order or when any order made is satisfied, discharged or quashed and there is no possibility of an appeal against the decision to quash the order. In a case where the application is withdrawn the application is concluded when the person who made the application notifies the withdrawal to the court.[5]

---

[1]   POCA, s 88(2).
[2]   POCA, s 85(3)–(5).
[3]   POCA, s 85(6)–(8).
[4]   POCA, ss 19, 20, 27 and 28.
[5]   POCA, s 86(1).

4   *Reconsideration of benefit*

POCA s 40(5) The court, on application by the prosecutor may make a new calculation of benefit and increase the confiscation order if evidence is presented that was not available at the time the original order was made.

A restraint order can be made if such an application has been made by the prosecutor and not concluded, or the court believes that such application is to be made and there is reasonable cause to believe that the court will decide that the amount found under the new calculations of the defendant's benefit exceeds the relevant amount (ie that the new benefit figure will exceed the value of the former confiscation order).

5   *Reconsideration of the available amount*

POCA, s 40(6) On the application of the prosecutor or an enforcement receiver the court may increase the order when it appears that the value of the defendant's realisable property is more than that found at the time the confiscation order was made. The court may increase the order to a just figure, provided that it does not exceed the defendant's benefit.

A restraint order can be made if such application has been made by the prosecutor and not concluded or the court believes that such application is to be made and there is reasonable cause to believe that the court will decide that the amount found under the new calculation of the available amount exceeds the relevant amount (ie that the available amount as revised exceeds the value of the former confiscation order).

3.3   There is no express provision in POCA which requires the prosecutor to establish a risk of dissipation of assets in order to obtain a restraint order. Case law,[6] however, establishes that there must be a real risk that the defendant will dissipate his assets. Consequently, if the prosecutor delays in applying for a restraint order and the assets have not been dissipated, it will be harder for the prosecutor to assert that there is a real risk that the defendant (or offender) will do so in the future. Anyone facing a charge or investigation which involves serious organised criminality may have an uphill struggle in convincing the court that there is no risk that they will dissipate their assets. Nonetheless, the prosecutor should not take it for granted that restraint orders will be granted in these circumstances. Any delay in applying for the order will make it subject to greater scrutiny.

Scope and duration of restraint orders

3.4   Under POCA, s 41(1), if any condition set out in s 40 is satisfied the Crown Court may make a restraint order prohibiting any specified person from dealing with any realisable property held by him.

---

[6]   *Re AJ and DJ* (unreported) 9 December 1992.

Property restrained by the order

3.5   Under POCA, s 41(2):

'A restraint order may provide that it applies to—

(a)   all realisable property held by the specified person whether or not the property is described in the order;

(b)   to realisable property transferred to the specified person after the order is made.'

Realisable property

3.6   Realisable property includes any free property held by the defendant and any free property held by the recipient of a tainted gift. Property is free unless an order is in force in relation to it.

This includes both legally and illegally acquired property and property held both in England and Wales and overseas.

Property

3.7   Property is all property wherever situated and includes:

(a)   money;

(b)   all forms of real or personal property;

(c)   things in action and other intangible or incorporeal property.[7]

The definition of property

3.8   POCA, s 84(2) defines 'property'.

(a)   Property is held by a person if he holds an interest in it.

(b)   Property is obtained by a person if he obtained an interest in it.

(c)   Property is transferred by one person to another if the first one transfers or grants an interest in it to the second.

(d)   References to property held by a person include references to property vested in his trustee in bankruptcy, permanent or interim trustee or liquidator.

(e)   References to an interest held by person beneficially in property include references to an interest which would be held by him beneficially if the property were not so vested.

(f)   References to an interest in relation to land in England and Wales or Northern Ireland are to any legal estate or equitable interest or power.

---

7   POCA, s 84.

(g)   References to an interest in relation to land in Scotland, are to any estate interest servitude or other heritable right in or overland including a heritable security.

(h)   References to an interest in relation to property other than land, include references to a right (including a right to possession).

The court should make a pragmatic assessment of property ownership.

Where the defendant does not have a criminal lifestyle, and where the defendant's benefit cannot be easily assessed, the prosecutor should not restrain assets significantly in excess of that benefit.

3.9   Assets of limited companies will not normally constitute realisable property since limited companies have a legal personality of their own. There are, however, two exceptions to this:

1   Property gifted to a company will be caught in the same way as property gifted to any other third party.

2   The corporate veil can be lifted, or pierced, in circumstances where a company is under the control of the defendant and has been used to facilitate the commission of criminal offences with which either he has been charged or which are subject to investigation. The assets of the company may then be treated as being the assets of the defendant.

Once a restraint order without notice is made, it remains in effect until the court makes an order varying or discharging it. Any person affected by a restraint order can apply for it to be varied or discharged by giving two clear days notice. Prosecutors should, however, consider in each case whether it is appropriate for the court to make an open-ended order or whether there should be a return date to consider whether the order should remain in force.

Money that can be released from restraint

3.10   POCA s 41(3) provides:

'A restraint order may be made subject to exceptions, and an exception may in particular—

(a)   make provision for reasonable living expenses and reasonable legal expenses;

(b)   make provision for the purpose of enabling any person to carry on any trade, business, profession or occupation;

(c)   be made subject to conditions.'

The right to draw on restrained funds ends once the confiscation order has been made, or any outstanding avenues of appeal have been exhausted.

Reasonable living expenses

3.11   This is typically in the sum of £350 a week for the payment of general living expenses. In addition, where a restraint order prevents a spouse or partner of the defendant from dealing with realisable property the order should also make provision to meet his or her reasonable living expenses unless he or she has access to unrestrained funds. The defendant should also be able to deal freely with any state benefits.

3.12   If the defendant considers the amount payable is insufficient for his legitimate needs he should, in the first instance, invite the prosecutor to agree to the order being varied by consent. If agreement cannot be reached then the defendant will make a formal variation application to the court.

Businesses

3.13   Restraint orders will not be allowed to operate in such a way as to prevent a business in which the defendant has an interest from trading profitably and legitimately. Indeed it is likely to be in the interest of realising funds to meet a subsequent confiscation order to allow the business to continue trading.

3.14   The court will, however, usually require safeguards to be incorporated to prevent abuse of the company accounts. In particular the court is likely to insist on accounts and other business records being produced to the prosecutor at regular intervals. If the business is particularly complex, or has a high turnover and it is suggested that it has been used to facilitate commercial criminal offences, the appointment of a management receiver may well be appropriate.

There is no express power to vary the terms of the order to pay third-party creditors.

Legal expenses

3.15   There are strict limitations on the court's power to release funds to pay reasonable legal expenses. Funds cannot be released to pay for legal expenses relating to the restraint proceedings or the criminal proceedings relating to the underlying offence, nor can funds be released to pay for the legal expenses incurred by recipients of tainted gifts.[8]

3.16   In essence, restrained funds may only be released to meet legal fees incurred in proceedings wholly unrelated to the criminal prosecution. Even then a court will carefully scrutinise the funds being released and require the defendant to name the source of the funds and provide a breakdown and justification of the legal costs incurred.

3.17   A defendant can nominate any restrained source to be released for payment of legal fees or general living expenses, including sources alleged by the Crown to have

---

8   POCA, s 41(4).

been illegitimately acquired. The defendant should, however, bear in mind that any source nominated will be inferred to belong to him and any suggestion otherwise at a later date will be treated unsympathetically by the court.

3.18 Occasionally cash seized becomes a prosecution exhibit. There is no bar on this money being released unless it is essential that the original cash must be produced in criminal proceedings.

Applications to vary and discharge restraint orders

3.19 Under POCA s 42(3), an application to discharge or vary a restraint order may be made to the Crown Court by the person who applied for the order or any person affected by the order. An application to vary or discharge must always be made before embarking on appeal.

3.20 Once proceedings are concluded the restraint order must be discharged. The court has no discretion in the matter. Proceedings are, however, only concluded upon the satisfaction of any confiscation order. The prosecutor should apply promptly for the order to be discharged if the defendant is acquitted or on the satisfaction of the order. If this is not done the defendant is at a liberty to make an application for the order to be discharged.

3.21 Since the order imposes great restrictions upon the defendant, once the order is made the prosecution should move to prosecuting any criminal proceedings expeditiously. In the event that there is undue delay in commencing proceedings, the court should discharge the order.[9]

3.22 A procedural irregularity made by the prosecution in applying for the restraint order may be sufficient basis to seek its discharge only if it is not capable of remedy. The application can also be based on an argument where the statutory criteria that have to be met before a restraint order can be made have not been established. However, applications on this basis should be confined to cases where there is no evidence to show that one or more of the statutory criteria exist.

3.23 Applications for restraint orders are often made without notice to the defendant: clearly there is a real risk that putting the defendant on notice might cause him to dissipate the assets prior to the hearing. The prosecutor must, therefore, give 'full and frank disclosure' of all material facts in witness statements in support of his application, including any weaknesses in his case of which he is aware and any information that might be favourable to the defendant. Failure to comply with this duty may well result in the order being discharged.[10] It is, however, open to the prosecutor to produce subsequent witness statements to remedy any defect.

---

[9] POCA, s 42(7).

[10] Though in *Jennings v CPS* [2005] 4 All ER 391 the court observed that in the majority of cases where full and frank disclosure had not been made the prosecutor could be penalised in costs without the order being discharged.

Procedure for applying for variation

3.24 It is for the applicant to satisfy the court that it would be just to vary the order. If there is evidence that the applicant has hidden assets, the applicant may be required to show that any requested release of funds cannot be met from those assets.

3.25 The court must balance the need to preserve assets for confiscation against legitimate reasonable expenditure.

The principles under which the court is required to act when exercising its powers under the Act

3.26 POCA, s 69 applies to the powers conferred on a court by ss 41–59 and 62–67 and the powers of a receiver appointed under s 48 or 50.

'(2) The powers—

(a)   must be exercised with a view to the value for the time being of realisable property being made available (by the property's realisation) for satisfying any confiscation order that has been or may be made against the defendant;

(b)   must be exercised, in a case where a confiscation order has not been made, with a view to securing that there is no diminution in the value of realisable property;

(c)   must be exercised without taking account of any obligation of the defendant or a recipient of a tainted gift if the obligation conflicts with the object of satisfying any confiscation order that has been or may be made against the defendant;

(d)   may be exercised in respect of a debt owed by the Crown.

(3) Subsection (2) has effect subject to the following rules—

(a)   the powers must be exercised with a view to allowing the person other than the defendant or a recipient of a tainted gift to retain or recover the value of any interest held by him;

(b)   in the case of realisable property held by a recipient of a tainted gift, the powers must be exercised with a view to realising no more than the value for the time being of the gift;

(c)   in a case where a confiscation order has not been made against the defendant, property must not be sold if the court so orders under subsection (4).

(4) If on an application by the defendant, or by the recipient of a tainted gift, the court decides that property cannot be replaced it may order that it must not be sold.

(5) An order under subsection (4) may be revoked or varied.'

Seizure of assets

3.27   POCA, s 45 provides:

'(1) if a restraint order is in force a constable or customs officer may seize any realisable property to which it applies to prevent its removal from England and Wales.'

Property seized under subs (1) must be dealt with in accordance with the directions of the court which made the order.

POCA appears to give an unlimited discretion to the court as to the directions that can be given as to how seized property should be dealt with. The court must, however, exercises powers in accordance with s 69.

Disclosure orders

3.28   A prosecutor making a restraint order will have considerable information about the defendant's realisable assets, although full knowledge remains with the defendant. Prosecutors therefore routinely ask courts making restraint orders to include a provision requiring the defendant to swear an affidavit disclosing the full extent of his realisable property.[11]

3.29   In producing the required affidavit, the defendant is at risk of incriminating himself. To provide protection for the defendant an affidavit produced in compliance with the order cannot be used as evidence in any criminal proceedings against the maker.[12]

3.30   Disclosure may not be ordered against the prosecutor for the purposes of assisting a defendant to comply with a restraint order. Defendants in custody are restricted in their ability to obtain information. In such circumstances if the information sought by the defendant is in the possession of the prosecution, the judge may invite the prosecution to make voluntary disclosure as they feel appropriate.[13]

Repatriation orders

3.31   It is common for defendants charged with offences involving large sums of money to have money and assets abroad. Whilst there is some international co-operation in facilitating the restraint of assets this is usually a complex and long drawn out procedure. It is simpler for the prosecutor to seek a repatriation order requiring the defendant to bring the asset in question within the jurisdiction of the

---

[11]   The power to do so is derived from POCA, s 41(7) which enables the court to 'make such order as it believes appropriate for the purpose of ensuring the restraint order is effective'.

[12]   POCA, s 360.

[13]   *Re S and W* (unreported), 7 February 2000.

court. The power to order repatriation is a discretionary one and the court will not make the order in every case where assets are located overseas.

Enforcement

3.32 Orders made are only effective if there are sanctions for breach.

Typical breaches include the defendant or third party dealing or attempting to deal with restrained assets, failing to comply with the terms of an order, or obstructing a receiver in the performance of his duties.

3.33 Curiously POCA does not give the prosecutor or receiver any specific remedy in relation to breaches of orders. A breach is simply treated as a contempt of court, with the court having the power to commit the contemnor to prison, or if the contemnor is a body corporate, sequestrating the company's assets.

3.34 The maximum sentence for contempt of court is two years' imprisonment. If a number of matters of contempt are sentenced at the same time the court is restricted to a maximum of two years imprisonment, although further consecutive terms of imprisonment can be imposed on subsequent occasions. Sentences are subject to the provisions for early release, ie the contemnor is released unconditionally after serving one-half of his sentence if he has been committed for less than 12 months, or one-third of the sentence if he has been committed for more than 12 months.

3.35 The court treats breaches of orders extremely seriously, especially where assets have been dissipated. The defendant should expect to receive an immediate sentence of imprisonment. If the contemnor is already serving a sentence of imprisonment at the time of being sentenced for contempt the sentence for contempt will be consecutive to the earlier sentence unless the court directs otherwise.

3.36 The court has the power to direct that an order for committal be suspended for such a period or such terms or conditions as it may specify. In the context of restraint orders this provision gives the court jurisdiction to suspend the committal provided that the defendant remedies his breach, or complies with the order, even if this has the ultimate effect of suspending the committal indefinitely.

3.37 A court also retains a discretion to refuse to hear a person who is in contempt until such time as the contempt has been purged. This would prevent, for example, the defendant applying for a variation of a restraint order.

3.38 The defendant in prison for contempt has the right to go back to court at any time on the ground that he has purged his contempt. This would generally require him to convince the judge that he will henceforth comply with the order. Proposals as to how this will be achieved will be of assistance to his application.

3.39 The whole objective of the contempt procedures is to encourage the defendant to comply with the order of the court. Any proposals put forward by the defendant for compliance are likely to be given a sympathetic hearing.

3.40   The procedure to be followed in the Crown Court regarding contempt matters is contained within the Criminal Procedure Rules 2010,[14] particularly Part 62. These state that the court must not exercise its power to punish for contempt of court in the respondent's absence unless he has had at least 14 days in which to make representations and introduce evidence. An application for proceedings for contempt must be made in writing identifying the respondent and giving details of any conduct which is considered to amount to contempt. The application must also include a warning notice that the court can impose imprisonment or a fine or both in that the court may deal with the application in the respondent's absence. The application must be handed to the person accused.

3.41   The court has the power to strike out a committal application if it appears:

(a)   that the application or the evidence in support of it disclose no reasonable grounds for alleging that the respondent is guilty of contempt;

(b)   that the procedure is an abuse of process; or

(c)   that there has been a failure to comply with a rule, practice direction or court order.

There may be grounds for the defendant to argue abuse of process if the prosecution has unreasonably delayed in bringing contempt proceedings, particularly in a case where the contempt proceedings fall to be heard at the same time as a criminal trial.

3.42   The prosecutor is required to prove the case beyond reasonable doubt. The hearing takes place before the judge alone. The prosecutor can call witnesses and read affidavits and the defendant has the opportunity to do the same.

Management receivers

3.43   The appointment of a management receiver is provided for in POCA, s 48. In some cases a restraint order alone will not be an effective means of preserving the value of the defendant's assets pending the determination of the proceedings. Real assets, for example, houses, sports cars and yachts may be abandoned if the defendant is in custody. Complex businesses run by the defendant may need close supervision.

3.44   The court may appoint a receiver in respect of any realisable property to which the restraint order applies.[15] The court has the power, on the application of the prosecutor, to appoint a receiver to take possession of and manage the defendant's realisable property pending the conclusion of proceedings. Management receivers are distinct from enforcement receivers. The latter realise the assets in order to satisfy the order; the former preserve the assets.

3.45   The costs and disbursements of management receivers are to be paid from the estate even when the defendant is acquitted. The costs of appointing a receiver

---

[14]   SI 2010/60.
[15]   POCA, s 48(2).

should, however, be proportionate to the benefits to be derived from the appointment. The receiver should also be discharged once the objective of his appointment has been achieved.

3.46 Only the prosecutor may make an application for the appointment of management receiver. There is no power for the defendant or an affected third party to do so.

3.47 Powers of the management receiver are set out in POCA, s 49. Essentially the management receiver has all the powers of an owner of the property to manage and transact with the property in the interest of preserving its value. The receiver cannot transact with the property or receive payments from the estate without giving notice to persons holding an interest in the property and giving them a reasonable opportunity to make representations. This, however, does not apply where property is perishable or ought to be disposed of before its value diminishes. The prosecutor or receiver should exercise its power sparingly and with appropriate justification, particularly where the property concerned may hold sentimental value.

3.48 Appointing a management receiver is a serious step and the court must be satisfied that a restraint order alone will not be sufficient to prevent the dissipation of the defendant's realisable property. Receivers are expensive creatures and the court must also consider whether the cost may ultimately outweigh the benefit.

3.49 A set of guidelines were prepared in the case of *Capewell v Customs and Excise Commissioners*.[16] These are considered to be a useful checklist (see 3.54).

On appointment a management receiver becomes an officer of the court and therefore accountable to the court. The prosecutor has no right to direct him to exercise his powers in a particular way. Therefore any obstruction of the receiver in his duties under a court order will constitute a contempt of court.

3.50 Both the defendant and the receiver have duties in relation to the assets. The defendant can play a part in ensuring that costs do not escalate by co-operating with the receiver in providing information. Indeed a wilful failure to co-operate with the receiver may amount to obstruction of the performance of the receiver and contempt proceedings may follow. The receiver for his part has a duty of care to those affected by his actions during the course of the receivership.

3.51 A letter of agreement is drawn up between the receiver and the prosecution authority. This should set out the receiver's agreed hourly rate. The receiver will typically be required to provide regular accounts and reports, to the court, the prosecutor and the defendant. All parties served with the receiver's accounts can apply for an order permitting them to inspect any document in the possession of the receiver relevant to those accounts, and within 14 days of being served with the accounts any party may object to an item in the accounts, giving reason for the objection and requiring the receiver – within 14 days – to either accept the objection or apply for examination of the accounts in relation to the contested item.

---

[16] [2005] 1 All ER 900.

3.52 The receiver is entitled to look only to the estate in management for the payment of his remuneration and expenses. The remuneration and expenses must be approved by the court. This gives the defendant the right to make representations if he considers the receiver's claims excessive. The receiver is entitled to exercise a lien over the assets forming part of the receivership estate for the payment of his remuneration and expenses.

Discharge of the receiver

3.53 The discharge of the receiver is governed by POCA, s 63. The receiver, the prosecutor and any person affected by the order can apply for the discharge or variation of receivership orders. It is a matter of discretion whether the receivership order should be discharged or not, unless a particular condition required for the continuation of the order has now been satisfied. The overriding consideration is whether the receivership is still serving a valid purpose. Even if there are insufficient grounds to justify the discharge of the receiver, a defendant or affected third party is entitled to seek the court's directions if he considers the receiver is abusing his power. POCA, s 64 provides for the discharge of management receivers on the appointment of enforcement receiver. This section requires the management receiver to hand over the assets to the enforcement receiver save for those assets required to fulfil his reasonably incurred expenses and remuneration.

The Capewell guidelines[17]

3.54 These guidelines were prepared by the Court of Appeal (Civil Division) to be used when the court is considering appointing a management receiver.

'**Application by the prosecutor**

1   Within the witness statement in support of the application to appoint a management receiver, the prosecutor should set out the reasons the prosecutor seeks the appointment of a receiver, and what purpose the prosecutor believes the receivership will serve.

2   The witness statement in support of the application should also give an indication of the type of work that it is envisaged the receiver may need to undertake, based on the facts known to prosecutor at the time of the appointment.

3   The witness statement in support of the application should specifically draw to the Court's attention the proposition that the assets over which the receiver is appointed be used to pay the costs, disbursements and other expenses of the receivership (even if the defendant is acquitted or the receivership subsequently discharged).

4   The letter of acceptance of appointment from the receiver, which must

---

[17]   [2005] 1 All ER 900.

be exhibited to the applicant's witness statement, should contain the time charging rates of the staff the receiver anticipates he may need to deploy.

5   In appropriate cases, where it is possible, and this will not be in every case, the receiver should give in his letter of acceptance an estimate as to how much the receivership is likely to cost.

6   The prosecutor's witness statement in support of the application should inform the court of the nature of the assets and their approximate value (if known) and the income the assets might produce (if known).

Upon appointment

7   If the prosecutor or receiver is unable to comply with any of the above requirements the prosecutor should explain the reasons for the failure in the prosecutor's application to the court and the matter will be left at the discretion of the court.

8   Upon the appointment of a receiver, the Judge should consider whether it is appropriate, in all the circumstances, to reserve any future applications to himself with a view to minimising costs.

9   Upon the appointment of a receiver, the Judge should consider whether it is appropriate, in all the circumstances, to set a return date, balancing the need for such a hearing with the interests of the defendant, who ultimately will bear the costs of such a hearing.

10   The receiver should inform the parties by written report as soon as reasonably practicable, if it appears to him that any initial cost estimate will be exceeded, or receivership costs are increasing or are likely to increase to a disproportionate level. Such report should also be filed with the Court. In such circumstances the parties and the receiver shall be at liberty to seek directions from the Court.

Reporting requirements

11   Unless the Court directs otherwise, the receiver should report 28 days after his appointment and quarterly thereafter.

12   Unless the court directs otherwise, the report should be served on the prosecutor and the defendant and filed with the Court.

13   Every report should set out the costs incurred to date; the work done; projected costs until the next report; a summary of how those costs attached to the matters that led to the appointment or to the matters that may have arisen; and, where appropriate, an estimated final outcome statement.

14   Every report should contain a statement that the receiver believes that his costs are reasonable and proportionate in all the circumstances.

15 If the receiver is unable to fulfil any of the above reporting requirements, he should give, as soon as reasonably practicable, an explanation, by way of written report to be filed at Court and served on the parties, of why this is the case, and those parties shall be at liberty to seek directions from the Court.

Lawyers and other agents

16 The parties should always be told that lawyers or other agents have been instructed unless it is not practicable or in the interests of justice to do so (for example, to make an urgent without notice application to secure assets).

17 If lawyers or other agents are instructed, the receiver should ask for monthly bills or fee notes. The receiver should endeavour to keep a close control on such fees and satisfy himself that the costs being incurred are reasonable and proportionate in all the circumstances.

18 The receiver should notify the parties as soon as reasonably practicable, if it appears to him that any lawyer's or other agent's costs are rising to a disproportionate level, and those parties shall be at liberty to apply to the Court for directions.

General

19 Nothing in these guidelines should be read as supplanting the appropriate rules of court particularly CPR 69 and the relevant statutory provisions.

20 Judges appointing receivers should always bear in mind that the costs of the receivership may fall on an innocent man. They should also bear in mind that the interests of justice dictate that receiverships are a necessary and essential tool of the criminal justice process for preserving and managing assets to satisfy confiscation orders if the defendant is convicted.

21 Management receivership orders should be endorsed with the appropriate penal notice. It will be a term of most orders that defendants should cooperate with and comply with, as soon as possible forthwith, directions and requests of the receiver, so as to enable the receiver to efficiently and cost-effectively carry out the duties, functions and obligations of his office. It is therefore in the defendant's interest to avoid, as far as possible, the need for the receiver to return to Court for further orders or directions, the cost of which will ultimately fall on the defendant's estate.'

Restraint basic question and answer checklist

3.55

1 I've been made the subject of an order, what can I do about it?

Apply for a variation or discharge giving two clear days' notice. The best prospect for a discharge of the order is if there has been a delay on the part of prosecution in seeking the order and there has been no dissipation of assets.

2   Can I pay my lawyers from restrained funds?

Only for proceedings not connected with confiscation or the trial that preceded it.

3   What happens if I don't comply with an order?

You are likely to be found in contempt of court and may be sent to prison.

4   Can I object to the appointment of a management receiver?

Yes, particularly if you feel the appointment is unnecessary and can show why this is the case.

5   Will I have to bear the costs of the receiver even if I am acquitted?

Yes.

Chapter 4   Practice and procedure

'Cab drivers are living proof that practice does not make perfect'
Howard Ogden

Contents Summary

Orders to provide information – prosecution statement of information – defence response – defence proof of evidence – evidence to be served by the defence – privilege against self incrimination – defence witnesses – forensic accountants – service of documents – avoiding a contested hearing – useful tactics for negotiation of agreement – co-defendants – the hearing – practical issues – defence testimony – defence attendance at court for order to be made

---

Typical procedural steps for making of the confiscation order

1   Defendant convicted.[1]

2   Court sets directions timetable[2] for:

  (i)   any disclosure of information under POCA, s 18;

  (ii)   service of prosecutor's statement of information under POCA, s 16;

  (iii)   service of defence response under POCA, s 17;

  (iv)   service of any defence expert report;

  (v)   service of prosecution material.

3   Parties will be asked to estimate the length of any final contested hearing and indicate witnesses likely to be called, particularly expert witnesses.[3]

4   If either party is struggling to comply with orders for disclosure the case can be listed for mention.

5   The amount of order may be agreed between the parties, avoiding the need for a contested hearing. The agreement is subject to judicial approval.

6   The parties may come to an agreement on some issues, resulting in reduced hearing time whilst a narrow range of issues are contested.

---

[1]   Although no conviction required for civil recovery procedure – see CHAPTER 8.
[2]   Typically at conviction but before sentence.
[3]   This is typically done at a pre trial hearing.

Orders to provide information

4.1   Section 18(2) of POCA enables the court to order the defendant to provide information 'at any time' for the purpose of assisting the court to carry out its confiscatory function ('section 18 request'). In practice, section 18 requests by the prosecution are set out in a pro forma and usually made upon conviction requiring the defendant to provide details of all assets. The response to the document is then used by the prosecution to inform the production of the section 16 ('statement of information') document ('section 16 document'). Section 18 requests can also be made to force the defendant to provide further information to assist the court in assessing the veracity of the defendant's assertions.

4.2   If the defendant fails to comply with the order without reasonable excuse, s 18(4) allows the court to draw any inference it feels appropriate. This is in addition to the court's powers to find the defendant in contempt for failure to comply.

Prosecution statement of information

4.3   Under POCA, s 16, once the court has decided to proceed under the confiscation provisions (either on request from the prosecutor or of its own motion), the prosecutor will provide the court and the defendant with a statement of information. The statements vary widely in format and the level of detail provided, but typically follow the following format:

1   The offences that the defendant has been convicted of and description of the facts of the case, date of conviction and sentence passed. This may also include references to evidence at trial and relevant sentencing remarks – particularly as to the judge's findings as to the defendant's overall culpability, or role within a conspiracy or any basis of plea.

2   Personal facts pertaining to the defendant, including previous convictions.

3   History of the proceedings including details of any restraint applications.

4   Whether the prosecution allege the case is one of general or particular criminal conduct and, if the case is one of general criminal conduct or a lifestyle offence, reference to the assumptions that the court is being invited to draw.

5   The extent of the benefit alleged and a breakdown of how the figure is reached.

6   A schedule of the defendant's realisable assets.

7   Whether the prosecution maintains that the defendant has hidden assets and the nature (and potential location) of those assets.

8   The final amount of the Order that the prosecution is seeking.

9   Any particular case law or statutory references to support the prosecution position in relation to any of the above.

Crucially the prosecutor should make it clear whether a criminal lifestyle is alleged.

4.4   Whilst the statement will usually be prepared either by or with the assistance of a specialist financial investigator, this will invariably be an employee of the agency preparing the report. The financial analysis varies widely in depth and quality between agencies, regions and even from case to case.

A copy must also be served on the defendant (or his representative).[4]

4.5   The section 16 statement of information must be served 'within the period the court orders'. Typically directions for service of the section 16 document will be made upon conviction. A court will often serve a section 18 request for information at the time of conviction, and the receipt of this information will then be used to formulate the section 16 document.

4.6   The statement of information can be accepted or disputed by the defendant, in whole or in part.

If the whole or part of the document is accepted this will save evidence being adduced on the matters at any subsequent hearing. It is therefore in the interests of the prosecution to produce a sufficiently detailed document to avoid either protracted correspondence with the defence or lengthy legal argument at the ultimate hearing. It also provides the judge with the basis of the case.

4.7   The prosecution is at liberty to provide supplementary section 16 documents and will typically provide a further section 16 document in response to the defence section 17 response document (see 4.8).

The defence response

4.8   The defendant's response to the statement of information is dealt with under POCA, s 17. The defendant needs to consider the prosecution statement of information very carefully and produce a written response either accepting or denying each paragraph. As such the response is analogous to civil pleadings.

4.9   In relation to those paragraphs that are disputed the defendant must be careful to set out the nature of the dispute, and if appropriate serve evidence to support his position. This is particularly the case in relation to expert reports which must be served on the prosecution with sufficient time for the prosecution to make a meaningful response.

4.10   The defendant should also set out in the response any case law supporting his position either on the law or the facts, and would be wise to serve copies of the same on the prosecution and the court.

4.11   Any statements served by either party for the purposes of confiscation proceedings should contain a statement of truth.[5] Defence responses are often simply signed by the defendant. Any assertion, to be compelling, will need to be backed by

---

[4]   CPR, r 58.1(2).
[5]   CPR, r 57.7.

evidence, preferably independent, and the defendant, to have any hope of his assertions being accepted, will either have to give evidence on oath, or call witnesses.

4.12 If the defendant fails to produce a response or remains silent in his response to assertions made by the prosecution, he is liable to be treated as agreeing to all the assertions put forward. The burden of proving that the defendant has benefited from his conduct still remains on the prosecution. Assuming that the prosecution discharge their burden (on the balance of probabilities), if the defence has produced no response an order is likely to be made in the full sum of the benefit.

Defence proof of evidence and the practicalities of taking instructions

4.13 Similar to a standard criminal trial, it is good practice to obtain a signed proof of evidence from the defendant with all responses to the section 18 document, some of which may not be appropriate to be disclosed. This will avoid matters being overlooked and provide protection for both lawyer and client in the event of a complaint. In particular a defence representative should take early instructions on the following matters (see also the list of defence evidence to be served):

- Bank accounts. Are the prosecution assertions about the accounts and the ownership of the contents correct? Are there any significant legitimate credits?

- Are there any other accounts, especially accounts abroad?

- Did the defendant have any legitimate income in the relevant period?

- Did the defendant pay all required taxes?

- Does anyone else have an interest in the assets?

- Were any of the properties obtained through fraudulent mortgage applications?

- Has the defendant made any transfers at an apparent undervalue? Are there any legitimate reasons for this?

- Can the defendant explain any unidentified assets in the accounts?

- Does the defendant have any witnesses (preferably without criminal records) that can testify as to the truth of his explanations?

4.14 In order that financial and legal documentation can be released to the defendant's representatives it is wise to get a generic authority of release signed at an early stage. Access to defendants in prison is very restricted and even those visits planned are frequently foiled by sudden bad weather, prison lock downs, prisoner transfers etc. It is therefore wise to plan prison visits in advance to make the most of the time available.

4.15 Whilst it is convenient for defendants to have financial information to work on whilst in custody, some defendants are understandably reluctant to have information disclosing their ownership of large amounts of assets accessible to their cellmates who may take an opportunistic view. Representatives should be sympathetic to the position and if necessary aim to provide information in a restricted format.

4.16 Typically defendants are not allowed to have access to computers in custody and legal representatives are not allowed to take computers into prison visits. Where a vast amount of financial information is provided by the prosecution in an electronic format, permission can be sought for the defendant to be provided with a laptop (disabled from accessing the internet!) and a hard drive, as storing numerous lever arch files in a cell is hardly practicable. Similarly legal representatives can seek advance permission to take laptops into prison. Permission will usually be granted if merited by the circumstances of the case.

4.17 Where an interpreter is required, fees will usually need to be negotiated in advance with the Legal Services Commission; otherwise there may be some difficulties in recovering the fees at a later stage. Also take steps to ensure the independence of the interpreter; the passing of information between co-defendants is not unknown particularly if the interpreter is used by more than one defendant, although this is generally less problematic at the confiscation stage than at trial. It is frequently helpful for section 16 documents to be disclosed between co-defendants to ensure that available assets are correctly assigned.

Evidence to be served by the defence

4.18 Confiscation proceedings are essentially a tracing exercise. The more comprehensive the tracing exercise performed by the defence to identify the source and ultimate destination of assets received the greater the chance of the defence account being accepted and any suggestion of hidden assets being avoided. As a minimum, evidence should be gained, considered and if appropriate served with regard to the following:

- Property – an up-to-date valuation is required. These can usually be obtained free of charge from a local estate agent. It is helpful to obtain three valuations and take an average figure. Alternatively a more official valuation can be obtained from a property assessor. Frequently valuations obtained early on in the proceedings are out of date by the time the order falls to be made. Remember also that solicitors and conveyancing fees can be deducted from the figure. Whilst this may only amount to a few thousand pounds this can make a big difference to a small order.

- Cars – an up-to-date valuation is required. Details of similar second hand cars for sale are easily available on the internet. Evidence of the ownership of the vehicle may also be relevant. This can be obtained from many independent companies advertising online.

- Jewellery and antiques – an up-to-date valuation is required. The resale value of jewellery will be affected by a number of factors, such as fluctuations in the price of gold and precious stones and the market for that particular type of jewellery. Valuations of jewellery for court proceedings may require the instruction of a specialist valuer – typically high street jewellers are not able or willing to provide valuations suitable for court proceedings.

- Bank accounts. The starting point is any account details and statements provided during the course of the trial; however, it may be appropriate to look at the activity on all the defendant's bank accounts over the relevant period. If the prosecution have obtained copies of the relevant bank accounts it may be quicker to request the statements direct from the prosecution. Frequently the prosecution simply obtains balance figures and it is then down to the defence to identify if there are any credits to the accounts that have an innocent explanation. Similarly there are frequently transfers between accounts that are double counted. A forensic accountant can assist with these matters but the statements need to be obtained in order to be analysed and in order to receive instructions upon them. Bank statements can take some time to be released – allow at least six weeks – therefore they should be requested as early as possible in the proceedings.

- Cheques – unidentified credits are frequently cheques. Obtaining a copy of the cheque may enable identification of the writer and establish an innocent source. Copies of cheques take a long time to be received, therefore should be requested as soon as possible, ideally as soon as the bank statements are received and unidentified cheque payments are discovered.

- Third-party interests – serve any evidence which supports an assertion that a third party may have a legitimate interest in the property (eg spouses). This can often be evidenced from the conveyancing files and mortgage applications.

- Tax returns – enquire whether appropriate tax has been paid, eg capital gains tax on the sale of property, tax on any rental income, tax on income from self-employed position.

- Conveyancing files and mortgage applications. Obtaining copies of conveyancing files of disputed properties may be of assistance to show that the funds used for payment of the deposit were legitimate. Frequently where money is laundered unlawful mortgage applications are made. If the mortgage was obtained unlawfully this is of itself criminal conduct, and even if the deposit monies were lawfully obtained, any equity in the property is therefore likely to be regarded as part of the benefit.

- Evidence of advice from professional advisers – the defendant may provide instructions to the effect that his general financial and mortgage arrangements were not a device to attempt to launder money but a legitimate arrangement to avoid tax as suggested by a professional adviser. Evidence will therefore need to be sought from the adviser as to whether this is indeed the case. Professional advisers are notoriously reluctant to respond to such requests and will often only do so upon receipt of an order from the court. Since this evidence can be difficult to secure it is as well to make the request early and chase for an early response. This will allow time for an order to be obtained if necessary.

- Evidence from witnesses abroad – the Legal Services Commission is generally reluctant to pay for fact-finding trips to exotic locations. All other options need to be explored for obtaining the statements by other means – video link or, more usually, instructing a solicitor in that country to obtain a statement. If there are sound grounds for the defence legal representative to make a trip then a request for funding needs to be sought at an early stage.

Privilege against self incrimination

4.19   To encourage the defendant to make full and frank disclosure, both POCA, ss 17 and 18 contain protection against self incrimination (ss 17(6) and 18(9)).

4.20   Under s 17(6):

'No acceptance under section 17 [the defendant's response to the prosecutors statement] that the defendant has benefited from criminal conduct is admissible in evidence in proceedings for an offence.'

Section 18 contains analogous wording in relation to the provision of information.

4.21   The privilege against self incrimination does not, however, prevent the prosecution using the information provided as the basis for further investigation into criminal activities and obtaining further admissible evidence. The protection also only extends to matters of self incrimination; incrimination of others in an effort to minimise the defendant's role, or to explain the ultimate destination of monies remains entirely possible. Whether the defendant's testimony would ever be regarded as a credible basis for any consequent prosecution is doubtful.

Defence witnesses

4.22   Given the defence problems with credibility the defendant's best hope of being believed is to call witnesses. The convicted are, however, frequently abandoned in their time of need by friends and associates. In the preparation of the defence case it is therefore wise to take signed statements at an early stage. If the witnesses are required to give evidence consider well in advance of the hearing whether a witness summons may be required. A written application to the judge is required for a summons to be granted giving reasons why the witness is unlikely to attend voluntarily.

4.23   To avoid the difficulties with the attendance and credibility of lay witnesses it preferable to have as much of the defence case as possible prepared and presented by expert witnesses.

Forensic accountants

4.24   A forensic accountant's report can be invaluable to both the defence and the court to achieve the following:

● To scrutinise the prosecution assessment of the defendant's assets (regrettably the Crown's figures are frequently incorrect).

- To propose an alternative assessment of which assets should be included in the defendant's benefit.

- To identify third party interests.

- To check for double counting between accounts.

- To present financial material in a manner more easily understandable by the court and witnesses.

- To identify explained and unexplained credits and give the defendant an opportunity to comment on the unexplained credits.

- Expertise in the operation of banking systems, particularly international systems, in order to facilitate the provision of relevant financial evidence.

4.25 Defence forensic accountancy evidence is also frequently agreed and accepted by the Crown resulting in a narrowing of the issues and significant time and cost savings. It is therefore surprising that judges are increasingly reluctant to allow adjournments for an accountant's report to be prepared, and the Legal Services Commission increasingly reluctant to authorise expenditure. Lawyers may find the list above useful in formulating arguments in favour of the preparation of reports.

Service of documents

4.26 Defendants (and their representatives) should be cautious to serve required responses on the correct agency. Typically the CPS will hand the confiscation proceedings post trial over to another agency upon which papers should be served. Documents erroneously served on the CPS may fall into an administrative black hole from which they may take weeks to emerge, if they emerge at all. The court will be unsympathetic to delays incurred as a result. Procedural requirements for the service of documents are given in the Criminal Procedure Rules.[6]

Avoiding a contested hearing

4.27 If an agreement can be reached that is satisfactory to both prosecution and defence a contested hearing can be avoided and the agreed order simply endorsed by the court. The majority of hearings are resolved by agreement for the following reasons:

- Contested proceedings are costly and time consuming for the prosecution.

- Contested hearings are risky for the defence since discharging the burden is tricky without compelling factual evidence or an innovative and original legal argument. Judges are significantly less inclined than juries to give the defendant the benefit of the doubt and, since the judge dealing with the matter is likely to be the judge who sat on the defendant's original trial, judicial evidential mis- or re-interpretation is highly unlikely.

---

6   Criminal Procedure Rules 2010, SI 2010/60. See APPENDIX 2.

- A contested hearing may require the defendant to give evidence to have any prospect of success. Depending on the case this may result in further embarrassing publicity and prejudice the prospects of any outstanding appeal. (Where possible it is always wise to adjourn any confiscation proceedings to after an appeal against conviction, although judges are frequently unsympathetic to delays on these grounds and will ask for details of the nature of the appeal before making a decision. It is therefore helpful to provide drafted grounds of appeal in advance of any application to adjourn.)

- The court is not limited to the prosecutor's statement and a hearing may throw up additional information that had been missed.

- The court is not limited to the jury's finding at the trial (in so far as it can be assessed). The judge is entitled to take into account all the evidence he has heard during the trial and make his own findings of fact when determining the question of the defendant's benefit. The judge must, however, act consistently with the verdict and its basis.

- Where a basis of plea is offered for sentencing that basis of plea is not binding for the purpose of confiscation (unless expressly agreed to be binding). The Crown, however, should make it clear at the time of accepting the basis of plea that they do not consider it to be so binding.

- The court is also not limited to the offences charged providing it is satisfied to the criminal standard that other offences have been committed. The judge is entitled to so find on the basis of evidence heard during the course of the trial.

Useful tactics for negotiation of agreement

4.28 Unlike a criminal trial success in confiscation proceeding requires full and frank disclosure from the defence. This can be hard for defendants to grasp – indeed the whole nature of confiscation proceedings is more akin to civil than criminal proceedings, and it is worth explaining this at some length to avoid confusion. The fuller and franker the disclosure the greater time and effort will be required by the prosecution to process and respond. Some prosecutors may take the view that if a reasonable settlement is offered the time and effort required to deal with the peripheral arguments is simply not worth it.

4.29 Frequently much of the statement of information is agreed but certain issues remain between the parties – often the existence and whereabouts of hidden assets. It is becoming increasingly frequent for the parties to draw up a list of agreed and contested issues and ringfence areas of agreement prior to the hearing which will then not be the subject of cross examination.

Co-defendants

4.30 Whatever the historic state of the relationship between co-defendants, it is generally in everyone's interests to co-operate for the purposes of confiscation, if only to avoid double counting. It is frequently the case that the financial affairs of co-defendants in a conspiracy are so intricately interwoven it is virtually impossible to deal with them separately. To this end it is usual for each co-defendant to serve copies of their section 16 statements on all others directly linked and to co-operate in obtaining evidence.

The hearing – practical issues

4.31 It is important that all parties have paginated bundles in advance of the hearing. Even where extended legal argument is not anticipated it is usually helpful for the parties to prepare a summary of agreed and disputed issues. The content of the bundles should be agreed with the other side beforehand. The court should be on notice of any legal arguments, and skeleton arguments and authorities must be served on the judge in good time prior to the hearing. Case law in this area is changing rapidly and it is as well to check the current position before embarking on a hearing that you may have prepared in advance.[7] All parties should be clear in advance which witnesses are likely to be called and provide an approximate time estimate. If any of the evidence requires use of electronic equipment in the court room be sure to check this in advance – frequently the court will not be able to play certain types of DVDs. It may be possible instead to plug a laptop into the court system.

Defence testimony

4.32 A defendant needs to be carefully advised before the hearing as to whether it is wise for him to give evidence. It is difficult for the assumptions to be rebutted in the absence of testimony from the defendant, although evidence from other witnesses may serve instead and be more compelling. There is little point in the defendant going into the witness box if he truly has no answers to the questions that are likely to be put. If the defendant chooses not to give evidence at the hearing then it is wise to get written confirmation of this choice since the likely upshot is that an order will be made in the full amount of the benefit.

Defence attendance at court for order to be made

4.33 Defendants are often unenthusiastic about being produced simply for the purposes of an agreed order being made by the court, particularly as they may be at a stage of their sentence where they are in a lower category prison; production invariably means at least one night in remand conditions and frequently up to a week.

4.34 It is possible for a final order to be made in the defendant's absence in these circumstances[8] providing the defence representative is fully briefed.

---

7   Crimeline provides an excellent free regular legal update service (http://www.crimeline.info/).
8   *R v Gavin* [2010] EWCA Crim 2727.

Confiscation hearing checklist

4.35

1   Have orders and directions been made for the service of documents and responses, including any expert evidence?

2   Has a proof of evidence been taken from the defendant?

3   Have statements been taken from relevant witnesses?

4   Has consideration been given to any additional evidence not arising in the course of the trial that may be of assistance?

5   Should there be an exchange of documents between co-defendants?

6   Are the witnesses willing to attend court?

7   Should the defendant give evidence?

8   Have the issues in dispute with the prosecution been identified?

9   Is it possible to negotiate a favourable agreement with the prosecution?

10   If not, is it possible to narrow the issues and restrict lines of cross examination?

Chapter 5   Cash seizures

'This is a court of law, young man, not a court of justice.'
Oliver Wendell Holmes, Jr.

Contents summary

Grounds for seizure – similarities with civil recovery – powers of the investigator – procedure and practice – further detention applications – further detention applications – applications for forfeiture – interest bearing accounts – remedies available to the respondent – remedies available to the owner/loser – costs – funding – compensation – appeals

Grounds for seizure: POCA, s 294(1)

5.1

'A customs officer, a constable or an accredited financial investigator may seize any cash if he has reasonable grounds for suspecting that it is—

(a)   recoverable property, or

(b)   intended by any person for use in unlawful conduct.'

Cash may also be seized if at least part of it is recoverable or intended for use in unlawful conduct.[1] 'Cash' bears an extended meaning in this context and is defined so as to include 'notes and coins, postal orders, cheques of any kind including travellers cheques, bankers drafts, bearer bonds and bearer shares'[2] or any other kind of monetary instrument.[3] There is a minimum threshold currently set at £1,000 below which cash may not be seized pursuant to these powers.[4]

Similarities with civil recovery

5.2   There are a number of important similarities between cash seizure proceedings and those in respect of forfeiture proceedings (see CHAPTER 4). Each of the provisions listed below bear the same meaning and have the same application within cash seizure proceedings as they do in proceedings for civil recovery:

•   unlawful conduct: s 241;

•   recoverable property: s 304;

---

[1]   POCA, s 294(2).
[2]   POCA, s 289(6).
[3]   POCA, s 289(7).
[4]   POCA, s 294 provides for a minimum amount (currently set at £1,000) by the Proceeds of Crime Act 2002 (Recovery of Cash in Summary Proceedings Minimum Amount) Order 2006, SI 2006/1699.

- tracing: s 305 (if cash represents the sale proceeds of property obtained through unlawful conduct then it will be recoverable);

- mixed property: s 306;

- accruing profits: s 307;

- granting interests: s 310.

The exceptions to recovery as set out in ss 308 and 309 also apply.[5]

Just as in civil recovery proceedings, the action is *in rem* as against the property and not against the person holding the property.

Powers of the investigator

5.3 Applications for production orders and search and seizure orders may be made to the High Court under a 'detained cash investigation' (see Serious Crime Act 2007).

5.4 POCA, s 290 provides that a magistrate or police inspector (or higher rank) or equivalent ranking Customs officer or an accredited financial investigator[6] may give 'prior approval' for a search for cash under s 289. If it is not practicable to obtain prior approval and officers are already lawfully on premises and form a reasonable suspicion that there may be recoverable cash then they may search for it.[7] If a search is conducted without prior approval and no cash is seized or any cash which is seized is not detained for more than 48 hours, the officer who seized it must make a report to a person appointed by the Home Office[8] setting out why it was believed that the powers were exercisable and why it was not practicable to obtain prior authority.

Procedure and practice

Standard of proof

5.5 The standard of proof is that of a balance of probabilities

Questioning the holder of cash

5.6 In order for the officer to form a reasonable suspicion that the cash is recoverable property or that it is intended for use in unlawful conduct s/he will almost invariably seek an explanation from the person as to the origin or intended use of the cash from the person/s in possession of it. It is worth noting that if questions are asked, there is no need to caution the person to whom they are directed, nor does

---

5 POCA, ss 308–310 create a number of exceptions and exemptions which mean that property ceases to be recoverable in certain circumstances – see CHAPTER 8.

6 POCA, s 290(2)–(5) as amended by the Serious Crime Act 2007 (Commencement No 2 and Transitional and Transitory Provisions and Savings) Order 2008, SI 2008/755.

7 POCA, s 289(1) as amended by the Serious Crime Act 2007 (Commencement No 2 and Transitional and Transitory Provisions and Savings) Order 2008, SI 2008/755.

8 POCA, s 290(7) and (8).

PACE 1984, s 78 apply.[9] Should the person when questioned decline to provide an explanation then 'A failure to give an explanation at all is also capable of giving rise to an inference that there is no innocent explanation'.[10] However, just as the protections which apply to criminal suspects do not apply, the powers of the police in criminal matters are also absent. Thus there is no power to arrest someone in the course of inquiries. There is a power to detain someone who the officer believes is carrying cash which is recoverable property or intended for use in unlawful conduct for as long as is necessary in order to search him or any article upon his person.[11]

Previous convictions

5.7   Subject to relevance and exclusionary rules under the civil rules of evidence, previous convictions are admissible.[12]

What must be proved?

5.8   The degree to which 'unlawful conduct' must be specified is the same as in civil recovery cases: see *Angus v United Kingdom Border Agency*[13] in which the court applied the test as propounded in *Director of the Assets Recovery Agency v Green*.[14]

Suspicious cash – the type of criminal conduct must be identified

5.9   Many cases arise where persons are found to be in possession of large amount of cash in suspicious circumstances, for example at airport. If such a person gives an account as to provenance or future purpose to which the cash will be put, then that in itself has been held to be capable of giving rise to an inference sufficient to prove the case, even though no particular unlawful conduct giving rise to the cash had been identified.[15] 'All that has to be identified is that the source was criminal activity or that the intended destination was to be used for criminal activity. A lie in that context may well entitle the fact finding body to infer what the source or intention for which the cash was to be used was in reality on the balance of probabilities'.[16] However in *Angus* the court observed that Moses J had not heard argument upon the construction of s 242(2)(b) and concluded that 'in a case of cash forfeiture, a customs officer does have to show that the property seized was obtained through conduct of one of a number of kinds each of which would have been unlawful conduct'.[17] Angus had given what she later accepted to be a false account as to the provenance of £40,000 in cash in her possession at an airport. Furthermore, witnesses called on her behalf at

---

9   *Revenue and Customs Commissioners v Pisciotto* [2009] EWHC 1991 (Admin).

10 *Commissioners of HMRC v Pisciotto* [2009] EWHC 1991 (Admin) at [15] .Though the extent that this reasoning will continue to apply remains in doubt following the decision in *Angus v United Kingdom Border Agency* [2011] EWHC 461 (Admin) (see 5.8, 5.9 below).

11 POCA, s 289(2) and (3). Note that the suspicion must relate to cash to the value of at least £1,000.

12 *Ali v Best* (1997) 161 JP 393.

13 [2011] EWHC 461 (Admin).

14 [2005] EWHC 3168 (Admin).

15 *Bujar Muneka v Customs and Excise Commissioners* [2005] EWHC 495 (Admin).

16 [2005] EWHC 495 (Admin) per Moses J at [12].

17 *Angus v United Kingdom Border Agency* [2011] EWHC 461 (Admin) at [29].

the final hearing were described as evasive and inconsistent and their evidence was found not to be credible.[18] A forfeiture order was made on the basis that the cash was the result of criminal activity, but the nature of that activity was not and did not require to be identified or specified. The respondent contended that this was sufficient.[19] The question for the court was: 'In a case of cash forfeiture does a customs officer have to show that the property seized was obtained through conduct of one of a number of kinds each of which would have been unlawful conduct or is it sufficient for the officer to point to criminal conduct of an unspecified kind?' The court held that it is not sufficient for the enforcement authority simply to point to criminal conduct of an unspecified kind. It would seem therefore that the approach taken in *Muneka* is now no longer appropriate; some kind of unlawful activity will have be identified and proved.

Procedure

5.10   Neither the Civil Procedure Rules nor the Criminal Procedure Rules apply in cash seizure cases. Procedure is instead provided for in the Magistrates Court (Detention and Forfeiture of Cash) Rules 2002[20] as amended by the Magistrates Courts (Miscellaneous Amendments) Rules 2003.[21]

5.11   The authorities are given time to investigate the provenance or future purpose of the cash.

The timetable envisaged by the statute is that Customs or the police are given an initial period of 48 hours to investigate the origin of the cash. Therefore so long as Customs or the police continue to have reasonable grounds for suspicion they may detain the cash for a period not exceeding 48 hours.[22] The 48-hour period excludes any Saturday or Sunday, Christmas Day, Good Friday or any Bank Holiday.[23] Any further application for the detention of cash must be made within 48 hours. The 48-hour rule is an important one and must be strictly adhered to (see *Walsh v Customs and Excise*[24] and *R v Uxbridge Magistrates Court ex p Henry*[25]). Further detention of cash for up to three months per application is permitted but in any event the total period of detention must not exceed two years.[26]

Further detention applications

5.12   Each and every application for further detention must be considered afresh on its merits. POCA, s 295(5) provides as to the test to be applied at further detention hearings:

[18]   [2011] EWHC 461 (Admin) at [5].
[19]   [2011] EWHC 461 (Admin) at [7]
[20]   SI 2002/2998.
[21]   SI 2003/1236.
[22]   POCA, s 295(1).
[23]   POCA, s 295(1B) as amended by the Serious Organised Crime and Police Act 2005.
[24]   [2001] EWHC Admin 426.
[25]   [1994] Crim LR 581. Both these cases were decided under other legislation but apply to POCA.
[26]   POCA, s 295(2).

'The first condition is that there are reasonable grounds for suspecting that the cash is recoverable property and that either—

(a)   its continued detention is justified whilst its derivation is further investigated or consideration is given to bringing (in the United Kingdom or elsewhere) proceedings against any person for an offence with which the cash is connected, or

(b)   proceedings against any person for an offence with which the cash is connected have been started and have not been concluded.'

Subsection (6) is in identical terms save that it relates to circumstances where there are reasonable grounds to suspect that the cash is to be used in unlawful conduct.

5.13   Each application for detention requires the court to have regard to the matters in s 295(5) or (6) depending on how the case is put.

5.14   Applications may be made by a constable or an officer of Revenue and Customs for production orders[27] and search and seizure warrants.[28] Such applications are heard in the High Court.

Procedure

5.15   The procedure is governed by the Magistrates Courts (Detention and Forfeiture of Cash) Rules 2002[29] as amended by the Magistrates Courts (Miscellaneous Amendments) Rules 2003.[30]

Form A

5.16   An application for continued detention must be in writing, and may be made by serving Form A on the court.[31] The court should fix a date for the hearing and notice of the hearing must be served upon the person from whom the cash was seized and to every person previously notified of prior orders.[32]

What happens if the application is refused?

5.17   The enforcement authority may seek to prove the case based on the material already has in its possession. If so minded it has 48 hours to make an application for forfeiture.[33] Alternatively it may concede the case and agree to the release of the cash.

---

[27]   POCA, s 345.

[28]   POCA, ss 352–354 as amended by Serious Crime Act 2007, ss 75–77.

[29]   SI 2002/2998.

[30]   SI 2003/1236.

[31]   Magistrates Court (Detention and Forfeiture of Cash) Rules 2002, r 5(1).

[32]   Magistrates Court (Detention and Forfeiture of Cash) Rules 2002, r 5(3).

[33]   See *Chief Constable of Lancashire Constabulary v Burnley Magistrates Court* (2003) EWHC (Admin) 3508.

What if the cash was not seized from a person but from an unattended despatch such as a letter?

5.18 The fact that the cash was not seized from any person is not bar to the institution of proceedings. The enforcement authority is, however, obliged to give notice of the hearing and provide copies of the application to the sender and intended recipient of the despatch.[34]

Applications for forfeiture

Form G

5.19 An application for the forfeiture of detained cash may be made on Form G.[35] It must be served on the magistrates' court and on any other person affected by the application. Form G must state the grounds upon which the application is made. Upon receipt of Form G the clerk to the justices will set a date for a directions hearing.

What happens if no-one appears to oppose the application at the directions hearing?

5.20 The court may order forfeiture at that stage if no one appears to oppose the application.[36] However, if the respondent can show that s/he had no notice of the application any order for forfeiture is liable to be quashed in judicial review proceedings.[37]

Forms

5.21 The forms used in cash seizure proceedings are as follows:

Form A:	Applications for the continued detention of cash under s 295(4).
Form B:	Court is required to record the date, time and place of seizure of cash, and the date, the amount and the amounts released since the last order for the continued detention of seized cash (if any).
Form C:	Notice to persons affected by an order for continued detention of seized cash. Any person from who the cash was seized may apply for the release of the detained cash or any part of it under s 297 of the Act.
Forms D, E, F:	No longer required to be used.
Form G:	See above at 5.19.

---

[34] Magistrates Court (Detention and Forfeiture of Cash) Rules 2002, r 4(4).

[35] Magistrates Court (Detention and Forfeiture of Cash) Rules 2002, r 7(1).

[36] Magistrates Courts (Detention and Forfeiture of Cash) Rules 2002, r 7(6).

[37] *R v Birmingham Magistrates Court and the Chief Constable of West Midlands Police, ex p Harrison* [2011] EWCA Civ 332 in which Hooper LJ urged the Lord Chief Justice to consider amending the Rules so that a person may show that notwithstanding purported service of the notice it had not been received, for example because the intended receipient had moved address. Pending such amendment, Hooper LJ invited magistrates to be 'particularly prudent' about proceeding in the absence of a respondent pending such amendment and indicated that it might be worthwhile to give notice of any application to solicitors known to act on behalf of the respondent in criminal proceedings.(at [55]–[56])

Interest-bearing accounts

5.22 Cash seized must be placed in an interest-bearing account at the first reasonable opportunity if it is detained for a period in excess of 48 hours.[38] What constitutes the first reasonable opportunity obviously depends on the circumstances. It is not infrequently the case that cash is submitted for a forensic examination of the bank notes to ascertain whether the level of prohibited drugs is higher than that found on bank notes normally in circulation. This is known as 'Mass Spec' analysis.

Remedies available to the respondent

5.23 The respondent need not wait until the case is fixed for trial. If so advised s/he may apply to the court for the release of detained cash, either in whole or in part, by virtue of POCA, s 297(2). Only the person from whom the cash was seized may make such an application and importantly, the burden of proof is upon the respondent to prove on a balance of probabilities that the conditions for further detention in s 295(5) and (6) no longer apply.[39] The application for release of the cash must be made in writing and submitted at the magistrates' court, which is then responsible for notifying the applicant and setting a date for the hearing.[40]

Remedies available to the owner/loser

5.24 Under POCA, s 301, if the person seeking release of the detained cash is not the person from whom it was seized but claims to be either the lawful owner of it or the loser of it, that person may apply for the release of detained cash either at an application for further detention or at the forfeiture hearing itself, or at any other time:

'If it appears to the court ... concerned that—

(a)   the applicant was deprived of the cash to which the application relates, or of property which it represents, by unlawful conduct,

(b)   the property he was deprived of was not, immediately before he was deprived of it, recoverable property, and

(c)   that cash belongs to him,

the court ... may order the cash to which the application relates to be released to the applicant.'

5.25 POCA, s 297(4) permits an officer to return detained cash in whole or in part if he is satisfied that the conditions for detention are no longer met. From a practical

---

[38] POCA, s 296(1). By virtue of subs (3) this requirement does not apply if the cash is required as evidence of an offence or in proceedings under Part V.

[39] *R (Chief Constable of Greater Manchester) v City of Salford Magistrates; R (Sarwar and Sons (Knitwear) Ltd) v Chief Constable of Greater Manchester Police* [2008] EWHC 1651 (Admin).

[40] Magistrates Court (Detention and Forfeiture of Cash) Rules 2002, r 6(1)–(4).

point of view, therefore, it is always advisable to seek to persuade the enforcement authority that the conditions for further detention are no longer met before making a formal application to the court.

Costs

5.26 The Civil Procedure Rules do not apply to cash seizure cases. Under s 64 of the Magistrates' Courts Act 1980 a successful party may apply for costs. The normal rule that costs follow the event is modified to this extent: the courts have held that there is a legitimate public interest in not discouraging the authorities from seizing cash in the honestly and reasonably held belief that it is recoverable property or intended for use in unlawful conduct. To award costs against them simply because the case was ultimately not proved might well have this effect. In deciding to award costs to a successful respondent the court will focus on whether the police had reasonable grounds to seize and detain the cash and their conduct thereafter; if the authority has behaved reasonably, the successful applicant is unlikely to get his costs.[41]

Funding

5.27 There is no express provision which enables the court to order the release of any part of the detained cash in order to pay for the respondent's legal representation. The absence of such an express power has been held, in the context of earlier related legislation to mean that there is none.[42] The only available route to public funding is through Community Legal Service.

Compensation

5.28 POCA, s 302 provides that if the application for forfeiture fails the court may make a compensation order[43] 'if the circumstances are exceptional'.[44] The amount of compensation is 'a sum which the court thinks reasonable to compensate for any loss suffered as a result of the detention'. If there are no exceptional circumstances then the amount is limited to lost interest for any period when the cash was not in an interest-bearing account.

Appeals

5.29 Any party aggrieved by an order in respect of a forfeiture application may appeal to the Crown Court and such appeal will result in a hearing *de novo*.[45] Alternatively appeal may be made to the Divisional Court on a point of law.

---

41 *R (Perinpanathan) v City of Westminster Magistrates' Court* [2010] 1 WLR 1508.
42 *Customs and Excise Commissioners v Harris* (1999) 163 JP 408.
43 POCA, s 302(1).
44 POCA, s 302(4).
45 POCA, s 299.The appeal must be made within 30 days of the order complained of (s 299(2)).

Chapter 6   Enforcement, reconsideration of orders and appeals and the dead, absconded and insolvent

'Every society gets the kind of criminal it deserves. What is equally true is that every community gets the kind of law enforcement it insists on.'
Robert Kennedy

Contents Summary

Magistrates' court – distress warrants-orders against banks – third party debt orders – activation of the default sentence – legal representation – applications for adjournments – time for payment – delay – appointment of enforcement receivers – reconsideration of the order: benefit, increase in available amount, inadequacy of available amount – discharge of the order – defendants who die, abscond or become insolvent – appeals

---

Reconsideration of the order

Section	Provision
19	reconsideration of the case where no confiscation order was originally made
20	reconsideration of benefit where no confiscation order was originally made
21	reconsideration of benefit where a confiscation order has been made
22	reconsideration due to increase in available amount
23	reconsideration due to inadequacy of available amount
24, 25	power to discharge the order
27	power to make a confiscation order against a defendant who absconds post conviction
28	power to make a confiscation order against a defendant who absconds pre conviction
Part 9	the insolvent defendant
Appeals	
43	restraint order appeals
65	receivership order appeals
31	confiscation order appeals

Magistrates' court

6.1   The magistrates' court is the venue for enforcement of orders. Defaulters will typically all be listed on the same day in an enforcement court, often before a district judge who may take a robust approach to enforcement.

6.2   The sole function of the magistrates' court is to enquire into the defendant's proposals for payment and decide what form of enforcement might be effective. If there appear to be, on enquiry, no effective proposals for payment, the court will simply issue a warrant of commitment and the default sentence will be activated.

6.3   The magistrates' court has purely an enforcement role and will not question the validity of the order or whether the defendant does in fact have the means to pay. Any such objections to the confiscation order made by the Crown Court should be addressed by way of appeal to the Court of Appeal.

6.4   Confiscation orders are enforced in the magistrates' court in the same way as fines.[1] The magistrates have four primary routes to secure compliance:

- distress warrants (bailiff);
- orders against banks and building societies;
- third-party debt orders;
- activation of the default sentence.

Distress warrants[2]

6.5   The distress warrant is the traditional bailiff method of seizing the defendant's property (if he has any) and selling it for what can be realised. A distress warrant will also allow the prosecutor to see any goods in his possession belonging to the defendant that the defendant refuses to hand over.

Orders against banks[3]

6.6   The court can direct banks and building societies holding money belonging to the defendant to pay it to the court.

Third-party debt orders[4]

6.7   This enables the court to enforce the debt from funds held by third parties via the county court. The funds will initially be frozen by the county court, then a further hearing may direct the funds to be paid to satisfy the order. The court can also make an order for deduction from benefits.

---

[1]   POCA, s 35 provides that ss 139(1)–(4) and 140(1) of the Powers of Criminal Court (Sentencing) Act 2000 shall apply to the enforcement of confiscation orders in the same way as they do to fines.

[2]   Magistrates' Courts Act 1980, s 76.

[3]   POCA, s 67.

[4]   Magistrates' Courts Act 1980, s 87.

Activation of the default sentence[5]

6.8   The court must issue a warrant of commitment to activate the default sentence imposed by the Crown Court. A hearing will be listed and the defendant required to attend. The default sentence cannot be activated in the absence of the defendant so if the defendant does not attend the hearing a warrant will be issued for his arrest. If the default sentence has already been served there is no power to issue further warrants to secure the defendant's attendance at court to consider other enforcement measures.[6] The upshot of the decision in *R (on the application of Rustim Necip) v City of London Magistrates' Court* is that there is now no power to compel the attendance of defendants at court to pursue civil enforcement when the default sentence cannot be activated, and in the absence of the defendant, no power to enforce the debt by civil means.

6.9   Whilst the court is not required to compel the attendance of the prosecutor at an enforcement hearing, the prosecutor has the right to attend and make representations when a warrant of commitment is being considered. Two Home Office circulars, 98/1986 and 10/1988, advise that liaison between the court and the prosecutor should take place. Since the prosecutor is in a position to advise the court on the current position regarding enforcement proceedings and relevant facts pertaining to the defendant it would seem prudent to seek the views of the prosecutor before making any order.[7] It would further be contrary to the purpose of the Act to send the defendant to prison where it is difficult for him to pay the order when there is a real prospect of him making payments if he remains at liberty.

The default sentence will be served consecutive to the sentence for the substantive offence and serving the sentence does not extinguish the debt.

Legal representation

6.10   State funding is available in appropriate circumstances for a solicitor, but does not extend to an advocate in court.[8]

Applications for adjournments

6.11   The court will usually be sympathetic to an adjournment if there is evidence that steps are being taken to make payment but the defendant's efforts are being

---

5   Magistrates' Courts Act 1980, s 76.
6   *R (on the application of Rustim Necip) v City of London Magistrates' Court* [2009] EWHC 755 (Admin).
7   *R v Harrow Justices ex p DPP* [1991] 1 WLR 395; *R (on the application of Garrote) v City of London Magistrates Court* [2002] EWHC 2009.
8   Criminal Defence Service (General) (No 2) Regulations 2001, SI 2001/1473, reg 12 is not met, which states:
    '(1)   A representation order for the purpose of proceedings before a magistrates' court may only include representation by an advocate in the case of:
        (a)   any indictable offence, including an offence which is triable either way; or
        (b)   extradition hearings under the Extradition Act 2003
        where the court is of the opinion that because of the circumstances which make the proceedings unusually grave or difficult, representation by both a litigator and an advocate would be desirable.'

frustrated by matters beyond his control (typically house sales falling through).[9] The court is likely to be less sympathetic if the failure to pay is as a consequence of the defendant's assets failing to realise the amount anticipated, and the defendant has made no application for a certificate of inadequacy or variation of the order to address the shortfall,[10] or there is an absence of co-operation and evidence of effort to comply with the order.

Time for payment

6.12   The Crown Court in POCA cases has a discretion to extend the time for payment up to a maximum of 12 months, but not beyond. The magistrates' court has no discretion to extend the time for payment or to waive interest payments.

Delay

6.13   An unreasonable delay in taking enforcement proceedings may act as a bar to the activation of the default sentence. Whether the delay is unreasonable must be considered in the context of each case. A confiscation order made on 21 June 1996 with an 18-month default sentence where committal did not take place until 9 October 2002 was held to be a breach of the defendant's rights under Article 6.1 of the European Convention on Human Rights to a fair trial (ie trial within a reasonable period of time).

Although the obligation is on the defendant to fulfil the confiscation order, the power to institute enforcement proceedings vests with the prosecution and they must do so within a reasonable time.[11]

Delay will be considered to be less prejudicial if the enforcement proposed does not involve loss of liberty, for example, the appointment of an enforcement receiver.

6.14   Mere delay of itself will not be sufficient to justify a stay; the delay must be one for which the enforcement agency is responsible, and which is unreasonable on the facts. If the defendant himself has contributed to the delay then it will not normally be appropriate for a stay to be granted.[12]

Where the delay occurs as a consequence of the defendant exercising his rights to appeal the court will be reluctant to stay enforcement unless there was an unreasonable delay of the appeal process itself for which the state was responsible.[13]

The court is far less inclined to stay delayed enforcement by civil means, which can be challenged under the law of abuse of process.[14]

---

[9]   *Barnett v Director of Public Prosecutions* [2009] EWHC 2004 (Admin).
[10]   *R v Liverpool Magistrates Court ex p Ansen* [1998] 1 All ER 692.
[11]   *R (on the application of Lloyd) v Bow Street Magistrates' Court* [2003] EWHC Admin 2294.
[12]   *R (on the application of Deamer) v Southampton Magistrates' Court* [2006] EWHC Admin 2221.
[13]   *Minshall v Marylebone Magistrates' Court* [2008] EWHC 2800; *Bullen and Soneji v The United Kingdom* [2009] ECHR 28.
[14]   *R (on the application of Joyce) v Dover Magistrates Court* [2008] EWHC Admin 1448.

Appointment of enforcement receivers

6.15   The Crown Court has the power, at its discretion, to appoint an enforcement receiver, on the application of the prosecutor, for the purpose of enforcing confiscation orders. The purpose of the enforcement receiver is to realise the assets in satisfaction of a confiscation order.

The power to appoint the receiver arises where a confiscation order is made, it is not satisfied and it is not subject to appeal.[15] The appointment can be made as soon as the order has been made.

6.16   The enforcement receiver has powers equivalent to an owner to manage and dispose of property, albeit the defendant must be given notice and given an opportunity to make representations in respect of the management, realisation of property and orders to make payments from the defendant's beneficial interests.[16]

Since the receiver is entitled to recover his costs from the defendant's estate[17] then before appointment the court should consider whether there is a less costly method of enforcement and give the defendant every opportunity to discharge the order voluntarily.

6.17   The defendant can object to the appointment of the receiver; however, his grounds for doing so are limited, particularly if he is in custody and the time limit for payment of the order has expired. He is generally best advised to consent to the appointment, or alternatively serve a statement setting out his proposals to fulfil the order.

On appointment the enforcement receiver becomes an officer of the court and operates independently of the prosecutor.

Reconsideration of the order

6.18   Whilst every effort is made accurately to assess the value of the defendant's assets at the time the order is made, it is often the case that at the time of sale the assets realise a different sum (usually less, but occasionally more). There is, therefore, power within POCA to adjust the order to take account of the variation.

No confiscation hearing originally made

6.19   The prosecutor can apply for an order under POCA, s 19 if new evidence has come to light which makes an order appropriate when one was not previously. It does not allow a prosecutor to apply for an order at a subsequent date when the evidence to do so was available at the time of conviction or at a time when the court decided not to proceed to make an order.

---

15   POCA, s 50.
16   POCA, s 51(8).
17   *Re HN & Others* [2005] EWHC 2982.

Section 19 provides:

'(1) This section applies if—

(a) the first condition in section 6 is satisfied, and no court has proceeded under that section;

(b) there is evidence which was not available to the prosecutor on the relevant date;

(c) before the end of the period of six years starting with the date of conviction the prosecutor applies to the Crown Court to consider the evidence; and

(d) after considering the evidence the court believes it appropriate to proceed under section 6.

...

(9) The "relevant date" is—

(a) if the court made a decision not to proceed under section 6, the date of that decision; or

(b) if the court did not make such a decision, the date of conviction.

(10) The "date of conviction" is—

(a) the date on which the defendant was convicted of the offence concerned, or

(b) if there were two or more offences and the convictions were on different dates, the date of the latest.'

Reconsideration of benefit

6.20 Section 20 of POCA applies if at the time when the court considered the provisions of s 6 it was concluded that the defendant had not benefited from his conduct, and therefore no order was made.

Two conditions[18] must be satisfied in order for the court to now proceed under s 6.

The first condition is that:

(a) the defendant has a criminal lifestyle but has not benefited from his general criminal conduct; or

(b) the defendant does not have a criminal lifestyle and has not benefited from his particular criminal conduct.

The second condition is that:

---

[18] POCA, s 20(2) and (4).

(a)   there is evidence that was not available to the prosecutor when the court decided that the defendant had not benefited from his general or particular criminal conduct;

(b)   before the end of the period of six years starting with the date on which the prosecutor applies to the Crown Court to consider the evidence; and

(c)   after considering the evidence the court concludes that it would have decided that the defendant would have benefited from his general or particular criminal conduct (as the case may be) if the evidence had been available to it.

6.21   Section 21 of POCA applies if evidence comes to light after the order has been made to suggest that the defendant's benefit was greater than was found when the order was originally made. It applies if:

(a)   the court has made a confiscation order;

(b)   there is evidence which was not available to the prosecutor at the relevant time;

(c)   the prosecutor believes that if the court were to find the amount of the defendant's benefit in pursuance of this section, it would exceed the relevant amount;

(d)   before the end of the period of six years starting from the date of conviction the prosecutor applies to the Crown Court to consider the evidence; and

(e)   after considering the evidence the court believes it is appropriate for it to proceed under this section.

6.22   There is no limit on the number of times that the prosecutor may return to the Crown Court to seek a reconsideration providing the applications are within six years of the date of conviction.

When reconsidering the defendant's benefit under s 21(4) the court must:

(a)   take account of conduct occurring up to the time it decided the defendant's benefit for the purposes of the confiscation order;

(b)   take account of property obtained up to that time;

(c)   take account of property obtained after that time if it was obtained as a result of or in connection with conduct occurring before that time.

6.23   The relevant time is:[19]

(a)   when the court calculated the defendant's benefit for the purposes of the confiscation order, if this section has not been applied previously

(b)   When the court last calculated the defendant's benefit in pursuance of this section, if the section has applied previously.

6.24   The relevant amount is:[20]

---

[19]   POCA, s 21(12).
[20]   POCA, s 21(13).

(a) the amount found as the defendant's benefit for the purposes of the confiscation order, if this section has not been applied previously;

(b) the amount last found as the defendant's benefit in pursuance of this section, if this section has applied previously.

6.25 The date of conviction is:[21]

(a) the date on which the defendant was convicted of the offence concerned; or

(b) if there are two or more offences and the convictions are on different dates, the date of the latest.

Operation of the 'criminal lifestyle' assumptions under POCA, s 10[22]

6.26 When benefit is being reconsidered the following applies to the assumptions:

(a) the first and second assumptions do not apply with regard to property first held by the defendant after the time the court decided his benefit for the purposes of the confiscation order;

(b) the third assumption does not apply with regard to expenditure incurred by him after that time;

(c) the fourth assumption does not apply with regard to property obtained (or assumed to have been obtained) by him after that time.

6.27 The objective in applying for reconsideration of benefit under s 21 must ultimately be for the prosecutor to apply to increase the recoverable amount. There would seem little point in making the application otherwise. Assuming the new calculation of the defendant's benefit exceeds the relevant amount, the court must make a new calculation of the recoverable amount and if it exceeds the amount required to be paid under the order previously made, the court may vary the order by substituting such amount to be paid as it considers 'is just'.

6.28 When considering the figure that is just, the court must have regard to any other financial orders made against the defendant in the context of the proceedings since the confiscation order was initially made.[23]

In assessing whether one amount exceeds another the court must also take account of any changes in the value of money.[24]

Increase in available amount

6.29 Section 22 of POCA allows the court to recalculate the available amount where the defendant now has funds not available when the order was made, and consequently the order was made in a lesser amount than the benefit. Such orders are

---

[21] POCA, s 21(14).
[22] POCA, s 21(6).
[23] POCA, s 21(9).
[24] POCA, s 21(11).

typically made if the prosecution becomes aware that the defendant has come into funds for example through an inheritance, or less likely, a lottery win.

6.30   The section applies if:[25]

(a)   a court has made a confiscation order;

(b)   the amount required to be paid was the amount found under that s 7(2); and

(c)   an applicant falling within s 22(2) applies to the Crown Court to make a new calculation of the available amount.

6.31   If the amount found under the new order exceeds the relevant amount the court may vary the order by substituting for the amount required to be paid such amount as it believes to be just, but does not exceed the amount found as the defendant's benefit from the conduct concerned. When considering what is just, the court must have regard to any other financial penalties or orders imposed on the defendant in the context of the proceedings which had not already been taken into account when the previous order was made.[26]

Whilst no time limit has been set for applications under s 22 the reasonable time requirement under Article 6(1) of the European Convention of Human Rights applies.[27]

Inadequacy of available amount

6.32   The POCA procedure under s 23 replaces the previous requirement to obtain a certificate of inadequacy from the High Court. Proceedings are in the Crown Court, and any application for public funding for representation for the hearing should be made to the Crown Court.

6.33   It applies if:

(a)   a court has made a confiscation order; and

(b)   the defendant, or a receiver appointed under s 50 of POCA applies to the Crown Court to vary the order under s 23.

The court must calculate the available amount as though the confiscation order was being determined at the time the s 23 application is being considered.[28]

6.34   The court may disregard any inadequacy which it believes is attributable (wholly or partly) to anything done by the defendant for the purpose of preserving property in circumstances where it is held by the recipient of a tainted gift.[29]

---

[25]   POCA, s 22(1).
[26]   POCA, s 22(5).
[27]   *Re Saggar (Confiscation Order: Delay)* [2005] EWCA Civ 174.
[28]   POCA, s 23(2).
[29]   POCA, s 23(5).

If the court then finds that the recalculated available amount is insufficient to meet the order outstanding it may reduce the order to a value it thinks just.[30]

The defendant is required to produce clear evidence of his reduced circumstances, in particular why assets available at the time the order was made are now reduced.

Practice

6.35 In the case of *Re B*[31] the court provided principles for the consideration of inadequacy applications under the Criminal Justice Act 1988. It is submitted that these general principles (summarised below) are of relevance in POCA, s 23 proceedings:

- The burden lies on the applicant to prove on the balance of probabilities that his realisable property is inadequate for the payment of the confiscation order.

- Realisable property must include his assets as a whole at the time of applying for the reconsideration; any property acquired since the order was made also falls to be considered.

- The application is not a back door route to reconsidering a previous finding as to the defendant's realisable assets. Any such challenge must be made by way of appeal of the order.

- It is not sufficient simply to say that the assets no longer meet the confiscation order. Evidence must be submitted to show why property existing at the time the order was made is no longer available.

- Reconsideration is only granted where there has been a genuine change in the defendant's financial circumstances as a consequence of events occurring after the confiscation order was made.

- The hearing is not an opportunity to raise arguments or adduce evidence that could properly have been raised at the time of the confiscation hearing.

- Any third-party interest may have to be made in an order post confiscation in a civil court.

- The defendant needs to show that it is impossible to recover a sum, not that it is merely difficult.[32]

The court is required to give reasons if it decides to disregard any inadequacy.[33]

---

[30] POCA, s 23(3).
[31] [2008] EWHC 3217.
[32] See also *R v Liverpool Justices ex p Ansen* [1998] 1 All ER 692, notable for its reference to a loan made by the defendant to his junior counsel which was proving difficult to recover.
[33] *Re Forwell* [2003] EWCA Civ 1608.

Hidden assets

6.36 If the Crown Court concluded in the original confiscation proceedings that the defendant had hidden assets, any application suggesting that these hidden assets are somehow now diminished such that the order cannot be met is unlikely to be successful.[34]

Powers to discharge the confiscation order

6.37 Powers exist under POCA for the relevant officer of the magistrates' court to apply to discharge the confiscation order either if the amount outstanding is less than £1,000 and the shortfall is caused by currency fluctuations,[35] or if the amount outstanding is less than £50.[36]

Defendants who die or abscond or become insolvent

6.38 These matters are dealt with in POCA, ss 27 and 28.

There is no power to make a confiscation order under POCA against a defendant who dies following his conviction but before the confiscation order is made. In appropriate cases civil recovery proceedings against 'recoverable property' may be commenced as an alternative: see CHAPTER 8.

There is power to make an order against a defendant who absconds post conviction if the conditions under s 6 are fulfilled, an application to the court is made and the court believes it is appropriate to proceed.[37]

6.39 The court proceeds are per a standard application subject to the safeguards in s 27. In summary:

- assumptions under s 10 are disregarded;

- no response by the defendant is required (s 17 or 18);

- any person the court believes is likely to be affected by an order is entitled to appear before the court and make representations;

- the court must not make an order unless the prosecutor has taken reasonable steps to contact the defendant.

Confiscation orders can be made even if the defendant absconds pre conviction

6.40 POCA, s 28 states as follows:

'(1) This section applies if the following two conditions are satisfied.

(2) The first condition is that—

---

[34] *Telli v Revenue and Customs Prosecutions Office* [2007] EWHC 2233.
[35] POCA, s 24.
[36] POCA, s 25.
[37] POCA, s 27(2), (3).

(a)   proceedings for an offence or offences are started against a defendant but are not concluded,

(b)   he absconds, and

(c)   the period of two years (starting with the date the court believes he absconded) has ended.

(3) The second condition is that—

(a)   the prosecutor applies to the Crown Court to proceed under this section, and

(b)   the court believes it is appropriate to do so.'

Similar conditions as apply under s 27 – any person who is likely to be affected by an order under s 6 is entitled to appear before the court and make representations. The prosecutor must also take reasonable steps to contact the defendant.

6.41   Under POCA, s 21, reconsideration of benefit cannot have effect whilst the defendant is an absconder.

If the court makes an order under s 28 and the defendant is later tried for the offence(s) and acquitted the Crown Court must discharge the confiscation order made in his absence on his application.[38]

6.42   In the event that the defendant ceases to be an absconder when a confiscation order has been made pre conviction, but the prosecutor no longer intends to proceed with the prosecution, the defendant can apply to the court to discharge the order and the court has a discretion to do so.[39]

A court discharging the confiscation order under s 30 has the power to make such other orders as it believes appropriate.[40]

The insolvent defendant (POCA, Part 9)

Bankruptcy

6.43   The bankruptcy of the defendant is covered by POCA, ss 417–419.

Where the bankruptcy post dates the restraint order the restrained assets shall be excluded from the defendant's estate for the purposes of bankruptcy.[41]

If the bankruptcy order is first in time the court may not make restraint or receivership orders in respect of any property referred to in it. However, in *R v Shahid*,[42] the Court of Appeal held that the fact a bankrupt's assets are in the hands of the trustee in bankruptcy

---

[38]   POCA, s 30(1), (2).
[39]   POCA, s 30(3).
[40]   POCA, s 30(5).
[41]   POCA, s 417.
[42]   [2009] EWCA Crim 831.

does not affect the power of the court to make a confiscation order, albeit that the bankruptcy may be 'highly relevant' when it comes to enforcement of the confiscation order. At this stage the powers of the prosecution to enforce the order 'may well be severely restricted' (per Keith J). At the enforcement stage therefore, a pre-existing order for bankruptcy will take precedence over a confiscation order.

Winding up of companies

6.44   Similarly, under POCA, s 426, if a winding-up order has been made a restraint order that post dates the winding up order cannot restrict the functions of the liquidator. If the restraint order is made before the winding up order, the functions of the liquidator may not be made in relation to property subject to restraint.

Insolvency practitioners who mistakenly deal with realisable property are not liable to pay damages unless they are negligent.[43]

Appeals

6.45   There are three types of appeal under POCA:

1   Appeal by the prosecutor against a confiscation order, or a failure of the Crown Court to make a confiscation order.[44]

2   Appeals about restraint orders.[45]

3   Appeals about receivers.[46]

Restraint order appeals

6.46   Under POCA, s 43, the prosecutor has the right to appeal to the Court of Appeal against the refusal of the Crown Court to make a restraint order. The Court of Appeal may either confirm the decision or make such order as it believes is appropriate. There is no right of appeal against the making of a restraint order; the defendant must first apply for the variation or discharge of the order. If that application fails then the defendant can appeal to the Court of Appeal.

6.47   Appeals can only be made with the leave of the court. Leave will only be given where:

(a)   the Court of Appeal considers that the appeal would have a real prospect of success; or

(b)   there is some other compelling reason why the appeal should be heard.

An appeal to the Supreme Court lies from the Court of Appeal.[47]

---

[43]   POCA, s 432(1) and (2).
[44]   POCA, s 43.
[45]   POCA, s 44.
[46]   POCA, s 65.
[47]   POCA, s 44.

Receivership order appeals

6.48 If, on an application for a receivership order, the court decides not to make such an order, the person who applied for the order can appeal to the Court of Appeal.[48] Equally if the court makes an order under any of ss 48–51 of POCA the person who applied for the order or any person affected by the order may appeal to the Court of Appeal in respect of the decision.[49]

6.49 If an application is made under POCA, s 62 for an order giving directions as to the exercise of the receiver's powers, if the court decides not to make the order applied for, the person who applied for the order may appeal to the Court of Appeal.[50]

6.50 Where an application is made to discharge or vary the powers of the receiver under s 63 of POCA, an appeal may be made to the Court of Appeal against the decision of the Crown Court by any person who applied for the order in respect of which the application was made; or any person affected by the court's decision; or the receiver.

An appeal lies only with the leave of the court.

6.51 An appeal also lies to the Supreme Court from the decision of the Court of Appeal on an appeal under POCA, s 65. This may be made by any person who was a party to the proceedings before the Court of Appeal and on appeal the Supreme Court may confirm the decision of the Court of Appeal or make such order as it believes is appropriate.

Confiscation order appeals

6.52 Appeals are made to the Court of Appeal (Criminal Division).

A confiscation order forms part of a sentence for the purpose of s 9 of the Criminal Appeal Act 1968. The grounds must either be mistake of law or mistake of fact.

The burden rests upon the appellant to show that his acceptance of any allegation in a prosecutor's statement was the result of a mistake of law or fact.

6.53 In the case of *R v Emmett*[51] guidance was given by Lord Steyn in relation to appeals (summarised below):

- The question will be not what mistake counsel made but what mistake the defendant made.

- In respect of matters peculiarly within the knowledge of the defendant the burden of proving the mistake will not easily be discharged.

---

48 POCA, s 65(1).
49 POCA, s 65(2).
50 POCA, s 65(5).
51 [1998] AC 773.

- The focus in these cases will be on a material and causatively relevant mistake, ie a material mistake which in fact caused the defendant to accept the correctness of a prosecutor's statement.

- Even if the defendant can persuade the court on the above points, the court must consider, whether in the absence of the material mistake, a particular confiscation order would nonetheless have been inevitable.

The Court of Appeal is reluctant to interfere with the discretion of the trial judge and will only do so where there has been a failure to exercise a discretion, failure to take into account a material consideration or a taking into account of an immaterial consideration.[52]

6.54 The lodging of an appeal does not affect the time to pay the order, which continues to run.

The prosecution have a right to appeal to the Court of Appeal against the making of a confiscation order,[53] and can also appeal against the decision not to make an order.[54]

On an application by the prosecutor the Court of Appeal has the power to confirm, quash or vary the confiscation order.[55] The court has the power to make a confiscation order if one was not previously made or direct the case back to the Crown Court to proceed under POCA, s 6.

6.55 An appeal lies to the Supreme Court from a decision of the Court of Appeal under POCA, s 31. The Supreme Court can confirm the decision or direct the Crown Court to proceed under s 6 if it believes the decision was wrong.

If in the meantime the Crown Court has imposed a related financial order on the defendant, then the court is required to take this into account when considering the confiscation order.[56]

---

[52] *R v Quinn* [1996] Crim LR 516.
[53] POCA, s 31(1).
[54] POCA, s 31(2).
[55] *R v Hockey* [2008] Crim LR 59.
[56] POCA, s 32(4).

Chapter 7 Case law

Contents Summary

Basic principles – three legitimate aims of confiscation – criminal lifestyle where the indictment is over six months but the criminal activity is not – basis of pleas – meaning of 'obtains' – benefit – value of goods – operation of the assumptions – pecuniary advantage – apportionment – companies, partnerships and the corporate veil – money launderers – property and mortgages – available amount – defendant's failure to testify – defendant's failure to respond – power to proceed in the defendant's absence – hidden assets – tainted gifts – imprisonment in default – delay – payment of prosecution costs – restraint orders – risk of dissipation – legal expenses – privilege against self incrimination – disclosure and third parties – funding of management receivers – management receiver's power of sale – application to vary and discharge restraint orders – contempt – management of proceedings – burden and standard of proof – abuse of process – how confiscation proceedings differ from criminal proceedings – evidence – inadequacy – enforcement – status of interim receiver – cash seizure – third parties and restraint – appeals – civil recovery

7.1 Confiscation proceedings have spawned a plethora of case law. Significant decisions have been listed below under relevant headings along with a summary of the findings.

Basic principles

R v May;[1] CPS v Jennings;[2] R v Green[3]

7.2 All three cases were decided by a single joint opinion of the Law Lords. Paragraph 48 of *May* (below) contains an endnote which is a statement of the relevant principles.

> '1. The legislation is intended to deprive defendants of the benefit they have gained from relevant criminal conduct, whether or not they have retained such benefit, within the limits of their available means. It does not provide for confiscation in the sense understood by schoolchildren and others, nor does it operate by way of a fine. The benefit gained is the total value of the property or advantage obtained, not the defendant's net profit after deduction of any expenses or any amounts payable to co-conspirators.
>
> 2. The court should proceed by asking the three questions posed above:

---

1 [2008] UKHL 28.
2 [2008] UKHL 29.
3 [2008] UKHL 30.

    (i)   Has the defendant (D) benefited from the relevant criminal conduct?

    (ii)   If so, what is the value of the benefit D has so obtained?

    (iii)   What sum is recoverable from D?[4]

3.   In addressing these questions the court must first establish the facts as best it can on the material available, relying as appropriate on the statutory assumptions. In very many cases the factual findings will be decisive.

4.   In addressing the questions the court should focus very closely on the language of the statutory provision in the question in the context of the statute and in the light of any statutory definition. The language used is not arcane or obscure and any judicial gloss or exegesis should be viewed with caution. Guidance should ordinarily be sought in the statutory language rather than in the proliferating case law.

5.   In determining, under the 2002 Act, whether D has obtained property or a pecuniary advantage and, if so, the value of any property or advantage so obtained, the court should (subject to any relevant statutory definition) apply ordinary common law principles to the facts as found. The exercise of this jurisdiction involves no departure from familiar rules governing entitlement and ownership. While the answering of the third question calls for enquiry into the financial resources of D at the date of determination, the answering of the first two questions plainly calls for a historical inquiry into past transactions.

6.   D ordinarily obtains property in law if he owns it, whether alone or jointly, which will ordinarily connote a power of disposition or control, as where a person directs a payment or conveyance of property to someone else. He ordinarily obtains a pecuniary advantage if (among other things) he evades a liability to which he is personally subject. Mere couriers or custodians or other very minor contributors to an offence, rewarded by a specific fee and having no interest in the property or proceeds of sale, are unlikely to be found to have obtained the property. It may be otherwise with money launderers.'

Other useful statements of principle

7.3   *Jennings*[5] (para 14):

' "Obtained" means obtained by the relevant defendant.'

---

4   Where issues of criminal lifestyle arise the questions must be modified. These are separate questions calling for separate answers, and the questions and answers must not be elided. (see CHAPTER 2).

5   [2008] UKHL 29.

A defendant's act may contribute significantly to property or to a pecuniary advantage being obtained without that defendant obtaining it.

Green[6] (para 15):

'Where two or more defendants obtain property jointly, each is to be regarded as obtaining the whole of it. Where property is obtained by one conspirator, what matters is the capacity in which he receives it, that is whether it is for his own personal benefit, or on behalf of others, or jointly on behalf of himself and others. This has to be decided on the evidence.'

See also *R v Cadman-Smith*.[7]

R v Sivaraman[8] set out general principles distilled from *May*, *Jennings* and *Green*:

'(1) The legislation is intended to deprive the offender of benefit he has gained from his relevant criminal conduct within his available means. It does not operate as a fine.

(2) The benefit gained is the total value of the property or pecuniary advantage gained, not his net profit.

(3) In considering what is the value of the benefit which the offender has obtained, the court should focus on the language of the statute and apply its ordinary meaning (subject to any statutory definition) to the facts of the case.

(4) "Obtained" means obtained by the relevant defendant.

(5) A defendant's act may contribute significantly to property being obtained without that defendant obtaining it.

(6) Where two or more defendants obtain property jointly each is to be regarded as obtaining the whole of it. Where property is received by one conspirator, what matters is the capacity in which he receives it, that is whether for his own personal benefit, or on behalf of others, or jointly on behalf of himself and others. This has to be decided on the evidence. By parity of reasoning two or more defendants may or may not obtain a joint pecuniary advantage: it depends on the facts.'[9]

In *R v Forte*:[10]

'the legislation can be considered to have a dual purpose. It is aimed at depriving offenders of the proceeds of their criminal conduct, and it is also an act which has the purpose of punishing convicted offenders in order to deter

6   [2008] UKHL 30.
7   (2002) 2 Cr App R (S) 37.
8   [2008] Crim 1736.
9   [2008] Crim 1736 at [12].
10 [2004] EWCA Crim 3188.

the commission of further offences so as to reduce the profits available to fund further criminal enterprises. In that respect it is therefore described as penal, or indeed draconian in operation.'

The three legitimate aims of confiscation

R v Rezvi, R v Benjafield[11]

7.4   The three aims of confiscation are to 'punish convicted offenders, deter the commission of further offences, and to reduce the profits available to fund further criminal enterprises'.

Criminal lifestyle where the indictment is over six months, but the defendant's criminal activity is less than six months

R v Bajwa[12]

7.5   The decision of the court:

'In our view the wording "it is an offence committed over a period of at least six months" must relate to the particular defendant's part in an offence, so that the defendant being considered must have committed the offence for at least six months.'

Their Lordships identified four reasons for their decision on this issue:

1   This approach is consistent with the object of s 75, which is to identify particular defendants who have a 'criminal lifestyle'.

2   Section 75(2)(c) is the third set of 'tests' for establishing whether a defendant has a criminal lifestyle. It only needs be considered if a defendant does not fulfil the other two. It should be construed consistently with s 75(2)(a) and (b) in which the first question is whether the particular defendant has committed the offences identified in those paragraphs.

3   Their Lordships observed that if it were enough for s 75(2)(c) that 'the offence' at large was committed over a period of at least six months, it produces a startling anomaly. It would mean that in a case where there is only one defendant involved in the offence, it would have to be demonstrated that he had committed the offence concerned for at least six months. But if there is more than one defendant involved in the same offence, then (on that construction) the defendant (A) committing the offence only on the last day of a period of at least six months would be caught by the paragraph, but only if it could be demonstrated, for at least one other co-defendant (B), that the offence had been

---

11   [2003] 1 AC 1099.
12   [2011] EWCA 1093.

committed over at least six months. For example, if there was a long-standing conspiracy to smuggle counterfeit cigarettes into the UK with the intention of fraudulently evading the duty payable and one defendant (of previous good character) was engaged, for a fee of £5.00, to be the driver on the day prior to the last run before all the defendants were arrested, he would be caught by this paragraph. Yet it would seem almost perverse to describe that driver as having a 'criminal lifestyle'.

4   The practical consequences of the alternative view would produce the following difficulty: No matter how short a period a particular defendant (A) was involved in a conspiracy, so long as one other co-defendant was involved for at least six months then defendant (A) could never enter a basis of plea that would avoid him being treated as having a 'criminal lifestyle'.

See also *R v Takkar*[13] where the Court of Appeal agreed with the submission that the issue of whether the appellant had committed an offence over a period of six months or longer was to be determined by reference to the facts and not simply by reference to the dates pleaded in the indictment.[14]

Basis of pleas and the scope of offending as identified at trial

R v Chambers;[15] R v Byatt;[16] R v Lazarus; R v Lunnon[17]

7.6   *General principle*: Where a basis of plea has been agreed by the Crown it will be treated as binding for the purposes of confiscation proceedings unless the prosecution has given a clear indication to the contrary. For the avoidance of doubt when a basis of plea is agreed in cases where confiscation is likely to be relevant the parties should make the position with regard to confiscation clear in the written basis.

R v Sangha[18]

7.7   Similarly the court is not limited to the finding of the jury for the purposes of confiscation.

R v Briggs Price[19]

7.8   Nor is the court limited to considering only the offences charged if there has been evidence at trial to satisfy the judge to the criminal standard that other offences have been committed.

---

13   [2011] EWCA Crim 646.
14   [2011] EWCA Crim 646 at [28].
15   [2008] EWCA Crim 2467.
16   [2006] EWCA Crim 904.
17   (2005) 1 Cr App R (S) 24.
18   [2008] EWCA Crim 2562.
19   [2009] UKHL 19.

Meaning of 'obtains'

7.9 *General principle*: the word obtain implies ownership, including a power of disposition or control.

In *Jennings* it was stated:

> '[the defendant] cannot, and should not be deprived of what he has never obtained or its equivalent, because that is a fine. The rationale of the confiscation regime is that the defendant is deprived of what he has gained or its equivalent. This must ordinarily mean that he has obtained property so as to own it whether alone or jointly, which will ordinarily connote a power of disposition or control, as where a person directs a payment or conveyance of property to someone else.

> A person's act may contribute significantly to property (as defined in the Act) being obtained without his obtaining it. But under section 71(4) [of the CJA 1988] a person benefits from an offence if he obtains property as a result of or in connection with its commission, and his benefit is the value of the property so obtained, which must be read as meaning "obtained by him".'

R v Cadman-Smith[20]

7.10 It makes no difference if the property once it was obtained was destroyed, damaged or forfeited.

R v Mitchell[21]

7.11 If you are not an importer or co-importer of goods, simply a loader on a fixed fee, you have not 'obtained' the goods.

R v Olupitan[22]

7.12 A defendant obtained nothing in circumstances where he had only joined a conspiracy to defraud on the day that police action had brought it to an end.

Benefit

R v Waya[23]

7.13 In 2003, Mr Waya obtained a loan of £465,000. He combined it with £310,000 of his own money and purchased a property for £775,000. The mortgage was redeemed in 2005 and the property was remortgaged with a different lender. In July

---

20 [2002] 1 WLR 54.
21 [2009] EWCA Crim 214.
22 [2004] 2 Cr App R (S) 14.
23 [2011] 1 Cr App R (S) 4.

2007, Mr Waya was convicted of making false statements in obtaining the £465,000 loan. There was no suggestion of any dishonesty in his obtaining of the second mortgage. By the time of confiscation proceedings in 2008, the value of the property was £1,850,000. Mr Waya had paid back the £465,000 three years earlier. The judge assessed Mr Waya's 'benefit' as the value of the property at the time of trial, less his original untainted contribution of £310,000. This led to an order being made in the sum of £1,540,000. Mr Waya appealed.

Relying on the dictum in the case of *R v Preddy*[24], Mr Waya submitted that he had not 'obtained' the money loaned to him. It had merely been paid to his solicitor as part of the conveyancing process. As such, he obtained no 'benefit' for himself and no confiscation order should have been made against him.

The Court of Appeal rejected that argument. It held that all that was necessary for a person to obtain a 'benefit' for the purposes of s 76 of POCA was that the person obtained 'property' as a result of or in connection with criminal conduct. The property he purchased was held to constitute 'property' for the purposes of POCA, s 84.

All parties agreed that the trial judge had erred in his calculation of the 'benefit' at £1,540,000. But they did not agree on what the figure should be. Mr Waya argued that if he did receive a 'benefit' it was no more than the amount of the loan he had obtained dishonestly: £465,000. The Crown argued that his 'benefit' was the proportion that the dishonest loan represented as 60% of the original purchase price. Accordingly, his 'benefit' under POCA was 60% of the current value: £1,100,000.

The Court of Appeal agreed with the Crown. It found that it was necessary to trace the character of the money financing the purchase of the property. Accordingly it was the proportion, not simply the amount that the money represented, that was important.

The issues certified for determination by the Supreme Court were:

1   whether, where a person obtains a 'benefit' within the meaning of Part 2 of POCA where he/she obtains a money transfer by deception and thereby causes a lending institution to transfer funds to his/her solicitor by way of a mortgage advance to enable the purchase of a property;

2. if so, whether the value of this 'benefit' is the value of the loan advanced, the person's interest in the property concerned or some other value; and

3   if not, whether the person obtains a 'pecuniary advantage' for the purposes of Part 2 of POCA.

---

[24]   [1996] 1 AC 815.

R v Frost[25]

7.14 The defendant secured a dishonest overpayment of VAT via his employment which was paid into his employer's bank account. He was held only to have obtained for the purposes of the Act those monies that he extracted for his use, and not the whole of the overpaid sum. Whilst his actions had demonstrated a power of disposition or control over monies in that he had caused them to be paid into his employer's bank account, he never 'got his hands' on those monies and so therefore not be said to have obtained a benefit in respect of them.

Value of goods and drugs

R v Islam[26]

7.15 *General principle*: all goods have a market value. Where they are legitimate goods this is the legitimate market value, where they are illegitimate their black market value can be calculated. However, since unlawful goods cannot be sold the value of unlawful goods cannot form part of the available amount.

Operation of the assumptions

R v Jones (Confiscation Orders)[27]

7.16 The court must not make the assumptions if there would be serious risk of injustice to the offender. However, 'serious risk of injustice' does not refer to hardship that would be sustained to the offender by virtue of the making of the order, and the phrase does not operate to provide a discretion to the court as to whether it would be fair to make any order at all.

R v Redbourne[28]

7.17 The assumption can be made by the court at any stage of the enquiry.

> 'An assumption … is the acceptance of something as true which is not already known or proved, and therefore may or may not be true. If the Crown is directed or empowered to make an assumption, that means that the court must or may take the assumed fact as true.'

---

[25] [2009] EWCA Crim 1737.
[26] [2009] UKHL 30.
[27] The Times 8 August 2006.
[28] [1992] 1 WLR 1182.

R v Walbrook and Glasgow[29]

7.18 If a defendant wants to succeed in showing the assumptions are incorrect he must produce clear and cogent evidence.

Pecuniary advantage

R v White; R v Dennard; R v Perry; R v Rowbotham[30]

7.19 The Act does not define pecuniary advantage. However, it seems to be generally accepted that a pecuniary advantage is an unlawful evasion or deferment of liability. The test seems to be – if the fraud succeeded, would the defendant have been better off – either as a result of property obtained, or as a result of money he does not need to pay out? If the latter, then he has obtained a pecuniary advantage.

These four appeals, not otherwise linked, against the imposition of confiscation orders involved the smuggling of tobacco into the UK for resale and had been listed together because they raised similar issues. The evasion by a smuggler of duty or VAT constituted, for the purposes of confiscation proceedings, the obtaining of a pecuniary advantage only if he personally owed that duty or VAT. This was established by the House of Lords in *R v May*[31] and *R v Jennings*.[32] The relevant Regulations would determine whether a defendant personally owed duty or VAT, subject to the compatibility of those regulations with the primary domestic legislation and the relevant EC Directive. Before the law was clarified by the House of Lords in *R v May* and *R v Jennings*, the regulations were generally unimportant in confiscation hearings since whether the defendant personally owed the duty or VAT did not matter because he would normally have contributed to the evasion of the duty or VAT by another. In each of these four cases the prosecution had relied on the Excise Goods (Holding, Movement, Warehousing and REDS) Regulations 1992[33] not knowing that they had been superseded (so far as tobacco products were concerned) on 1 June 2001 by the Tobacco Products Regulations 2001.[34] The error was discovered during the course of the appeal in *R v Chambers*[35] but the court in that case refused to adjourn the case for further argument because the prosecution had failed in its duty to put before the court at first instance the relevant statutory provisions. In these appeals, the compatibility of the Regulations with the relevant Council Directive 92/12/EEC and with s 1(4) of the Finance (No 2) Act 1992 had been considered with the benefit of argument from counsel who specialised in European Community law.

---

[29] [1994] Crim LR 613.
[30] [2010] EWCA Crim 978.
[31] [2008] AC 1028.
[32] [2008] AC 1046.
[33] SI 1992/3135.
[34] SI 2001/1712.
[35] [2008] EWCA Crim 2467.

R v Mitchell[36]

7.20 Mitchell was convicted of being knowingly concerned in the fraudulent evasion of duty on the importation of tobacco. He contended that he had been paid £100 for helping to load dutiable tobacco and this was his only benefit. Regulation 13(1) of the Tobacco Products Regulations 2001 provides that the person liable to pay the duty is the person holding the products at the excise point. Regulation 13(3) makes any person who 'caused the tobacco products to reach' the excise point jointly and severally liable for the duty.

The court did not accept that anybody who contributed to the importation (eg by loading) would be a person who 'caused' the goods to reach the excise duty point. Instead the court found that the phrase appeared to be directed at that person or body who had real and immediate responsibility for causing the product to reach that point, which will typically and ordinarily be the consignor. Therefore the court accepted that the defendant did not have a personal liability to pay the duty and his benefit was limited to £100.

R v Sivaraman[37]

7.21 Sivaraman in his capacity as manager of a petrol station accepted a number of deliveries of red diesel which had been converted for sale to the general public. The petrol was purchased by his employer and he was paid £15,000 for his role. It was accepted that he was not a joint purchaser with his employer and therefore there was no liability that he had evaded. His benefit was therefore limited to £15,000.

R v Chambers[38]

7.22 Chambers pleaded guilty to being knowingly concerned in the fraudulent evasion of excise duty but asserted that he only started work at the warehouse on the day of his arrest. His work involved handling the goods but he had not been involved in their purchase.

The court came to the following conclusions (summarised):

- A benefit is obtained by way of a pecuniary advantage if the defendant dishonestly evaded a personal liability to pay duty.

- The court must look carefully at the levels of benefit obtained where someone has simply helped someone else to evade duty. The helper may obtain benefit by way of a fixed fee for services.

See also *R v Dimsey and Allen*:[39] if a defendant defers or evades payment of tax then he obtains a pecuniary advantage equal to the tax evaded or deferred.

---

36 [2009] EWCA Crim 214.
37 [2008] EWCA Crim 1736.
38 [2008] EWCA Crim 2467.
39 (2000) 1 Cr App R (S) 497.

A-G v Moran[40]

7.23 In cases of tax evasion the benefit is held to be the underpayment of tax with interest, rather than the whole of the undeclared profits.

R v Cadman-Smith[41]

7.24 Where contraband cigarettes were seized before the defendant had a chance to sell them it was held that it was immaterial that the defendant had not had a chance to sell them. He had obtained a pecuniary advantage at the point of importation.

> '... where a person misappropriates money from a company as an essential part of a fraud on the Inland Revenue, and is convicted of that fraud, he is liable to a confiscation order in the amount of the monies which he has misappropriated on the ground that the monies are property obtained as a result of or in connection with the fraud.'

See also *R v Foggon*.[42]

Apportionment

7.25 *General principles*: if co-conspirators are acting jointly, then each benefits to the full sum obtained. If defendants are not acting jointly then the court should look carefully at the facts of the case to determine the relationships between the parties and the role of each defendant to appropriately apportion the benefit.

R v Clark and Severn[43]

7.26 C and S assisted in the shipment of stolen cars to East Africa through their limited company which provided storage and shipping facilities. The cars were stowed in containers at the company's premises. C was the organiser and facilitator of the container operation, and S arranged for the haulage of the containers to the port. C submitted that the judge misapplied the decision of the House of Lords in *May*,[44] and failed to take account of subsequent decisions of the Court of Appeal such as *Sivaraman*,[45] *Allpress*,[46] and *Anderson*.[47] C contended that the judge was wrong to fix C with the burden of the full value of the cars when his role, significant as it may have been for the purpose of the conspiracy, was only to facilitate the export of the cars. The confiscation order was quashed and the case remitted to the Crown Court for a redetermination. C was not a courier or custodian of money or drugs, but he was, through his company, a bailee of the cars for the purpose of containerising and

---

40 [2001] EWCA Crim 1770.
41 [2002] 1 WLR 54.
42 [2003] EWCA Crim 270.
43 [2011] EWCA Crim 15.
44 [2008] 1 AC 1028.
45 [2009] 1 Cr App R (S) 80.
46 [2009] 2 Cr App R (S) 58.
47 [2010] EWCA Crim 615.

transporting them in preparation for their shipment to East Africa. He was an 'integral facilitator', but there was nothing to link him either with the original thefts or with the onward sales in Africa or the proceeds of such sales. 'His role was no doubt an important part of the overall handling conspiracy, but there was nothing apart from the importance of that role to suggest that the cars were jointly owned by him (or Severn) with other principal conspirators.' The Court added: 'As pointed out in *Jennings* … and again in *Allpress* … a defendant may play an important role in a conspiracy without obtaining property for the purpose of the test of benefit.'

R v Green[48]

7.27

'where money or property is received by one defendant on behalf of several defendants jointly, each defendant is to be regarded as having received the whole of it … it does not matter that proceeds of sale may have been received by one conspirator who retains his share before passing on the remainder; what matters is that capacity in which he receives them.'

R v Patel[49]

7.28 It is not relevant what a defendant who receives money does with the money afterwards; even if a share of the money is paid to an accomplice after it is received, the defendant who forwards it to him is still regarded as having the benefit of the full sum.

R v Sharma[50]

7.29 However, in a separate case the defendants had not jointly obtained the benefit, but there had been a disposal of by one member of the criminal enterprise to another. Each is treated as a recipient of a benefit to the extent of the value of the money which has come into the possession of each of them.

R v Gibbons[51]

7.30 Yet where there is no evidence before the court to enable a finding that the sum had been jointly obtained or how the proceeds had been divided, it was appropriate for the sum obtained to be divided by the four defendants.

R v Sivaraman[52]

7.31 The greater the involvement in the conspiracy, the greater the appropriate level of punishment; but it does not follow that the greater the involvement, the

---

48 [2008] UKHL 30.
49 [2000] 2 Cr App R (S) 10, CA.
50 [2006] 2 Cr App R (S) 416.
51 [2003] 2 Cr App R (S) 169, CA.
52 [2008] EWCA Crim 1736.

greater the benefit to the defendant. A mere employee accepting deliveries of fuel on which duty was not paid only had the benefit of his fee for accepting the fuel, not the full value of the duty evaded.

Companies, partnerships and the corporate veil

R v Grainger;[53] R v W Stephenson & Sons and Bick[54]

7.32 *General principle*: payments made to companies or a partnership as a separate legal entity become the benefit of those legal entities and not any other individual, although in certain circumstances it may be appropriate to pierce the corporate veil, if the company is simply being used as a vehicle or facade by the offender to conceal criminal activity.

R v Dimsey[55]

7.33 In this case (at 772) Laws LJ applied the principle laid down by Diplock LJ in *Snook v London and West Riding Investments Ltd*[56] (at 802).

The court cannot pierce the corporate veil simply where it considers it just to do so. There must be evidence of impropriety and dishonesty. The courts have identified three situations where the corporate veil can be pierced in the context of criminal cases:

1   If an offender attempts to shelter behind a corporate facade, or veil, to hide his crime and his benefits from it.

2   Where an offender does acts in the name of the company which with the necessary *mens rea* constitute a criminal offence which leads to the offenders conviction, then 'the veil of incorporation is not so much pierced as rudely torn away'; per Lord Bingham in *CPS v Jennings*[57] (at [16]).

3.   Where the transaction or business structures constitute a 'device', 'cloak' or 'sham' ie an attempt to disguise the true nature of the transaction or structure so as to deceive third parties or the courts.

These principles were applied to the case of *R v Seager and Blatch*[58] where it was held that the corporate veil should not be pierced. Mr Blatch was operating as a company director when disqualified from doing so, but the company itself was engaged in legitimate business. Similarly Mr Seager did not use the company for illegal activities or as a facade to hide the benefits of his crime.

---

53   [2008] EWCA Crim 2506.
54   [2008] EWCA Crim 273.
55   [2000] QB 744.
56   [1967] 2 QB 786.
57   [2008] UKHL 29.
58   [2009] EWCA Crim 1703.

Re D[59]

7.34 In *Re D*, the company was set up just prior to the defendant being sent to prison for non payment of the order. The RCPO applied for the restraint order to be varied to include the assets of the company. The company applied to remove reference to the company assets on the basis that the corporate veil should not have been lifted. This was rejected.

Ouseley J observed:

> 'The object of the Act is to enable proceeds of crime to be ascertained, protected and realised. The first question therefore is whether there are corporate assets which should be treated as a the defendant's assets and the second question is whether, if that is the case, a restraint and receivership order of the extent sought is necessary. The position, in my judgment, is the same where there is an intermingling of the assets of a criminal, who is seeking to evade the effects of a confiscation order, with the assets of innocent business partners of a company. If it is established that some or all of the assets of the company are to be treated as assets of the defendant, the question of how their intermingling with assets of someone who is innocent of wrongdoing is to be dealt with, is a matter for resolution by deciding whether an order should be made and if so on what terms, rather than a matter, which has to be resolved by simply asking whether the corporate veil should be pierced. As I have said, the question is whether it is necessary to impose an order in the terms sought bearing in mind that there would be, necessarily, someone who is innocent whose interests would be adversely affected by such an order ... There would obviously be a very considerable lacuna in the ability of the Act to achieve its objective if in principle because such a company was not a one man band or wholly criminal in its origin, funding or activities, assets held in it could not be subject to receivership or restraint order provisions.'

Re D was decided against the backdrop of an unfulfilled order, a history of breaches of restraint orders and evidence of cash investment. The company represented some of the funds that the defendant had sought to put out of the reach of the RCPO.

Ouseley J stated:

> 'it would be absurd not to treat the company's assets as being his in part. Any other approach would enable, as I have said, someone with criminal proceeds to incorporate himself with one other, who might be an innocent dupe, and thereby put his assets beyond the reach of the R&CPO.'

---

[59]   [2006] EWHC Admin 254.

Re H (Restraint Order: Realisable Property)[60]

7.35 An excellent analysis of the principles of separate corporate identity and when the corporate veil should be pierced is given in *Re H (Restraint Order: Realisable Property)*[61] citing *Adams v Cape Industries plc*:[62]

'... The court also assumed to be correct the proposition that the court will lift the corporate veil where the defendant by the device of a corporate structure attempts to evade (i) limitations imposed on his conduct by law ... clearly as a matter of law, the corporate veil can be lifted in appropriate circumstances.'

R v K[63]

7.36 The court is entitled to lift the corporate veil even if the company is engaged in significant legitimate trading activity. Asking whether the corporate veil should be lifted may be misleading in this context; a better question to ask is whether the assets of the company may be treated as realisable property of the defendant.

Money launderers

R v Allpress[64]

7.37 *General principle*: money laundering is not a special category of case. Payment of money into a bank account in the defendant's name suggests that the money was his property in the absence of evidence that the money, although technically in the defendant's name, was operated by another person for his benefit.

In this case the defendant couriered money for a fee. The court considered whether her benefit was the money couriered or the fee.

'... if D's only role in relation to property connected with his criminal conduct, whether in the form of cash or otherwise, was to act as a courier on behalf of another, such property does not amount to property obtained by him within the meaning of POCA 2002.'

Property and mortgages

7.38 *General principle*: where it can be shown that tainted funds have been used to pay the deposit on a house, but the remainder was legitimately obtained, the house has not been obtained as a result of or in connection with the commission of criminal offences.

---

60 [1996] 2 All ER 391.
61 [1996] 2 All ER 391.
62 [1990] Ch 433.
63 [2005] EWCA Crim 619.
64 [2009] EWCA Crim 8.

R v Walls[65]

7.39　The defendant's benefit in mortgaged property is the value of the equity.

R v Roach[66]

7.40　Where the defendant's interest in a property comes partly from tainted and partly from legitimate funds the legitimate part should not be regarded as the proceeds of crime.

R v Ward[67]

7.41　Mortgage payments from legitimate funds:

'... the legitimacy of the source of the moneys is not sufficient to displace the assumption. What must be shown in addition is that the property in question, here the remortgage money, was obtained lawfully, and that the appellant's criminal lifestyle was irrelevant to its obtaining. Because of his general lack of credibility, the appellant failed to show that the moneys had been obtained lawfully ... moreover the false accounts made it virtually impossible for the appellant to displace the statutory assumption.'

See also *R v Agombar*.[68]

Available amount – what can be realised?

R v Chen[69]

7.42　Pension policies can form part of the available amount, but only if they can be realised.

Re Adams[70]

7.43　A consultancy contract for the defendant's services was not 'realisable property' but a chose in action personal to the party because the services had to be provided by the defendant.

See also *R v May* (above): legitimately acquired assets may be treated as realisable property.[71]

---

65   [2003] 1 WLR 731.
66   [2008] EWCA Crim 2649.
67   [2008] EWCA Civ 2955.
68   [2009] EWCA Crim 903.
69   [2009] EWCA Crim 2669.
70   (2005) LS Gaz January 13, 28, QBD (Lightman J).
71   [2008] UKHL 28 at [41].

Defendant's failure to testify

R v Siddique;[72] R v Benjafield;[73] R v Comiskey[74]

7.44   *General principle*: if the defendant fails to give evidence and thereby persuade the court that the amount of his realisable assets is less than the amount of his benefit, the order is likely to be made in the full amount of the benefit. If a defendant is convicted after a trial at which he was disbelieved:

'the fact that his credibility may already have been badly damaged is not a shield behind which he can hide. If it were, defendants in the position of the appellant could refuse to give evidence and yet successfully maintain that their realisable assets were less than the benefit. Such a position would be nonsensical ...'[75]

However, the court is not bound to reject a defendant's case that his realisable assets are less than the benefit figure merely because he does not testify. The court can look at other sources of evidence to form a just and proportionate view of the facts.

R v Mcintosh and Marsden[76]

7.44A

'In the light of *Glaves*[77] and *May* (supra) there is no principle that a court is bound to reject a defendant's case that his current realisable assets are less than the full amount of the benefit, merely because it concludes that the defendant has not revealed their true extent or value, or has not participated in any revelation at all. The court must answer the statutory question in s.71(6) in a just and proportionate way. The court may conclude that a defendant's realisable assets are less than the full value of the benefit on the basis of the facts as a whole. A defendant who is found not to have told the truth or who has declined to give truthful disclosure will inevitably find it difficult to discharge the burden imposed upon him. But it may not be impossible for him to do so. Other sources of evidence, apart from the defendant himself, and a view of the case as a whole, may persuade a court that the assets available to the defendant are less than the full value of the benefit.'[78]

'... there is no power to make a lesser order once the defendant has failed to satisfy the evidential burden imposed on him. That is correct so far as it goes. But it must always be recognised that a just and proportionate view of the facts *as a whole* may enable a defendant to satisfy that evidential burden even when

72   [2005] EWCA Crim 1812.
73   (2002) 2 Cr App R(S) 70.
74   (1991) 93 Cr App R 227.
75   Per Bennett J at [27]. This case was decided under the Drug Trafficking Act 1994 but the reasoning applies to cases decided under POCA 2002.
76   [2011] EWCA Crim 1501.
77   *Glaves v CPS* [2011] EWCA Civ 69.
78   [2011] EWCA Crim 1501 at [15].

his own evidence proves to be an untruthful and unreliable or even non-existent source of the nature and extent of his current assets.'[79]

See also *Telli v Revenue and Customs Prosecutions Office*:[80]

'absent identification of all the realisable property held by him, a defendant will normally be unable to satisfy the court that the amounts that might be realised at the time the confiscation order is made is less than the amount assessed to be the proceeds of his drug trafficking.'

Defendant's failure to respond to the section 16 statement

R v Layode[81]

7.45   If the defendant fails to respond to the section 16 statement or give evidence at the hearing and the judge makes an unfavourable ruling on appeal it was held 'the appellant had nobody but himself to blame'.

Power to proceed in the defendant's absence

R v Gavin[82]

7.46   *General principle*: if the defendant is well aware of the proceedings against him and has voluntarily absented himself then an order can be made in the defendant's absence.

Hidden assets

R v Barwick[83]

7.47   It is for the defendant to satisfy the court that his realisable assets are less than the sum of the benefit.

R v Barnham[84]

7.48   The Crown is not required to make out a prima facie case of hidden assets.

---

[79]   [2011] EWCA Crim 1501 at [19].
[80]   [2007] EWHC 2233.
[81]   (unreported) 12 March 1993, CA.
[82]   [2010] EWCA Crim 2727.
[83]   (2001) 1 Cr App R(S) 129.
[84]   [2005] EWCA Crim 1049.

Tainted gifts

R v Richards[85]

7.49   Where property is transferred as a tainted gift the benefit vests in the person making the gift and the benefit should not be found against the person holding the bare legal title.

Imprisonment in default

R v Popple[86]

7.50   The imposition of a default sentence is mandatory and must be served consecutively to any sentence of imprisonment.

R v Szrajber[87]

7.51   The sentence periods in default are maximum sentences, and the judge has a discretion to impose a sentence within the band. The court should have regard to the circumstances of the case, the overall seriousness of the matter, and the purpose for which the default sum was being imposed, namely to ensure payment of the sum ordered to be confiscated.

Togher v Revenue and Customs Prosecutions Office[88]

7.52   The question the judge should consider when imposing the sentence in default is the following: what period of imprisonment not exceeding the statutory maximum is necessary to coerce the defendant into realising and paying the sum under the confiscation order?

Delay

Bullen and Soneji v UK[89]

7.53   An unreasonable delay in the final determination of proceedings may amount of a breach of Art 6.1 of the European Convention on Human Rights. Delay must be assessed with reference to the overall circumstances of the case, including its complexity and seriousness, the conduct of the applicants and the relevant authorities. In this case five years six months was held to be a breach.

---

85   [2008] EWCA Crim 1841.
86   [1992] Crim LR 675.
87   (1994) 15 Cr App R (S) 821.
88   [2007] EWCA Civ 686.
89   [2009] ECtHR 28.

Lloyd v Bow Street Magistrates Court;[90] R (on the application of Deamer) v Southampton Crown Court;[91] Minshall v Marylebone Magistrates Court[92]

7.54 A delay in enforcement action may be held to be a breach if the breach involves implementing the default sentence but each case must be considered with respect to the circumstances.

Payment of prosecution costs

R v Szrajber[93]

7.55 If the whole of the defendant's assets have been taken by the confiscation order it not appropriate for a further order for costs in addition to be made.

Restraint

Windsor v CPS[94]

7.56 Is there reasonable cause to believe that the defendant has benefited from his criminal conduct?

The court must sharply focus on the statutory test: is the judge satisfied that there is a reasonable cause to believe that the alleged offender has benefited from his criminal conduct? The presence of uncertainties does not prevent there being reasonable cause to believe, but the judge must still be satisfied that there is reasonable cause to believe. A complex application should be listed before a judge with sufficient time to read and absorb the papers and with sufficient time to conduct a proper hearing. It would be preferable to list such applications before a High Court Judge sitting in the Crown Court with experience of complex frauds or a Circuit Judge with similar experience. The hearing should be listed some days before the day on which any arrests were to occur. In the interests of the absent alleged offenders, the hearing must be as fair as is possible in the circumstances: 'Giving those affected an early opportunity to apply to set aside or vary the restraint orders and receivership orders (whilst important) is not a substitute for a fair ex parte hearing.' It is vital that the judge is given the material on which he can reach the conclusion himself or herself that there is 'reasonable cause'. The judge cannot find it just because he is told that an investigation has confirmed the suspicions of the relevant authorities. In the instant case, the judge did not seek to identify the nature and extent of those assets of the company in which the alleged offenders might have a beneficial interest, or which might represent their benefit from criminal conduct; he did not make any attempt to separate the proceeds of crime from the proceeds of legitimate trading; he did not

---

90   [2003] EWHC Admin 2294.
91   [2006] EWHC 2221 (Admin).
92   [2008] EWHC 2800.
93   (1994) Crim LR 543.
94   [2011] EWCA Crim 143.

advert to the consequences of the orders upon the companies or their minority shareholders, or indeed to the other creditors of the companies.

Director of the Serious Fraud Office v A[95]

7.57 The prosecution has a duty of full and frank disclosure.

Re AJ and DJ[96]

7.58 Where there has been material non disclosure the court may discharge a restraint order.

Risk of dissipation

Re AJ and DJ[97]

7.59 The applicant for the order must establish that there is a reasonable apprehension that if the order is not granted then assets will be dissipated. Where there has been some delay in seeking the order and the defendants have had the opportunity to dissipate the assets but do not do so, the judge has a discretion not to grant the order or discharge orders made ex parte.

However:

'... in many and perhaps the substantial majority of cases where offences concerning a gain exceeding £10,000 are concerned, the circumstances of the alleged offences will lead to a reasonable apprehension that, without a restraint or charging order, realisable assets are likely to be dissipated. In drug trafficking offences, this is likely to be so in almost every case. Thus the onus on the prosecution will often not be difficult to satisfy.'

Jennings v CPS[98]

7.60 The test to be applied was held to be as follows:

'The principal question for the court must always be whether the protection of a restraint order is on the facts necessary to ensure so far as possible that any confiscation order will be effacious.'

'Delay ... maybe relevant if there has been delay between the defendant being charged and the date of the application, if there has been no dissipation of the assets meanwhile. It is then incumbent on the Crown to explain why dissipation was not seen as a major risk but now is.'

---

95 [2007] EWCA Crim 1927.
96 (unreported) 9 December 1992.
97 (unreported) 9 December 1992.
98 [2005] 4 All ER 391.

R v Chrastny (No 2)[99]

7.61   Restraint orders can be made in relation to any free property held by the defendant, or the recipient of a tainted gift, up to the full amount of the benefit.

Re G[100]

7.62   Restraint orders are required to allow business to continue to trade profitably if there is legitimate as well as fraudulent, activity. It may not be appropriate to treat the assets of the company as being the assets of the defendant in such circumstances.

R v B[101]

7.63   A Crown Court judge should normally give reasons for making a restraint order.

Legal expenses

Custom and Excise Commissioners v S[102]

7.64   The prohibition on the release of restrained funds to meet legal expenses applies equally to restraint proceedings as to the criminal trial. The court noted that the prohibition extended to the legal expenses of recipients of tainted gifts, and that the Access to Justice Act 1999 was amended to make public funding available in relation to restraint proceedings.

AP & U Limited v CPS and Revenue and Prosecutions Office[103]

7.65   The rationale for the restriction on the use of restrained funds to cover legal expenses was given in this case.

Lathan LJ said:

> 'To permit..monies which could well be the proceeds of crime being used to pay lawyers for the benefit of the defendant who is either suspected of being, or has been found to be, a criminal raises a clear social issue. Parliament ... is entitled to take the view that funds which have criminal origins should not be so used.'

---

[99]   [1991] 1 WLR 1385.
[100]   [2001] EWHC (Admin) 606.
[101]   [2008] EWCA Crim 1374.
[102]   [2005] 1 WLR 1338.
[103]   [2007] EWCA Crim 3128.

Re P[104]

7.66 The court was unsympathetic to the release of funds from a restraint order to pursue a case in the European Court of Human Rights after an appeal to the Court of Appeal had been dismissed.

Funds for general living expenses

Re O[105]

7.67 The court will be reluctant to increase payments for general living expenses in the absence of full disclosure from the defendant.

Stodgell v Stodgell[106]

7.68 In this case a wife was refused leave to appeal against a decision to stop payment of general living expenses whilst the order remained unpaid in its entirety.

'Unless and until the confiscation order has been satisfied in full, both the wife and (the child) will have to live at the standard and by the means provided by the state out of welfare and other benefits and entitlements.'

Privilege against self incrimination

Re a Defendant[107]

7.69 Disclosure orders are only permitted to come into effect upon the prosecutor giving an undertaking:

'not to use any of the information obtained as a result of compliance with the order for any purpose or in connection with any criminal proceedings taken or contemplated against the defendant or for any purpose other than for a purpose arising under the Drug Trafficking Offences Act 1986.'

Disclosure and third parties

Re D (Restraint Order: Non party)[108]

7.70 Disclosure orders can bind third parties not charged with any offence.

---

[104] [1998] EWHC Admin 1049.
[105] [1991] 1 All ER 330.
[106] [2009] EWCA Civ 243.
[107] The Independent, 2 April 1987.
[108] The Times, 26 January 1995.

Re W[109]

7.71   Disclosure orders may be made against solicitors.

In the leading case of *Re W* the prosecutor sought disclosure from solicitors as to when they first received instructions to act, whether the instructions were oral or in writing, the identity of the person who instructed them, and their address and telephone number. The prosecutor also sought disclosure of the date on which funds were remitted to the solicitors to cover the cost of the proceedings, the identity of the person remitting the funds and the sort code and account number of any cheque transfer. The solicitors provided the names and addresses sought but not the date that they were instructed or the financial information requested. The judge ordered that all information be provided on the grounds that the disclosure sought would be of value to the enforcement receiver and for the purpose of advancing the enforcement of the confiscation order and hindering the manifest attempts of the defendant in evading it. Significantly the information sought was not covered by legal professional privilege since it had nothing to do with the provision of legal advice by the solicitor to the client.

R v Central Criminal Court ex p Francis and Francis[110]

7.72   Information is not protected from legal professional privilege if it is held with the intention of furthering a criminal purpose.

Funding of management receivers

Hughes v Customs and Excise Commissioners[111]

7.73   The costs and disbursements of management receivers are to be paid from the estate under management, even when the defendant is acquitted. The receiver's remuneration, however, must be approved by the court.

Mirror Group Newspapers v Maxwell[112]

7.74   The test for determining whether a receiver had acted properly is:

'... whether a reasonable prudent man, faced with the same circumstances in relation to his own affairs, would lay out or hazard his own money in doing what the office holders have done.'

---

[109]   [2008] EWHC 2780.
[110]   [1988] 3 All ER 77.
[111]   [2002] 4 All ER 633.
[112]   [1998] BCC 324.

Management receiver's powers of sale

Re P (Restraint Order: Sale of Assets)[113]

7.75 A defendant resisted the sale by the receiver of his racehorses, which he regarded as much loved family pets. The Court of Appeal agreed.

Simon Brown LJ:

> '... I see as the primary task of an interim receiver the safeguarding of the defendant's assets from dissipation and secretion rather than their realisation so as to maximise the amount of any confiscation order.'

> 'There was no suggestion that the defendant was dissipating his assets (in the sense that he was incurring excessive or unusual expenditure beyond what for him was the norm), still less that he was attempting to salt them away. Whilst the defendant remains unconvicted his assets should not be sold against his wishes except for compelling reason. The possibility, even the probability, that these horses could more profitably be sold now than at some future date is not such a compelling reason.'

Mellor v Mellor[114]

7.76 The receiver has a lien over the assets forming part of the receivership estate for payment of his remuneration and expenses.

Applications to vary and discharge restraint orders

Re AJ and DJ[115]

7.77 When there was a delay in excess of two years between the defendants being charged and an application for a restraint order being made and during this time the defendants made no attempt to dissipate their assets, a restraint order was discharged.

Jennings v CPS[116]

7.78 The court should be slow to discharge a restraint order even where there have been failings on the part of the prosecution if it can be shown that the restraint order is justified. Any failure by the prosecutor to comply with the duty of 'full frank disclosure' might instead result in a costs order against them.

---

[113] [2000] 1 WLR 473.
[114] [1992] 1 WLR 517.
[115] (unreported) 9 December 1992.
[116] [2005] 4 All ER 391.

Contempt proceedings

Togher v Customs and Excise Commissioners[117]

7.79 Those facing contempt proceedings and at risk of imprisonment should be legally represented.

CPS v Ellis[118]

7.80 Contempt is always regarded as a serious matter and the sentence should reflect this.

Griffin v Griffin[119]

7.81 Committal can be suspended on terms that the defendant comply with the order.

Importance of proper management of confiscation proceedings

R (on the application of BERR) v Baden Lowe[120]

7.82

'It is essential that the court hearing the proceedings finds and sets out all the relevant facts in its ruling (or judgment) including the facts that are agreed before it. It is evident that many confiscation hearings are not prepared in advance as they should be. There are many complaints that defence statements are inadequate. Timetables set out in the criminal procedure rules or the courts directions frequently slip. Sometimes it is only at the last minute, either immediately before the court sits or even in the outset of a hearing that some matters are agreed and the real issues emerge, considerably burdening the task of the judge hearing the proceedings. If identifying the issues is left to the last minute, then insufficient detail is paid to ensuring that any procedural steps needed for the evidence to be admissible are taken. Difficulties are from time to time compounded by the lack of a properly paginated bundle. It is, in the experience of many in this court, that, for reasons such as those we have outlined, it is not always clear from the ruling (or judgment) below what the facts were on which the issues which arose were determined. As the task of the court hearing the confiscation proceedings is to apply the statutory provisions to the facts (as agreed or found), it is essential that the ruling (or judgment) sets out all the relevant facts, as agreed and as found.'

---

117 [2001] EWCA Civ 474.
118 [2009] EWHC 876 (Admin).
119 The Times 28 April 2000.
120 [2009] EWCA Crim 194.

R v Hockey[121]

7.83 The potential for third party claims is not a matter that the court should speculate upon when making the order. It is a matter for interested third parties to put their claim into the court early.

Burden and standard of proof and hidden assets

R v Barnham[122]

7.84

> 'Once the prosecution has established the benefit there is no requirement on it to provide a prima facie case. At the second stage the burden of proof shifts to a defendant to establish, if he can, his realisable assets to the satisfaction of the court. By the second stage a defendant will know exactly how the court has determined the benefit attributable to him and must prove by evidence what his realisable assets are. It is for him to show why the confiscation order should not be the value of (his) proceeds of drug trafficking. If he proves that he has no, or appreciably less, realisable assets than the amount of the benefit determined by the court the order will be made in the lesser sum. Provided the judge keeps well in mind the principle that serious injustice to the defendant must be avoided and does not just pay lip service to the principle, the order will be in the amount assessed as either the amount of benefit or such other sum as the defendant shows represents his realisable assets.'

> 'To hold that the prosecution must in some way show a prima facie case that the defendant has hidden assets in our judgment would defeat the object of the legislation. It is designed to enable the court to confiscate a criminal's ill gotten gains. The expression "hidden assets" is indicative of the fact that the prosecution can have no means of knowing how and where a defendant may have dealt with or disposed of the proceeds of his criminal activities.'

R v Granger[123]

7.85 Moreover it is not enough for a defendant to accept that he had money and say in general terms that it disappeared. A defendant seeking to avert or minimise a proposed confiscation order needs to be specific about where his money has come from and gone to, if the judge is to be invited to hold that a defendant has no realisable assets.

---

[121] [2008] Crim LR 59.
[122] [2005] Crim LR 657.
[123] [2007] EWCA Crim 139.

Abuse of process

R v Shabir[124]

7.86   The power of the court to stay confiscation proceedings as an abuse of process should only be exercised with considerable caution.

Where a pharmacist had submitted false inflated claims to the value of £179,000 but was entitled to all of the money bar £494, it was held to be inappropriate to proceed to confiscation.

R v Morgan[125]

7.87   Where the defendant has voluntarily paid full compensation to the victim or victims, or is ready, willing and able immediately to repay all of the victims to the full amount of their losses, and has not otherwise profited from this, it may be inappropriate for the prosecution to bring confiscation proceedings.

R v Carter[126]

7.88   Where the defendant has received employment as a consequence of a false representation, the wages may be his benefit, but the link between criminality and the payment may be too remote.

R v Clarke (Joseph)[127]

7.89   There is no power to instigate confiscation proceedings where there has been an absolute or conditional discharge.

R v Steel and Shevki[128]

7.90   Once exceptional circumstances for the postponement of a confiscation order have been found it is not necessary to find further exceptional circumstances for further postponements.

R v Emmett[129]

7.91   The defendant's acceptance of assertions in the section 16 statement will not necessarily be treated as binding on appeal.

---

124   [2008] EWCA Crim 1809.
125   [2009] 1 Cr App R (S) 60.
126   [2006] EWCA Crim 416.
127   [2009] EWCA Crim 1074.
128   [2001] 2 Cr App R(S) 40.
129   [1997] 3 WLR 1119.

How confiscation proceedings differ from criminal proceedings

R v Levin[130]

7.92

1   The court could make far-reaching assumptions.

2   The court could require the defendant to provide information and could draw inferences from the failure to do so.

3   The court might rely on evidence given at trial and any relevant information properly obtained either before the trial or thereafter in order to determine a defendant's benefit and the amounts to be recovered.

4   These factors did and were intended to separate the confiscation proceedings from the criminal proceedings.

R v Atkinson[131]

7.93   The court is not limited to the prosecutor's section 16 statement for the purposes of confiscation.

R v Sangha[132]

7.94   Neither is the court limited to the jury's findings.

R v Briggs-Price[133]

7.95   Nor is it limited to the offences charged.

Evidence

R v Clipston[134]

7.96   The Court of Appeal, Criminal Division, held that hearsay evidence was admissible in confiscation proceedings and the hearsay provisions of the Criminal Justice Act 2003 were applicable in such proceedings.

Dickens[135]

7.97   In considering whether the defendant has benefited from his criminal conduct the conclusion will be drawn:

---

130   The Times, 20 February 2004.
131   [1992] Crim LR 749.
132   [2008] EWCA Crim 2562.
133   [2009] UKHL 19.
134   [2011] EWCA Crim 446 (judgment delivered 4 March 2011).
135   [1990] 2 All ER 626.

'in part from the trial, if there has been one, in part from the statements rendered by the parties to the court and in part from evidence adduced before the court.'

Inadequacy of available amount

R v B[136]

7.98 In *R v B* (at para 74) a set of principles were set down with regard to the consideration of inadequacy applications in a CJA matter (although the principles are of general application to inadequacy applications under POCA 2002).

1   The burden lies on the applicant to prove, on the balance of probabilities, that his realisable property is inadequate for the payment of the confiscation order.

2   The reference to realisable property must be to whatever are his realisable assets as a whole at the time he applies for the certificate of inadequacy. If they include assets he did not have at the time the confiscation order was made, that is by no means a reason for leaving such fresh assets out of consideration.

3   A section 83 (inadequacy) application cannot be used to go behind a finding made at the confiscation hearing or embodied in the confiscation order as to the amount of the defendant's realisable assets. Such a finding can only be challenged by way of an appeal against the confiscation order

4   It is insufficient for a defendant to say under s 83 'that his assets are inadequate to meet the confiscation order, unless at the same time he condescends to demonstrate what has happened since the making of the order to the realisable property found by the trial judge to have existed when the order was made'.

5   The confiscation hearing provided an opportunity for the defendant to show that his realisable property was worth less than the prosecution alleged. It also enabled the defendant to identify any specific assets which he contended should be treated as the only realisable property. The section 83 procedure is intended to be used only where there has been a genuine change in the defendant's financial circumstances. It is a safety net intended to provide for post confiscation order events.

6   A section 83 application is not to be used as a second bite of the cherry. It is not an opportunity to adduce evidence or to present arguments which could have been put before the Crown Court judge at the confiscation hearing.

7   The clarification of a third party's interest in property may be a post confiscation order event. The extent of any such interest may have to be decided by a civil court.

8   In a section 83 application the definition of realisable property includes a chose in action or a right to a sum of money which the applicant is entitled to recover,

---

[136] [2008] EWHC 3217 (Admin).

irrespective of any difficulty in its actual recovery, unless the applicant proves on the balance of probabilities that it is impossible to recover that sum.

Telli v Revenue and Customs Prosecutions Office[137]

7.99   Where there has been a finding of hidden assets it will be near impossible to obtain a certificate of inadequacy:

'absent identification of all the realisable property held by him, a defendant will normally be unable to satisfy the court that the amounts that might be realised at the time the confiscation order is made is less than the amount assessed to be the proceeds of his drug trafficking. Assets that he hides from the gaze of Customs and Excise may, for all anyone knows, be equal to or in excess of the value of his proceeds of drug trafficking. For that reason, no court should be satisfied that they are to be quantified at a lesser amount.

Secondly it is incumbent upon a court to assess the current value of the realisable property in order to determine whether it is inadequate now to meet the outstanding amount ... If a defendant fails to identify all the assets he holds no-one will know their true value, and by the time of the application, the value of the assets he failed to identify may have increased.'

Re O'Donoghue[138]

7.100   The burden of proof is on the defendant to establish that the value of his assets were inadequate to satisfy the whole value of the confiscation order.

R v Liverpool Justices ex p Ansen[139]

7.101   Assets need to be impossible, not merely difficult, to realise.

Re Forwell[140]

7.102   The court must give a reason for disregarding any inadequacy.

---

[137] [2007] EWCA Civ 1385.
[138] [2004] EWHC (Admin) 176.
[139] [1998] 1 All ER 692.
[140] [2003] EWCA Civ 1608.

Enforcement of confiscation proceedings

R (on the application of Garrote) v City of London Magistrates Court[141]

7.103   The prosecutor should be given the opportunity to attend and make representations. A committal warrant was quashed where the enforcing magistrates' court failed to adjourn the case to give the prosecutor an opportunity to attend.

Barnett v Director of Public Prosecutions[142]

7.104   The defendant had genuine difficulties in selling a property and requested that enforcement proceedings be adjourned. The prosecutor consented to the adjournment. The case nonetheless remained in the list and the district judge committed the defendant for the default sentence. The divisional court held the district judge has been wrong to refuse the adjournment and activate the default sentence as other methods of enforcement were available.

Hansford v Southampton Magistrates' Court[143]

7.105   The court has no discretion to waive interest payments.

R v City of London ex p Chapman[144]

7.106   A default sentence is liable to be served consecutively immediately following the period in custody in respect of the offence.

R v Harrow Justices ex p DPP[145]

7.107   A warrant of commital should only be issued after considering all the other available enforcement options and concluding that they are unlikely to be effective.

Delay in instituting enforcement proceedings

R (on the application of Deamer) v Southampton Magistrates Court[146]

7.108   A stay on enforcement action will only be granted where the delay by the enforcing authority was unreasonable and unjustified. Mere delay by itself is insufficient; it must be a delay for which the enforcing authority is responsible.

---

[141] [2002] EWHC 2909.
[142] [2009] EWHC 2004 (Admin).
[143] [2008] EWHC 67 (Admin).
[144] (1998) 162 JP 359.
[145] [2008] 4 All ER 432.
[146] [2006] EWHC Admin 2221.

Lloyd v Bow Street Magistrates' Court[147]

7.109 An order had been made against the defendant in June 1996, but the warrant of commitment was not issued until October 2002.

The order was quashed by the high court. The court stated

'... there is nothing surprising about a requirement that, if the prosecuting authorities seek to enforce a confiscation order, they should do so within a reasonable time. It is potentially very unfair on a defendant that he should be committed to prison for non payment of sums due under a confiscation order many years after the time for payment has expired, and long after he has been released from custody and resumed work and family life.'

Joyce v Dover Magistrates' Court[148]

7.110 The court is less inclined to stay civil enforcement actions.

Status and independence of the interim receiver

Director of the Assets Recovery Agency v Jackson[149]

7.111 An interim receiver should be considered an independent officer of the court. An interim receiver is the court's investigator and is not a witness for the enforcement authority. His report as to recoverable property should be given persuasive weight but is not considered binding.

R (on the application of the Director of the Assets Recovery Agency) v Jia Jin He (No 2)[150]

7.112 The receiver has a duty to report as soon as practicable.

Cash seizure

R v Dover and East Kent Magistrates' Court ex p Steven Gore[151]

7.113 Provisions are civil in nature

R v NW SW RC and CC[152]

7.114 The Crown is required to identify the class of crime in question:

---

[147] [2003] EWHC Admin 2294.
[148] [2008] EWHC Admin 1448.
[149] [2007] EWCA 2553 (QB).
[150] [2004] EWHC 3021 (Admin).
[151] (unreported) 23 May 1996, QBD.
[152] [2008] EWCA Crim 2.

'… we do not consider that parliament can have intended a state of affairs in which in any given instance, no particulars whatever need be given or proved of a cardinal element of the case, namely the criminal conduct relied on. It is a requirement … of elementary fairness.'

Chief Constable of Merseyside Police v Hickman[153]

7.115 Seized money can be re-seized at any time.

R v Payton[154]

7.116 Cash seizure hearings are often adjourned pending the criminal trial to avoid prejudice to the defendant.

R v West London Magistrates Court ex p Lamai[155]

7.117 There is no discretion to extend the 30-day deadline for appeal against forfeiture.

Third parties and restraint orders

Re D[156]

7.118 Third parties cannot obtain funding from the property which they assert they have an interest in, when their interest is being disputed.

Re G (Restraint Order)[157]

7.119 The basis upon which a prosecutor may apply for a restraint order prohibiting dealings in the assets of a company controlled by the defendant, but against which no criminal charge is to be made is as follows:

1   that the company holds realisable property within the meaning of the (applicable) Act;

2   that the company has no genuine separate existence from the defendant, and is used by him as a device for fraud.

Serious Fraud Office v Lexi Holdings Plc (In Administration)[158]

7.120 Restraint orders may not be varied to pay off unsecured third party creditors.

---

153 [2006] EWHC (Admin) 451.
154 (2006) 150 SJ 741.
155 (unreported) 6 July 2000, QBD.
156 [2006] EWHC (Admin) 1519.
157 [2001] EWHC Admin 606.
158 [2008] EWCA Crim 1443.

Re Norris[159]

7.121   There is no right for third parties to be heard at the confiscation stage:

'The court is merely concerned with the arithmetical exercise of computing what is, in effect a statutory debt. That process does not involve any assessment, in our judgement, of the way in which that debt may ultimately be paid, any more than the assessment of any other debt …

Different considerations will however arise if the debt is not met and the prosecution determine to take enforcement action … this is the stage of the proceedings where the third party rights can not only be taken into account, but resolved.

A third party who gives evidence on behalf of the defendant in confiscation proceedings is not prevented thereby from subsequently raising an interest at the enforcement stage.'

See also *R v Ahmed and Quereshi*.[160]

Appeals

R v Johnson[161]

7.122   An appeal against a confiscation order lies as part of the sentencing process.

R v Hirani[162]

7.123   The Court of Appeal may substitute a new order in place of the original.

R v Emmett[163]

7.124   A right of appeal exists against a confiscation order in all cases, unless expressly or implied excluded by the relevant Act. However:

'it is of course true that if there is an appeal, the Court of Appeal may have to take account of the fact that a Judge has decided to treat an acceptance of an allegation in a prosecution statement as conclusive, and the Court of Appeal may have to give proper and due weight to that consideration.'

---

159 [2001] 1 WLR 1388.
160 [2004] EWCA Crim 2599.
161 [1991] 2 QB 249.
162 [2008] EWCA Crim 1463.
163 [1998] AC 773.

Expert evidence on appeal

R v Stroud[164]

7.125   The same rules apply in relation to the admissibility of expert evidence in appeals against confiscation orders as to appeals against conviction.

R v Hockey[165]

7.126   The Court of Appeal can confirm, quash or vary the confiscation order.

Civil recovery

SOCA v David Gale, Teresa Mandy Gale David Kenneth Gale, June Patricia Peel[166]

7.127   The Serious Organised Crime Agency brought civil recovery proceedings under Part 5 of the Proceeds of Crime Act 2005 in relation to recoverable property owned by David Gale either in his own name or in the names of his former wife, his son and his mother. The court found that although specific offences had not been identified by SOCA in support of its claim for a civil recovery order, on the balance of probabilities, the evidence established that significant assets had been acquired as a direct consequence of money laundering and drug trafficking and on this basis an order was granted.[167]

Serious Organised Crime Agency v Pelekanos[168]

7.128   The applicant agency applied for a recovery order under Part 5 of the Proceeds of Crime Act 2002 against the respondent (P) in respect of five properties.

Police intelligence to the effect that P was involved in drug trafficking had provided a starting point for the agency's investigation into his affairs. The agency argued that the only inference that could sensibly be drawn from the evidence gleaned from its investigation was that P derived his income through unlawful conduct in the form of drug trafficking and money laundering. It further argued that, almost without exception, every mortgage application made by P in relation to the relevant properties contained false information about his income and the source of that income. That, it submitted, also amounted to unlawful conduct. It was held that:

---

[164]   [2004] EWCA Crim 1048.
[165]   [2008] Crim LR 59.
[166]   3 September 2009, High Court.
[167]   For both civil recovery and cash seizure cases it is necessary to identify that the property or cash obtained through one of a number of kinds, each of which would have been unlawful conduct see *Angus v UK Border Agency* [2011] EWHC 461(Admin).
[168]   [2009] EWHC 2307 (QB).

1   The allegation of drug trafficking, which relied on police intelligence and P's association with individuals with drug convictions, had not been proven. The same went for the allegation of money laundering. However, with one exception, the agency had made out its case on mortgage fraud. P had made substantially false statements as to his income and he had intended and expected those statements to be relied on.

2   (Obiter) The case illustrated the breadth of application of the civil recovery legislation. As the law stood, any person, however otherwise law-abiding, could be the subject of a recovery order if he made a deliberately false statement in a mortgage application form. It was important that that should be more widely known, and it would be desirable for mortgage-providers to spell out in their application forms that possible consequence of a misstatement.

Chapter 8 Civil recovery

'Sin cannot be conceived in a natural state, but only in a civil state, where it is decreed by common consent what is good or bad.'
Baruch Spinoza

Contents summary

What are Part V proceedings – why was Part V enacted – who may bring an action – what is the target of the proceedings – what is recoverable property – the trustee for civil recovery – how is 'property' defined – what must be proved – can a claim be based purely on unexplained lifestyle – applications of principles in practice – mixed and associated property – accruing profits – granting interests – consequences of the civil nature of proceedings

---

The basic provisions

Section	Provision
240(1)	The general purpose of Part V proceedings is to enable the enforcement authority to recover property which is or represents property obtained through 'unlawful conduct'.
241(1) and (2)	Define 'unlawful conduct, as being criminal offences in the UK or abroad (so long as the conduct relied upon would also have been unlawful under the law of a part of the UK).
242(1)	In order for property to have been obtained through unlawful conduct it must be property 'obtained by or in return for unlawful conduct' whether that conduct is that of the respondent or of another.
316	Defines 'property' as in effect all forms of property and including interests held in property.
304(1)	Defines 'recoverable property'. It is 'property obtained through unlawful conduct'.
304–305	Tracing: Operates in two ways. First, if recoverable property is disposed of to a third party it may, depending on the circumstances of the disposal, be followed into the hands of the new owner or successive owners (but see s 308). Secondly, if recoverable property is used by the respondent to purchase assets or otherwise invested the asset or investment is recoverable property. Where property is or has been recoverable property, property which 'represents' it, is recoverable property.

307	Provides for the recovery of 'accruing profits'. These may be either capital gains or income generated by the investment of recoverable property in other assets.
308	Tracing will not be permitted if the third party who acquires the recoverable property does so in good faith, for value and without notice that it was recoverable property.
242(2)(b)	It is not necessary to show that the conduct was of a particular kind as long as it is shown that the property was obtained through one of a number of kinds, each of which would have been unlawful conduct.
241(3)	The standard of proof is that of proof on the balance of probabilities.
245(1)	Associated property is property which is not in itself recoverable but is held by the respondent or by a third party and is linked to recoverable property.
272	Empowers the court to make an order for the associated property to be recovered and payment made to the owner of it; or
243(1)	The claim must be served on the person that the enforcement authority thinks holds the recoverable property and on any person who holds associated property which the enforcement authority wishes to recover.
308–309	Exemptions and exceptions to recoverable property.
310	Granting interests.

What are Part V proceedings?

8.1 Part V proceedings are a civil action for the recovery of property obtained through unlawful conduct.

Why was Part V enacted?

8.2

> 'The clear intention of Parliament was to ensure that, so far as possible, criminals should be deprived of the possibility of benefiting from their crimes.'[1]

Who may bring such an action?

8.3 Only an 'enforcement agency' as defined by POCA, s 316 may bring such an action. Current authorised enforcement agencies are: the Serious Organised Crime Agency (SOCA), the Serious Fraud Office, the Director of Public Prosecutions, HMRC and the Crown Prosecution Service. These agencies are all subject to the

---

1   *Director of Assets Recovery Agency v Singh* [2004] EWHC Admin 2335, per Latham LJ.

same statutory guidance as to the execution of this function, namely that it be utilised in the way best calculated to reduce crime. In general,[2] this is best achieved by the institution of criminal proceedings.[3] The minimum value of any claim must be at least £10,000.[4]

Who, or rather what, is the target of the proceeding?

8.4 Unlike criminal confiscation proceedings, it is recoverable property itself and not the respondent (or defendant), who is the target of the proceedings.

What is 'recoverable property'?

8.5 POCA, s 304(1) states that 'Property obtained through unlawful conduct is recoverable property'. If the court is satisfied that any property is recoverable, then subject to limited exceptions contained within s 266, it must make a recovery order, ie an order vesting the recoverable property in the trustee for civil recovery.[5]

8.6 If the court is satisfied that property is recoverable it must make a recovery order. However, the court may not make an order if the respondent (a) obtained the property in good faith, (b) he took steps which he would not otherwise have taken if he had not obtained it or he took such steps in the belief that he was going to obtain the property, (c) making the order would be detrimental to him in light of those steps and (d) he had no notice that the property was recoverable property. If those conditions are satisfied and the court thinks it would not be just and equitable to make the order, it may decline to make a recovery order. In deciding whether to do so the court must have regard to the degree of detriment that would be suffered by the respondent, as well as to the enforcement authority's interest in receiving the realised proceeds of the recoverable property.[6] The court, therefore, has a limited discretion not to make the order in certain circumstances. Finally, the court may not make any provision within a recovery order which would be incompatible with any provision of the European Convention on Human Rights.[7]

The trustee for civil recovery

8.7 The trustee for civil recovery is a person nominated by the enforcement authority and appointed by the court to give effect to the recovery order.[8] A recovery order vests identified recoverable or associated property in the trustee for civil

---

[2] See the Attorney General Guidance to prosecuting bodies on their asset recovery powers under the Proceeds of Crime Act 2002 (reproduced at Appendix 4) and also abuse of process in Chapter 2.

[3] POCA, s 2A and 2A(4).

[4] See POCA, s 287 and the Proceeds of Crime Act 2002 (Financial Threshold for Civil Recovery) Order 2003 (SI 2003/175).

[5] See POCA, s 266(1) and (2). See 8.7 below concerning the trustee.

[6] POCA, s 266(4).

[7] POCA, s 266(3)(b).

[8] POCA, s 267(1) and (2).

recovery.[9].The functions of the trustee are to 'secure the detention, custody or preservation of any property vested in him by a recovery order' and in the case of property other than money, to realise the value of the property for the benefit of the enforcement trustee.[10] The court may impose conditions as to how the trustee may deal with property which is made the subject of the recovery order.[11]

How is 'property' defined?

8.8   The definition of property is widely drawn. It includes 'property, **wherever situated**',[12] being money, all forms of real or personal property, things/choses in action, and all other intangible and incorporeal property[13] as well as any interest in land or property[14] (emphasis supplied).

Examples of circumstances in which an action might be brought:

(i)   Following the acquittal of an accused in a criminal trial.

(ii)   Where there is thought to be insufficient evidence for a criminal prosecution to succeed.[15] A case which illustrates how an action for civil recovery might arise is *Serious Organised Crime Agency v Pelekanos*.[16] Mr Pelekanos was investigated for drug-trafficking offences but was never charged due to a lack of evidence. The Serious Organised Crime Agency then unsuccessfully sought to prove in civil recovery proceedings that he was in possession of recoverable property as a result of being a drug dealer. However, the investigation revealed that he had made material misstatements in a number of mortgage applications:

'This began as a case about drug trafficking. It has ended up as a case about mortgage fraud. As such it illustrates the breadth of application of the civil recovery legislation. As the law stands, any person, however otherwise law abiding may be the subject of a civil recovery order if he makes a deliberately false statement in a mortgage application form.'

(iii)   Where the proposed respondent has died or is abroad and cannot be extradited.[17]

(iv)   The crime which led to the property being obtained was committed abroad and there is no extra territorial jurisdiction to prosecute.[18]

---

9   POCA, s 266(2).
10   POCA, s 267. Schedule 7 to POCA lists the powers of the trustee which include powers to sell and manage the property vested in him.
11   POCA, s 266(8).
12   In *Perry v Serious Organised Crime Agency* [2011] EWCA Civ 578 the court rejected the submission that the power of the court to make a recovery order was confined to property within the jurisdiction.
13   POCA, s 316(4).
14   POCA, s 316(6), (7).
15   POCA, s 241(3) provides that the standard of proof is that of proof on a balance of probabilities. For a fuller analysis of how this has been interpreted by the courts, see 8.21 below.
16   [2009] EWHC 2307(QB).
17   *Director of the Assets Recovery Agency v Green* [2005] EWHC 3168 (Admin) at [40] at which the court reviews paragraph 5.5. of the Explanatory Notes to the Act.
18   See *Green* (above) at [40].

(v) Where the prosecution in criminal proceedings has accepted a basis of plea which has the effect of making criminal confiscation proceedings unsustainable.[19]

What must be proved?

8.9 The property must be proved to have been obtained through unlawful conduct. Under POCA, s 241(1) unlawful conduct is defined as conduct which is contrary to the criminal law in the part of the United Kingdom in which it occurs or if occurs in country outside the UK, is unlawful according to the laws of that country and would be unlawful if it had occurred in a part of the UK. Thus a drug dealer in Spain who chooses to repatriate his proceeds to this country may be the subject of an action.

8.10 Under POCA, s 242(1)(b) it is not necessary for a specific offence to be proved. Moreover, 'it is not necessary to show that the conduct was of a particular kind if it is shown that property was obtained through conduct of one of a number of kinds, each of which would have been unlawful conduct'.[20]

Can a claim be made simply on the basis of the unexplained lifestyle of the respondent?

8.11 The leading case is the *Director of the Assets Recovery Agency v Green*.[21] The question in that case was:

'Whether a claim for civil recovery can be determined on the basis of conduct in relation to property without the identification of any particular unlawful conduct, the question to include whether the claimant can sustain a case for civil recovery in circumstances where a respondent has no identifiable lawful income to warrant the lifestyle and purchases of that respondent.'

Sullivan J embarked upon a review of the legislation and authorities and held that:

'Any litigant in civil proceedings seeking to recover property upon the basis that it had been obtained by unlawful conduct would be expected to identify a) the property and b) the conduct that was said to be unlawful. The former is an obvious requirement. As far as the latter is concerned, it has long been the position that fraud and illegality must be specifically pleaded. The requirement is now to be found in CPR 16 para 8.2. Subsection (3) in s 243 recognises the practical difficulties which the Director may face in specifying the property which has been obtained through unlawful conduct and enables the Director to describe the property "in general terms". There is no similar relaxation in the rules of pleading in respect of the necessary allegation of unlawful conduct. There does not need to be, since sections 240 to 242 have made it plain that the

---

[19] See *Director of the Assets Recovery Agency v Olupitan* [2007] EWHC 162 at [39] and [40].
[20] POCA, s 242(2)(b).
[21] [2005] EWHC 3168 (Admin).

Director need not allege a specific criminal offence or offences and need only describe (alleged matters which constitute) a particular kind or kinds of unlawful conduct' [para 23]

'Although proceedings under Part 5 of the Act are, in rem, directed at the property and not at the criminality of any particular individual, form should not be allowed to obscure substance. Part 5 proceedings are not concerned with any property, however obtained. They are concerned only with property which has been obtained through conduct which is unlawful under the criminal law. It would be surprising if a claimant in civil proceedings, who had to allege criminal conduct as a necessary part of his claim in rem, was not required to give to the respondent and the court at least some particulars of what that conduct was said to be. The requirement that fraud or illegality be specifically pleaded is not simply a procedural nicety. Rather, it reflects the requirements of elementary fairness. In my judgement, the Act deliberately steered a careful middle course between, at the one extreme, requiring the Director to prove (on the balance of probabilities) the commission of a specific criminal offence or offences by a particular individual or individuals and, at the other, being able to make a wholly unparticularised allegation of "unlawful conduct" and in effect require a respondent to justify his lifestyle.' [para 25]

'For the purposes of s 240 and 241(1) and (2) a description of the conduct in relatively general terms should suffice, "importing and supplying controlled drugs", "trafficking women for the purposes of prostitution", "brothel keeping", "money laundering" are all examples of conduct which, if it occurs in the United Kingdom is unlawful under the criminal law. It is possible that more detail might be required if conduct outside the United Kingdom is relied upon, but that is an inevitable consequence of the Director having to establish that the conduct in question was unlawful in both the foreign country and the United Kingdom.' [para 17]

How are these principles applied in practice?

8.12   The cases below are fact specific; however they do illustrate certain differences in approach whilst at the same time purporting to apply the same test as propounded in *Green*.

A   In *Serious Organised Crime Agency v Kelly*[22] it was held that:

'... the court is entitled to take a global approach when considering whether property is recoverable, and is not obliged to consider whether a particular unlawful act by a respondent at a particular time can be shown to have enabled a particular property transaction.[23] ... though a claim for civil recovery cannot be sustained solely on the basis that a respondent

---

[22] [2010] EWHC 3565 (QB).
[23] The reference to a property transaction is specific to the facts of this case but the principle would no doubt apply to any other type of alleged unlawful conduct.

has no identifiable income to warrant his lifestyle, the lack of any such income may be very relevant in painting the overall picture, particularly if the respondent concerned has failed to provide any explanation for his income or has deliberately provided an untruthful explanation.' [para 20 per Maddison J]

B   A similar approach taken by the court in *Director of the Assets Recovery Agency v Olupitan*:

'… it is the whole picture which has to be balanced. For example, it is one thing to point to an unexplained lifestyle, it may be another if an explanation is offered but rejected as untruthful; and taken with other evidence might be more or less persuasive' [para 23]

Having heard evidence Langley J approached the matter in this way:

'the Director has fully satisfied me on a balance of probabilities that Mr Olupitan is a dishonest man who has employed dishonesty to obtain or seek to obtain property (the mortgage fraud and his conviction for conspiracy) and to seek to obtain an immigration status to which he knew and knows he was not entitled. The Director has also satisfied me that Mr Olupitan has had no significant legitimate source of income whilst living in this country and has lied again and again in his evidence about the sources of the money (in particular cash) which undoubtedly came into his bank accounts. On that basis and on all the evidence I conclude that **any** significant asset of Mr Olupitan was obtained by or was the proceeds of his dishonest acquisitive criminal conduct and is recoverable property." [para 67] (emphasis supplied)

C   In *Angus v UK Border Agency*,[24] the appellant provided two conflicting explanations as to the origin of £40,000 cash which was seized from her at Gatwick Airport. The first explanation was provided by her when she was initially questioned by Customs and the second provided by her solicitor on her behalf in correspondence following the seizure of the cash. The respondent enforcement authority submitted that in cash forfeiture cases no specific particular criminal conduct is required to be identified and relied upon the inconsistencies in her explanations to provide an inference that the cash must have been derived from unlawful conduct. The court rejected this argument. Notwithstanding the discrepancies in the accounts provided by the appellant, the application for forfeiture of the cash failed as SOCA were unable to specify with sufficient particularity the unlawful conduct by which the property was said to have been obtained; the matters which were alleged to constitute the particular kind or kinds of conduct by or in return for which property was obtained had to be set out. The court confirmed that the interpretation of POCA, s 242(2)(b) was the same whether the proceedings are for cash forfeiture or civil recovery.

---

24   [2011] EWHC 461. Although this is a cash seizure case, the court confirmed that the same principles applied in relation to civil recovery proceedings.

D   In *Serious Organised Crime Agency v Bosworth*[25] the judge found the case advanced by SOCA to be vague and lacking in particularity:

> 'It was difficult to avoid the conclusion that the essential basis for the claims made in this action was simply that Mr Bosworth had been caught in possession of assets for the lawful acquisition of which he could not satisfy SOCA. In my judgment, the effect of the material provisions of POCA is not that a person has to satisfy SOCA, or anyone else, that a particular asset had been acquired out of funds obtained lawfully. The true position is that, if SOCA alleges that particular property is recoverable property, it has to prove, on a balance of probabilities, that that property was obtained by unlawful conduct.' [para 56]

Mixed and associated property

8.13   The Act recognises that recoverable property may be mixed or associated with property which is not itself obtained through unlawful conduct. In either instance it matters not whether such mixed or associated property is owned by the respondent or a third party.

Associated property (POCA, s 245)

8.14

> '(1) Associated property means property of any of the following descriptions (including property held by the respondent) which is not itself the recoverable property—
>
> (a)   any interest in the recoverable property,
>
> (b)   any other interest in the property in which the recoverable property subsists,
>
> (c)   if the recoverable property is a tenancy in common, the tenancy of the other tenant,
>
> (d)   if (in Scotland) the recoverable property is owned in common, the interest of the other owner,
>
> (e)   if the recoverable property is part of a larger property, but not a separate part, the remainder of that property.'

As is evident from the wording of s 245, associated property may be property owned by third parties or it may be property owned by the respondent. A simple example of associated property is provided in the Explanatory Notes to the Act: if the respondent steals a painting and has it framed in a picture frame which she has lawfully obtained, the frame is associated property, whereas the painting is and remains recoverable property. Associated property may be treated as recoverable, but only if the holder of

---

[25]   [2010] EWHC 645 (QB).

119

the associated property and the claimant are unable to reach agreement for the holder to make a payment to the trustee for civil recovery which represents the value of the recoverable property[26] and the court thinks it is 'just and equitable' to make the order for recovery.[27] In that circumstance the recovery order may provide (a) for the trustee to pay an amount to the person who holds the associated property or who is an excepted joint owner or (b) for the creation of interests in favour of that person, or for the creation of liabilities and conditions in relation to the property vested in the trustee.[28] Associated property may be subject to a property freezing order.

Mixing property (POCA, s 306)

8.15 It may be that recoverable property is mixed with other property which is not obtained through unlawful conduct. In that instance the 'portion of the mixed property which is attributable to the recoverable property represents the property obtained through unlawful conduct'[29] and remains recoverable. Statutory examples of mixed property include where a person uses recoverable property to increase funds in a bank account, or in part payment for the acquisition of an asset or for the restoration or improvement of land.[30] Mixed property may be entirely or partly owned by the respondent or a part of it may be equally owned by a third party.

8.16 In *Pelekanos*[31] the court considered the approach where property had been acquired partly with monies obtained by mortgage fraud and partly with legitimate funds; the loan money was recoverable property as it has been obtained by unlawful conduct, namely mortgage fraud. Applying POCA, s 306(2)[32] the recovery order could only apply in relation to that portion of the property which was attributable to the fraudulently obtained loan money. The portion of the property attributable to legitimate funds was not recoverable.[33]

Accruing profits

8.17 Under POCA, s 307, if recoverable property is invested or otherwise deployed so that it grows in value or produces a yield, the resulting profits are known as 'accruing profits' and as such are also deemed to be recoverable property.

Tracing

8.18 POCA, s 305(1) states:

---

[26] POCA, s 271.
[27] POCA, s 272(1)(b).
[28] POCA, s 272(3).
[29] POCA, s 306(2).
[30] POCA, s 306(3)(a)–(c).
[31] *Serious Organised Crime Agency v Pelekanos* [2009] EWHC 2307 (QB).
[32] Section 306(2) reads 'The portion of the mixed property which is attributable to the recoverable property represents the property obtained through unlawful conduct'.
[33] See also *Director of the Assets Recovery Agency v Olupitan* [2008] EWCA Civ 104 to the same effect.

'Where property obtained through unlawful conduct (the original property) is or has been recoverable property, property which represents the original property is also recoverable property.'

By virtue of subss (2) and (3), the ability to follow the property into the hands of another subsists no matter how many subsequent disposals of the recoverable property, or that which represents it, there may be. Property obtained through unlawful conduct does not cease to be recoverable property merely because it is sold, given away or invested in some way. Any increase in value will also be recoverable property.[34] The concept extends to bequests in wills. However, if the person who acquires the recoverable property 'does so in good faith, for value and without notice that it was recoverable property ... it ceases to be recoverable'.[35]

Granting interests

8.19   Section 310 of POCA provides:

'If a person grants an interest in his recoverable property, the question of whether the interest is also recoverable is determined in the same manner as it is on any other disposal of recoverable property.'

Thus

'(a) where the property in question is property obtained through unlawful conduct, the interest is also to be treated as obtained through that conduct;

(b) where the property in question represents property in his hands obtained through unlawful conduct, the interest is also to be treated as representing, in his hands, the property so obtained.'[36]

Exceptions and exemptions

8.20   Property ceases to be recoverable if it is acquired by a person in good faith for value without notice that it is recoverable property.[37]

Other principal exceptions include where the property has been vested, forfeited or otherwise disposed of in pursuance of Part V powers or is otherwise restrained under POCA, s 40, 120 or 190 or there has been a successful civil claim whereby the claimant has obtained payment, or the claimant has otherwise received property from the defendant which would otherwise be recoverable, then such property ceases to be recoverable. Similarly if a payment is made for compensation under s 130 of the Powers of the Criminal Courts (Sentencing) Act 2000 or for restitution under s 148(2) of the same Act the payment/property ceases to be recoverable.[38]

---

34   POCA, s 307 (accruing interests).
35   POCA, s 308(1)(b).
36   POCA, s 310(2)(a), (b).
37   POCA, s 308(1).
38   POCA, s 308(3).

POCA, s 309 provides exceptions to recovery if it is 'prescribed property' or disposed of pursuant to a prescribed enactment. Prescribed property means prescribed by an order made by the Secretary of State.[39]

The consequences of the civil nature of proceedings

8.21

(a) *The standard of proof:* POCA, s 241(3) provides that the court must decide the claim on a balance of probabilities. However, '[t]he more serious the allegation or the more serious the consequences of the allegation if proved, the stronger must be the evidence before the court will find the allegation proved on a balance of probabilities' (see *Serious Organised Crime Agency v Kelly,*[40] citing with approval what was said in *R (on the application of N) v Mental Health Review Tribunal (Northern Region)*).[41]

(b) *Limitation Act 1980*: Under s 27A of the Limitation Act 1980, as amended by POCA, s 288, an action for civil recovery may not be commenced after the expiry of 12 years from the date on which the cause of action accrued.

(c) *Summary judgment*: Under CPR r 24.2 summary judgment is available to the claimant where the respondent has no real prospect of defending the claim and where there is no compelling reason why the case ought not to be disposed of before a hearing

(d) *Form*: Part V proceedings are brought under CPR Part 8. As such there is no requirement for the claimant to serve particulars of claim. Notwithstanding there may be cases in which one is highly desirable: 'In my judgement it was not just or fair for SOCA to serve a 24 page witness statement and 468 pages of exhibited documentation and to say, in effect, "if you read all of that, you will able to work out what is the case you have meet".'[42]

(e) *Mediation*: Like all civil claims there is nothing to prevent the parties from seeking to arrive at a negotiated settlement in respect of the claim. A further alternative to which all parties to civil litigation are now duty bound to consider is mediation. There may be serious costs implications to either party who fails to consider alternative dispute resolution.

(f) The respondent is not at risk of conviction.

(g) Enforcement is not in the magistrates' court but via the trustee for civil recovery.

---

[39] POCA, s 309(4).
[40] [2010] EWHC 3565 (QB) at [20].
[41] [2006] QB 468.
[42] See *Serious Organised Crime Agency v Bosworth* [2010] EWHC 645 (QB) at [26].

Chapter 9 Third-party interests

'The interest in life does not lie in what people do, nor even in their relations to each other, but largely in the power to communicate with a third party, antagonistic, enigmatic, yet perhaps persuadable, which one may call life in general.'
Virginia Woolf

Contents Summary

Third-party interests in Part V proceedings – recoverable property and associated property – funding – compensation – third-party interests in criminal confiscation proceedings – third-party interests in enforcement proceedings – burden of proof – where the third party is not the legal owner

9.1 Whenever a recovery or restraint order is sought there is the possibility that the property rights of third parties who have an interest in the property will be affected. Such third parties may well be entirely innocent of any unlawful conduct or even complicity in the wrongdoing of another; the Act seeks to strike a balance between protecting the interests of third parties whilst at the same time ensuring that recognition of those interests does not frustrate the purpose of the legislation.

Third-party interests in Part V proceedings (civil recovery)

Civil restraint

9.2 Section 245A of POCA (as inserted by s 98 of the Serious Organised Crime and Police Act 2005 (SOCPA)) empowers an enforcement authority to seek a 'property freezing order (whether before or after starting proceedings)'. Both 'recoverable property' and 'associated property' may be the subject of a property freezing order (PFO) so that a third party may find his assets restrained as a result.[1] The court has a discretion as to whether to grant a PFO. The court must give any person affected by the PFO an opportunity to be heard.[2] The court must vary or set aside a PFO if it concludes that property restrained under the terms of the order is neither associated nor recoverable property.[3]

---

[1] POCA, s 245A(5).
[2] POCA, s 245B(5).
[3] POCA, s 245B(4).

Recoverable property and associated property

9.3 Associated property may belong to the respondent or to a third party. Associated property is property which is not in itself the recoverable property but which has an interest in recoverable property or an interest in the property in which the recoverable property subsists or if the recoverable property is a tenancy in common, the tenancy of the other tenant.[4] Such property may be frozen and subsequently made recoverable. In essence the holder of associated property is given the option of buying out the recoverable part of the property by reaching agreement with the claimant; in default of such agreement the recovery order may provide for payment to be made to the holder of the associated property in respect of it.[5] (See 8.14 above.)

9.4 Receivership orders may also be made in respect of associated property.[6]

Funding

9.5 Unlike the position in criminal proceedings a respondent may be permitted to access frozen funds to instruct lawyers to contest the proceedings. The total amount must be specified and be 'limited to reasonable legal expenses'. In deciding whether to permit the release of funds the court must have regard to the desirability of the person being represented and, where he is the respondent, disregard the possibility of public funding.[7] If permitted, the mechanics of the arrangement are that the respondent has to approach the claimant's solicitors for permission to undertake particular tasks and agree on the time considered reasonable to discharge the agreed task as well as the level of fees. The power to release money for the purposes of defending the proceedings must not be exercised in such a way so that the rights of the enforcement authority to recover property obtained by unlawful conduct are unduly prejudiced.[8]

Compensation

9.6 If the holder of associated property suffers loss as a result of a property freezing order or interim receiving order and the court subsequently rules that the property is neither recoverable nor associated property, the court may order the enforcement authority to pay compensation to the owner of the property.[9] The amount payable is that which the court considers reasonable.[10] Any application for compensation must be made within three months of the conclusion of the proceedings or three months from the date on which they were discontinued.[11]

---

[4] POCA, s 245(1)(a), (b).
[5] POCA, ss 271 and 272.
[6] POCA, ss 245A–245G.
[7] POCA, s 252(4) as amended by the Serious Organised Crime and Police Act 2005, s 98 and Sch 6, paras 14(2) and (3).
[8] POCA, s 252(6).
[9] POCA, ss 283(1) and 316(1).
[10] POCA, s 272(6).
[11] POCA, s 283(3) and (4).

Third party interests in criminal confiscation proceedings

Restraint

9.7   Under POCA, s 41(1), '[i]f any condition set out in s 40 is satisfied the Crown Court may make an order (a restraint order) prohibiting any specified person from dealing with any realisable property held by him'.[12] It is clear from the wording of the section that the property rights of persons other than the defendant may be affected by the terms of a restraint order. Third parties may apply to vary restraint orders which adversely affect them. Section 41(3) of POCA provides that:

> 'A restraint order may be made subject to exceptions, and an exception may in particular—
>
> (a)   make provision for reasonable living expenses and reasonable legal expenses;[13]
>
> (b)   make provision for the purpose of enabling **any** person to carry on any trade or business profession or occupation;
>
> (c)   be made subject to conditions.'(emphasis added)

9.8   Criminal confiscation proceedings are against the defendant in personam and not as against the property in rem. As a consequence third parties who assert an interest in allegedly realisable property have no locus in the substantive proceedings. A third party does, however, have the right to apply to the court to vary or discharge a restraint order which affects his property rights.[14] This would include an application to vary the restraint order so as to provide for the reasonable living expenses of a third party, for example the spouse or partner of a defendant whose funds have been restrained. Any person affected by the order resulting from the application to vary or discharge the order has a right of appeal to the Court of Appeal.[15]

The making of the confiscation order and third parties

9.9

> 'Provisions designed to protect the interests of third parties are conspicuously absent from the rules of procedure that apply at the stage of the hearing at the Crown Court. Third parties are not entitled to participate in the criminal proceedings in that court'[16]

---

[12]   The conditions in s 40 are that a criminal investigation has been started or concluded and it is believed that the alleged offender has benefited from his criminal conduct, or that an application has been made for either the benefit figure or the available amount to be reconsidered or if no confiscation order was made, an application for an order based on fresh evidence has been submitted.

[13]   However POCA, s 41(4) and (5) operate so as to prevent the release of restrained monies to defend the criminal proceedings and challenges to the restraint order see *Customs and Excise v S* [2005] 1 WLR 1338.

[14]   POCA, s 42(3)(b).

[15]   POCA, s 43(2).

[16]   *In re Norris* [2001] UKHL 34 at [5] per Lord Hope of Craighead. *In re Norris* concerned the Drug Trafficking Act 1986 but the observation applies with equal vigour to POCA proceedings.

In *R v Ahmed and Qureshi*[17] the Court of Appeal held that the Crown Court has no discretion as to whether or not to include the defendant's share in the matrimonial home, even if the sale of it would render the wife and children homeless (see paras 2 and 13 of the judgment).

'The Court is merely concerned with the arithmetic exercise of computing what is, in the effect, a statutory debt. That process does not involve any assessment ... of the way in which that debt may ultimately be paid, any more than the assessment of any other debt. No questions therefore arise under Article 8 at this stage of the process. Different considerations will however arise if the debt is not met and the prosecution determine to take enforcement action, for example by obtaining an order for a receiver. As the House of Lords explained in *Re Norris* this is the stage in the procedure in which the third party's rights can not only be taken into account but resolved ... It would be at that stage that the court would have to consider whether or not it would be proportionate to make an order selling the home in the circumstances of the particular case ... The court would undoubtedly be concerned to ensure that proper weight is given to the public policy objective behind the making of confiscation orders, which is to ensure that criminals do not profit from their crime. And the court will have a range of enforcement options available with which to take account of the rights of third parties such as other members of the Ahmed family.' [paras 11 and 12]

9.10   Thus the property rights of a third party affected by a confiscation order are ignored at the point at which the order is made; should they exist, account will only be taken of such interests at the enforcement stage. This includes the right of a wife to apply for ancillary relief under the Matrimonial Causes Act 1973.[18] There is of course nothing to prevent an interested third party appearing as a witness on behalf of the defendant in the confiscation proceedings in the hope of persuading the court that for example the third party is in fact the beneficial owner of some or all of the allegedly realisable property and that consequently the property is not 'realisable' as against the defendant. In *In re Norris*[19] the wife held unencumbered legal title to a property which Customs alleged was in truth beneficially owned by the defendant, her husband, who had been convicted of drug trafficking offences. Mrs Norris gave evidence on behalf of her husband in the confiscation proceedings. The judge at first instance disbelieved the evidence of the defendant's wife and found that the home belonged to the defendant and was accordingly properly to be treated as a realisable asset. Importantly, the House of Lords ruled that the fact that a third party had been disbelieved when called as a witness for the defendant at the confiscation hearing,

---

[17]   (2004) EWCA Crim 2559.
[18]   See *Webber v Webber* [2006] EWHC (Fam) 2893 at [44]. The court in this case stated that it was plainly preferable that the ancillary relief application should be disposed of first' so that the Crown Court would be in a position to judge the amount available, the High Court having already resolved the claim of the wife in ancillary relief proceedings.
[19]   [2001] 1 WLR 1388.

does not prevent such a third party from subsequently seeking to assert his rights at the enforcement stage as a party to those proceedings. The matter can and will be examined *de novo*.

Third party interests in enforcement proceedings in the Crown Court

9.11   Where an order remains unsatisfied, upon application by the enforcement authority, the court may appoint an enforcement receiver to step into the shoes of the defendant and realise (ie sell), property which belongs to him.

> 'Once a confiscation order has been made, the Crown is entitled to demand the appointment of an enforcement receiver in order to realise the funds with which to discharge the confiscation order. That after all, is no more than the legislative steer in section 82(2) would normally demand. The effect of the ruling is potentially to throw on to the defendant's assets the burden of meeting the receiver's costs, disbursements and fee. It may be proper, in an appropriate case, to defer the appointment of a receiver for a short period to give the defendant the opportunity himself (subject, of course, to suitable safeguards) to realise the assets – something he may perhaps be able to do advantageously and at lesser expense than a receiver.'[20]

9.12   If a third party seeks to assert a beneficial interest in such property, or raise any other legal argument, it is at this stage that s/he needs to apply to become an interested party in the proceedings. To ensure that affected persons are afforded an opportunity to be heard, POCA, s 51(8) provides that the court must not confer upon the receiver the power to manage or otherwise deal with the property or to realise it unless an affected person has been given a reasonable opportunity to make representations to the court.

9.13   Issues which frequently arise in relation to third parties are proportionality, contributions to the property and the right to family life. However, it must be noted that just as a third party may assert that s/he has a beneficial interest in property without being the apparent legal owner of it, equally the enforcement authority may argue that the defendant is the part or sole beneficial owner of a property to which he has no title. A case which is illustrative of some of the issues that can arise in this context is *Gibson v Revenue and Customs Prosecution Office*.[21] In that case the defendant's wife held 50% legal title to the home. The Revenue and Customs Prosecution Office sought confiscation of the whole property in the following circumstances: the defendant had made substantial cash payments into bank accounts from which he made mortgage and endowment repayments. The judge found that Mrs Gibson must have known that not all of the cash in the household, including

---

20   *Re HN* [2005] EWHC 2982 (Admin) at [27], per Munby J (a case decided under the Drug Trafficking Act 1994; but the general approach is the same although qualified to some extent in that third-party interests are to be ignored at the confiscation stage but must be considered in the context of enforcement proceedings. For the wide ranging powers of the receiver generally see POCA, s 51.
21   [2008] EWCA Civ 645.

money used to pay the mortgage, was legitimate in origin. The court approached the matter by seeking to ascertain the intention of the parties at the time that they acquired the property; was it their intention that Mr Gibson should acquire a greater beneficial interest in the property than the 50% interest which was reflected in his half legal ownership? The court found not.

9.14   In addressing the effect of the Mrs Gibson's complicity in her spouse's wrongdoing the court observed that she applies

> 'for no transfer in her favour and no exercise of the Courts discretion. It is the prosecution who have to establish a public policy jurisdiction entitling the court to confiscate her assets when she was not convicted ; when no confiscation order has been made against her ..." [para 14]

> 'Declining to order the transfer to a complicit spouse of property which is not hers is one thing: confiscating property which she already owns is quite another.' [para 20]

In other words whilst knowledge or complicity in offending might assume great relevance where the third party seeks the relief of the court, the principle that that he who comes to equity must come with 'clean hands' is of less importance where the property rights of the third party are reflected in the legal title.

9.15

> 'In the civil proceedings the starting point is that Mrs Norris is the registered freehold owner of the property and in occupation of it. Her apparent title has to be displaced by evidence. If she is considered to have only a partial interest, which she recognises is a possible view, the extent of that interest has still to be determined. No presumptions are to be made against her. The burden of proof is upon the Customs and Excise.'[22]

Cases where the third party is not the legal owner and has knowledge that tainted money has been used

9.16   In *Crown Prosecution Service v Richards*,[23] 'it was successfully contended by the prosecution that public policy demanded that drug dealers were deprived of the fruits of their crimes and that those fruits should not be distributed to others, least of all those who had guilty knowledge of the origin of the assets'. That case concerned a husband's assets which were the subject of confiscation proceedings. The wife was seeking a discretionary order in her favour to transfer the assets to her. The court declined to exercise the discretion in her favour because the assets were tainted and she was complicit.[24]

---

[22] See *In re Norris* [2001] 1 WLR 1388 at [25].
[23] [2006] 2 FLR 1220 as summarised in *Gibson v Revenue and Customs Prosecution Office* [2008] EWCA Civ 645 at [12].
[24] *Gibson v Revenue and Customs Prosecution Office* [2008] EWCA Civ 645 at [12] and [14].

9.17 The position is different where the wife is divorcing the defendant and her claim for ancillary or financial relief is in conflict with claims made under POCA by an enforcement authority. In *Customs and Excise v A*[25] the Court of Appeal roundly rejected any suggestion that the jurisdiction of the courts under Part II of the Matrimonial Causes Act 1973 was ousted by or secondary to confiscation proceedings.[26] In circumstances where the applicant wife is seeking discretionary financial relief under Matrimonial Causes Act 1973 the court identified the following factors as relevant:

(a) the fact that one or both parties to the marriage had engaged in drug trafficking and that one or more of them had been made the subject of a confiscation order;

(b) the extent to which their assets and their standard of living derived from drug trafficking.[27]

Applying *Customs and Excise v A* the court in *Stodgell v Stodgell*[28] stayed ancillary relief claims for a wife and child pending satisfaction of a confiscation order against the husband in favour of the Revenue for unpaid tax and penalties. This was despite the fact that the judge found that the wife was not complicit in the crime; non-complicity is a necessary, but not necessarily sufficient, condition for a spouse to succeed when in competition with a confiscation order.

Other relevant factors are whether or not the third party spouse has made mortgage contributions;[29] knowledge or complicity in the offending behaviour; whether the spouse will be dependent upon state funds if the order is enforced.[30]

Tainted gifts

9.18 Realisable property includes 'any free property held by the recipient of a tainted gift'.[31]

'The underlying purpose of the tainted gift provisions is plain. No self respecting organised criminal would expect to be caught with high value goods in his own name readily identifiable, particularly since the enactment of legislation. As a matter of standard practice he is likely to have taken steps to transfer high value assets to nominee companies, offshore companies or trusted

---

25 [2002] EWCA Civ 1039.
26 This case was decided under the Drug Trafficking Act 1994. Although note that the learned authors of *Millington and Sutherland Williams on the Proceeds of Crime* (3rd edn) express the view that it is now arguable that POCA does indeed oust the Matrimonial Causes Act 1973 since POCA, s 58(5) provides that where a restraint order has been applied for or made under POCA any other action may be stayed (at para 16.126).
27 *Customs and Excise v A* [2002] EWCA Civ 1039 at [12] and [13].
28 [2009] EWCA Civ 243.
29 *Cowcher v Cowcher* [1972] 1 WLR 425. Such payments are to be treated as though they were payments towards the purchase price of the property.
30 *Customs & Excise Commissioners v A* [2003] 2 WLR 210.
31 POCA, s 83(b).

associates which is designed to strip such criminals of their profits. Parliament has sought to address that mischief in various ways including the tainted gift provisions.'[32]

Tainted gifts include transfers of property made for significantly less than the market value at the time of transfer.[33] To the extent that it conflicts with the object of satisfying the confiscation order any obligation of a recipient of tainted gift must be ignored.[34]

The legislative steer and protecting the property rights of innocent third parties

9.19 The powers of the court and of the receiver contained in the Act must be exercised with a view to the value of realisable property being made available for satisfying any confiscation order that has been made or may be made against the defendant. However, the primary objective of satisfying the order is subject to POCA, s 69(3)(a) which provides that 'the powers must be exercised with a view to allowing a person other than a defendant or the recipient of a tainted gift to retain or recover the value of any interest held by him'. The Act therefore seeks to protect the property interests of innocent third parties who have an interest in the property. However, the protection afforded by the Act is not absolute and even innocent holders of property may find their property rights overridden and the property in which they hold an interest sold. In that instance the third party's interest in the property will be recognised by payment made from the proceeds of sale.

Sale of third party assets: POCA, s 51

9.20 The court may direct the receiver to sell the asset and pay to the third party the value of his share in the asset,[35] or it may order a third party to buy out the defendant's share of an asset and pay a sum equivalent to that share to the receiver; once payment has been made the defendant will cease to have an interest in the property as any interest he did have will have been transferred to the third party.[36] If the confiscation order has been satisfied in full and the receiver has surplus funds he must distribute such funds to persons who held an interest in the property concerned and the court must give such persons a reasonable opportunity to be heard before directing the proportions in which payment of the surplus funds is to be made.[37]

---

[32] *R v Michael Richards* [2008] EWCA Crim 1841, per Toulson LJ.
[33] POCA, s 78.
[34] POCA, s 69(2)(c).
[35] POCA, s 51.
[36] POCA, s 51(6)(a) and (b).
[37] POCA, s 54(3) and (4).

Appendix 1

PROCEEDS OF CRIME ACT 2002

(2002 CHAPTER 29)

An Act to establish the Assets Recovery Agency and make provision about the appointment of its Director and his functions (including Revenue functions), to provide for confiscation orders in relation to persons who benefit from criminal conduct and for restraint orders to prohibit dealing with property, to allow the recovery of property which is or represents property obtained through unlawful conduct or which is intended to be used in unlawful conduct, to make provision about money laundering, to make provision about investigations relating to benefit from criminal conduct or to property which is or represents property obtained through unlawful conduct or to money laundering, to make provision to give effect to overseas requests and orders made where property is found or believed to be obtained through criminal conduct, and for connected purposes

[24 July 2002]

PART 1
[INTRODUCTORY]¹

1 ...²

...²

Amendments
1   Substituted by the Serious Crime Act 2007, s 74(2)(*f*), Sch 8, Pt 6, paras 121, 122.
2   Repealed by the Serious Crime Act 2007, ss 74(2)(*f*), 92, Sch 8, Pt 6, paras 121, 123, Sch 14.

2 ...¹

...¹

Amendments
1   Repealed by the Serious Crime Act 2007, ss 74(2)(*f*), 92, Sch 8, Pt 6, paras 121, 123, Sch 14.

[2A   Contribution to the reduction of crime

(1)   A relevant authority must exercise its functions under this Act in the way which it considers is best calculated to contribute to the reduction of crime.

(2)   In this section 'a relevant authority' means–

(*a*)   SOCA,

(*b*)   the Director of Public Prosecutions,

(*c*)   the Director of Public Prosecutions for Northern Ireland, (*d*)   the Director of Revenue and Customs Prosecutions, or

(*e*)   the Director of the Serious Fraud Office.

(3)   In considering under subsection (1) the way which is best calculated to contribute to the reduction of crime a relevant authority must have regard to any guidance given to it by–

    (*a*)   in the case of SOCA, the Secretary of State,

    (*b*)   in the case of the Director of Public Prosecutions, the Director of Revenue and Customs Prosecutions or the Director of the Serious Fraud Office, the Attorney General, and

    (*c*)   in the case of the Director of Public Prosecutions for Northern Ireland, the Advocate General for Northern Ireland.

(4)   The guidance must indicate that the reduction of crime is in general best secured by means of criminal investigations and criminal proceedings.

(5)   The reference in this section to the Advocate General for Northern Ireland is to be read, before the coming into force of section 27(1) of the Justice (Northern Ireland) Act 2002 (c. 26), as a reference to the Attorney General for Northern Ireland.][1]

Amendments
1   Inserted by the Serious Crime Act 2007, s 74(2)(*f*), Sch 8, Pt 6, paras 121, 124.

[2B SOCA and members of SOCA's staff

(1)   For the purposes of this Act SOCA is the Serious Organised Crime Agency.

(2)   Anything which SOCA is authorised or required to do under this Act (whether directly or through its staff) may be done by a person providing services under arrangements made by SOCA if the person is authorised by SOCA (whether generally or specifically) for that purpose.

(3)   References in this Act to members of SOCA's staff are to be read in accordance with paragraph 8(4) of Schedule 1 to the Serious Organised Crime and Police Act 2005 (c. 15) (employees of SOCA or persons seconded to SOCA to serve as members of its staff).][1]

Amendments
1   Inserted by the Serious Crime Act 2007, s 74(2)(*f*), Sch 8, Pt 6, paras 121, 124.

[2C Prosecuting authorities

(1)   Anything which the Director of Public Prosecutions is authorised or required to do under, or in relation to, Part 5 or 8 of this Act may be done by a member of his staff if the member of staff is authorised by the Director (generally or specifically) for that purpose.

(2)   Anything which the Director of Revenue and Customs Prosecutions or the Director of the Serious Fraud Office is authorised or required to do under, or in relation to, Part 5 or 8 of this Act may be done by a member of his staff if the member of staff is authorised by the Director concerned (generally or specifically) for that purpose.

(3)   Anything which a relevant Director or a member of his staff is authorised or required to do under, or in relation to, Part 5 or 8 of this Act may be done by a person providing

services under arrangements made by the relevant Director if the person is authorised by the relevant Director (whether generally or specifically) for that purpose.

[(3A) Subsection (3) does not apply to the functions of the Director of Public Prosecutions for Northern Ireland and the Director of Revenue and Customs Prosecutions under section 302A.][1]

(4) In this section 'relevant Director' means–

    (*a*)   the Director of Public Prosecutions,

    (*b*)   the Director of Public Prosecutions for Northern Ireland,

    (*c*)   the Director of Revenue and Customs Prosecutions, or

    (*d*)   the Director of the Serious Fraud Office.][1]

Amendments

1   Inserted by the Serious Crime Act 2007, ss 74(2)(*f*), 84(2), Sch 8, Pt 6, paras 121, 124.

3 Accreditation and training

(1) The [National Policing Improvement Agency][1] must [provide][1] a system for the accreditation of financial investigators.

(2) The system of accreditation must include provision for—

    (*a*)   the monitoring of the performance of accredited financial investigators, and

    (*b*)   the withdrawal of accreditation from any person who contravenes or fails to comply with any condition subject to which he was accredited.

(3) A person may be accredited—

    (*a*)   in relation to this Act;

    (*b*)   in relation to particular provisions of this Act.

(4) But the accreditation may be limited to specified purposes.

(5) A reference in this Act to an accredited financial investigator is to be construed accordingly.

(6) ...[2]

(7) The [National Policing Improvement Agency][1] must make provision for the training of persons in—

    (*a*)   financial investigation, and

    (*b*)   the operation of this Act.

(8) ...[2]

Amendments

1   Substituted by the Serious Crime Act 2007, s 74(2)(*e*), Sch 8, Pt 5, para 120.
2   Repealed by the Serious Crime Act 2007, ss 74(2)(*e*), 92, Sch 8, Pt 5, para 120, Sch 14.

4 ...[1]

   [1]
...

Amendments

1   Repealed by the Serious Crime Act 2007, ss 74(2)(*f*), 92, Sch 8, Pt 6, paras 121, 125, Sch 14.

5   ...[1]

  ...[1]

Amendments

1   Repealed by the Serious Crime Act 2007, ss 74(2)(*f*), 92, Sch 8, Pt 6, paras 121, 125, Sch 14.

PART 2
CONFISCATION: ENGLAND AND WALES

Confiscation orders

6   Making of order

(1)   The Crown Court must proceed under this section if the following two conditions are satisfied.

(2)   The first condition is that a defendant falls within any of the following paragraphs—

     (*a*)   he is convicted of an offence or offences in proceedings before the Crown Court;

     (*b*)   he is committed to the Crown Court for sentence in respect of an offence or offences under section 3, 4 or 6 of the Sentencing Act;

     (*c*)   he is committed to the Crown Court in respect of an offence or offences under section 70 below (committal with a view to a confiscation order being considered).

(3)   The second condition is that—

     (*a*)   the prosecutor ...[1] asks the court to proceed under this section, or

     (*b*)   the court believes it is appropriate for it to do so.

(4)   The court must proceed as follows—

     (*a*)   it must decide whether the defendant has a criminal lifestyle;

     (*b*)   if it decides that he has a criminal lifestyle it must decide whether he has benefited from his general criminal conduct;

     (*c*)   if it decides that he does not have a criminal lifestyle it must decide whether he has benefited from his particular criminal conduct.

(5)   If the court decides under subsection (4)(*b*) or (*c*) that the defendant has benefited from the conduct referred to it must—

     (*a*)   decide the recoverable amount, and

     (*b*)   make an order (a confiscation order) requiring him to pay that amount.

(6)   But the court must treat the duty in subsection (5) as a power if it believes that any victim of the conduct has at any time started or intends to start proceedings against the defendant in respect of loss, injury or damage sustained in connection with the conduct.

(7)   The court must decide any question arising under subsection (4) or (5) on a balance of probabilities.

(8) The first condition is not satisfied if the defendant absconds (but section 27 may apply).

(9) References in this Part to the offence (or offences) concerned are to the offence (or offences) mentioned in subsection (2).

Amendments
1   Repealed by the Serious Crime Act 2007, ss 74(2)(*a*), 92, Sch 8, Pt 1, paras 1, 2, Sch 14.

7 Recoverable amount

(1) The recoverable amount for the purposes of section 6 is an amount equal to the defendant's benefit from the conduct concerned.

(2) But if the defendant shows that the available amount is less than that benefit the recoverable amount is—

  (*a*) the available amount, or

  (*b*) a nominal amount, if the available amount is nil.

(3) But if section 6(6) applies the recoverable amount is such amount as—

  (*a*) the court believes is just, but

  (*b*) does not exceed the amount found under subsection (1) or (2) (as the case may be).

(4) In calculating the defendant's benefit from the conduct concerned for the purposes of subsection (1), any property in respect of which—

  (*a*) a recovery order is in force under section 266, or

  (*b*) a forfeiture order is in force under section 298(2),

  must be ignored.

(5) If the court decides the available amount, it must include in the confiscation order a statement of its findings as to the matters relevant for deciding that amount.

8 Defendant's benefit

(1) If the court is proceeding under section 6 this section applies for the purpose of—

  (*a*) deciding whether the defendant has benefited from conduct, and

  (*b*) deciding his benefit from the conduct.

(2) The court must—

  (*a*) take account of conduct occurring up to the time it makes its decision;

  (*b*) take account of property obtained up to that time.

(3) Subsection (4) applies if—

  (*a*) the conduct concerned is general criminal conduct,

  (*b*) a confiscation order mentioned in subsection (5) has at an earlier time been made against the defendant, and

  (*c*) his benefit for the purposes of that order was benefit from his general criminal conduct.

(4)   His benefit found at the time the last confiscation order mentioned in subsection (3)(*c*) was made against him must be taken for the purposes of this section to be his benefit from his general criminal conduct at that time.

(5)   If the conduct concerned is general criminal conduct the court must deduct the aggregate of the following amounts—

    (*a*)   the amount ordered to be paid under each confiscation order previously made against the defendant;

    (*b*)   the amount ordered to be paid under each confiscation order previously made against him under any of the provisions listed in subsection (7).

(6)   But subsection (5) does not apply to an amount which has been taken into account for the purposes of a deduction under that subsection on any earlier occasion.

(7)   These are the provisions—

    (*a*)   the Drug Trafficking Offences Act 1986 (c. 32);

    (*b*)   Part 1 of the Criminal Justice (Scotland) Act 1987 (c. 41);

    (*c*)   Part 6 of the Criminal Justice Act 1988 (c. 33);

    (*d*)   the Criminal Justice (Confiscation) (Northern Ireland) Order 1990 (S.I. 1990/2588 (N.I. 17));

    (*e*)   Part 1 of the Drug Trafficking Act 1994 (c. 37);

    (*f*)   Part 1 of the Proceeds of Crime (Scotland) Act 1995 (c. 43);

    (*g*)   the Proceeds of Crime (Northern Ireland) Order 1996 (S.I. 1996/1299 (N.I. 9));

    (*h*)   Part 3 or 4 of this Act.

(8)   The reference to general criminal conduct in the case of a confiscation order made under any of the provisions listed in subsection (7) is a reference to conduct in respect of which a court is required or entitled to make one or more assumptions for the purpose of assessing a person's benefit from the conduct.

9   Available amount

(1)   For the purposes of deciding the recoverable amount, the available amount is the aggregate of—

    (*a*)   the total of the values (at the time the confiscation order is made) of all the free property then held by the defendant minus the total amount payable in pursuance of obligations which then have priority, and

    (*b*)   the total of the values (at that time) of all tainted gifts.

(2)   An obligation has priority if it is an obligation of the defendant—

    (*a*)   to pay an amount due in respect of a fine or other order of a court which was imposed or made on conviction of an offence and at any time before the time the confiscation order is made, or

    (*b*)   to pay a sum which would be included among the preferential debts if the defendant's bankruptcy had commenced on the date of the confiscation order or his winding up had been ordered on that date.

(3)   'Preferential debts' has the meaning given by section 386 of the Insolvency Act 1986 (c. 45).

10   Assumptions to be made in case of criminal lifestyle

(1)   If the court decides under section 6 that the defendant has a criminal lifestyle it must make the following four assumptions for the purpose of—

(*a*)   deciding whether he has benefited from his general criminal conduct, and

(*b*)   deciding his benefit from the conduct.

(2)   The first assumption is that any property transferred to the defendant at any time after the relevant day was obtained by him—

(*a*)   as a result of his general criminal conduct, and

(*b*)   at the earliest time he appears to have held it.

(3)   The second assumption is that any property held by the defendant at any time after the date of conviction was obtained by him—

(*a*)   as a result of his general criminal conduct, and

(*b*)   at the earliest time he appears to have held it.

(4)   The third assumption is that any expenditure incurred by the defendant at any time after the relevant day was met from property obtained by him as a result of his general criminal conduct.

(5)   The fourth assumption is that, for the purpose of valuing any property obtained (or assumed to have been obtained) by the defendant, he obtained it free of any other interests in it.

(6)   But the court must not make a required assumption in relation to particular property or expenditure if—

(*a*)   the assumption is shown to be incorrect, or

(*b*)   there would be a serious risk of injustice if the assumption were made.

(7)   If the court does not make one or more of the required assumptions it must state its reasons.

(8)   The relevant day is the first day of the period of six years ending with—

(*a*)   the day when proceedings for the offence concerned were started against the defendant, or

(*b*)   if there are two or more offences and proceedings for them were started on different days, the earliest of those days.

(9)   But if a confiscation order mentioned in section 8(3)(*c*) has been made against the defendant at any time during the period mentioned in subsection (8)—

(*a*)   the relevant day is the day when the defendant's benefit was calculated for the purposes of the last such confiscation order;

(*b*)   the second assumption does not apply to any property which was held by him on or before the relevant day.

(10)   The date of conviction is—

(*a*)   the date on which the defendant was convicted of the offence concerned, or

(*b*)   if there are two or more offences and the convictions were on different dates, the date of the latest.

137

11   Time for payment

(1)   The amount ordered to be paid under a confiscation order must be paid on the making of the order; but this is subject to the following provisions of this section.

(2)   If the defendant shows that he needs time to pay the amount ordered to be paid, the court making the confiscation order may make an order allowing payment to be made in a specified period.

(3)   The specified period—

    (*a*)   must start with the day on which the confiscation order is made, and

    (*b*)   must not exceed six months.

(4)   If within the specified period the defendant applies to the Crown Court for the period to be extended and the court believes there are exceptional circumstances, it may make an order extending the period.

(5)   The extended period—

    (*a*)   must start with the day on which the confiscation order is made, and

    (*b*)   must not exceed 12 months.

(6)   An order under subsection (4)—

    (*a*)   may be made after the end of the specified period, but

    (*b*)   must not be made after the end of the period of 12 months starting with the day on which the confiscation order is made.

(7)   The court must not make an order under subsection (2) or (4) unless it gives—

    (*a*)   the prosecutor, ...[1]

    (*b*)   ...[1]

an opportunity to make representations.

Amendments

1   Repealed by the Serious Crime Act 2007, ss 74(2)(*a*), 92, Sch 8, Pt 1, paras 1, 3, Sch 14.

12   Interest on unpaid sums

(1)   If the amount required to be paid by a person under a confiscation order is not paid when it is required to be paid, he must pay interest on the amount for the period for which it remains unpaid.

(2)   The rate of interest is the same rate as that for the time being specified in section 17 of the Judgments Act 1838 (c. 110) (interest on civil judgment debts).

(3)   For the purposes of this section no amount is required to be paid under a confiscation order if—

    (*a*)   an application has been made under section 11(4),

    (*b*)   the application has not been determined by the court, and

    (*c*)   the period of 12 months starting with the day on which the confiscation order was made has not ended.

(4)   In applying this Part the amount of the interest must be treated as part of the amount to be paid under the confiscation order.

13 Effect of order on court's other powers

(1) If the court makes a confiscation order it must proceed as mentioned in subsections (2) and (4) in respect of the offence or offences concerned.

(2) The court must take account of the confiscation order before—

(*a*) it imposes a fine on the defendant, or

(*b*) it makes an order falling within subsection (3).

(3) These orders fall within this subsection—

(*a*) an order involving payment by the defendant, other than an order under section 130 of the Sentencing Act (compensation orders);

(*b*) an order under section 27 of the Misuse of Drugs Act 1971 (c. 38) (forfeiture orders);

(*c*) an order under section 143 of the Sentencing Act (deprivation orders);

(*d*) an order under section 23 [or 23A]¹ of the Terrorism Act 2000 (c. 11) (forfeiture orders).

(4) Subject to subsection (2), the court must leave the confiscation order out of account in deciding the appropriate sentence for the defendant.

(5) Subsection (6) applies if—

(*a*) the Crown Court makes both a confiscation order and an order for the payment of compensation under section 130 of the Sentencing Act against the same person in the same proceedings, and

(*b*) the court believes he will not have sufficient means to satisfy both the orders in full.

(6) In such a case the court must direct that so much of the compensation as it specifies is to be paid out of any sums recovered under the confiscation order; and the amount it specifies must be the amount it believes will not be recoverable because of the insufficiency of the person's means.

Amendments
1   Inserted by the Counter-Terrorism Act 2008, s 39, Sch 3, para 7.

Procedural matters

14 Postponement

(1) The court may—

(*a*) proceed under section 6 before it sentences the defendant for the offence (or any of the offences) concerned, or

(*b*) postpone proceedings under section 6 for a specified period.

(2) A period of postponement may be extended.

(3) A period of postponement (including one as extended) must not end after the permitted period ends.

(4) But subsection (3) does not apply if there are exceptional circumstances.

(5) The permitted period is the period of two years starting with the date of conviction.

(6)   But if—

    (*a*)   the defendant appeals against his conviction for the offence (or any of the offences) concerned, and

    (*b*)   the period of three months (starting with the day when the appeal is determined or otherwise disposed of) ends after the period found under subsection (5),

    the permitted period is that period of three months.

(7)   A postponement or extension may be made—

    (*a*)   on application by the defendant;

    (*b*)   on application by the prosecutor …[1];

    (*c*)   by the court of its own motion.

(8)   If—

    (*a*)   proceedings are postponed for a period, and

    (*b*)   an application to extend the period is made before it ends,

    the application may be granted even after the period ends.

(9)   The date of conviction is—

    (*a*)   the date on which the defendant was convicted of the offence concerned, or

    (*b*)   if there are two or more offences and the convictions were on different dates, the date of the latest.

(10)   References to appealing include references to applying under section 111 of the Magistrates' Courts Act 1980 (c. 43) (statement of case).

(11)   A confiscation order must not be quashed only on the ground that there was a defect or omission in the procedure connected with the application for or the granting of a postponement.

(12)   But subsection (11) does not apply if before it made the confiscation order the court—

    (*a*)   imposed a fine on the defendant;

    (*b*)   made an order falling within section 13(3);

    (*c*)   made an order under section 130 of the Sentencing Act (compensation orders).

Amendments

1   Repealed by the Serious Crime Act 2007, ss 74(2)(*a*), 92, Sch 8, Pt 1, paras 1, 4, Sch 14.

15   Effect of postponement

(1)   If the court postpones proceedings under section 6 it may proceed to sentence the defendant for the offence (or any of the offences) concerned.

(2)   In sentencing the defendant for the offence (or any of the offences) concerned in the postponement period the court must not—

    (*a*)   impose a fine on him,

    (*b*)   make an order falling within section 13(3), or

    (*c*)   make an order for the payment of compensation under section 130 of the Sentencing Act.

(3)   If the court sentences the defendant for the offence (or any of the offences) concerned in the postponement period, after that period ends it may vary the sentence by—

    (*a*)   imposing a fine on him,

    (*b*)   making an order falling within section 13(3), or

    (*c*)   making an order for the payment of compensation under section 130 of the Sentencing Act.

(4)   But the court may proceed under subsection (3) only within the period of 28 days which starts with the last day of the postponement period.

(5)   For the purposes of—

    (*a*)   section 18(2) of the Criminal Appeal Act 1968 (c. 19) (time limit for notice of appeal or of application for leave to appeal), and

    (*b*)   paragraph 1 of Schedule 3 to the Criminal Justice Act 1988 (c. 33) (time limit for notice of application for leave to refer a case under section 36 of that Act),

the sentence must be regarded as imposed or made on the day on which it is varied under subsection (3).

(6)   If the court proceeds to sentence the defendant under subsection (1), section 6 has effect as if the defendant's particular criminal conduct included conduct which constitutes offences which the court has taken into consideration in deciding his sentence for the offence or offences concerned.

(7)   The postponement period is the period for which proceedings under section 6 are postponed.

16   Statement of information

(1)   If the court is proceeding under section 6 in a case where section 6(3)(*a*) applies, the prosecutor ...[1] must give the court a statement of information within the period the court orders.

(2)   If the court is proceeding under section 6 in a case where section 6(3)(*b*) applies and it orders the prosecutor to give it a statement of information, the prosecutor must give it such a statement within the period the court orders.

(3)   If the prosecutor ...[1] believes the defendant has a criminal lifestyle the statement of information is a statement of matters the prosecutor ...[1] believes are relevant in connection with deciding these issues—

    (*a*)   whether the defendant has a criminal lifestyle;

    (*b*)   whether he has benefited from his general criminal conduct;

    (*c*)   his benefit from the conduct.

(4)   A statement under subsection (3) must include information the prosecutor ...[1] believes is relevant—

    (*a*)   in connection with the making by the court of a required assumption under section 10;

    (*b*)   for the purpose of enabling the court to decide if the circumstances are such that it must not make such an assumption.

(5)   If the prosecutor ...[1] does not believe the defendant has a criminal lifestyle the statement of information is a statement of matters the prosecutor ...[1] believes are relevant in connection with deciding these issues—

(a)   whether the defendant has benefited from his particular criminal conduct;

(b)   his benefit from the conduct.

(6)   If the prosecutor ...[1] gives the court a statement of information—

(a)   he may at any time give the court a further statement of information;

(b)   he must give the court a further statement of information if it orders him to do so, and he must give it within the period the court orders.

(7)   If the court makes an order under this section it may at any time vary it by making another one.

Amendments

1   Repealed by the Serious Crime Act 2007, ss 74(2)(a), 92, Sch 8, Pt 1, paras 1, 5, Sch 14.

17   Defendant's response to statement of information

(1)   If the prosecutor ...[1] gives the court a statement of information and a copy is served on the defendant, the court may order the defendant—

(a)   to indicate (within the period it orders) the extent to which he accepts each allegation in the statement, and

(b)   so far as he does not accept such an allegation, to give particulars of any matters he proposes to rely on.

(2)   If the defendant accepts to any extent an allegation in a statement of information the court may treat his acceptance as conclusive of the matters to which it relates for the purpose of deciding the issues referred to in section 16(3) or (5) (as the case may be).

(3)   If the defendant fails in any respect to comply with an order under subsection (1) he may be treated for the purposes of subsection (2) as accepting every allegation in the statement of information apart from—

(a)   any allegation in respect of which he has complied with the requirement;

(b)   any allegation that he has benefited from his general or particular criminal conduct.

(4)   For the purposes of this section an allegation may be accepted or particulars may be given in a manner ordered by the court.

(5)   If the court makes an order under this section it may at any time vary it by making another one.

(6)   No acceptance under this section that the defendant has benefited from conduct is admissible in evidence in proceedings for an offence.

Amendments

1   Repealed by the Serious Crime Act 2007, ss 74(2)(a), 92, Sch 8, Pt 1, paras 1, 6, Sch 14.

18 Provision of information by defendant

(1) This section applies if—

    (*a*) the court is proceeding under section 6 in a case where section 6(3)(*a*) applies, or

    (*b*) it is proceeding under section 6 in a case where section 6(3)(*b*) applies or it is considering whether to proceed.

(2) For the purpose of obtaining information to help it in carrying out its functions the court may at any time order the defendant to give it information specified in the order.

(3) An order under this section may require all or a specified part of the information to be given in a specified manner and before a specified date.

(4) If the defendant fails without reasonable excuse to comply with an order under this section the court may draw such inference as it believes is appropriate.

(5) Subsection (4) does not affect any power of the court to deal with the defendant in respect of a failure to comply with an order under this section.

(6) If the prosecutor ...[1] accepts to any extent an allegation made by the defendant—

    (*a*) in giving information required by an order under this section, or

    (*b*) in any other statement given to the court in relation to any matter relevant to deciding the available amount under section 9,

the court may treat the acceptance as conclusive of the matters to which it relates.

(7) For the purposes of this section an allegation may be accepted in a manner ordered by the court.

(8) If the court makes an order under this section it may at any time vary it by making another one.

(9) No information given under this section which amounts to an admission by the defendant that he has benefited from criminal conduct is admissible in evidence in proceedings for an offence.

Amendments
1   Repealed by the Serious Crime Act 2007, ss 74(2)(*a*), 92, Sch 8, Pt 1, paras 1, 7, Sch 14.

Reconsideration

19 No order made: reconsideration of case

(1) This section applies if—

    (*a*) the first condition in section 6 is satisfied but no court has proceeded under that section,

    (*b*) there is evidence which was not available to the prosecutor on the relevant date,

    (*c*) before the end of the period of six years starting with the date of conviction the prosecutor ...[1] applies to the Crown Court to consider the evidence, and

    (*d*) after considering the evidence the court believes it is appropriate for it to proceed under section 6.

(2) If this section applies the court must proceed under section 6, and when it does so subsections (3) to (8) below apply.

(3)   If the court has already sentenced the defendant for the offence (or any of the offences) concerned, section 6 has effect as if his particular criminal conduct included conduct which constitutes offences which the court has taken into consideration in deciding his sentence for the offence or offences concerned.

(4)   Section 8(2) does not apply, and the rules applying instead are that the court must—

    (*a*)   take account of conduct occurring before the relevant date;

    (*b*)   take account of property obtained before that date;

    (*c*)   take account of property obtained on or after that date if it was obtained as a result of or in connection with conduct occurring before that date.

(5)   In section 10—

    (*a*)   the first and second assumptions do not apply with regard to property first held by the defendant on or after the relevant date;

    (*b*)   the third assumption does not apply with regard to expenditure incurred by him on or after that date;

    (*c*)   the fourth assumption does not apply with regard to property obtained (or assumed to have been obtained) by him on or after that date.

(6)   The recoverable amount for the purposes of section 6 is such amount as—

    (*a*)   the court believes is just, but

    (*b*)   does not exceed the amount found under section 7.

(7)   In arriving at the just amount the court must have regard in particular to—

    (*a*)   the amount found under section 7;

    (*b*)   any fine imposed on the defendant in respect of the offence (or any of the offences) concerned;

    (*c*)   any order which falls within section 13(3) and has been made against him in respect of the offence (or any of the offences) concerned and has not already been taken into account by the court in deciding what is the free property held by him for the purposes of section 9;

    (*d*)   any order which has been made against him in respect of the offence (or any of the offences) concerned under section 130 of the Sentencing Act (compensation orders).

(8)   If an order for the payment of compensation under section 130 of the Sentencing Act has been made against the defendant in respect of the offence or offences concerned, section 13(5) and (6) above do not apply.

(9)   The relevant date is—

    (*a*)   if the court made a decision not to proceed under section 6, the date of the decision;

    (*b*)   if the court did not make such a decision, the date of conviction.

(10)   The date of conviction is—

    (*a*)   the date on which the defendant was convicted of the offence concerned, or

    (*b*)   if there are two or more offences and the convictions were on different dates, the date of the latest.

Amendments
1   Repealed by the Serious Crime Act 2007, ss 74(2)(*a*), 92, Sch 8, Pt 1, paras 1, 8, Sch 14.

20   No order made: reconsideration of benefit

(1)   This section applies if the following two conditions are satisfied.

(2)   The first condition is that in proceeding under section 6 the court has decided that—

   (*a*)   the defendant has a criminal lifestyle but has not benefited from his general criminal conduct, or

   (*b*)   the defendant does not have a criminal lifestyle and has not benefited from his particular criminal conduct.

(3)   ...[1]

(4)   ...[1] The second condition is that—

   (*a*)   there is evidence which was not available to the prosecutor when the court decided that the defendant had not benefited from his general or particular criminal conduct,

   (*b*)   before the end of the period of six years starting with the date of conviction the prosecutor ...[1] applies to the Crown Court to consider the evidence, and

   (*c*)   after considering the evidence the court concludes that it would have decided that the defendant had benefited from his general or particular criminal conduct (as the case may be) if the evidence had been available to it.

(5)   If this section applies the court—

   (*a*)   must make a fresh decision under section 6(4)(*b*) or (*c*) whether the defendant has benefited from his general or particular criminal conduct (as the case may be);

   (*b*)   may make a confiscation order under that section.

(6)   Subsections (7) to (12) below apply if the court proceeds under section 6 in pursuance of this section.

(7)   If the court has already sentenced the defendant for the offence (or any of the offences) concerned, section 6 has effect as if his particular criminal conduct included conduct which constitutes offences which the court has taken into consideration in deciding his sentence for the offence or offences concerned.

(8)   Section 8(2) does not apply, and the rules applying instead are that the court must—

   (*a*)   take account of conduct occurring before the date of the original decision that the defendant had not benefited from his general or particular criminal conduct;

   (*b*)   take account of property obtained before that date;

   (*c*)   take account of property obtained on or after that date if it was obtained as a result of or in connection with conduct occurring before that date.

(9)   In section 10—

   (*a*)   the first and second assumptions do not apply with regard to property first held by the defendant on or after the date of the original decision that the defendant had not benefited from his general or particular criminal conduct;

   (*b*)   the third assumption does not apply with regard to expenditure incurred by him on or after that date;

(c)   the fourth assumption does not apply with regard to property obtained (or assumed to have been obtained) by him on or after that date.

(10)   The recoverable amount for the purposes of section 6 is such amount as—

    (a)   the court believes is just, but

    (b)   does not exceed the amount found under section 7.

(11)   In arriving at the just amount the court must have regard in particular to—

    (a)   the amount found under section 7;

    (b)   any fine imposed on the defendant in respect of the offence (or any of the offences) concerned;

    (c)   any order which falls within section 13(3) and has been made against him in respect of the offence (or any of the offences) concerned and has not already been taken into account by the court in deciding what is the free property held by him for the purposes of section 9;

    (d)   any order which has been made against him in respect of the offence (or any of the offences) concerned under section 130 of the Sentencing Act (compensation orders).

(12)   If an order for the payment of compensation under section 130 of the Sentencing Act has been made against the defendant in respect of the offence or offences concerned, section 13(5) and (6) above do not apply.

(13)   The date of conviction is the date found by applying section 19(10).

Amendments
1   Repealed by the Serious Crime Act 2007, ss 74(2)(a), 92, Sch 8, Pt 1, paras 1, 9, Sch 14.

21 Order made: reconsideration of benefit

(1)   This section applies if—

    (a)   a court has made a confiscation order,

    (b)   there is evidence which was not available to the prosecutor ...[1] at the relevant time,

    (c)   the prosecutor ...[1] believes that if the court were to find the amount of the defendant's benefit in pursuance of this section it would exceed the relevant amount,

    (d)   before the end of the period of six years starting with the date of conviction the prosecutor ...[1] applies to the Crown Court to consider the evidence, and

    (e)   after considering the evidence the court believes it is appropriate for it to proceed under this section.

(2)   The court must make a new calculation of the defendant's benefit from the conduct concerned, and when it does so subsections (3) to (6) below apply.

(3)   If a court has already sentenced the defendant for the offence (or any of the offences) concerned section 6 has effect as if his particular criminal conduct included conduct which constitutes offences which the court has taken into consideration in deciding his sentence for the offence or offences concerned.

(4)   Section 8(2) does not apply, and the rules applying instead are that the court must—

(a)   take account of conduct occurring up to the time it decided the defendant's benefit for the purposes of the confiscation order;

(b)   take account of property obtained up to that time;

(c)   take account of property obtained after that time if it was obtained as a result of or in connection with conduct occurring before that time.

(5)   In applying section 8(5) the confiscation order must be ignored.

(6)   In section 10—

(a)   the first and second assumptions do not apply with regard to property first held by the defendant after the time the court decided his benefit for the purposes of the confiscation order;

(b)   the third assumption does not apply with regard to expenditure incurred by him after that time;

(c)   the fourth assumption does not apply with regard to property obtained (or assumed to have been obtained) by him after that time.

(7)   If the amount found under the new calculation of the defendant's benefit exceeds the relevant amount the court—

(a)   must make a new calculation of the recoverable amount for the purposes of section 6, and

(b)   if it exceeds the amount required to be paid under the confiscation order, may vary the order by substituting for the amount required to be paid such amount as it believes is just.

(8)   In applying subsection (7)(a) the court must—

(a)   take the new calculation of the defendant's benefit;

(b)   apply section 9 as if references to the time the confiscation order is made were to the time of the new calculation of the recoverable amount and as if references to the date of the confiscation order were to the date of that new calculation.

(9)   In applying subsection (7)(b) the court must have regard in particular to—

(a)   any fine imposed on the defendant for the offence (or any of the offences) concerned;

(b)   any order which falls within section 13(3) and has been made against him in respect of the offence (or any of the offences) concerned and has not already been taken into account by the court in deciding what is the free property held by him for the purposes of section 9;

(c)   any order which has been made against him in respect of the offence (or any of the offences) concerned under section 130 of the Sentencing Act (compensation orders).

(10)   But in applying subsection (7)(b) the court must not have regard to an order falling within subsection (9)(c) if a court has made a direction under section 13(6).

(11)   In deciding under this section whether one amount exceeds another the court must take account of any change in the value of money.

(12)   The relevant time is—

147

(*a*)   when the court calculated the defendant's benefit for the purposes of the confiscation order, if this section has not applied previously;

(*b*)   when the court last calculated the defendant's benefit in pursuance of this section, if this section has applied previously.

(13)   The relevant amount is—

(*a*)   the amount found as the defendant's benefit for the purposes of the confiscation order, if this section has not applied previously;

(*b*)   the amount last found as the defendant's benefit in pursuance of this section, if this section has applied previously.

(14)   The date of conviction is the date found by applying section 19(10).

Amendments

1   Repealed by the Serious Crime Act 2007, ss 74(2)(*a*), 92, Sch 8, Pt 1, paras 1, 10, Sch 14.

22   Order made: reconsideration of available amount

(1)   This section applies if—

(*a*)   a court has made a confiscation order,

(*b*)   the amount required to be paid was the amount found under section 7(2), and

(*c*)   an applicant falling within subsection (2) applies to the Crown Court to make a new calculation of the available amount.

(2)   These applicants fall within this subsection—

(*a*)   the prosecutor;

(*b*)   ...[1]

(*c*)   a receiver appointed under section 50 ...[1].

(3)   In a case where this section applies the court must make the new calculation, and in doing so it must apply section 9 as if references to the time the confiscation order is made were to the time of the new calculation and as if references to the date of the confiscation order were to the date of the new calculation.

(4)   If the amount found under the new calculation exceeds the relevant amount the court may vary the order by substituting for the amount required to be paid such amount as—

(*a*)   it believes is just, but

(*b*)   does not exceed the amount found as the defendant's benefit from the conduct concerned.

(5)   In deciding what is just the court must have regard in particular to—

(*a*)   any fine imposed on the defendant for the offence (or any of the offences) concerned;

(*b*)   any order which falls within section 13(3) and has been made against him in respect of the offence (or any of the offences) concerned and has not already been taken into account by the court in deciding what is the free property held by him for the purposes of section 9;

(*c*)   any order which has been made against him in respect of the offence (or any of the offences) concerned under section 130 of the Sentencing Act (compensation orders).

(6)   But in deciding what is just the court must not have regard to an order falling within subsection (5)(*c*) if a court has made a direction under section 13(6).

(7)   In deciding under this section whether one amount exceeds another the court must take account of any change in the value of money.

(8)   The relevant amount is—

(*a*)   the amount found as the available amount for the purposes of the confiscation order, if this section has not applied previously;

(*b*)   the amount last found as the available amount in pursuance of this section, if this section has applied previously.

(9)   The amount found as the defendant's benefit from the conduct concerned is—

(*a*)   the amount so found when the confiscation order was made, or

(*b*)   if one or more new calculations of the defendant's benefit have been made under section 21 the amount found on the occasion of the last such calculation.

Amendments
1   Repealed by the Serious Crime Act 2007, ss 74(2)(*a*), 92, Sch 8, Pt 1, paras 1, 11, Sch 14.

23   Inadequacy of available amount: variation of order

(1)   This section applies if—

(*a*)   a court has made a confiscation order, and

(*b*)   the defendant, or a receiver appointed under section 50 ...[1], applies to the Crown Court to vary the order under this section.

(2)   In such a case the court must calculate the available amount, and in doing so it must apply section 9 as if references to the time the confiscation order is made were to the time of the calculation and as if references to the date of the confiscation order were to the date of the calculation.

(3)   If the court finds that the available amount (as so calculated) is inadequate for the payment of any amount remaining to be paid under the confiscation order it may vary the order by substituting for the amount required to be paid such smaller amount as the court believes is just.

(4)   If a person has been adjudged bankrupt or his estate has been sequestrated, or if an order for the winding up of a company has been made, the court must take into account the extent to which realisable property held by that person or that company may be distributed among creditors.

(5)   The court may disregard any inadequacy which it believes is attributable (wholly or partly) to anything done by the defendant for the purpose of preserving property held by the recipient of a tainted gift from any risk of realisation under this Part.

(6)   In subsection (4) 'company' means any company which may be wound up under the Insolvency Act 1986 (c. 45) or the Insolvency (Northern Ireland) Order 1989 (S.I. 1989/2405 (N.I. 19)).

Amendments
1   Repealed by the Serious Crime Act 2007, ss 74(2)(*a*), 92, Sch 8, Pt 1, paras 1, 12, Sch 14.

24 Inadequacy of available amount: discharge of order

(1)   This section applies if—

    (*a*)   a court has made a confiscation order,

    (*b*)   [the designated officer for a magistrates' court][1] applies to the Crown Court for the discharge of the order, and

    (*c*)   the amount remaining to be paid under the order is less than £1,000.

(2)   In such a case the court must calculate the available amount, and in doing so it must apply section 9 as if references to the time the confiscation order is made were to the time of the calculation and as if references to the date of the confiscation order were to the date of the calculation.

(3)   If the court—

    (*a*)   finds that the available amount (as so calculated) is inadequate to meet the amount remaining to be paid, and

    (*b*)   is satisfied that the inadequacy is due wholly to a specified reason or a combination of specified reasons,

it may discharge the confiscation order.

(4)   The specified reasons are—

    (*a*)   in a case where any of the realisable property consists of money in a currency other than sterling, that fluctuations in currency exchange rates have occurred;

    (*b*)   any reason specified by the Secretary of State by order.

(5)   The Secretary of State may by order vary the amount for the time being specified in subsection (1)(*c*).

Amendments
1   Substituted by the Courts Act 2003, s 109(1), Sch 8, para 406(*a*).

25 Small amount outstanding: discharge of order

(1)   This section applies if—

    (*a*)   a court has made a confiscation order,

    (*b*)   [the designated officer for a magistrates' court][1] applies to the Crown Court for the discharge of the order, and

    (*c*)   the amount remaining to be paid under the order is £50 or less.

(2)   In such a case the court may discharge the order.

(3)   The Secretary of State may by order vary the amount for the time being specified in subsection (1)(*c*).

Amendments
1   Substituted by the Courts Act 2003, s 109(1), Sch 8, para 406(*b*).

26 Information

(1) This section applies if—

(a) the court proceeds under section 6 in pursuance of section 19 or 20, or

(b) the prosecutor …[1] applies under section 21.

(2) In such a case—

(a) the prosecutor …[1] must give the court a statement of information within the period the court orders;

(b) section 16 applies accordingly (with appropriate modifications where the prosecutor …[1] applies under section 21);

(c) section 17 applies accordingly;

(d) section 18 applies as it applies in the circumstances mentioned in section 18(1).

Amendments
1 Repealed by the Serious Crime Act 2007, ss 74(2)(a), 92, Sch 8, Pt 1, paras 1, 13, Sch 14.

Defendant absconds

27 Defendant convicted or committed

(1) This section applies if the following two conditions are satisfied.

(2) The first condition is that a defendant absconds after—

(a) he is convicted of an offence or offences in proceedings before the Crown Court,

(b) he is committed to the Crown Court for sentence in respect of an offence or offences under [section 3, 3A, 3B, 3C, 4, 4A or 6][1] of the Sentencing Act, or

(c) he is committed to the Crown Court in respect of an offence or offences under section 70 below (committal with a view to a confiscation order being considered).

(3) The second condition is that—

(a) the prosecutor …[2] applies to the Crown Court to proceed under this section, and

(b) the court believes it is appropriate for it to do so.

(4) If this section applies the court must proceed under section 6 in the same way as it must proceed if the two conditions there mentioned are satisfied; but this is subject to subsection (5).

(5) If the court proceeds under section 6 as applied by this section, this Part has effect with these modifications—

(a) any person the court believes is likely to be affected by an order under section 6 is entitled to appear before the court and make representations;

(b) the court must not make an order under section 6 unless the prosecutor …[2] has taken reasonable steps to contact the defendant;

(c) section 6(9) applies as if the reference to subsection (2) were to subsection (2) of this section;

(d) sections 10, 16(4), 17 and 18 must be ignored;

(*e*)   sections 19, 20 and 21 must be ignored while the defendant is still an absconder.

(6)   Once the defendant ceases to be an absconder section 19 has effect as if subsection (1)(*a*) read—

'(*a*)   at a time when the first condition in section 27 was satisfied the court did not proceed under section 6,.'

(7)   If the court does not believe it is appropriate for it to proceed under this section, once the defendant ceases to be an absconder section 19 has effect as if subsection (1)(*b*) read—

'(*b*)   there is evidence which was not available to the prosecutor ...[2] on the relevant date,.'

Amendments

1   Substituted by the Criminal Justice Act 2003, s 41, Sch 3, Pt 2, para 75(1), (3).
2   Repealed by the Serious Crime Act 2007, ss 74(2)(*a*), 92, Sch 8, Pt 1, paras 1, 14, Sch 14.

28   Defendant neither convicted nor acquitted

(1)   This section applies if the following two conditions are satisfied.

(2)   The first condition is that—

(*a*)   proceedings for an offence or offences are started against a defendant but are not concluded,

(*b*)   he absconds, and

(*c*)   the period of two years (starting with the day the court believes he absconded) has ended.

(3)   The second condition is that—

(*a*)   the prosecutor ...[1] applies to the Crown Court to proceed under this section, and

(*b*)   the court believes it is appropriate for it to do so.

(4)   If this section applies the court must proceed under section 6 in the same way as it must proceed if the two conditions there mentioned are satisfied; but this is subject to subsection (5).

(5)   If the court proceeds under section 6 as applied by this section, this Part has effect with these modifications—

(*a*)   any person the court believes is likely to be affected by an order under section 6 is entitled to appear before the court and make representations;

(*b*)   the court must not make an order under section 6 unless the prosecutor ...[1] has taken reasonable steps to contact the defendant;

(*c*)   section 6(9) applies as if the reference to subsection (2) were to subsection (2) of this section;

(*d*)   sections 10, 16(4) and 17 to 20 must be ignored;

(*e*)   section 21 must be ignored while the defendant is still an absconder.

(6)   Once the defendant has ceased to be an absconder section 21 has effect as if references to the date of conviction were to—

(a)   the day when proceedings for the offence concerned were started against the defendant, or

(b)   if there are two or more offences and proceedings for them were started on different days, the earliest of those days.

(7)   If—

(a)   the court makes an order under section 6 as applied by this section, and

(b)   the defendant is later convicted in proceedings before the Crown Court of the offence (or any of the offences) concerned,

section 6 does not apply so far as that conviction is concerned.

Amendments

1   Repealed by the Serious Crime Act 2007, ss 74(2)(a), 92, Sch 8, Pt 1, paras 1, 15, Sch 14.

29   Variation of order

(1)   This section applies if—

(a)   the court makes a confiscation order under section 6 as applied by section 28,

(b)   the defendant ceases to be an absconder,

(c)   he is convicted of an offence (or any of the offences) mentioned in section 28(2)(a),

(d)   he believes that the amount required to be paid was too large (taking the circumstances prevailing when the amount was found for the purposes of the order), and

(e)   before the end of the relevant period he applies to the Crown Court to consider the evidence on which his belief is based.

(2)   If (after considering the evidence) the court concludes that the defendant's belief is well founded—

(a)   it must find the amount which should have been the amount required to be paid (taking the circumstances prevailing when the amount was found for the purposes of the order), and

(b)   it may vary the order by substituting for the amount required to be paid such amount as it believes is just.

(3)   The relevant period is the period of 28 days starting with—

(a)   the date on which the defendant was convicted of the offence mentioned in section 28(2)(a), or

(b)   if there are two or more offences and the convictions were on different dates, the date of the latest.

(4)   But in a case where section 28(2)(a) applies to more than one offence the court must not make an order under this section unless it is satisfied that there is no possibility of any further proceedings being taken or continued in relation to any such offence in respect of which the defendant has not been convicted.

30   Discharge of order

(1)   Subsection (2) applies if—

    (*a*)   the court makes a confiscation order under section 6 as applied by section 28,

    (*b*)   the defendant is later tried for the offence or offences concerned and acquitted on all counts, and

    (*c*)   he applies to the Crown Court to discharge the order.

(2)   In such a case the court must discharge the order.

(3)   Subsection (4) applies if—

    (*a*)   the court makes a confiscation order under section 6 as applied by section 28,

    (*b*)   the defendant ceases to be an absconder,

    (*c*)   subsection (1)(*b*) does not apply, and

    (*d*)   he applies to the Crown Court to discharge the order.

(4)   In such a case the court may discharge the order if it finds that—

    (*a*)   there has been undue delay in continuing the proceedings mentioned in section 28(2), or

    (*b*)   the prosecutor does not intend to proceed with the prosecution.

(5)   If the court discharges a confiscation order under this section it may make such a consequential or incidental order as it believes is appropriate.

Appeals

31   Appeal by prosecutor ...[1]

(1)   If the Crown Court makes a confiscation order the prosecutor ...[1] may appeal to the Court of Appeal in respect of the order.

(2)   If the Crown Court decides not to make a confiscation order the prosecutor ...[1] may appeal to the Court of Appeal against the decision.

(3)   Subsections (1) and (2) do not apply to an order or decision made by virtue of section 19, 20, 27 or 28.

Amendments
1   Repealed by the Serious Crime Act 2007, ss 74(2)(*a*), 92, Sch 8, Pt 1, paras 1, 16, Sch 14.

32   Court's powers on appeal

(1)   On an appeal under section 31(1) the Court of Appeal may confirm, quash or vary the confiscation order.

(2)   On an appeal under section 31(2) the Court of Appeal may confirm the decision, or if it believes the decision was wrong it may—

    (*a*)   itself proceed under section 6 (ignoring subsections (1) to (3)), or

    (*b*)   direct the Crown Court to proceed afresh under section 6.

(3)   In proceeding afresh in pursuance of this section the Crown Court must comply with any directions the Court of Appeal may make.

(4)   If a court makes or varies a confiscation order under this section or in pursuance of a direction under this section it must—

   (*a*)   have regard to any fine imposed on the defendant in respect of the offence (or any of the offences) concerned;

   (*b*)   have regard to any order which falls within section 13(3) and has been made against him in respect of the offence (or any of the offences) concerned, unless the order has already been taken into account by a court in deciding what is the free property held by the defendant for the purposes of section 9.

(5)   If the Court of Appeal proceeds under section 6 or the Crown Court proceeds afresh under that section in pursuance of a direction under this section subsections (6) to (10) apply.

(6)   If a court has already sentenced the defendant for the offence (or any of the offences) concerned, section 6 has effect as if his particular criminal conduct included conduct which constitutes offences which the court has taken into consideration in deciding his sentence for the offence or offences concerned.

(7)   If an order has been made against the defendant in respect of the offence (or any of the offences) concerned under section 130 of the Sentencing Act (compensation orders)—

   (*a*)   the court must have regard to it, and

   (*b*)   section 13(5) and (6) above do not apply.

(8)   Section 8(2) does not apply, and the rules applying instead are that the court must—

   (*a*)   take account of conduct occurring before the relevant date;

   (*b*)   take account of property obtained before that date;

   (*c*)   take account of property obtained on or after that date if it was obtained as a result of or in connection with conduct occurring before that date.

(9)   In section 10—

   (*a*)   the first and second assumptions do not apply with regard to property first held by the defendant on or after the relevant date;

   (*b*)   the third assumption does not apply with regard to expenditure incurred by him on or after that date;

   (*c*)   the fourth assumption does not apply with regard to property obtained (or assumed to have been obtained) by him on or after that date.

(10)   Section 26 applies as it applies in the circumstances mentioned in subsection (1) of that section.

(11)   The relevant date is the date on which the Crown Court decided not to make a confiscation order.

33   Appeal to [Supreme Court][1]

(1)   An appeal lies to the [Supreme Court][1] from a decision of the Court of Appeal on an appeal under section 31.

(2)   An appeal under this section lies at the instance of—

   (*a*)   the defendant or the prosecutor ...[2];

   (*b*)   ...[2]

(3)   On an appeal from a decision of the Court of Appeal to confirm, vary or make a confiscation order the [Supreme Court]¹ may confirm, quash or vary the order.

(4)   On an appeal from a decision of the Court of Appeal to confirm the decision of the Crown Court not to make a confiscation order or from a decision of the Court of Appeal to quash a confiscation order the [Supreme Court]¹ may—

    (*a*)   confirm the decision, or

    (*b*)   direct the Crown Court to proceed afresh under section 6 if it believes the decision was wrong.

(5)   In proceeding afresh in pursuance of this section the Crown Court must comply with any directions the [Supreme Court]¹ may make.

(6)   If a court varies a confiscation order under this section or makes a confiscation order in pursuance of a direction under this section it must—

    (*a*)   have regard to any fine imposed on the defendant in respect of the offence (or any of the offences) concerned;

    (*b*)   have regard to any order which falls within section 13(3) and has been made against him in respect of the offence (or any of the offences) concerned, unless the order has already been taken into account by a court in deciding what is the free property held by the defendant for the purposes of section 9.

(7)   If the Crown Court proceeds afresh under section 6 in pursuance of a direction under this section subsections (8) to (12) apply.

(8)   If a court has already sentenced the defendant for the offence (or any of the offences) concerned, section 6 has effect as if his particular criminal conduct included conduct which constitutes offences which the court has taken into consideration in deciding his sentence for the offence or offences concerned.

(9)   If an order has been made against the defendant in respect of the offence (or any of the offences) concerned under section 130 of the Sentencing Act (compensation orders)—

    (*a*)   the Crown Court must have regard to it, and

    (*b*)   section 13(5) and (6) above do not apply.

(10)   Section 8(2) does not apply, and the rules applying instead are that the Crown Court must—

    (*a*)   take account of conduct occurring before the relevant date;

    (*b*)   take account of property obtained before that date;

    (*c*)   take account of property obtained on or after that date if it was obtained as a result of or in connection with conduct occurring before that date.

(11)   In section 10—

    (*a*)   the first and second assumptions do not apply with regard to property first held by the defendant on or after the relevant date;

    (*b*)   the third assumption does not apply with regard to expenditure incurred by him on or after that date;

    (*c*)   the fourth assumption does not apply with regard to property obtained (or assumed to have been obtained) by him on or after that date.

(12) Section 26 applies as it applies in the circumstances mentioned in subsection (1) of that section.

(13) The relevant date is—

> (*a*) in a case where the Crown Court made a confiscation order which was quashed by the Court of Appeal, the date on which the Crown Court made the order;

> (*b*) in any other case, the date on which the Crown Court decided not to make a confiscation order.

Amendments

1   Substituted by the Constitutional Reform Act 2005, s 40(4), Sch 9, Pt 1, para 77(1), (2).
2   Repealed by the Serious Crime Act 2007, ss 74(2)(*a*), 92, Sch 8, Pt 1, paras 1, 17, Sch 14.

. . .*¹*

34   ...¹

. . .¹

Amendments

1   Repealed by the Serious Crime Act 2007, ss 74(2)(*a*), 92, Sch 8, Pt 1, paras 1, 18, Sch 14.

[Enforcement as fines]¹

35   Director not appointed as enforcement authority

(1) This section applies if a court—

> (*a*) makes a confiscation order, ...²

> (*b*) ...²

(2) Sections 139(2) to (4) and (9) and 140(1) to (4) of the Sentencing Act (functions of court as to fines and enforcing fines) apply as if the amount ordered to be paid were a fine imposed on the defendant by the court making the confiscation order.

(3) In the application of Part 3 of the Magistrates' Courts Act 1980 (c. 43) to an amount payable under a confiscation order—

> (*a*) ignore section 75 of that Act (power to dispense with immediate payment);

> (*b*) such an amount is not a sum adjudged to be paid by a conviction for the purposes of section 81 (enforcement of fines imposed on young offenders) or a fine for the purposes of section 85 (remission of fines) of that Act;

> (*c*) in section 87 of that Act ignore subsection (3) (inquiry into means).

Amendments

1   Substituted by the Serious Crime Act 2007, s 74(2)(*a*), Sch 8, Pt 1, paras 1, 19(1), (2).
2   Repealed by the Serious Crime Act 2007, ss 74(2)(*a*), 92, Sch 8, Pt 1, paras 1, 19(1), (3), Sch 14.

36   ...¹

. . .¹

Amendments

1   Repealed by the Serious Crime Act 2007, ss 74(2)(*a*), 92, Sch 8, Pt 1, paras 1, 20, Sch 14.

37   ...[1]

... [1]

Amendments

1   Repealed by the Serious Crime Act 2007, ss 74(2)(*a*), 92, Sch 8, Pt 1, paras 1, 20, Sch 14.

38   Provisions about imprisonment or detention

(1)   Subsection (2) applies if—

   (*a*)   a warrant committing the defendant to prison or detention is issued for a default in payment of an amount ordered to be paid under a confiscation order in respect of an offence or offences, and

   (*b*)   at the time the warrant is issued the defendant is liable to serve a term of custody in respect of the offence (or any of the offences).

[(1A) An individual who is not a member of the Office may be appointed by the Director to appear in–

   (*a*)   specified proceedings, or

   (*b*)   a specified class or description of proceedings,

   in which the Director or a Prosecutor would otherwise appear by virtue of section 302A of the Proceeds of Crime Act 2002 (cash recovery proceedings).][1]

(2)   In such a case the term of imprisonment or of detention under section 108 of the Sentencing Act (detention of persons aged 18 to 20 for default) to be served in default of payment of the amount does not begin to run until after the term mentioned in subsection (1)(*b*) above.

(3)   The reference in subsection (1)(*b*) to the term of custody the defendant is liable to serve in respect of the offence (or any of the offences) is a reference to the term of imprisonment, or detention in a young offender institution, which he is liable to serve in respect of the offence (or any of the offences).

(4)   For the purposes of subsection (3) consecutive terms and terms which are wholly or partly concurrent must be treated as a single term and the following must be ignored—

   (*a*)   any sentence suspended under [section 189(1) of the Criminal Justice Act 2003][2] which has not taken effect at the time the warrant is issued;

   (*b*)   in the case of a sentence of imprisonment passed with an order under section 47(1) of the Criminal Law Act 1977 (c. 45) (sentences of imprisonment partly served and partly suspended) any part of the sentence which the defendant has not at that time been required to serve in prison;

   (*c*)   any term of imprisonment or detention fixed under section 139(2) of the Sentencing Act (term to be served in default of payment of fine etc) for which a warrant committing the defendant to prison or detention has not been issued at that time.

(5)   If the defendant serves a term of imprisonment or detention in default of paying any amount due under a confiscation order, his serving that term does not prevent the confiscation order from continuing to have effect so far as any other method of enforcement is concerned.

Amendments
1   Inserted by the Serious Crime Act 2007, s 84(3).
2   Substituted by the Criminal Justice Act 2003, s 304, Sch 32, Pt 1, para 141.

39   Reconsideration etc: variation of prison term

(1)   Subsection (2) applies if—

(*a*)   a court varies a confiscation order under section 21, 22, 23, 29, 32 or 33,

(*b*)   the effect of the variation is to vary the maximum period applicable in relation to the order under section 139(4) of the Sentencing Act, and

(*c*)   the result is that that maximum period is less than the term of imprisonment or detention fixed in respect of the order under section 139(2) of the Sentencing Act.

[(1A) The Director may designate a member of the Office to appear in–

(*a*)   specified proceedings, or

(*b*)   a specified class or description of proceedings,

in which the Director or a Prosecutor would otherwise appear by virtue of section 302A of the Proceeds of Crime Act 2002 (cash recovery proceedings).][1]

(2)   In such a case the court must fix a reduced term of imprisonment or detention in respect of the confiscation order under section 139(2) of the Sentencing Act in place of the term previously fixed.

(3)   Subsection (4) applies if paragraphs (*a*) and (*b*) of subsection (1) apply but paragraph (*c*) does not.

(4)   In such a case the court may amend the term of imprisonment or detention fixed in respect of the confiscation order under section 139(2) of the Sentencing Act.

(5)   If the effect of section 12 is to increase the maximum period applicable in relation to a confiscation order under section 139(4) of the Sentencing Act, on the application of the [prosecutor][2] the Crown Court may amend the term of imprisonment or detention fixed in respect of the order under section 139(2) of that Act.

(6)   ...[3]

Amendments
1   Inserted by the Serious Crime Act 2007, s 84(4).
2   Substituted by the Serious Crime Act 2007, s 74(2)(*a*), Sch 8, Pt 1, paras 1, 21(1), (2).
3   Repealed by the Serious Crime Act 2007, ss 74(2)(*a*), 92, Sch 8, Pt 1, paras 1, 21(1), (3), Sch 14.

Restraint orders

40   Conditions for exercise of powers

(1)   The Crown Court may exercise the powers conferred by section 41 if any of the following conditions is satisfied.

(2)   The first condition is that—

    (*a*)   a criminal investigation has been started in England and Wales with regard to an offence, and

    (*b*)   there is reasonable cause to believe that the alleged offender has benefited from his criminal conduct.

(3)   The second condition is that—

    (*a*)   proceedings for an offence have been started in England and Wales and not concluded, and

    (*b*)   there is reasonable cause to believe that the defendant has benefited from his criminal conduct.

(4)   The third condition is that—

    (*a*)   an application by the prosecutor ...[1] has been made under section 19, 20, 27 or 28 and not concluded, or the court believes that such an application is to be made, and

    (*b*)   there is reasonable cause to believe that the defendant has benefited from his criminal conduct.

(5)   The fourth condition is that—

    (*a*)   an application by the prosecutor ...[1] has been made under section 21 and not concluded, or the court believes that such an application is to be made, and

    (*b*)   there is reasonable cause to believe that the court will decide under that section that the amount found under the new calculation of the defendant's benefit exceeds the relevant amount (as defined in that section).

(6)   The fifth condition is that—

    (*a*)   an application by the prosecutor ...[1] has been made under section 22 and not concluded, or the court believes that such an application is to be made, and

    (*b*)   there is reasonable cause to believe that the court will decide under that section that the amount found under the new calculation of the available amount exceeds the relevant amount (as defined in that section).

(7)   The second condition is not satisfied if the court believes that—

    (*a*)   there has been undue delay in continuing the proceedings, or

    (*b*)   the prosecutor does not intend to proceed.

(8)   If an application mentioned in the third, fourth or fifth condition has been made the condition is not satisfied if the court believes that—

    (*a*)   there has been undue delay in continuing the application, or

    (*b*)   the prosecutor ...[1] does not intend to proceed.

(9)   If the first condition is satisfied—

    (*a*)   references in this Part to the defendant are to the alleged offender;

    (*b*)   references in this Part to the prosecutor are to the person the court believes is to have conduct of any proceedings for the offence;

(c)   section 77(9) has effect as if proceedings for the offence had been started against the defendant when the investigation was started.

Amendments

1   Repealed by the Serious Crime Act 2007, ss 74(2)(*a*), 92, Sch 8, Pt 1, paras 1, 22, Sch 14.

41   Restraint orders

(1)   If any condition set out in section 40 is satisfied the Crown Court may make an order (a restraint order) prohibiting any specified person from dealing with any realisable property held by him.

(2)   A restraint order may provide that it applies—

(a)   to all realisable property held by the specified person whether or not the property is described in the order;

(b)   to realisable property transferred to the specified person after the order is made.

(3)   A restraint order may be made subject to exceptions, and an exception may in particular—

(a)   make provision for reasonable living expenses and reasonable legal expenses;

(b)   make provision for the purpose of enabling any person to carry on any trade, business, profession or occupation;

(c)   be made subject to conditions.

(4)   But an exception to a restraint order must not make provision for any legal expenses which—

(a)   relate to an offence which falls within subsection (5), and

(b)   are incurred by the defendant or by a recipient of a tainted gift.

(5)   These offences fall within this subsection—

(a)   the offence mentioned in section 40(2) or (3), if the first or second condition (as the case may be) is satisfied;

(b)   the offence (or any of the offences) concerned, if the third, fourth or fifth condition is satisfied.

(6)   Subsection (7) applies if—

(a)   a court makes a restraint order, and

(b)   the applicant for the order applies to the court to proceed under subsection (7) (whether as part of the application for the restraint order or at any time afterwards).

(7)   The court may make such order as it believes is appropriate for the purpose of ensuring that the restraint order is effective.

(8)   A restraint order does not affect property for the time being subject to a charge under any of these provisions—

(a)   section 9 of the Drug Trafficking Offences Act 1986 (c. 32);

(b)   section 78 of the Criminal Justice Act 1988 (c. 33);

(*c*)   Article 14 of the Criminal Justice (Confiscation) (Northern Ireland) Order 1990 (S.I. 1990/2588 (N.I. 17));

(*d*)   section 27 of the Drug Trafficking Act 1994 (c. 37);

(*e*)   Article 32 of the Proceeds of Crime (Northern Ireland) Order 1996 (S.I. 1996/1299 (N.I. 9)).

(9)   Dealing with property includes removing it from England and Wales.

42 Application, discharge and variation

(1)   A restraint order—

(*a*)   may be made only on an application by an applicant falling within subsection (2);

(*b*)   may be made on an ex parte application to a judge in chambers.

(2)   These applicants fall within this subsection—

(*a*)   the prosecutor;

(*b*)   ...¹

(*c*)   an accredited financial investigator.

(3)   An application to discharge or vary a restraint order or an order under section 41(7) may be made to the Crown Court by—

(*a*)   the person who applied for the order;

(*b*)   any person affected by the order.

(4)   Subsections (5) to (7) apply to an application under subsection (3).

(5)   The court—

(*a*)   may discharge the order;

(*b*)   may vary the order.

(6)   If the condition in section 40 which was satisfied was that proceedings were started or an application was made, the court must discharge the order on the conclusion of the proceedings or of the application (as the case may be).

(7)   If the condition in section 40 which was satisfied was that an investigation was started or an application was to be made, the court must discharge the order if within a reasonable time proceedings for the offence are not started or the application is not made (as the case may be).

Amendments
1   Repealed by the Serious Crime Act 2007, ss 74(2)(*a*), 92, Sch 8, Pt 1, paras 1, 23, Sch 14.

43 Appeal to Court of Appeal

(1)   If on an application for a restraint order the court decides not to make one, the person who applied for the order may appeal to the Court of Appeal against the decision.

(2)   If an application is made under section 42(3) in relation to a restraint order or an order under section 41(7) the following persons may appeal to the Court of Appeal in respect of the Crown Court's decision on the application—

(*a*)   the person who applied for the order;

(*b*)   any person affected by the order.

(3)   On an appeal under subsection (1) or (2) the Court of Appeal may—

(*a*)   confirm the decision, or

(*b*)   make such order as it believes is appropriate.

44   Appeal to [Supreme Court]¹

(1)   An appeal lies to the [Supreme Court]¹ from a decision of the Court of Appeal on an appeal under section 43.

(2)   An appeal under this section lies at the instance of any person who was a party to the proceedings before the Court of Appeal.

(3)   On an appeal under this section the [Supreme Court]¹ may—

(*a*)   confirm the decision of the Court of Appeal, or

(*b*)   make such order as it believes is appropriate.

Amendments
1   Substituted by the Constitutional Reform Act 2005, s 40(4), Sch 9, Pt 1, para 77(1), (3).

45   Seizure

(1)   If a restraint order is in force a constable[, an accredited financial investigator]¹ or a customs officer may seize any realisable property to which it applies to prevent its removal from England and Wales.

(2)   Property seized under subsection (1) must be dealt with in accordance with the directions of the court which made the order.

[(3)   The reference in subsection (1) to an accredited financial investigator is a reference to an accredited financial investigator who falls within a description specified in an order made for the purposes of that subsection by the Secretary of State under section 453.]¹

Amendments
1   Inserted by the Serious Crime Act 2007, s 78(1), (2).

46   Hearsay evidence

(1)   Evidence must not be excluded in restraint proceedings on the ground that it is hearsay (of whatever degree).

(2)   Sections 2 to 4 of the Civil Evidence Act 1995 (c. 38) apply in relation to restraint proceedings as those sections apply in relation to civil proceedings.

(3)   Restraint proceedings are proceedings—

(*a*)   for a restraint order;

(*b*)   for the discharge or variation of a restraint order;

(*c*)   on an appeal under section 43 or 44.

(4)   Hearsay is a statement which is made otherwise than by a person while giving oral evidence in the proceedings and which is tendered as evidence of the matters stated.

(5)   Nothing in this section affects the admissibility of evidence which is admissible apart from this section.

47 Supplementary

(1)   The registration Acts—

    (*a*)   apply in relation to restraint orders as they apply in relation to orders which affect land and are made by the court for the purpose of enforcing judgments or recognisances;

    (*b*)   apply in relation to applications for restraint orders as they apply in relation to other pending land actions.

(2)   The registration Acts are—

    (*a*)   the Land Registration Act 1925 (c. 21);

    (*b*)   the Land Charges Act 1972 (c. 61);

    (*c*)   the Land Registration Act 2002 (c. 9).

(3)   But no notice may be entered in the register of title under the Land Registration Act 2002 in respect of a restraint order.

(4)   The person applying for a restraint order must be treated for the purposes of section 57 of the Land Registration Act 1925 (inhibitions) as a person interested in relation to any registered land to which—

    (*a*)   the application relates, or

    (*b*)   a restraint order made in pursuance of the application relates.

Management receivers

48 Appointment

(1)   Subsection (2) applies if—

    (*a*)   the Crown Court makes a restraint order, and

    (*b*)   the applicant for the restraint order applies to the court to proceed under subsection (2) (whether as part of the application for the restraint order or at any time afterwards).

(2)   The Crown Court may by order appoint a receiver in respect of any realisable property to which the restraint order applies.

49 Powers

(1)   If the court appoints a receiver under section 48 it may act under this section on the application of the person who applied for the restraint order.

(2)   The court may by order confer on the receiver the following powers in relation to any realisable property to which the restraint order applies—

    (*a*)   power to take possession of the property;

    (*b*)   power to manage or otherwise deal with the property;

    (*c*)   power to start, carry on or defend any legal proceedings in respect of the property;

    (*d*)   power to realise so much of the property as is necessary to meet the receiver's remuneration and expenses.

(3)   The court may by order confer on the receiver power to enter any premises in England and Wales and to do any of the following—

(a)   search for or inspect anything authorised by the court;

(b)   make or obtain a copy, photograph or other record of anything so authorised;

(c)   remove anything which the receiver is required or authorised to take possession of in pursuance of an order of the court.

(4)   The court may by order authorise the receiver to do any of the following for the purpose of the exercise of his functions—

(a)   hold property;

(b)   enter into contracts;

(c)   sue and be sued;

(d)   employ agents;

(e)   execute powers of attorney, deeds or other instruments;

(f)   take any other steps the court thinks appropriate.

(5)   The court may order any person who has possession of realisable property to which the restraint order applies to give possession of it to the receiver.

(6)   The court—

(a)   may order a person holding an interest in realisable property to which the restraint order applies to make to the receiver such payment as the court specifies in respect of a beneficial interest held by the defendant or the recipient of a tainted gift;

(b)   may (on the payment being made) by order transfer, grant or extinguish any interest in the property.

(7)   Subsections (2), (5) and (6) do not apply to property for the time being subject to a charge under any of these provisions—

(a)   section 9 of the Drug Trafficking Offences Act 1986 (c. 32);

(b)   section 78 of the Criminal Justice Act 1988 (c. 33);

(c)   Article 14 of the Criminal Justice (Confiscation) (Northern Ireland) Order 1990 (S.I. 1990/2588 (N.I. 17));

(d)   section 27 of the Drug Trafficking Act 1994 (c. 37);

(e)   Article 32 of the Proceeds of Crime (Northern Ireland) Order 1996 (S.I. 1996/1299 (N.I. 9)).

(8)   The court must not—

(a)   confer the power mentioned in subsection (2)(b) or (d) in respect of property, or

(b)   exercise the power conferred on it by subsection (6) in respect of property,

unless it gives persons holding interests in the property a reasonable opportunity to make representations to it.

[(8A) Subsection (8), so far as relating to the power mentioned in subsection (2)(b), does not apply to property which–

(*a*)   is perishable; or

(*b*)   ought to be disposed of before its value diminishes.]¹

(9)   The court may order that a power conferred by an order under this section is subject to such conditions and exceptions as it specifies.

(10)   Managing or otherwise dealing with property includes—

(*a*)   selling the property or any part of it or interest in it;

(*b*)   carrying on or arranging for another person to carry on any trade or business the assets of which are or are part of the property;

(*c*)   incurring capital expenditure in respect of the property.

Amendments
1   Inserted by the Serious Crime Act 2007, s 82(1).

Enforcement receivers

50 Appointment

(1)   This section applies if—

(*a*)   a confiscation order is made,

(*b*)   it is not satisfied, and

(*c*)   it is not subject to appeal.

(2)   On the application of the prosecutor the Crown Court may by order appoint a receiver in respect of realisable property.

51 Powers

(1)   If the court appoints a receiver under section 50 it may act under this section on the application of the prosecutor.

(2)   The court may by order confer on the receiver the following powers in relation to the realisable property—

(*a*)   power to take possession of the property;

(*b*)   power to manage or otherwise deal with the property;

(*c*)   power to realise the property, in such manner as the court may specify;

(*d*)   power to start, carry on or defend any legal proceedings in respect of the property.

(3)   The court may by order confer on the receiver power to enter any premises in England and Wales and to do any of the following—

(*a*)   search for or inspect anything authorised by the court;

(*b*)   make or obtain a copy, photograph or other record of anything so authorised;

(*c*)   remove anything which the receiver is required or authorised to take possession of in pursuance of an order of the court.

(4)   The court may by order authorise the receiver to do any of the following for the purpose of the exercise of his functions—

(a)   hold property;

(b)   enter into contracts;

(c)   sue and be sued;

(d)   employ agents;

(e)   execute powers of attorney, deeds or other instruments;

(f)   take any other steps the court thinks appropriate.

(5)   The court may order any person who has possession of realisable property to give possession of it to the receiver.

(6)   The court—

    (a)   may order a person holding an interest in realisable property to make to the receiver such payment as the court specifies in respect of a beneficial interest held by the defendant or the recipient of a tainted gift;

    (b)   may (on the payment being made) by order transfer, grant or extinguish any interest in the property.

(7)   Subsections (2), (5) and (6) do not apply to property for the time being subject to a charge under any of these provisions—

    (a)   section 9 of the Drug Trafficking Offences Act 1986 (c. 32);

    (b)   section 78 of the Criminal Justice Act 1988 (c. 33);

    (c)   Article 14 of the Criminal Justice (Confiscation) (Northern Ireland) Order 1990 (S.I. 1990/2588 (N.I. 17));

    (d)   section 27 of the Drug Trafficking Act 1994 (c. 37);

    (e)   Article 32 of the Proceeds of Crime (Northern Ireland) Order 1996 (S.I. 1996/1299 (N.I. 9)).

(8)   The court must not—

    (a)   confer the power mentioned in subsection (2)(b) or (c) in respect of property, or

    (b)   exercise the power conferred on it by subsection (6) in respect of property,

unless it gives persons holding interests in the property a reasonable opportunity to make representations to it.

[(8A)   Subsection (8), so far as relating to the power mentioned in subsection (2)(b), does not apply to property which–

    (a)   is perishable; or

    (b)   ought to be disposed of before its value diminishes.][1]

(9)   The court may order that a power conferred by an order under this section is subject to such conditions and exceptions as it specifies.

(10)   Managing or otherwise dealing with property includes—

    (a)   selling the property or any part of it or interest in it;

    (b)   carrying on or arranging for another person to carry on any trade or business the assets of which are or are part of the property;

    (c)   incurring capital expenditure in respect of the property.

Amendments

1   Inserted by the Serious Crime Act 2007, s 82(2).

52 ...[1]

...[1]

Amendments

1   Repealed by the Serious Crime Act 2007, ss 74(2)(*a*), 92, Sch 8, Pt 1, paras 1, 24, Sch 14.

53 ...[1]

...[1]

Amendments

1   Repealed by the Serious Crime Act 2007, ss 74(2)(*a*), 92, Sch 8, Pt 1, paras 1, 24, Sch 14.

Application of sums

54   Enforcement receivers

(1)   This section applies to sums which are in the hands of a receiver appointed under section 50 if they are—

    (*a*)   the proceeds of the realisation of property under section 51;

    (*b*)   sums (other than those mentioned in paragraph (*a*)) in which the defendant holds an interest.

(2)   The sums must be applied as follows—

    (*a*)   first, they must be applied in payment of such expenses incurred by a person acting as an insolvency practitioner as are payable under this subsection by virtue of section 432;

    (*b*)   second, they must be applied in making any payments directed by the Crown Court;

    (*c*)   third, they must be applied on the defendant's behalf towards satisfaction of the confiscation order.

(3)   If the amount payable under the confiscation order has been fully paid and any sums remain in the receiver's hands he must distribute them—

    (*a*)   among such persons who held (or hold) interests in the property concerned as the Crown Court directs, and

    (*b*)   in such proportions as it directs.

(4)   Before making a direction under subsection (3) the court must give persons who held (or hold) interests in the property concerned a reasonable opportunity to make representations to it.

(5)   For the purposes of subsections (3) and (4) the property concerned is—

    (*a*)   the property represented by the proceeds mentioned in subsection (1)(*a*);

    (*b*)   the sums mentioned in subsection (1)(*b*).

(6) The receiver applies sums as mentioned in subsection (2)(*c*) by paying them to the appropriate [designated officer]¹ on account of the amount payable under the order.

(7) The appropriate [designated officer]¹ is the one for the magistrates' court responsible for enforcing the confiscation order as if the amount ordered to be paid were a fine.

Amendments

1   Substituted by the Courts Act 2003, s 109(1), Sch 8, para 407.

55 Sums received by [designated officer]¹

(1) This section applies if a [designated officer]¹ receives sums on account of the amount payable under a confiscation order (whether the sums are received under section 54 or otherwise).

(2) The [designated officer's]¹ receipt of the sums reduces the amount payable under the order, but he must apply the sums received as follows.

(3) First he must apply them in payment of such expenses incurred by a person acting as an insolvency practitioner as—

(*a*) are payable under this subsection by virtue of section 432, but

(*b*) are not already paid under section 54(2)(*a*).

(4) If the [designated officer]¹ received the sums under section 54 he must next apply them—

(*a*) first, in payment of the remuneration and expenses of a receiver appointed under section 48, to the extent that they have not been met by virtue of the exercise by that receiver of a power conferred under section 49(2)(*d*);

(*b*) second, in payment of the remuneration and expenses of the receiver appointed under section 50.

(5) If a direction was made under section 13(6) for an amount of compensation to be paid out of sums recovered under the confiscation order, the [designated officer]¹ must next apply the sums in payment of that amount.

(6) If any amount remains after the [designated officer]¹ makes any payments required by the preceding provisions of this section, the amount must be treated for the purposes of [section 38 of the Courts Act 2003]¹ (application of fines etc) as if it were a fine imposed by a magistrates' court.

[(7) Subsection (4) does not apply in relation to the remuneration of a receiver if the receiver is a person falling within subsection (8).]²

[(8) The following fall within this subsection—

(*a*) a constable,

(*b*) a person employed by a police authority in England and Wales under section 15 of the Police Act 1996 or a member of staff of the City of London police force,

(*c*) an accredited financial investigator,

(*d*) a member of staff of the Crown Prosecution Service,

(*e*) a member of staff of the Serious Fraud Office,

(*f*) a member of staff of the Revenue and Customs Prosecutions Office,

(g)   a member of staff of the Commissioners for Her Majesty's Revenue and Customs,

(h)   a member of staff of SOCA,

(i)   a member of staff of any government department not mentioned above.

(9)   It is immaterial for the purposes of subsection (7) whether a person falls within subsection (8) by virtue of a permanent or temporary appointment or a secondment from elsewhere.

(10)   The reference in subsection (8) to an accredited financial investigator is a reference to an accredited financial investigator who falls within a description specified in an order made for the purposes of that subsection by the Secretary of State under section 453.][3]

Amendments

1   Substituted by the Courts Act 2003, s 109(1), Sch 8, para 408.
2   Substituted by the Policing and Crime Act 2009, s 51(1), (2).
3   Inserted by the Policing and Crime Act 2009, s 51(1), (2).

56   ...[1]

...[1]

Amendments

1   Repealed by the Serious Crime Act 2007, ss 74(2)(a), 92, Sch 8, Pt 1, paras 1, 25, Sch 14.

57   ...[1]

...[1]

Amendments

1   Repealed by the Serious Crime Act 2007, ss 74(2)(a), 92, Sch 8, Pt 1, paras 1, 25, Sch 14.

Restrictions

58   Restraint orders

(1)   Subsections (2) to (4) apply if a court makes a restraint order.

(2)   No distress may be levied against any realisable property to which the order applies except with the leave of the Crown Court and subject to any terms the Crown Court may impose.

(3)   If the order applies to a tenancy of any premises, no landlord or other person to whom rent is payable may exercise a right within subsection (4) except with the leave of the Crown Court and subject to any terms the Crown Court may impose.

(4)   A right is within this subsection if it is a right of forfeiture by peaceable re-entry in relation to the premises in respect of any failure by the tenant to comply with any term or condition of the tenancy.

(5)   If a court in which proceedings are pending in respect of any property is satisfied that a restraint order has been applied for or made in respect of the property, the court may either stay the proceedings or allow them to continue on any terms it thinks fit.

(6)   Before exercising any power conferred by subsection (5), the court must give an opportunity to be heard to—

(*a*)   the applicant for the restraint order, and

(*b*)   any receiver appointed in respect of the property under section 48 [or 50]¹.

Amendments

1   Substituted by the Serious Crime Act 2007, s 74(2)(*a*), Sch 8, Pt 1, paras 1, 26.

59   Enforcement receivers

(1)   Subsections (2) to (4) apply if a court makes an order under section 50 appointing a receiver in respect of any realisable property.

(2)   No distress may be levied against the property except with the leave of the Crown Court and subject to any terms the Crown Court may impose.

(3)   If the receiver is appointed in respect of a tenancy of any premises, no landlord or other person to whom rent is payable may exercise a right within subsection (4) except with the leave of the Crown Court and subject to any terms the Crown Court may impose.

(4)   A right is within this subsection if it is a right of forfeiture by peaceable re-entry in relation to the premises in respect of any failure by the tenant to comply with any term or condition of the tenancy.

(5)   If a court in which proceedings are pending in respect of any property is satisfied that an order under section 50 appointing a receiver in respect of the property has been applied for or made, the court may either stay the proceedings or allow them to continue on any terms it thinks fit.

(6)   Before exercising any power conferred by subsection (5), the court must give an opportunity to be heard to—

(*a*)   the prosecutor, and

(*b*)   the receiver (if the order under section 50 has been made).

60   ...¹

...¹

Amendments

1   Repealed by the Serious Crime Act 2007, ss 74(2)(*a*), 92, Sch 8, Pt 1, paras 1, 27, Sch 14.

Receivers: further provisions

61   Protection

If a receiver appointed under section 48 [or 50]¹—

(*a*)   takes action in relation to property which is not realisable property,

(*b*)   would be entitled to take the action if it were realisable property, and

(*c*)   believes on reasonable grounds that he is entitled to take the action,

he is not liable to any person in respect of any loss or damage resulting from the action, except so far as the loss or damage is caused by his negligence.

Amendments

1   Substituted by the Serious Crime Act 2007, s 74(2)(*a*), Sch 8, Pt 1, paras 1, 28.

62 Further applications

(1)   This section applies to a receiver appointed under section 48 [or 50][1].

(2)   The receiver may apply to the Crown Court for an order giving directions as to the exercise of his powers.

(3)   The following persons may apply to the Crown Court—

   (*a*)   any person affected by action taken by the receiver;

   (*b*)   any person who may be affected by action the receiver proposes to take.

(4)   On an application under this section the court may make such order as it believes is appropriate.

Amendments
1   Substituted by the Serious Crime Act 2007, s 74(2)(*a*), Sch 8, Pt 1, paras 1, 29.

63 Discharge and variation

(1)   The following persons may apply to the Crown Court to vary or discharge an order made under any of sections 48 [to 51][1]—

   (*a*)   the receiver;

   (*b*)   the person who applied for the order ...[2];

   (*c*)   any person affected by the order.

(2)   On an application under this section the court—

   (*a*)   may discharge the order;

   (*b*)   may vary the order.

(3)   But in the case of an order under section 48 or 49—

   (*a*)   if the condition in section 40 which was satisfied was that proceedings were started or an application was made, the court must discharge the order on the conclusion of the proceedings or of the application (as the case may be);

   (*b*)   if the condition which was satisfied was that an investigation was started or an application was to be made, the court must discharge the order if within a reasonable time proceedings for the offence are not started or the application is not made (as the case may be).

Amendments
1   Substituted by the Serious Crime Act 2007, s 74(2)(*a*), Sch 8, Pt 1, paras 1, 30(*a*).
2   Repealed by the Serious Crime Act 2007, ss 74(2)(*a*), 92, Sch 8, Pt 1, paras 1, 30(*b*), Sch 14.

64 Management receivers: discharge

(1)   This section applies if—

   (*a*)   a receiver stands appointed under section 48 in respect of realisable property (the management receiver), and

   (*b*)   the court appoints a receiver under section 50 ...[1].

(2)   The court must order the management receiver to transfer to the other receiver all property held by the management receiver by virtue of the powers conferred on him by section 49.

(3)   ...[1]

(4)   Subsection (2) does not apply to property which the management receiver holds by virtue of the exercise by him of his power under section 49(2)(*d*).

(5)   If the management receiver complies with an order under subsection (2) he is discharged—

    (*a*)   from his appointment under section 48;

    (*b*)   from any obligation under this Act arising from his appointment.

(6)   If this section applies the court may make such a consequential or incidental order as it believes is appropriate.

Amendments

1   Repealed by the Serious Crime Act 2007, ss 74(2)(*a*), 92, Sch 8, Pt 1, paras 1, 31, Sch 14.

65   Appeal to Court of Appeal

(1)   If on an application for an order under any of sections 48 to 51 ...[1] the court decides not to make one, the person who applied for the order may appeal to the Court of Appeal against the decision.

(2)   If the court makes an order under any of sections 48 to 51 ...[1], the following persons may appeal to the Court of Appeal in respect of the court's decision—

    (*a*)   the person who applied for the order;

    (*b*)   any person affected by the order.

(3)   If on an application for an order under section 62 the court decides not to make one, the person who applied for the order may appeal to the Court of Appeal against the decision.

(4)   If the court makes an order under section 62, the following persons may appeal to the Court of Appeal in respect of the court's decision—

    (*a*)   the person who applied for the order;

    (*b*)   any person affected by the order;

    (*c*)   the receiver.

(5)   The following persons may appeal to the Court of Appeal against a decision of the court on an application under section 63—

    (*a*)   the person who applied for the order in respect of which the application was made ...[1];

    (*b*)   any person affected by the court's decision;

    (*c*)   the receiver.

(6)   On an appeal under this section the Court of Appeal may—

    (*a*)   confirm the decision, or

    (*b*)   make such order as it believes is appropriate.

Amendments
1   Repealed by the Serious Crime Act 2007, ss 74(2)(*a*), 92, Sch 8, Pt 1, paras 1, 32, Sch 14.

66   Appeal to [Supreme Court][1]

(1)   An appeal lies to the [Supreme Court][1] from a decision of the Court of Appeal on an appeal under section 65.

(2)   An appeal under this section lies at the instance of any person who was a party to the proceedings before the Court of Appeal.

(3)   On an appeal under this section the [Supreme Court][1] may—

    (*a*)   confirm the decision of the Court of Appeal, or

    (*b*)   make such order as it believes is appropriate.

Amendments
1   Substituted by the Constitutional Reform Act 2005, s 40(4), Sch 9, Pt 1, para 77(1), (3).

Seized money

67   Seized money

(1)   This section applies to money which—

    (*a*)   is held by a person, and

    (*b*)   is held in an account maintained by him with a bank or a building society.

(2)   This section also applies to money which is held by a person and which—

    (*a*)   has been seized by a constable under section 19 of the Police and Criminal Evidence Act 1984 (c. 60) (general power of seizure etc), and

    (*b*)   is held in an account maintained by a police force with a bank or a building society.

(3)   This section also applies to money which is held by a person and which—

    (*a*)   has been seized by a customs officer under section 19 of the 1984 Act as applied by order made under section 114(2) of that Act, and

    (*b*)   is held in an account maintained by the Commissioners of Customs and Excise with a bank or a building society.

(4)   This section applies if the following conditions are satisfied—

    (*a*)   a restraint order has effect in relation to money to which this section applies;

    (*b*)   a confiscation order is made against the person by whom the money is held;

    (*c*)   ...[1]

    (*d*)   a receiver has not been appointed under section 50 in relation to the money;

    (*e*)   any period allowed under section 11 for payment of the amount ordered to be paid under the confiscation order has ended.

(5)   In such a case a magistrates' court may order the bank or building society to pay the money to the [designated officer][2] for the court on account of the amount payable under the confiscation order.

(6)   If a bank or building society fails to comply with an order under subsection (5)—

    (*a*)   the magistrates' court may order it to pay an amount not exceeding £5,000, and

    (*b*)   for the purposes of the Magistrates' Courts Act 1980 (c. 43) the sum is to be treated as adjudged to be paid by a conviction of the court.

(7)   In order to take account of changes in the value of money the Secretary of State may by order substitute another sum for the sum for the time being specified in subsection (6)(*a*).

(8)   For the purposes of this section—

    (*a*)   a bank is a deposit-taking business within the meaning of the Banking Act 1987 (c. 22);

    (*b*)   'building society' has the same meaning as in the Building Societies Act 1986 (c. 53).

Amendments

1   Repealed by the Serious Crime Act 2007, ss 74(2)(*a*), 92, Sch 8, Pt 1, paras 1, 33, Sch 14.
2   Substituted by the Courts Act 2003, s 109(1), Sch 8, para 409.

Financial investigators

68   Applications and appeals

(1)   Subsections (2) and (3) apply to—

    (*a*)   an application under section 41, 42, 48, 49 or 63;

    (*b*)   an appeal under section 43, 44, 65 or 66.

(2)   An accredited financial investigator must not make such an application or bring such an appeal unless he falls within subsection (3).

(3)   An accredited financial investigator falls within this subsection if he is one of the following or is authorised for the purposes of this section by one of the following—

    (*a*)   a police officer who is not below the rank of superintendent,

    (*b*)   a customs officer who is not below such grade as is designated by the Commissioners of Customs and Excise as equivalent to that rank,

    (*c*)   an accredited financial investigator who falls within a description specified in an order made for the purposes of this paragraph by the Secretary of State under section 453.

(4)   If such an application is made or appeal brought by an accredited financial investigator any subsequent step in the application or appeal or any further application or appeal relating to the same matter may be taken, made or brought by a different accredited financial investigator who falls within subsection (3).

(5)   If—

    (*a*)   an application for a restraint order is made by an accredited financial investigator, and

    (*b*)   a court is required under section 58(6) to give the applicant for the order an opportunity to be heard, the court may give the opportunity to a different accredited financial investigator who falls within subsection (3).

Exercise of powers

69 Powers of court and receiver

(1)   This section applies to—

(*a*)   the powers conferred on a court by sections 41 to [59][1] and sections 62 to 67;

(*b*)   the powers of a receiver appointed under section 48 [or 50][1].

(2)   The powers—

(*a*)   must be exercised with a view to the value for the time being of realisable property being made available (by the property's realisation) for satisfying any confiscation order that has been or may be made against the defendant;

(*b*)   must be exercised, in a case where a confiscation order has not been made, with a view to securing that there is no diminution in the value of realisable property;

(*c*)   must be exercised without taking account of any obligation of the defendant or a recipient of a tainted gift if the obligation conflicts with the object of satisfying any confiscation order that has been or may be made against the defendant;

(*d*)   may be exercised in respect of a debt owed by the Crown.

(3)   Subsection (2) has effect subject to the following rules—

(*a*)   the powers must be exercised with a view to allowing a person other than the defendant or a recipient of a tainted gift to retain or recover the value of any interest held by him;

(*b*)   in the case of realisable property held by a recipient of a tainted gift, the powers must be exercised with a view to realising no more than the value for the time being of the gift;

(*c*)   in a case where a confiscation order has not been made against the defendant, property must not be sold if the court so orders under subsection (4).

(4)   If on an application by the defendant, or by the recipient of a tainted gift, the court decides that property cannot be replaced it may order that it must not be sold.

(5)   An order under subsection (4) may be revoked or varied.

Amendments

1   Substituted by the Serious Crime Act 2007, s 74(2)(*a*), Sch 8, Pt 1, paras 1, 34.

Committal

70 Committal by magistrates' court

(1)   This section applies if—

(*a*)   a defendant is convicted of an offence by a magistrates' court, and

(*b*)   the prosecutor asks the court to commit the defendant to the Crown Court with a view to a confiscation order being considered under section 6.

(2)   In such a case the magistrates' court—

    (*a*)   must commit the defendant to the Crown Court in respect of the offence, and

    (*b*)   may commit him to the Crown Court in respect of any other offence falling within subsection (3).

(3)   An offence falls within this subsection if—

    (*a*)   the defendant has been convicted of it by the magistrates' court or any other court, and

    (*b*)   the magistrates' court has power to deal with him in respect of it.

(4)   If a committal is made under this section in respect of an offence or offences—

    (*a*)   section 6 applies accordingly, and

    (*b*)   the committal operates as a committal of the defendant to be dealt with by the Crown Court in accordance with section 71.

(5)   If a committal is made under this section in respect of an offence for which (apart from this section) the magistrates' court could have committed the defendant for sentence under section 3(2) of the Sentencing Act (offences triable either way) the court must state whether it would have done so.

(6)   A committal under this section may be in custody or on bail.

71   Sentencing by Crown Court

(1)   If a defendant is committed to the Crown Court under section 70 in respect of an offence or offences, this section applies (whether or not the court proceeds under section 6).

(2)   In the case of an offence in respect of which the magistrates' court has stated under section 70(5) that it would have committed the defendant for sentence, the Crown Court—

    (*a*)   must inquire into the circumstances of the case, and

    (*b*)   may deal with the defendant in any way in which it could deal with him if he had just been convicted of the offence on indictment before it.

(3)   In the case of any other offence the Crown Court—

    (*a*)   must inquire into the circumstances of the case, and

    (*b*)   may deal with the defendant in any way in which the magistrates' court could deal with him if it had just convicted him of the offence.

Compensation

72   Serious default

(1)   If the following three conditions are satisfied the Crown Court may order the payment of such compensation as it believes is just.

(2)   The first condition is satisfied if a criminal investigation has been started with regard to an offence and proceedings are not started for the offence.

(3)   The first condition is also satisfied if proceedings for an offence are started against a person and—

    (*a*)   they do not result in his conviction for the offence, or

    (*b*)   he is convicted of the offence but the conviction is quashed or he is pardoned in respect of it.

(4)   If subsection (2) applies the second condition is that—

    (*a*)   in the criminal investigation there has been a serious default by a person mentioned in subsection (9), and

    (*b*)   the investigation would not have continued if the default had not occurred.

(5)   If subsection (3) applies the second condition is that—

    (*a*)   in the criminal investigation with regard to the offence or in its prosecution there has been a serious default by a person who is mentioned in subsection (9), and

    (*b*)   the proceedings would not have been started or continued if the default had not occurred.

(6)   The third condition is that an application is made under this section by a person who held realisable property and has suffered loss in consequence of anything done in relation to it by or in pursuance of an order under this Part.

(7)   The offence referred to in subsection (2) may be one of a number of offences with regard to which the investigation is started.

(8)   The offence referred to in subsection (3) may be one of a number of offences for which the proceedings are started.

(9)   Compensation under this section is payable to the applicant and—

    (*a*)   if the person in default was or was acting as a member of a police force, the compensation is payable out of the police fund from which the expenses of that force are met;

    (*b*)   if the person in default was a member of the Crown Prosecution Service or was acting on its behalf, the compensation is payable by the Director of Public Prosecutions;

    [(*ba*)   if the person in default was a member of staff of SOCA, the compensation is payable by SOCA;][1]

    (*c*)   if the person in default was a member of the Serious Fraud Office, the compensation is payable by the Director of that Office;

    [(*d*)   if the person in default was a member of or acting on behalf of the Revenue and Customs Prosecutions Office, the compensation is payable by the Director of Revenue and Customs Prosecutions;][2]

    (*e*)   if the person in default was an officer of the Commissioners of Inland Revenue, the compensation is payable by those Commissioners;

    [(*f*)   if the person in default was an accredited financial investigator and none of paragraphs (*a*) to (*e*) apply, the compensation is payable in accordance with paragraph (*a*), (*c*) or (*e*) of section 302(7A) (as the case may require).][1]

Amendments

1   Inserted by the Policing and Crime Act 2009, s 61(1), (2).
2   Substituted by the Commissioners for Revenue and Customs Act 2005, s 50(6), Sch 4, para 97.

73 Order varied or discharged

(1) This section applies if—

    (*a*)   the court varies a confiscation order under section 29 or discharges one under section 30, and

    (*b*)   an application is made to the Crown Court by a person who held realisable property and has suffered loss as a result of the making of the order.

(2) The court may order the payment of such compensation as it believes is just.

(3) Compensation under this section is payable—

    (*a*)   to the applicant;

    (*b*)   by the Lord Chancellor.

Enforcement abroad

74 Enforcement abroad

(1) This section applies if—

    (*a*)   any of the conditions in section 40 is satisfied,

    (*b*)   the prosecutor ...[1] believes that realisable property is situated in a country or territory outside the United Kingdom (the receiving country), and

    (*c*)   the prosecutor ...[1] sends a request for assistance to the Secretary of State with a view to it being forwarded under this section.

(2) In a case where no confiscation order has been made, a request for assistance is a request to the government of the receiving country to secure that any person is prohibited from dealing with realisable property.

(3) In a case where a confiscation order has been made and has not been satisfied, discharged or quashed, a request for assistance is a request to the government of the receiving country to secure that—

    (*a*)   any person is prohibited from dealing with realisable property,

    (*b*)   realisable property is realised and the proceeds are applied in accordance with the law of the receiving country.

(4) No request for assistance may be made for the purposes of this section in a case where a confiscation order has been made and has been satisfied, discharged or quashed.

(5) If the Secretary of State believes it is appropriate to do so he may forward the request for assistance to the government of the receiving country.

(6) If property is realised in pursuance of a request under subsection (3) the amount ordered to be paid under the confiscation order must be taken to be reduced by an amount equal to the proceeds of realisation.

(7) A certificate purporting to be issued by or on behalf of the requested government is admissible as evidence of the facts it states if it states—

    (*a*)   that property has been realised in pursuance of a request under subsection (3),

    (*b*)   the date of realisation, and

    (*c*)   the proceeds of realisation.

(8)   If the proceeds of realisation made in pursuance of a request under subsection (3) are expressed in a currency other than sterling, they must be taken to be the sterling equivalent calculated in accordance with the rate of exchange prevailing at the end of the day of realisation.

Amendments

1   Repealed by the Serious Crime Act 2007, ss 74(2)(*a*), 92, Sch 8, Pt 1, paras 1, 35, Sch 14.

Interpretation

75   Criminal lifestyle

(1)   A defendant has a criminal lifestyle if (and only if) the following condition is satisfied.

(2)   The condition is that the offence (or any of the offences) concerned satisfies any of these tests—

   (*a*)   it is specified in Schedule 2;

   (*b*)   it constitutes conduct forming part of a course of criminal activity;

   (*c*)   it is an offence committed over a period of at least six months and the defendant has benefited from the conduct which constitutes the offence.

(3)   Conduct forms part of a course of criminal activity if the defendant has benefited from the conduct and—

   (*a*)   in the proceedings in which he was convicted he was convicted of three or more other offences, each of three or more of them constituting conduct from which he has benefited, or

   (*b*)   in the period of six years ending with the day when those proceedings were started (or, if there is more than one such day, the earliest day) he was convicted on at least two separate occasions of an offence constituting conduct from which he has benefited.

(4)   But an offence does not satisfy the test in subsection (2)(*b*) or (*c*) unless the defendant obtains relevant benefit of not less than £5000.

(5)   Relevant benefit for the purposes of subsection (2)(*b*) is—

   (*a*)   benefit from conduct which constitutes the offence;

   (*b*)   benefit from any other conduct which forms part of the course of criminal activity and which constitutes an offence of which the defendant has been convicted;

   (*c*)   benefit from conduct which constitutes an offence which has been or will be taken into consideration by the court in sentencing the defendant for an offence mentioned in paragraph (*a*) or (*b*).

(6)   Relevant benefit for the purposes of subsection (2)(*c*) is—

   (*a*)   benefit from conduct which constitutes the offence;

   (*b*)   benefit from conduct which constitutes an offence which has been or will be taken into consideration by the court in sentencing the defendant for the offence mentioned in paragraph (*a*).

(7)   The Secretary of State may by order amend Schedule 2.

(8)   The Secretary of State may by order vary the amount for the time being specified in subsection (4).

76   Conduct and benefit

(1)   Criminal conduct is conduct which—

(*a*)   constitutes an offence in England and Wales, or

(*b*)   would constitute such an offence if it occurred in England and Wales.

(2)   General criminal conduct of the defendant is all his criminal conduct, and it is immaterial—

(*a*)   whether conduct occurred before or after the passing of this Act;

(*b*)   whether property constituting a benefit from conduct was obtained before or after the passing of this Act.

(3)   Particular criminal conduct of the defendant is all his criminal conduct which falls within the following paragraphs—

(*a*)   conduct which constitutes the offence or offences concerned;

(*b*)   conduct which constitutes offences of which he was convicted in the same proceedings as those in which he was convicted of the offence or offences concerned;

(*c*)   conduct which constitutes offences which the court will be taking into consideration in deciding his sentence for the offence or offences concerned.

(4)   A person benefits from conduct if he obtains property as a result of or in connection with the conduct.

(5)   If a person obtains a pecuniary advantage as a result of or in connection with conduct, he is to be taken to obtain as a result of or in connection with the conduct a sum of money equal to the value of the pecuniary advantage.

(6)   References to property or a pecuniary advantage obtained in connection with conduct include references to property or a pecuniary advantage obtained both in that connection and some other.

(7)   If a person benefits from conduct his benefit is the value of the property obtained.

77   Tainted gifts

(1)   Subsections (2) and (3) apply if—

(*a*)   no court has made a decision as to whether the defendant has a criminal lifestyle, or

(*b*)   a court has decided that the defendant has a criminal lifestyle.

(2)   A gift is tainted if it was made by the defendant at any time after the relevant day.

(3)   A gift is also tainted if it was made by the defendant at any time and was of property—

(*a*)   which was obtained by the defendant as a result of or in connection with his general criminal conduct, or

(*b*)   which (in whole or part and whether directly or indirectly) represented in the defendant's hands property obtained by him as a result of or in connection with his general criminal conduct.

(4)   Subsection (5) applies if a court has decided that the defendant does not have a criminal lifestyle.

(5)   A gift is tainted if it was made by the defendant at any time after—

(*a*)   the date on which the offence concerned was committed, or

(*b*)   if his particular criminal conduct consists of two or more offences and they were committed on different dates, the date of the earliest.

(6)   For the purposes of subsection (5) an offence which is a continuing offence is committed on the first occasion when it is committed.

(7)   For the purposes of subsection (5) the defendant's particular criminal conduct includes any conduct which constitutes offences which the court has taken into consideration in deciding his sentence for the offence or offences concerned.

(8)   A gift may be a tainted gift whether it was made before or after the passing of this Act.

(9)   The relevant day is the first day of the period of six years ending with—

(*a*)   the day when proceedings for the offence concerned were started against the defendant, or

(*b*)   if there are two or more offences and proceedings for them were started on different days, the earliest of those days.

78   Gifts and their recipients

(1)   If the defendant transfers property to another person for a consideration whose value is significantly less than the value of the property at the time of the transfer, he is to be treated as making a gift.

(2)   If subsection (1) applies the property given is to be treated as such share in the property transferred as is represented by the fraction—

(*a*)   whose numerator is the difference between the two values mentioned in subsection (1), and

(*b*)   whose denominator is the value of the property at the time of the transfer.

(3)   References to a recipient of a tainted gift are to a person to whom the defendant has made the gift.

79   Value: the basic rule

(1)   This section applies for the purpose of deciding the value at any time of property then held by a person.

(2)   Its value is the market value of the property at that time.

(3)   But if at that time another person holds an interest in the property its value, in relation to the person mentioned in subsection (1), is the market value of his interest at that time, ignoring any charging order under a provision listed in subsection (4).

(4)   The provisions are—

(*a*)   section 9 of the Drug Trafficking Offences Act 1986 (c. 32);

(*b*)   section 78 of the Criminal Justice Act 1988 (c. 33);

(*c*)   Article 14 of the Criminal Justice (Confiscation) (Northern Ireland) Order 1990 (S.I. 1990/2588 (N.I. 17));

(*d*)   section 27 of the Drug Trafficking Act 1994 (c. 37);

(*e*)   Article 32 of the Proceeds of Crime (Northern Ireland) Order 1996 (S.I. 1996/1299 (N.I. 9)).

(5)   This section has effect subject to sections 80 and 81.

80   Value of property obtained from conduct

(1)   This section applies for the purpose of deciding the value of property obtained by a person as a result of or in connection with his criminal conduct; and the material time is the time the court makes its decision.

(2)   The value of the property at the material time is the greater of the following—

(*a*)   the value of the property (at the time the person obtained it) adjusted to take account of later changes in the value of money;

(*b*)   the value (at the material time) of the property found under subsection (3).

(3)   The property found under this subsection is as follows—

(*a*)   if the person holds the property obtained, the property found under this subsection is that property;

(*b*)   if he holds no part of the property obtained, the property found under this subsection is any property which directly or indirectly represents it in his hands;

(*c*)   if he holds part of the property obtained, the property found under this subsection is that part and any property which directly or indirectly represents the other part in his hands.

(4)   The references in subsection (2)(*a*) and (*b*) to the value are to the value found in accordance with section 79.

81   Value of tainted gifts

(1)   The value at any time (the material time) of a tainted gift is the greater of the following—

(*a*)   the value (at the time of the gift) of the property given, adjusted to take account of later changes in the value of money;

(*b*)   the value (at the material time) of the property found under subsection (2).

(2)   The property found under this subsection is as follows—

(*a*)   if the recipient holds the property given, the property found under this subsection is that property;

(*b*)   if the recipient holds no part of the property given, the property found under this subsection is any property which directly or indirectly represents it in his hands;

(*c*)   if the recipient holds part of the property given, the property found under this subsection is that part and any property which directly or indirectly represents the other part in his hands.

(3)   The references in subsection (1)(*a*) and (*b*) to the value are to the value found in accordance with section 79.

82 Free property

Property is free unless an order is in force in respect of it under any of these provisions—

(*a*)   section 27 of the Misuse of Drugs Act 1971 (c. 38) (forfeiture orders);

(*b*)   Article 11 of the Criminal Justice (Northern Ireland) Order 1994 (S.I. 1994/2795 (N.I. 15)) (deprivation orders);

(*c*)   Part 2 of the Proceeds of Crime (Scotland) Act 1995 (c. 43) (forfeiture of property used in crime);

(*d*)   section 143 of the Sentencing Act (deprivation orders);

(*e*)   section 23[, 23A][1] or 111 of the Terrorism Act 2000 (c. 11) (forfeiture orders);

(*f*)   section [245A,][2] 246, [255A, 256,][2] 266, 295(2) or 298(2) of this Act.

Amendments

1   Inserted by the Counter-Terrorism Act 2008, s 39, Sch 3, para 7.
2   Inserted by the Serious Organised Crime and Police Act 2005, s 109, Sch 6, paras 4, 5.

83 Realisable property

Realisable property is—

(*a*)   any free property held by the defendant;

(*b*)   any free property held by the recipient of a tainted gift.

84 Property: general provisions

(1)   Property is all property wherever situated and includes—

(*a*)   money;

(*b*)   all forms of real or personal property;

(*c*)   things in action and other intangible or incorporeal property.

(2)   The following rules apply in relation to property—

(*a*)   property is held by a person if he holds an interest in it;

(*b*)   property is obtained by a person if he obtains an interest in it;

(*c*)   property is transferred by one person to another if the first one transfers or grants an interest in it to the second;

(*d*)   references to property held by a person include references to property vested in his trustee in bankruptcy, permanent or interim trustee (within the meaning of the Bankruptcy (Scotland) Act 1985 (c. 66)) or liquidator;

(*e*)   references to an interest held by a person beneficially in property include references to an interest which would be held by him beneficially if the property were not so vested;

(*f*)   references to an interest, in relation to land in England and Wales or Northern Ireland, are to any legal estate or equitable interest or power;

(*g*)   references to an interest, in relation to land in Scotland, are to any estate, interest, servitude or other heritable right in or over land, including a heritable security;

(*h*)　　references to an interest, in relation to property other than land, include references to a right (including a right to possession).

85　Proceedings

(1)　Proceedings for an offence are started—

(*a*)　　when a justice of the peace issues a summons or warrant under section 1 of the Magistrates' Courts Act 1980 (c. 43) in respect of the offence;

[(*aa*)　when a public prosecutor issues a written charge and requisition in respect of the offence;][1]

(*b*)　　when a person is charged with the offence after being taken into custody without a warrant;

(*c*)　　when a bill of indictment is preferred under section 2 of the Administration of Justice (Miscellaneous Provisions) Act 1933 (c. 36) in a case falling within subsection (2)(*b*) of that section (preferment by Court of Appeal or High Court judge).

(2)　If more than one time is found under subsection (1) in relation to proceedings they are started at the earliest of them.

(3)　If the defendant is acquitted on all counts in proceedings for an offence, the proceedings are concluded when he is acquitted.

(4)　If the defendant is convicted in proceedings for an offence and the conviction is quashed or the defendant is pardoned before a confiscation order is made, the proceedings are concluded when the conviction is quashed or the defendant is pardoned.

(5)　If a confiscation order is made against the defendant in proceedings for an offence (whether the order is made by the Crown Court or the Court of Appeal) the proceedings are concluded—

(*a*)　　when the order is satisfied or discharged, or

(*b*)　　when the order is quashed and there is no further possibility of an appeal against the decision to quash the order.

(6)　If the defendant is convicted in proceedings for an offence but the Crown Court decides not to make a confiscation order against him, the following rules apply—

(*a*)　　if an application for leave to appeal under section 31(2) is refused, the proceedings are concluded when the decision to refuse is made;

(*b*)　　if the time for applying for leave to appeal under section 31(2) expires without an application being made, the proceedings are concluded when the time expires;

(*c*)　　if on appeal under section 31(2) the Court of Appeal confirms the Crown Court's decision, and an application for leave to appeal under section 33 is refused, the proceedings are concluded when the decision to refuse is made;

(*d*)　　if on appeal under section 31(2) the Court of Appeal confirms the Crown Court's decision, and the time for applying for leave to appeal under section 33 expires without an application being made, the proceedings are concluded when the time expires;

(e) if on appeal under section 31(2) the Court of Appeal confirms the Crown Court's decision, and on appeal under section 33 the [Supreme Court][1] confirms the Court of Appeal's decision, the proceedings are concluded when the [Supreme Court][1] confirms the decision;

(f) if on appeal under section 31(2) the Court of Appeal directs the Crown Court to reconsider the case, and on reconsideration the Crown Court decides not to make a confiscation order against the defendant, the proceedings are concluded when the Crown Court makes that decision;

(g) if on appeal under section 33 the [Supreme Court][1] directs the Crown Court to reconsider the case, and on reconsideration the Crown Court decides not to make a confiscation order against the defendant, the proceedings are concluded when the Crown Court makes that decision.

(7) In applying subsection (6) any power to extend the time for making an application for leave to appeal must be ignored.

(8) In applying subsection (6) the fact that a court may decide on a later occasion to make a confiscation order against the defendant must be ignored.

[(9) In this section 'public prosecutor', 'requisition' and 'written charge' have the same meaning as in section 29 of the Criminal Justice Act 2003.][1]

Amendments
1   Inserted by the Criminal Justice Act 2003, s 331, Sch 36, Pt 2, para 15.
2   Substituted by the Constitutional Reform Act 2005, s 40(4), Sch 9, Pt 1, para 77(1), (4).

86 Applications

(1) An application under section 19, 20, 27 or 28 is concluded—

(a) in a case where the court decides not to make a confiscation order against the defendant, when it makes the decision;

(b) in a case where a confiscation order is made against him as a result of the application, when the order is satisfied or discharged, or when the order is quashed and there is no further possibility of an appeal against the decision to quash the order;

(c) in a case where the application is withdrawn, when the person who made the application notifies the withdrawal to the court to which the application was made.

(2) An application under section 21 or 22 is concluded—

(a) in a case where the court decides not to vary the confiscation order concerned, when it makes the decision;

(b) in a case where the court varies the confiscation order as a result of the application, when the order is satisfied or discharged, or when the order is quashed and there is no further possibility of an appeal against the decision to quash the order;

(c) in a case where the application is withdrawn, when the person who made the application notifies the withdrawal to the court to which the application was made.

87 Confiscation orders

(1) A confiscation order is satisfied when no amount is due under it.

(2) A confiscation order is subject to appeal until there is no further possibility of an appeal on which the order could be varied or quashed; and for this purpose any power to grant leave to appeal out of time must be ignored.

88 Other interpretative provisions

(1) A reference to the offence (or offences) concerned must be construed in accordance with section 6(9).

(2) A criminal investigation is an investigation which police officers or other persons have a duty to conduct with a view to it being ascertained whether a person should be charged with an offence.

(3) A defendant is a person against whom proceedings for an offence have been started (whether or not he has been convicted).

(4) A reference to sentencing the defendant for an offence includes a reference to dealing with him otherwise in respect of the offence.

(5) The Sentencing Act is the Powers of Criminal Courts (Sentencing) Act 2000 (c. 6).

(6) The following paragraphs apply to references to orders—

    (*a*) a confiscation order is an order under section 6;

    (*b*) a restraint order is an order under section 41.

(7) Sections 75 to 87 and this section apply for the purposes of this Part.

General

89 Procedure on appeal to the Court of Appeal

(1) An appeal to the Court of Appeal under this Part lies only with the leave of that Court.

(2) Subject to rules of court made under section 53(1) of the Supreme Court Act 1981 (c. 54) (distribution of business between civil and criminal divisions) the criminal division of the Court of Appeal is the division—

    (*a*) to which an appeal to that Court under this Part is to lie, and

    (*b*) which is to exercise that Court's jurisdiction under this Part.

(3) In relation to appeals to the Court of Appeal under this Part, the Secretary of State may make an order containing provision corresponding to any provision in the Criminal Appeal Act 1968 (c. 19) (subject to any specified modifications).

[(4) Subject to any rules made under section 91, the costs of and incidental to all proceedings on an appeal to the criminal division of the Court of Appeal under–

    (*a*) section 43(1) or (2) (appeals against orders made in restraint proceedings), or

    (*b*) section 65 (appeals against, or relating to, the making of receivership orders),

are in the discretion of the court.

(5) Such rules may in particular make provision for regulating matters relating to the costs of those proceedings, including prescribing scales of costs to be paid to legal or other representatives.

(6)   The court shall have full power to determine by whom and to what extent the costs are to be paid.

(7)   In any proceedings mentioned in subsection (4), the court may–

  (*a*)   disallow, or

  (*b*)   (as the case may be) order the legal or other representative concerned to meet,

  the whole of any wasted costs or such part of them as may be determined in accordance with rules under section 91.

(8)   In subsection (7) 'wasted costs' means any costs incurred by a party–

  (*a*)   as a result of any improper, unreasonable or negligent act or omission on the part of any legal or other representative or any employee of such a representative, or

  (*b*)   which, in the light of any such act or omission occurring after they were incurred, the court considers it is unreasonable to expect that party to pay.

(9)   'Legal or other representative', in relation to a party to proceedings means any person exercising a right of audience or right to conduct litigation on his behalf.][1]

Amendments
1   Inserted by the Courts Act 2003, s 94(1), (2).

90   Procedure on appeal to the [Supreme Court][1]

(1)   Section 33(3) of the Criminal Appeal Act 1968 (limitation on appeal from criminal division of the Court of Appeal) does not prevent an appeal to the [Supreme Court][1] under this Part.

(2)   In relation to appeals to the [Supreme Court][1] under this Part, the Secretary of State may make an order containing provision corresponding to any provision in the Criminal Appeal Act 1968 (subject to any specified modifications).

Amendments
1   Substituted by the Constitutional Reform Act 2005, s 40(4), Sch 9, Pt 1, para 77(1), (5).

91   Crown Court Rules

In relation to—

  (*a*)   proceedings under this Part, or

  (*b*)   receivers appointed under this Part,

  [Criminal Procedure Rules][1] may make provision corresponding to provision in Civil Procedure Rules.

Amendments
1   Substituted by the Courts Act 2003, s 109(1), Sch 8, para 410.

[*Sections 92 to 155 only apply to Scotland so are not reproduced in this title.*]

[*Sections 156 to 239 only apply to Northern Ireland so are not reproduced in this title.*]

PART 5
CIVIL RECOVERY OF THE PROCEEDS ETC. OF UNLAWFUL CONDUCT

CHAPTER 1
INTRODUCTORY

240   General purpose of this Part

(1)   This Part has effect for the purposes of—

    (*a*)   enabling the enforcement authority to recover, in civil proceedings before the High Court or Court of Session, property which is, or represents, property obtained through unlawful conduct,

    (*b*)   enabling cash which is, or represents, property obtained through unlawful conduct, or which is intended to be used in unlawful conduct, to be forfeited in civil proceedings before a magistrates' court or (in Scotland) the sheriff.

(2)   The powers conferred by this Part are exercisable in relation to any property (including cash) whether or not any proceedings have been brought for an offence in connection with the property.

241   'Unlawful conduct'

(1)   Conduct occurring in any part of the United Kingdom is unlawful conduct if it is unlawful under the criminal law of that part.

(2)   Conduct which—

    (*a*)   occurs in a country [or territory][1] outside the United Kingdom and is unlawful under the criminal law [applying in that country or territory][2], and

    (*b*)   if it occurred in a part of the United Kingdom, would be unlawful under the criminal law of that part,

is also unlawful conduct.

(3)   The court or sheriff must decide on a balance of probabilities whether it is proved—

    (*a*)   that any matters alleged to constitute unlawful conduct have occurred, or

    (*b*)   that any person intended to use any cash in unlawful conduct.

Amendments
1   Inserted by the Serious Organised Crime and Police Act 2005, s 109, Sch 6, paras 4, 8(*a*).
2   Substituted by the Serious Organised Crime and Police Act 2005, s 109, Sch 6, paras 4, 8(*b*).

242   'Property obtained through unlawful conduct'

(1)   A person obtains property through unlawful conduct (whether his own conduct or another's) if he obtains property by or in return for the conduct.

(2)   In deciding whether any property was obtained through unlawful conduct—

    (*a*)   it is immaterial whether or not any money, goods or services were provided in order to put the person in question in a position to carry out the conduct, (*b*)   it is not necessary to show that the conduct was of a particular kind if it is shown that the property was obtained through conduct of one of a number of kinds, each of which would have been unlawful conduct.

CHAPTER 2
CIVIL RECOVERY IN THE HIGH COURT OR COURT OF SESSION

Proceedings for recovery orders

243 Proceedings for recovery orders in England and Wales or Northern Ireland

(1)   Proceedings for a recovery order may be taken by the enforcement authority in the High Court against any person who the authority thinks holds recoverable property.

(2)   The enforcement authority must serve the claim form—

    (*a*)   on the respondent, and

    (*b*)   unless the court dispenses with service, on any other person who the authority thinks holds any associated property which the authority wishes to be subject to a recovery order,

wherever domiciled, resident or present.

(3)   If any property which the enforcement authority wishes to be subject to a recovery order is not specified in the claim form it must be described in the form in general terms; and the form must state whether it is alleged to be recoverable property or associated property.

(4)   The references above to the claim form include the particulars of claim, where they are served subsequently.

[(5)   Nothing in sections 245A to 255 limits any power of the court apart from those sections to grant interim relief in connection with proceedings (including prospective proceedings) under this Chapter.]¹

Amendments

1   Inserted by the Serious Organised Crime and Police Act 2005, s 109, Sch 6, paras 4, 9.

[*Section 244 only applies to Scotland so is not reproduced in this title.*]

245 'Associated property'

(1)   'Associated property' means property of any of the following descriptions (including property held by the respondent) which is not itself the recoverable property—

    (*a*)   any interest in the recoverable property,

    (*b*)   any other interest in the property in which the recoverable property subsists,

    (*c*)   if the recoverable property is a tenancy in common, the tenancy of the other tenant,

    (*d*)   if (in Scotland) the recoverable property is owned in common, the interest of the other owner, (*e*)   if the recoverable property is part of a larger property, but not a separate part, the remainder of that property.

(2)   References to property being associated with recoverable property are to be read accordingly.

(3)   No property is to be treated as associated with recoverable property consisting of rights under a pension scheme (within the meaning of sections 273 to 275).

[Property freezing orders (England and Wales and Northern Ireland)

245A Application for property freezing order

(1)   Where the enforcement authority may take proceedings for a recovery order in the High Court, the authority may apply to the court for a property freezing order (whether before or after starting the proceedings).

(2)   A property freezing order is an order that—

(*a*)   specifies or describes the property to which it applies, and

(*b*)   subject to any exclusions (see section 245C(1)(*b*) and (2)), prohibits any person to whose property the order applies from in any way dealing with the property.

(3)   An application for a property freezing order may be made without notice if the circumstances are such that notice of the application would prejudice any right of the enforcement authority to obtain a recovery order in respect of any property.

(4)   The court may make a property freezing order on an application if it is satisfied that the condition in subsection (5) is met and, where applicable, that the condition in subsection (6) is met.

(5)   The first condition is that there is a good arguable case—

(*a*)   that the property to which the application for the order relates is or includes recoverable property, and

(*b*)   that, if any of it is not recoverable property, it is associated property.

(6)   The second condition is that, if—

(*a*)   the property to which the application for the order relates includes property alleged to be associated property, and

(*b*)   the enforcement authority has not established the identity of the person who holds it,

the authority has taken all reasonable steps to do so.][1]

Amendments

1   Inserted by the Serious Organised Crime and Police Act 2005, s 98(1).

[245B Variation and setting aside of order

(1)   The court may at any time vary or set aside a property freezing order.

(2)   If the court makes an interim receiving order that applies to all of the property to which a property freezing order applies, it must set aside the property freezing order.

(3)   If the court makes an interim receiving order that applies to some but not all of the property to which a property freezing order applies, it must vary the property freezing order so as to exclude any property to which the interim receiving order applies.

(4)   If the court decides that any property to which a property freezing order applies is neither recoverable property nor associated property, it must vary the order so as to exclude the property.

(5)   Before exercising power under this Chapter to vary or set aside a property freezing order, the court must (as well as giving the parties to the proceedings an opportunity to be heard) give such an opportunity to any person who may be affected by its decision.

(6)   Subsection (5) does not apply where the court is acting as required by subsection (2) or (3).]¹

Amendments
1   Inserted by the Serious Organised Crime and Police Act 2005, s 98(1).

[245C Exclusions

(1)   The power to vary a property freezing order includes (in particular) power to make exclusions as follows—

(*a*)   power to exclude property from the order, and

(*b*)   power, otherwise than by excluding property from the order, to make exclusions from the prohibition on dealing with the property to which the order applies.

(2)   Exclusions from the prohibition on dealing with the property to which the order applies (other than exclusions of property from the order) may also be made when the order is made.

(3)   An exclusion may, in particular, make provision for the purpose of enabling any person—

(*a*)   to meet his reasonable living expenses, or

(*b*)   to carry on any trade, business, profession or occupation.

(4)   An exclusion may be made subject to conditions.

(5)   Where the court exercises the power to make an exclusion for the purpose of enabling a person to meet legal expenses that he has incurred, or may incur, in respect of proceedings under this Part, it must ensure that the exclusion—

(*a*)   is limited to reasonable legal expenses that the person has reasonably incurred or that he reasonably incurs,

(*b*)   specifies the total amount that may be released for legal expenses in pursuance of the exclusion, and

(*c*)   is made subject to the required conditions (see section 286A) in addition to any conditions imposed under subsection (4).

(6)   The court, in deciding whether to make an exclusion for the purpose of enabling a person to meet legal expenses of his in respect of proceedings under this Part—

(*a*)   must have regard (in particular) to the desirability of the person being represented in any proceedings under this Part in which he is a participant, and (*b*) must, where the person is the respondent, disregard the possibility that legal representation of the person in any such proceedings might, were an exclusion not made, be funded by the Legal Services Commission or the Northern Ireland Legal Services Commission.

(7) If excluded property is not specified in the order it must be described in the order in general terms.

(8) The power to make exclusions must, subject to subsection (6), be exercised with a view to ensuring, so far as practicable, that the satisfaction of any right of the enforcement authority to recover the property obtained through unlawful conduct is not unduly prejudiced.

(9) Subsection (8) does not apply where the court is acting as required by section 245B(3) or (4).][1]

Amendments
1   Inserted by the Serious Organised Crime and Police Act 2005, s 98(1).

[245D   Restriction on proceedings and remedies

(1) While a property freezing order has effect—

(*a*) the court may stay any action, execution or other legal process in respect of the property to which the order applies, and

(*b*) no distress may be levied against the property to which the order applies except with the leave of the court and subject to any terms the court may impose.

(2) If a court (whether the High Court or any other court) in which proceedings are pending in respect of any property is satisfied that a property freezing order has been applied for or made in respect of the property, it may either stay the proceedings or allow them to continue on any terms it thinks fit.

(3) If a property freezing order applies to a tenancy of any premises, no landlord or other person to whom rent is payable may exercise the right of forfeiture by peaceable re-entry in relation to the premises in respect of any failure by the tenant to comply with any term or condition of the tenancy, except with the leave of the court and subject to any terms the court may impose.

(4) Before exercising any power conferred by this section, the court must (as well as giving the parties to any of the proceedings concerned an opportunity to be heard) give such an opportunity to any person who may be affected by the court's decision.][1]

Amendments
1   Inserted by the Serious Organised Crime and Police Act 2005, s 98(1).

[245E   Receivers in connection with property freezing orders

(1) Subsection (2) applies if–

(*a*) the High Court makes a property freezing order on an application by an enforcement authority, and

(*b*) the authority applies to the court to proceed under subsection (2) (whether as part of the application for the property freezing order or at any time afterwards).

(2)   The High Court may by order appoint a receiver in respect of any property to which the property freezing order applies.

(3)   An application for an order under this section may be made without notice if the circumstances are such that notice of the application would prejudice any right of the enforcement authority to obtain a recovery order in respect of any property.

(4)   In its application for an order under this section, the enforcement authority must nominate a suitably qualified person for appointment as a receiver.

(5)   Such a person may be a member of staff of the enforcement authority.

(6)   The enforcement authority may apply a sum received by it under section 280(2) in making payment of the remuneration and expenses of a receiver appointed under this section.

(7)   Subsection (6) does not apply in relation to the remuneration of the receiver if he is a member of the staff of the enforcement authority (but it does apply in relation to such remuneration if the receiver is a person providing services under arrangements made by the enforcement authority).]¹

Amendments
1   Inserted by the Serious Crime Act 2007, s 83(1).

[245F   Powers of receivers appointed under section 245E

(1)   If the High Court appoints a receiver under section 245E on an application by an enforcement authority, the court may act under this section on the application of the authority.

(2)   The court may by order authorise or require the receiver–

        (*a*)   to exercise any of the powers mentioned in paragraph 5 of Schedule 6 (management powers) in relation to any property in respect of which the receiver is appointed,

        (*b*)   to take any other steps the court thinks appropriate in connection with the management of any such property (including securing the detention, custody or preservation of the property in order to manage it).

(3)   The court may by order require any person in respect of whose property the receiver is appointed–

        (*a*)   to bring the property to a place (in England and Wales or, as the case may be, Northern Ireland) specified by the receiver or to place it in the custody of the receiver (if, in either case, he is able to do so),

        (*b*)   to do anything he is reasonably required to do by the receiver for the preservation of the property.

(4)   The court may by order require any person in respect of whose property the receiver is appointed to bring any documents relating to the property which are in his possession or control to a place (in England and Wales or, as the case may be, Northern Ireland) specified by the receiver or to place them in the custody of the receiver.

(5)   In subsection (4) 'document' means anything in which information of any description is recorded.

194

(6)   Any prohibition on dealing with property imposed by a property freezing order does not prevent a person from complying with any requirements imposed by virtue of this section.

(7)   If–

    (*a*)   the receiver deals with any property which is not property in respect of which he is appointed under section 245E, and

    (*b*)   at the time he deals with the property he believes on reasonable grounds that he is entitled to do so by virtue of his appointment,

the receiver is not liable to any person in respect of any loss or damage resulting from his dealing with the property except so far as the loss or damage is caused by his negligence.]¹

Amendments

1   Inserted by the Serious Crime Act 2007, s 83(1).

[245G   Supervision of section 245E receiver and variations

(1)   Any of the following persons may at any time apply to the High Court for directions as to the exercise of the functions of a receiver appointed under section 245E–

    (*a*)   the receiver,

    (*b*)   any party to the proceedings for the appointment of the receiver or the property freezing order concerned,

    (*c*)   any person affected by any action taken by the receiver,

    (*d*)   any person who may be affected by any action proposed to be taken by the receiver.

(2)   Before giving any directions under subsection (1), the court must give an opportunity to be heard to–

    (*a*)   the receiver,

    (*b*)   the parties to the proceedings for the appointment of the receiver and for the property freezing order concerned,

    (*c*)   any person who may be interested in the application under subsection (1).

(3)   The court may at any time vary or set aside the appointment of a receiver under section 245E, any order under section 245F or any directions under this section.

(4)   Before exercising any power under subsection (3), the court must give an opportunity to be heard to–

    (*a*)   the receiver,

    (*b*)   the parties to the proceedings for the appointment of the receiver, for the order under section 245F or, as the case may be, for the directions under this section;

    (*c*)   the parties to the proceedings for the property freezing order concerned,

    (*d*)   any person who may be affected by the court's decision.]¹

Amendments

1   Inserted by the Serious Crime Act 2007, s 83(1).

Interim receiving orders (England and Wales and Northern Ireland)

246   Application for interim receiving order

(1)   Where the enforcement authority may take proceedings for a recovery order in the High Court, the authority may apply to the court for an interim receiving order (whether before or after starting the proceedings).

(2)   An interim receiving order is an order for—

(*a*)   the detention, custody or preservation of property, and

(*b*)   the appointment of an interim receiver.

(3)   An application for an interim receiving order may be made without notice if the circumstances are such that notice of the application would prejudice any right of the enforcement authority to obtain a recovery order in respect of any property.

(4)   The court may make an interim receiving order on the application if it is satisfied that the conditions in subsections (5) and, where applicable, (6) are met.

(5)   The first condition is that there is a good arguable case—

(*a*)   that the property to which the application for the order relates is or includes recoverable property, and

(*b*)   that, if any of it is not recoverable property, it is associated property.

(6)   The second condition is that, if—

(*a*)   the property to which the application for the order relates includes property alleged to be associated property, and

(*b*)   the enforcement authority has not established the identity of the person who holds it,

the authority has taken all reasonable steps to do so.

(7)   In its application for an interim receiving order, the enforcement authority must nominate a suitably qualified person for appointment as interim receiver, but the nominee may not be a member of the staff of the [enforcement authority][1].

(8)   The extent of the power to make an interim receiving order is not limited by sections 247 to 255.

Amendments

1   Substituted by the Serious Crime Act 2007, s 74(2)(*b*), Sch 8, Pt 2, paras 85, 86.

247   Functions of interim receiver

(1)   An interim receiving order may authorise or require the interim receiver—

(*a*)   to exercise any of the powers mentioned in Schedule 6,

(*b*)   to take any other steps the court thinks appropriate,

for the purpose of securing the detention, custody or preservation of the property to which the order applies or of taking any steps under subsection (2).

(2)   An interim receiving order must require the interim receiver to take any steps which the court thinks necessary to establish—

(*a*)   whether or not the property to which the order applies is recoverable property or associated property,

(*b*)   whether or not any other property is recoverable property (in relation to the same unlawful conduct) and, if it is, who holds it.

(3)   If—

(*a*)   the interim receiver deals with any property which is not property to which the order applies, and

(*b*)   at the time he deals with the property he believes on reasonable grounds that he is entitled to do so in pursuance of the order,

the interim receiver is not liable to any person in respect of any loss or damage resulting from his dealing with the property except so far as the loss or damage is caused by his negligence.

[Property freezing orders and interim receiving orders: registration][1]

248   Registration

(1)   The registration Acts—

(*a*)   apply in relation to [property freezing orders, and in relation to interim receiving orders,][2] as they apply in relation to orders which affect land and are made by the court for the purpose of enforcing judgements or recognisances,

(*b*)   apply in relation to applications for [property freezing orders, and in relation to applications for interim receiving orders,][2] as they apply in relation to other pending land actions.

(2)   The registration Acts are—

(*a*)   the Land Registration Act 1925 (c. 21),

(*b*)   the Land Charges Act 1972 (c. 61), and

(*c*)   the Land Registration Act 2002 (c. 9).

(3)   But no notice may be entered in the register of title under the Land Registration Act 2002 in respect of [a property freezing order or][1] an interim receiving order.

(4)   A person applying for an interim receiving order must be treated for the purposes of section 57 of the Land Registration Act 1925 (inhibitions) as a person interested in relation to any registered land to which—

(*a*)   the application relates, or

(*b*)   an interim receiving order made in pursuance of the application relates.

Amendments

1   Inserted by the Serious Organised Crime and Police Act 2005, s 109, Sch 6, paras 4, 10, 11(1), (4).
2   Substituted by the Serious Organised Crime and Police Act 2005, s 109, Sch 6, paras 4, 11(1), (2), (3).

[Section 249 only applies to Northern Ireland so is not reproduced in this title.]

[Interim receiving orders: further provisions][1]

250 Duties of respondent etc.

(1) An interim receiving order may require any person to whose property the order applies—

(a) to bring the property to a place (in England and Wales or, as the case may be, Northern Ireland) specified by the interim receiver or place it in the custody of the interim receiver (if, in either case, he is able to do so),

(b) to do anything he is reasonably required to do by the interim receiver for the preservation of the property.

(2) An interim receiving order may require any person to whose property the order applies to bring any documents relating to the property which are in his possession or control to a place (in England and Wales or, as the case may be, Northern Ireland) specified by the interim receiver or to place them in the custody of the interim receiver.

'Document' means anything in which information of any description is recorded.

Amendments

1   Inserted by the Serious Organised Crime and Police Act 2005, s 109, Sch 6, paras 4, 13.

251 Supervision of interim receiver and variation of order

(1) The interim receiver, any party to the proceedings and any person affected by any action taken by the interim receiver, or who may be affected by any action proposed to be taken by him, may at any time apply to the court for directions as to the exercise of the interim receiver's functions.

(2) Before giving any directions under subsection (1), the court must (as well as giving the parties to the proceedings an opportunity to be heard) give such an opportunity to the interim receiver and to any person who may be interested in the application.

(3) The court may at any time vary or set aside an interim receiving order.

(4) Before exercising any power under this Chapter to vary or set aside an interim receiving order, the court must (as well as giving the parties to the proceedings an opportunity to be heard) give such an opportunity to the interim receiver and to any person who may be affected by the court's decision.

252 Restrictions on dealing etc. with property

(1) An interim receiving order must, subject to any exclusions made in accordance with this section, prohibit any person to whose property the order applies from dealing with the property.

(2) Exclusions may be made when the interim receiving order is made or on an application to vary the order.

(3) An exclusion may, in particular, make provision for the purpose of enabling any person—

(a) to meet his reasonable living expenses, or

(b) to carry on any trade, business, profession or occupation,

and may be made subject to conditions.

[(4) Where the court exercises the power to make an exclusion for the purpose of enabling a person to meet legal expenses that he has incurred, or may incur, in respect of proceedings under this Part, it must ensure that the exclusion—

(*a*) is limited to reasonable legal expenses that the person has reasonably incurred or that he reasonably incurs,

(*b*) specifies the total amount that may be released for legal expenses in pursuance of the exclusion, and

(*c*) is made subject to the required conditions (see section 286A) in addition to any conditions imposed under subsection (3).][1]

[(4A) The court, in deciding whether to make an exclusion for the purpose of enabling a person to meet legal expenses of his in respect of proceedings under this Part—

(*a*) must have regard (in particular) to the desirability of the person being represented in any proceedings under this Part in which he is a participant, and

(*b*) must, where the person is the respondent, disregard the possibility that legal representation of the person in any such proceedings might, were an exclusion not made, be funded by the Legal Services Commission or the Northern Ireland Legal Services Commission.][2]

(5) If the excluded property is not specified in the order it must be described in the order in general terms.

(6) The power to make exclusions must[, subject to subsection (4A),][2] be exercised with a view to ensuring, so far as practicable, that the satisfaction of any right of the enforcement authority to recover the property obtained through unlawful conduct is not unduly prejudiced.

Amendments

1   Substituted by the Serious Organised Crime and Police Act 2005, s 109, Sch 6, paras 4, 14(1), (2).
2   Inserted by the Serious Organised Crime and Police Act 2005, s 109, Sch 6, paras 4, 14.

253   Restriction on proceedings and remedies

(1) While an interim receiving order has effect—

(*a*) the court may stay any action, execution or other legal process in respect of the property to which the order applies,

(*b*) no distress may be levied against the property to which the order applies except with the leave of the court and subject to any terms the court may impose.

(2) If a court (whether the High Court or any other court) in which proceedings are pending in respect of any property is satisfied that an interim receiving order has been applied for or made in respect of the property, the court may either stay the proceedings or allow them to continue on any terms it thinks fit.

(3) If the interim receiving order applies to a tenancy of any premises, no landlord or other person to whom rent is payable may exercise any right of forfeiture by peaceable re-entry in relation to the premises in respect of any failure by the tenant to comply with any term or condition of the tenancy, except with the leave of the court and subject to any terms the court may impose.

(4)   Before exercising any power conferred by this section, the court must (as well as giving the parties to any of the proceedings in question an opportunity to be heard) give such an opportunity to the interim receiver (if appointed) and any person who may be affected by the court's decision.

254   Exclusion of property which is not recoverable etc.

(1)   If the court decides that any property to which an interim receiving order applies is neither recoverable property nor associated property, it must vary the order so as to exclude it.

(2)   The court may vary an interim receiving order so as to exclude from the property to which the order applies any property which is alleged to be associated property if the court thinks that the satisfaction of any right of the enforcement authority to recover the property obtained through unlawful conduct will not be prejudiced.

(3)   The court may exclude any property within subsection (2) on any terms or conditions, applying while the interim receiving order has effect, which the court thinks necessary or expedient.

255   Reporting

(1)   An interim receiving order must require the interim receiver to inform the enforcement authority and the court as soon as reasonably practicable if he thinks that—

(*a*)   any property to which the order applies by virtue of a claim that it is recoverable property is not recoverable property,

(*b*)   any property to which the order applies by virtue of a claim that it is associated property is not associated property,

(*c*)   any property to which the order does not apply is recoverable property (in relation to the same unlawful conduct) or associated property, or

(*d*)   any property to which the order applies is held by a person who is different from the person it is claimed holds it,

or if he thinks that there has been any other material change of circumstances.

(2)   An interim receiving order must require the interim receiver—

(*a*)   to report his findings to the court,

(*b*)   to serve copies of his report on the enforcement authority and on any person who holds any property to which the order applies or who may otherwise be affected by the report.

[*Sections 255A to 265 only apply to Scotland so are not reproduced in this title.*]

Vesting and realisation of recoverable property

266   Recovery orders

(1)   If in proceedings under this Chapter the court is satisfied that any property is recoverable, the court must make a recovery order.

(2)   The recovery order must vest the recoverable property in the trustee for civil recovery.

(3)   But the court may not make in a recovery order—

(a) any provision in respect of any recoverable property if each of the conditions in subsection (4) or (as the case may be) (5) is met and it would not be just and equitable to do so, or

(b) any provision which is incompatible with any of the Convention rights (within the meaning of the Human Rights Act 1998 (c. 42)).

(4) In relation to a court in England and Wales or Northern Ireland, the conditions referred to in subsection (3)(a) are that—

(a) the respondent obtained the recoverable property in good faith,

(b) he took steps after obtaining the property which he would not have taken if he had not obtained it or he took steps before obtaining the property which he would not have taken if he had not believed he was going to obtain it,

(c) when he took the steps, he had no notice that the property was recoverable,

(d) if a recovery order were made in respect of the property, it would, by reason of the steps, be detrimental to him.

(5) In relation to a court in Scotland, the conditions referred to in subsection (3)(a) are that—

(a) the respondent obtained the recoverable property in good faith,

(b) he took steps after obtaining the property which he would not have taken if he had not obtained it or he took steps before obtaining the property which he would not have taken if he had not believed he was going to obtain it,

(c) when he took the steps, he had no reasonable grounds for believing that the property was recoverable,

(d) if a recovery order were made in respect of the property, it would, by reason of the steps, be detrimental to him.

(6) In deciding whether it would be just and equitable to make the provision in the recovery order where the conditions in subsection (4) or (as the case may be) (5) are met, the court must have regard to—

(a) the degree of detriment that would be suffered by the respondent if the provision were made,

(b) the enforcement authority's interest in receiving the realised proceeds of the recoverable property.

(7) A recovery order may sever any property.

(8) A recovery order may impose conditions as to the manner in which the trustee for civil recovery may deal with any property vested by the order for the purpose of realising it.

[(8A) A recovery order made by a court in England and Wales or Northern Ireland may provide for payment under section 280 of reasonable legal expenses that a person has reasonably incurred, or may reasonably incur, in respect of—

(a) the proceedings under this Part in which the order is made, or

(b) any related proceedings under this Part.

(8B) If regulations under section 286B apply to an item of expenditure, a sum in respect of the item is not payable under section 280 in pursuance of provision under subsection (8A) unless—

201

(*a*)   the enforcement authority agrees to its payment, or

(*b*)   the court has assessed the amount allowed by the regulations in respect of that item and the sum is paid in respect of the assessed amount.]¹

(9)   This section is subject to sections 270 to 278.

Amendments
1   Inserted by the Serious Organised Crime and Police Act 2005, s 109, Sch 6, paras 4, 15.

267   Functions of the trustee for civil recovery

(1)   The trustee for civil recovery is a person appointed by the court to give effect to a recovery order.

(2)   The enforcement authority must nominate a suitably qualified person for appointment as the trustee.

(3)   The functions of the trustee are—

(*a*)   to secure the detention, custody or preservation of any property vested in him by the recovery order,

(*b*)   in the case of property other than money, to realise the value of the property for the benefit of the enforcement authority, and

(*c*)   to perform any other functions conferred on him by virtue of this Chapter.

(4)   In performing his functions, the trustee acts on behalf of the enforcement authority and must comply with any directions given by the authority.

(5)   The trustee is to realise the value of property vested in him by the recovery order, so far as practicable, in the manner best calculated to maximise the amount payable to the enforcement authority.

(6)   The trustee has the powers mentioned in Schedule 7.

(7)   References in this section to a recovery order include an order under section 276 and references to property vested in the trustee by a recovery order include property vested in him in pursuance of an order under section 276.

[*Section 268 only applies to Scotland so is not reproduced in this title.*]

269   Rights of pre-emption, etc.

(1)   A recovery order is to have effect in relation to any property despite any provision (of whatever nature) which would otherwise prevent, penalise or restrict the vesting of the property.

(2)   A right of pre-emption, right of irritancy, right of return or other similar right does not operate or become exercisable as a result of the vesting of any property under a recovery order.

A right of return means any right under a provision for the return or reversion of property in specified circumstances.

(3)   Where property is vested under a recovery order, any such right is to have effect as if the person in whom the property is vested were the same person in law as the person who held the property and as if no transfer of the property had taken place.

(4)   References to rights in subsections (2) and (3) do not include any rights in respect of which the recovery order was made.

(5) This section applies in relation to the creation of interests, or the doing of anything else, by a recovery order as it applies in relation to the vesting of property.

270 Associated and joint property

(1) Sections 271 and 272 apply if the court makes a recovery order in respect of any recoverable property in a case within subsection (2) or (3).

(2) A case is within this subsection if—

    (*a*) the property to which the proceedings relate includes property which is associated with the recoverable property and is specified or described in the claim form or (in Scotland) application, and

    (*b*) if the associated property is not the respondent's property, the claim form or application has been served on the person whose property it is or the court has dispensed with service.

(3) A case is within this subsection if—

    (*a*) the recoverable property belongs to joint tenants, and

    (*b*) one of the tenants is an excepted joint owner.

(4) An excepted joint owner is a person who obtained the property in circumstances in which it would not be recoverable as against him; and references to the excepted joint owner's share of the recoverable property are to so much of the recoverable property as would have been his if the joint tenancy had been severed.

(5) Subsections (3) and (4) do not extend to Scotland.

271 Agreements about associated and joint property

(1) Where—

    (*a*) this section applies, and

    (*b*) the enforcement authority (on the one hand) and the person who holds the associated property or who is the excepted joint owner (on the other) agree,

the recovery order may, instead of vesting the recoverable property in the trustee for civil recovery, require the person who holds the associated property or who is the excepted joint owner to make a payment to the trustee

(2) A recovery order which makes any requirement under subsection (1) may, so far as required for giving effect to the agreement, include provision for vesting, creating or extinguishing any interest in property.

(3) The amount of the payment is to be the amount which the enforcement authority and that person agree represents—

    (*a*) in a case within section 270(2), the value of the recoverable property,

    (*b*) in a case within section 270(3), the value of the recoverable property less the value of the excepted joint owner's share.

(4) But if—

    (*a*) [a property freezing order, an interim receiving order, a prohibitory property order or an]¹ interim administration order applied at any time to the associated property or joint tenancy, and

203

(b)   the enforcement authority agrees that the person has suffered loss as a result of the [order mentioned in paragraph (a)]¹,

the amount of the payment may be reduced by any amount the enforcement authority and that person agree is reasonable, having regard to that loss and to any other relevant circumstances

(5)   If there is more than one such item of associated property or excepted joint owner, the total amount to be paid to the trustee, and the part of that amount which is to be provided by each person who holds any such associated property or who is an excepted joint owner, is to be agreed between both (or all) of them and the enforcement authority.

(6)   A recovery order which makes any requirement under subsection (1) must make provision for any recoverable property to cease to be recoverable.

Amendments

1   Substituted by the Serious Organised Crime and Police Act 2005, s 109, Sch 6, paras 4, 16.

272   Associated and joint property: default of agreement

(1)   Where this section applies, the court may make the following provision if—

(a)   there is no agreement under section 271, and

(b)   the court thinks it just and equitable to do so.

(2)   The recovery order may provide—

(a)   for the associated property to vest in the trustee for civil recovery or (as the case may be) for the excepted joint owner's interest to be extinguished, or

(b)   in the case of an excepted joint owner, for the severance of his interest.

(3)   A recovery order making any provision by virtue of subsection (2)(a) may provide—

(a)   for the trustee to pay an amount to the person who holds the associated property or who is an excepted joint owner, or

(b)   for the creation of interests in favour of that person, or the imposition of liabilities or conditions, in relation to the property vested in the trustee,

or for both

(4)   In making any provision in a recovery order by virtue of subsection (2) or (3), the court must have regard to—

(a)   the rights of any person who holds the associated property or who is an excepted joint owner and the value to him of that property or, as the case may be, of his share (including any value which cannot be assessed in terms of money),

(b)   the enforcement authority's interest in receiving the realised proceeds of the recoverable property.

(5)   If—

(a)   [a property freezing order, an interim receiving order, a prohibitory property order or an]¹ interim administration order applied at any time to the associated property or joint tenancy, and

(b)   the court is satisfied that the person who holds the associated property or who is an excepted joint owner has suffered loss as a result of the [order mentioned in paragraph (a)]¹, a recovery order making any provision by virtue of subsection (2) or (3) may require the enforcement authority to pay compensation to that person

(6)   The amount of compensation to be paid under subsection (5) is the amount the court thinks reasonable, having regard to the person's loss and to any other relevant circumstances.

[(7)   In subsection (5) the reference to the enforcement authority is, in the case of an enforcement authority in relation to England and Wales or Northern Ireland, a reference to the enforcement authority which obtained the property freezing order or interim receiving order concerned.]²

Amendments

1   Substituted by the Serious Organised Crime and Police Act 2005, s 109, Sch 6, paras 4, 17.
2   Inserted by the Serious Crime Act 2007, s 74(2)(*b*), Sch 8, Pt 2, paras 85, 88.

273   Payments in respect of rights under pension schemes

(1)   This section applies to recoverable property consisting of rights under a pension scheme.

(2)   A recovery order in respect of the property must, instead of vesting the property in the trustee for civil recovery, require the trustees or managers of the pension scheme—

(*a*)   to pay to the trustee for civil recovery within a prescribed period the amount determined by the trustees or managers to be equal to the value of the rights, and

(*b*)   to give effect to any other provision made by virtue of this section and the two following sections in respect of the scheme.

This subsection is subject to sections 276 to 278

(3)   A recovery order made by virtue of subsection (2) overrides the provisions of the pension scheme to the extent that they conflict with the provisions of the order.

(4)   A recovery order made by virtue of subsection (2) may provide for the recovery by the trustees or managers of the scheme (whether by deduction from any amount which they are required to pay to the trustee for civil recovery or otherwise) of costs incurred by them in—

(*a*)   complying with the recovery order, or

(*b*)   providing information, before the order was made, to the enforcement authority, [receiver appointed under section 245E,]¹ interim receiver or interim administrator.

(5)   None of the following provisions applies to a court making a recovery order by virtue of subsection (2)—

(*a*)   any provision of section 159 of the Pension Schemes Act 1993 (c. 48), section 155 of the Pension Schemes (Northern Ireland) Act 1993 (c. 49), section 91 of the Pensions Act 1995 (c. 26) or Article 89 of the Pensions (Northern Ireland) Order 1995 (S.I. 1995/3213 (N.I. 22)) (which prevent assignment and the making of orders that restrain a person from receiving anything which he is prevented from assigning),

(*b*)   any provision of any enactment (whenever passed or made) corresponding to any of the provisions mentioned in paragraph (*a*), (*c*)   any provision of the pension scheme in question corresponding to any of those provisions.

Amendments
1   Inserted by the Serious Crime Act 2007, s 83(2).

274   Consequential adjustment of liabilities under pension schemes

(1)   A recovery order made by virtue of section 273(2) must require the trustees or managers of the pension scheme to make such reduction in the liabilities of the scheme as they think necessary in consequence of the payment made in pursuance of that subsection.

(2)   Accordingly, the order must require the trustees or managers to provide for the liabilities of the pension scheme in respect of the respondent's recoverable property to which section 273 applies to cease.

(3)   So far as the trustees or managers are required by the recovery order to provide for the liabilities of the pension scheme in respect of the respondent's recoverable property to which section 273 applies to cease, their powers include (in particular) power to reduce the amount of—

(*a*)   any benefit or future benefit to which the respondent is or may be entitled under the scheme,

(*b*)   any future benefit to which any other person may be entitled under the scheme in respect of that property.

275   Pension schemes: supplementary

(1)   Regulations may make provision as to the exercise by trustees or managers of their powers under sections 273 and 274, including provision about the calculation and verification of the value at any time of rights or liabilities.

(2)   The power conferred by subsection (1) includes power to provide for any values to be calculated or verified—

(*a*)   in a manner which, in the particular case, is approved by a prescribed person, or

(*b*)   in accordance with guidance from time to time prepared by a prescribed person.

(3)   Regulations means regulations made by the Secretary of State after consultation with the Scottish Ministers; and prescribed means prescribed by regulations.

(4)   A pension scheme means an occupational pension scheme or a personal pension scheme; and those expressions have the same meaning as in the Pension Schemes Act 1993 (c. 48) or, in relation to Northern Ireland, the Pension Schemes (Northern Ireland) Act 1993 (c. 49).

(5)   In relation to an occupational pension scheme or a personal pension scheme, the trustees or managers means—

(*a*)   in the case of a scheme established under a trust, the trustees,

(*b*)   in any other case, the managers.

(6)   References to a pension scheme include—

(*a*)   a retirement annuity contract (within the meaning of Part 3 of the Welfare Reform and Pensions Act 1999 (c. 30) or, in relation to Northern Ireland, Part 4 of the Welfare Reform and Pensions (Northern Ireland) Order 1999),

(b)   an annuity or insurance policy purchased, or transferred, for the purpose of giving effect to rights under an occupational pension scheme or a personal pension scheme,

(c)   an annuity purchased, or entered into, for the purpose of discharging any liability in respect of a pension credit under section 29(1)(b) of the Welfare Reform and Pensions Act 1999 (c. 30) or, in relation to Northern Ireland, Article 26(1)(b) of the Welfare Reform and Pensions (Northern Ireland) Order 1999.

(7)   References to the trustees or managers—

(a)   in relation to a retirement annuity contract or other annuity, are to the provider of the annuity,

(b)   in relation to an insurance policy, are to the insurer.

(8)   Subsections (3) to (7) have effect for the purposes of this group of sections (that is, sections 273 and 274 and this section).

276 Consent orders

(1)   The court may make an order staying (in Scotland, sisting) any proceedings for a recovery order on terms agreed by the parties for the disposal of the proceedings if each person to whose property the proceedings, or the agreement, relates is a party both to the proceedings and the agreement.

(2)   An order under subsection (1) may, as well as staying (or sisting) the proceedings on terms—

(a)   make provision for any property which may be recoverable property to cease to be recoverable,

(b)   make any further provision which the court thinks appropriate.

(3)   Section 280 applies to property vested in the trustee for civil recovery, or money paid to him, in pursuance of the agreement as it applies to property vested in him by a recovery order or money paid under section 271.

277 Consent orders: pensions

(1)   This section applies where recoverable property to which proceedings under this Chapter relate includes rights under a pension scheme.

(2)   An order made under section 276—

(a)   may not stay (in Scotland, sist) the proceedings on terms that the rights are vested in any other person, but

(b)   may include provision imposing the following requirement, if the trustees or managers of the scheme are parties to the agreement by virtue of which the order is made.

(3)   The requirement is that the trustees or managers of the pension scheme—

(a)   make a payment in accordance with the agreement, and

(b)   give effect to any other provision made by virtue of this section in respect of the scheme.

(4)   The trustees or managers of the pension scheme have power to enter into an agreement in respect of the proceedings on any terms on which an order made under section 276 may stay (in Scotland, sist) the proceedings.

(5)   The following provisions apply in respect of an order under section 276, so far as it includes the requirement mentioned in subsection (3).

(6)   The order overrides the provisions of the pension scheme to the extent that they conflict with the requirement.

(7)   The order may provide for the recovery by the trustees or managers of the scheme (whether by deduction from any amount which they are required to pay in pursuance of the agreement or otherwise) of costs incurred by them in—

   (*a*)   complying with the order, or

   (*b*)   providing information, before the order was made, to the enforcement authority, [receiver appointed under section 245E,][1] interim receiver or interim administrator.

(8)   Sections 273(5) and 274 (read with section 275) apply as if the requirement were included in an order made by virtue of section 273(2).

(9)   Section 275(4) to (7) has effect for the purposes of this section.

Amendments
1   Inserted by the Serious Crime Act 2007, s 83(2).

278   Limit on recovery

(1)   This section applies if the enforcement authority seeks a recovery order—

   (*a*)   in respect of both property which is or represents property obtained through unlawful conduct and related property, or

   (*b*)   in respect of property which is or represents property obtained through unlawful conduct where such an order, or an order under section 276, has previously been made in respect of related property.

(2)   For the purposes of this section—

   (*a*)   the original property means the property obtained through unlawful conduct,

   (*b*)   the original property, and any items of property which represent the original property, are to be treated as related to each other.

(3)   The court is not to make a recovery order if it thinks that the enforcement authority's right to recover the original property has been satisfied by a previous recovery order or order under section 276.

(4)   Subject to subsection (3), the court may act under subsection (5) if it thinks that—

   (*a*)   a recovery order may be made in respect of two or more related items of recoverable property, but

   (*b*)   the making of a recovery order in respect of both or all of them is not required in order to satisfy the enforcement authority's right to recover the original property.

(5)   The court may in order to satisfy that right to the extent required make a recovery order in respect of—

   (*a*)   only some of the related items of property, or

(b)   only a part of any of the related items of property,

or both

(6)   Where the court may make a recovery order in respect of any property, this section does not prevent the recovery of any profits which have accrued in respect of the property.

(7)   If—

(a)   an order is made under section 298 for the forfeiture of recoverable property, and

(b)   the enforcement authority subsequently seeks a recovery order in respect of related property,

the order under section 298 is to be treated for the purposes of this section as if it were a recovery order obtained by the enforcement authority in respect of the forfeited property

(8)   If—

(a)   in pursuance of a judgment in civil proceedings (whether in the United Kingdom or elsewhere), the claimant has obtained property from the defendant ('the judgment property'),

(b)   the claim was based on the defendant's having obtained the judgment property or related property through unlawful conduct, and

(c)   the enforcement authority subsequently seeks a recovery order in respect of property which is related to the judgment property,

the judgment is to be treated for the purposes of this section as if it were a recovery order obtained by the enforcement authority in respect of the judgment property

In relation to Scotland, 'claimant' and 'defendant' are to be read as 'pursuer' and 'defender'

(9)   If—

(a)   property has been taken into account in deciding the amount of a person's benefit from criminal conduct for the purpose of making a confiscation order, and

(b)   the enforcement authority subsequently seeks a recovery order in respect of related property,

the confiscation order is to be treated for the purposes of this section as if it were a recovery order obtained by the enforcement authority in respect of the property referred to in paragraph (a)

(10)   In subsection (9), a confiscation order means—

(a)   an order under section 6, 92 or 156, or

(b)   an order under a corresponding provision of an enactment mentioned in section 8(7)(a) to (g),

and, in relation to an order mentioned in paragraph (b), the reference to the amount of a person's benefit from criminal conduct is to be read as a reference to the corresponding amount under the enactment in question

279   Section 278: supplementary

(1)   Subsections (2) and (3) give examples of the satisfaction of the enforcement authority's right to recover the original property.

(2)   If—

    (*a*)   there is a disposal, other than a part disposal, of the original property, and

    (*b*)   other property (the representative property) is obtained in its place,

the enforcement authority's right to recover the original property is satisfied by the making of a recovery order in respect of either the original property or the representative property

(3)   If—

    (*a*)   there is a part disposal of the original property, and

    (*b*)   other property (the representative property) is obtained in place of the property disposed of,

the enforcement authority's right to recover the original property is satisfied by the making of a recovery order in respect of the remainder of the original property together with either the representative property or the property disposed of

(4)   In this section—

    (*a*)   a part disposal means a disposal to which section 314(1) applies,

    (*b*)   the original property has the same meaning as in section 278.

280 Applying realised proceeds

(1)   This section applies to—

    (*a*)   sums which represent the realised proceeds of property which was vested in the trustee for civil recovery by a recovery order or which he obtained in pursuance of a recovery order,

    (*b*)   sums vested in the trustee by a recovery order or obtained by him in pursuance of a recovery order.

(2)   The trustee is to make out of the sums—

    (*a*)   first, any payment required to be made by him by virtue of section 272,

    [(*aa*)   next, any payment of legal expenses which, after giving effect to section 266(8B), are payable under this subsection in pursuance of provision under section 266(8A) contained in the recovery order,][1]

    (*b*)   [then][2], any payment of expenses incurred by a person acting as an insolvency practitioner which are payable under this subsection by virtue of section 432(10),

and any sum which remains is to be paid to the enforcement authority

[(3)   The [enforcement authority (unless it is the Scottish Ministers)][3] may apply a sum received by [it][3] under subsection (2) in making payment of the remuneration and expenses of—

    (*a*)   the trustee, or

    (*b*)   any interim receiver appointed in, or in anticipation of, the proceedings for the recovery order.

(4)   Subsection (3)(*a*) does not apply in relation to the remuneration of the trustee if the trustee is a member of the staff of the [enforcement authority concerned][3] [(but it does apply in relation to such remuneration if the trustee is a person providing services under arrangement made by that enforcement authority)][4].][1]

Amendments
1   Inserted by the Serious Organised Crime and Police Act 2005, ss 99(1), (2), 109, Sch 6, paras 4, 18(*a*).
2   Substituted by the Serious Organised Crime and Police Act 2005, s 109, Sch 6, paras 4, 18(*b*).
3   Substituted by the Serious Crime Act 2007, s 74(2)(*b*), Sch 8, Pt 2, paras 85, 88.
4   Inserted by the Serious Crime Act 2007 (Amendment of the Proceeds of Crime Act 2002) Order 2008, SI 2008/949, art 2.

Exemptions etc

281 Victims of theft, etc.

(1)   In proceedings for a recovery order, a person who claims that any property alleged to be recoverable property, or any part of the property, belongs to him may apply for a declaration under this section.

(2)   If the applicant appears to the court to meet the following condition, the court may make a declaration to that effect.

(3)   The condition is that—

   (*a*)   the person was deprived of the property he claims, or of property which it represents, by unlawful conduct,

   (*b*)   the property he was deprived of was not recoverable property immediately before he was deprived of it, and

   (*c*)   the property he claims belongs to him.

(4)   Property to which a declaration under this section applies is not recoverable property.

282 Other exemptions

(1)   Proceedings for a recovery order may not be taken against any person in circumstances of a prescribed description; and the circumstances may relate to the person himself or to the property or to any other matter.

In this subsection, prescribed means prescribed by an order made by the Secretary of State after consultation with the Scottish Ministers

(2)   Proceedings for a recovery order may not be taken in respect of cash found at any place in the United Kingdom unless the proceedings are also taken in respect of property other than cash which is property of the same person.

(3)   Proceedings for a recovery order may not be taken against the Financial Services Authority in respect of any recoverable property held by the authority.

(4)   Proceedings for a recovery order may not be taken in respect of any property which is subject to any of the following charges—

   (*a*)   a collateral security charge, within the meaning of the Financial Markets and Insolvency (Settlement Finality) Regulations 1999 (S.I. 1999/2979),

   (*b*)   a market charge, within the meaning of Part 7 of the Companies Act 1989 (c. 40),

   (*c*)   a money market charge, within the meaning of the Financial Markets and Insolvency (Money Market) Regulations 1995 (S.I. 1995/2049),

   (*d*)   a system charge, within the meaning of the Financial Markets and Insolvency Regulations 1996 (S.I. 1996/1469) or the Financial Markets and Insolvency Regulations (Northern Ireland) 1996 (S.R. 1996/252).

(5)   Proceedings for a recovery order may not be taken against any person in respect of any recoverable property which he holds by reason of his acting, or having acted, as an insolvency practitioner.

Acting as an insolvency practitioner has the same meaning as in section 433

Miscellaneous

283   Compensation

(1)   If, in the case of any property to which [a property freezing order, an interim receiving order, a prohibitory property order or an][1] interim administration order has at any time applied, the court does not in the course of the proceedings decide that the property is recoverable property or associated property, the person whose property it is may make an application to the court for compensation.

(2)   Subsection (1) does not apply if the court—

    (*a*)   has made a declaration in respect of the property by virtue of section 281, or

    (*b*)   makes an order under section 276.

(3)   If the court has made a decision by reason of which no recovery order could be made in respect of the property, the application for compensation must be made within the period of three months beginning—

    (*a*)   in relation to a decision of the High Court in England and Wales, with the date of the decision or, if any application is made for leave to appeal, with the date on which the application is withdrawn or refused or (if the application is granted) on which any proceedings on appeal are finally concluded,

    (*b*)   in relation to a decision of the Court of Session or of the High Court in Northern Ireland, with the date of the decision or, if there is an appeal against the decision, with the date on which any proceedings on appeal are finally concluded.

(4)   If, in England and Wales or Northern Ireland, the proceedings in respect of the property have been discontinued, the application for compensation must be made within the period of three months beginning with the discontinuance.

(5)   If the court is satisfied that the applicant has suffered loss as a result of the [order mentioned in subsection (1)][1], it may require the enforcement authority to pay compensation to him.

(6)   If, but for section 269(2), any right mentioned there would have operated in favour of, or become exercisable by, any person, he may make an application to the court for compensation.

(7)   The application for compensation under subsection (6) must be made within the period of three months beginning with the vesting referred to in section 269(2).

(8)   If the court is satisfied that, in consequence of the operation of section 269, the right in question cannot subsequently operate in favour of the applicant or (as the case may be) become exercisable by him, it may require the enforcement authority to pay compensation to him.

(9)   The amount of compensation to be paid under this section is the amount the court thinks reasonable, having regard to the loss suffered and any other relevant circumstances.

[(10)   In the case of an enforcement authority in relation to England and Wales or Northern Ireland–

(*a*)   the reference in subsection (5) to the enforcement authority is a reference to the enforcement authority which obtained the property freezing order or interim receiving order concerned, and

(*b*)   the reference in subsection (8) to the enforcement authority is a reference to the enforcement authority which obtained the recovery order concerned.]²

Amendments

1   Substituted by the Serious Organised Crime and Police Act 2005, s 109, Sch 6, paras 4, 19.
2   Inserted by the Serious Crime Act 2007, s 74(2)(*b*), Sch 8, Pt 2, paras 85, 89.

[*Sections 284 to 286 only apply to Scotland so are not reproduced in this title.*]

[286A   Legal expenses excluded from freezing: required conditions

(1)   The Lord Chancellor may by regulations specify the required conditions for the purposes of section 245C(5) or 252(4).

(2)   A required condition may (in particular)—

(*a*)   restrict who may receive sums released in pursuance of the exclusion (by, for example, requiring released sums to be paid to professional legal advisers), or

(*b*)   be made for the purpose of controlling the amount of any sum released in pursuance of the exclusion in respect of an item of expenditure.

(3)   A required condition made for the purpose mentioned in subsection (2)(*b*) may (for example)—

(*a*)   provide for sums to be released only with the agreement of the enforcement authority;

(*b*)   provide for a sum to be released in respect of an item of expenditure only if the court has assessed the amount allowed by regulations under section 286B in respect of that item and the sum is released for payment of the assessed amount;

(*c*)   provide for a sum to be released in respect of an item of expenditure only if—

(i)   the enforcement authority agrees to its release, or

(ii)   the court has assessed the amount allowed by regulations under section 286B in respect of that item and the sum is released for payment of the assessed amount.

(4)   Before making regulations under this section, the Lord Chancellor must consult such persons as he considers appropriate.]¹

Amendments

1   Inserted by the Serious Organised Crime and Police Act 2005, s 109, Sch 6, paras 4, 20.

[286B   Legal expenses: regulations for purposes of section 266(8B) or 286A(3)

(1)   The Lord Chancellor may by regulations—

(*a*)   make provision for the purposes of section 266(8B);

(*b*)   make provision for the purposes of required conditions that make provision of the kind mentioned in section 286A(3)(*b*) or (*c*).

(2)   Regulations under this section may (in particular)—

(*a*)   limit the amount of remuneration allowable to representatives for a unit of time worked;

(*b*)   limit the total amount of remuneration allowable to representatives for work done in connection with proceedings or a step in proceedings;

(*c*)   limit the amount allowable in respect of an item of expense incurred by a representative or incurred, otherwise than in respect of the remuneration of a representative, by a party to proceedings.

(3)   Before making regulations under this section, the Lord Chancellor must consult such persons as he considers appropriate.][1]

Amendments
1   Inserted by the Serious Organised Crime and Police Act 2005, s 109, Sch 6, paras 4, 20.

287   Financial threshold

(1)   At any time when an order specifying an amount for the purposes of this section has effect, the enforcement authority may not start proceedings for a recovery order unless the authority reasonably believes that the aggregate value of the recoverable property which the authority wishes to be subject to a recovery order is not less than the specified amount.

(2)   The power to make an order under subsection (1) is exercisable by the Secretary of State after consultation with the Scottish Ministers.

(3)   If the authority applies for [a property freezing order, an interim receiving order, a prohibitory property order or an][1] interim administration order before starting the proceedings, subsection (1) applies to the application instead of to the start of the proceedings.

(4)   This section does not affect the continuation of proceedings for a recovery order which have been properly started or the making or continuing effect of [a property freezing order, an interim receiving order, a prohibitory property order or an][1] interim administration order which has been properly applied for.

Amendments
1   Substituted by the Serious Organised Crime and Police Act 2005, s 109, Sch 6, paras 4, 21.

288   Limitation

(1)   After section 27 of the Limitation Act 1980 (c. 58) there is inserted—

'27A   Actions for recovery of property obtained through unlawful conduct etc.

(1)   None of the time limits given in the preceding provisions of this Act applies to any proceedings under Chapter 2 of Part 5 of the Proceeds of Crime Act 2002 (civil recovery of proceeds of unlawful conduct).

(2)   Proceedings under that Chapter for a recovery order in respect of any recoverable property shall not be brought after the expiration of the period of twelve years from the date on which the Director's cause of action accrued.

214

(3)   Proceedings under that Chapter are brought when—

  (*a*)   a claim form is issued, or

  (*b*)   an application is made for an interim receiving order,

  whichever is the earlier

(4)   The Director's cause of action accrues in respect of any recoverable property—

  (*a*)   in the case of proceedings for a recovery order in respect of property obtained through unlawful conduct, when the property is so obtained,

  (*b*)   in the case of proceedings for a recovery order in respect of any other recoverable property, when the property obtained through unlawful conduct which it represents is so obtained.

(5)   If—

  (*a*)   a person would (but for the preceding provisions of this Act) have a cause of action in respect of the conversion of a chattel, and

  (*b*)   proceedings are started under that Chapter for a recovery order in respect of the chattel,

  section 3(2) of this Act does not prevent his asserting on an application under section 281 of that Act that the property belongs to him, or the court making a declaration in his favour under that section

(6)   If the court makes such a declaration, his title to the chattel is to be treated as not having been extinguished by section 3(2) of this Act.

(7)   Expressions used in this section and Part 5 of that Act have the same meaning in this section as in that Part.'

(2)   After section 19A of the Prescription and Limitation (Scotland) Act 1973 (c. 52) there is inserted—

'19B   Actions for recovery of property obtained through unlawful conduct etc.

(1)   None of the time limits given in the preceding provisions of this Act applies to any proceedings under Chapter 2 of Part 5 of the Proceeds of Crime Act 2002 (civil recovery of proceeds of unlawful conduct).

(2)   Proceedings under that Chapter for a recovery order in respect of any recoverable property shall not be commenced after the expiration of the period of twelve years from the date on which the Scottish Ministers' right of action accrued.

(3)   Proceedings under that Chapter are commenced when—

  (*a*)   the proceedings are served, or

  (*b*)   an application is made for an interim administration order,

  whichever is the earlier

(4)   The Scottish Ministers' right of action accrues in respect of any recoverable property—

  (*a*)   in the case of proceedings for a recovery order in respect of property obtained through unlawful conduct, when the property is so obtained,

  (*b*)   in the case of proceedings for a recovery order in respect of any other recoverable property, when the property obtained through unlawful conduct which it represents is so obtained.

(5)   Expressions used in this section and Part 5 of that Act have the same meaning in this section as in that Part.'

(3)   After Article 72 of the Limitation (Northern Ireland) Order 1989 (SI 1989/1339 (N.I. 11)) there is inserted—

'72A   Actions for recovery of property obtained through unlawful conduct etc.

(1)   None of the time limits fixed by Parts II and III applies to any proceedings under Chapter 2 of Part 5 of the Proceeds of Crime Act 2002 (civil recovery of proceeds of unlawful conduct).

(2)   Proceedings under that Chapter for a recovery order in respect of any recoverable property shall not be brought after the expiration of the period of twelve years from the date on which the Director's cause of action accrued.

(3)   Proceedings under that Chapter are brought when—

(*a*)   a claim form is issued, or

(*b*)   an application is made for an interim receiving order,

whichever is the earlier

(4)   The Director's cause of action accrues in respect of any recoverable property—

(*a*)   in the case of proceedings for a recovery order in respect of property obtained through unlawful conduct, when the property is so obtained,

(*b*)   in the case of proceedings for a recovery order in respect of any other recoverable property, when the property obtained through unlawful conduct which it represents is so obtained.

(5)   If—

(*a*)   a person would (but for a time limit fixed by this Order) have a cause of action in respect of the conversion of a chattel, and

(*b*)   proceedings are started under that Chapter for a recovery order in respect of the chattel,

Article 17(2) does not prevent his asserting on an application under section 281 of that Act that the property belongs to him, or the court making a declaration in his favour under that section

(6)   If the court makes such a declaration, his title to the chattel is to be treated as not having been extinguished by Article 17(2).

(7)   Expressions used in this Article and Part 5 of that Act have the same meaning in this Article as in that Part.'

CHAPTER 3
RECOVERY OF CASH IN SUMMARY PROCEEDINGS

Searches

289   Searches

(1)   If a customs officer[, a constable or an accredited financial investigator][1] is lawfully on any premises [and][2] has reasonable grounds for suspecting that there is on the premises cash—

(a)   which is recoverable property or is intended by any person for use in unlawful conduct, and

(b)   the amount of which is not less than the minimum amount,

he may search for the cash there

(2)   If a customs officer[, a constable or accredited financial investigator][1] has reasonable grounds for suspecting that a person (the suspect) is carrying cash—

(a)   which is recoverable property or is intended by any person for use in unlawful conduct, and

(b)   the amount of which is not less than the minimum amount,

he may exercise the following powers

(3)   The officer[, constable or accredited financial investigator][1] may, so far as he thinks it necessary or expedient, require the suspect—

(a)   to permit a search of any article he has with him,

(b)   to permit a search of his person.

(4)   An officer[, constable or accredited financial investigator][1] exercising powers by virtue of subsection (3)(b) may detain the suspect for so long as is necessary for their exercise.

(5)   The powers conferred by this section—

(a)   are exercisable only so far as reasonably required for the purpose of finding cash,

(b)   are exercisable by a customs officer only if he has reasonable grounds for suspecting that the unlawful conduct in question relates to an assigned matter (within the meaning of the Customs and Excise Management Act 1979 (c. 2));

[(c)   are exercisable by an accredited financial investigator only in relation to premises or (as the case may be) suspects in England, Wales or Northern Ireland.][2]

(6)   Cash means—

(a)   notes and coins in any currency,

(b)   postal orders,

(c)   cheques of any kind, including travellers' cheques,

(d)   bankers' drafts,

(e)   bearer bonds and bearer shares,

found at any place in the United Kingdom

(7)   Cash also includes any kind of monetary instrument which is found at any place in the United Kingdom, if the instrument is specified by the Secretary of State by an order made after consultation with the Scottish Ministers.

(8)   This section does not require a person to submit to an intimate search or strip search (within the meaning of section 164 of the Customs and Excise Management Act 1979 (c. 2)).

Amendments

1   Substituted by the Serious Crime Act 2007, s 79, Sch 11, paras 1, 2(1), (2)(a), (3), (4).
2   Inserted by the Serious Crime Act 2007, s 79, Sch 11, paras 1, 2(1), (2)(b), (5).

290   Prior approval

(1)   The powers conferred by section 289 may be exercised only with the appropriate approval unless, in the circumstances, it is not practicable to obtain that approval before exercising the power.

(2)   The appropriate approval means the approval of a judicial officer or (if that is not practicable in any case) the approval of a senior officer.

(3)   A judicial officer means—

(*a*)   in relation to England and Wales and Northern Ireland, a justice of the peace,

(*b*)   in relation to Scotland, the sheriff.

(4)   A senior officer means—

(*a*)   in relation to the exercise of the power by a customs officer, a customs officer of a rank designated by the Commissioners of Customs and Excise as equivalent to that of a senior police officer,

(*b*)   in relation to the exercise of the power by a constable, a senior police officer;

[(*c*)   in relation to the exercise of the power by an accredited financial investigator, an accredited financial investigator who falls within a description specified in an order made for this purpose by the Secretary of State under section 453.][1]

(5)   A senior police officer means a police officer of at least the rank of inspector.

(6)   If the powers are exercised without the approval of a judicial officer in a case where—

(*a*)   no cash is seized by virtue of section 294, or

(*b*)   any cash so seized is not detained for more than 48 hours [(calculated in accordance with section 295(1B))][2],

the customs officer[, constable or accredited financial investigator][3] who exercised the powers must give a written report to the appointed person

(7)   The report must give particulars of the circumstances which led him to believe that—

(*a*)   the powers were exercisable, and

(*b*)   it was not practicable to obtain the approval of a judicial officer.

(8)   In this section and section 291, the appointed person means—

(*a*)   in relation to England and Wales and Northern Ireland, a person appointed by the Secretary of State,

(*b*)   in relation to Scotland, a person appointed by the Scottish Ministers.

(9)   The appointed person must not be a person employed under or for the purposes of a government department or of the Scottish Administration; and the terms and conditions of his appointment, including any remuneration or expenses to be paid to him, are to be determined by the person appointing him.

Amendments

1   Inserted by the Serious Crime Act 2007, s 79, Sch 11, paras 1, 3(1), (2).
2   Inserted by the Serious Organised Crime and Police Act 2005, s 100(1), (3).
3   Substituted by the Serious Crime Act 2007, s 79, Sch 11, paras 1, 3(1), (3).

291   Report on exercise of powers

(1)   As soon as possible after the end of each financial year, the appointed person must prepare a report for that year.

'Financial year' means—

(*a*)   the period beginning with the day on which this section comes into force and ending with the next 31 March (which is the first financial year), and

(*b*)   each subsequent period of twelve months beginning with 1 April

(2)   The report must give his opinion as to the circumstances and manner in which the powers conferred by section 289 are being exercised in cases where the customs officer[, constable or accredited financial investigator][1] who exercised them is required to give a report under section 290(6).

(3)   In the report, he may make any recommendations he considers appropriate.

(4)   He must send a copy of his report to the Secretary of State or, as the case may be, the Scottish Ministers, who must arrange for it to be published.

(5)   The Secretary of State must lay a copy of any report he receives under this section before Parliament; and the Scottish Ministers must lay a copy of any report they receive under this section before the Scottish Parliament.

Amendments
1   Substituted by the Serious Crime Act 2007, s 79, Sch 11, paras 1, 4.

292   Code of practice

(1)   The Secretary of State must make a code of practice in connection with the exercise by customs officers and (in relation to England and Wales and Northern Ireland) constables [and accredited financial investigators][1] of the powers conferred by virtue of section 289.

(2)   Where he proposes to issue a code of practice he must—

(*a*)   publish a draft,

(*b*)   consider any representations made to him about the draft by the Scottish Ministers or any other person,

(*c*)   if he thinks it appropriate, modify the draft in the light of any such representations.

(3)   He must lay a draft of the code before Parliament.

(4)   When he has laid a draft of the code before Parliament he may bring it into operation by order.

(5)   He may revise the whole or any part of the code issued by him and issue the code as revised; and subsections (2) to (4) apply to such a revised code as they apply to the original code.

(6)   A failure by a customs officer[, a constable or an accredited financial investigator][2] to comply with a provision of the code does not of itself make him liable to criminal or civil proceedings.

(7)   The code is admissible in evidence in criminal or civil proceedings and is to be taken into account by a court or tribunal in any case in which it appears to the court or tribunal to be relevant.

Amendments
1   Inserted by the Serious Crime Act 2007, s 79, Sch 11, paras 1, 5(1), (2).
2   Substituted by the Serious Crime Act 2007, s 79, Sch 11, paras 1, 5(1), (3).

[*Section 293 only applies to Scotland so is not reproduced in this title.*]

Seizure and detention

294   Seizure of cash

(1)   A customs officer[, a constable or an accredited financial investigator][1] may seize any cash if he has reasonable grounds for suspecting that it is—

   (*a*)   recoverable property, or

   (*b*)   intended by any person for use in unlawful conduct.

(2)   A customs officer or constable may also seize cash part of which he has reasonable grounds for suspecting to be—

   (*a*)   recoverable property, or

   (*b*)   intended by any person for use in unlawful conduct,

   if it is not reasonably practicable to seize only that part

(3)   This section does not authorise the seizure of an amount of cash if it or, as the case may be, the part to which his suspicion relates, is less than the minimum amount.

[(4)   This section does not authorise the seizure by an accredited financial investigator of cash found in Scotland.][2]

Amendments
1   Substituted by the Serious Crime Act 2007, s 79, Sch 11, paras 1, 6(1), (2).
2   Inserted by the Serious Crime Act 2007, s 79, Sch 11, paras 1, 6(1), (3).

295   Detention of seized cash

(1)   While the customs officer[, constable or accredited financial investigator][1] continues to have reasonable grounds for his suspicion, cash seized under section 294 may be detained initially for a period of 48 hours.

[(1A)   The period of 48 hours mentioned in subsection (1) is to be calculated in accordance with subsection (1B).

(1B)   In calculating a period of 48 hours in accordance with this subsection, no account shall be taken of—

   (*a*)   any Saturday or Sunday,

   (*b*)   Christmas Day,

   (*c*)   Good Friday,

   (*d*)   any day that is a bank holiday under the Banking and Financial Dealings Act 1971 in the part of the United Kingdom within which the cash is seized, or

   (*e*)   any day prescribed under section 8(2) of the Criminal Procedure (Scotland) Act 1995 as a court holiday in a sheriff court in the sheriff court district within which the cash is seized.][2]

(2) The period for which the cash or any part of it may be detained may be extended by an order made by a magistrates' court or (in Scotland) the sheriff; but the order may not authorise the detention of any of the cash—

    (*a*)   beyond the end of the period of [six months][3] beginning with the date of the order,

    (*b*)   in the case of any further order under this section, beyond the end of the period of two years beginning with the date of the first order.

(3) A justice of the peace may also exercise the power of a magistrates' court to make the first order under subsection (2) extending the period.

(4) An application for an order under subsection (2)—

    (*a*)   in relation to England and Wales and Northern Ireland, may be made by the Commissioners of Customs and Excise[, a constable or an accredited financial investigator][1],

    (*b*)   in relation to Scotland, may be made by the Scottish Ministers in connection with their functions under section 298 or by a procurator fiscal,

and the court, sheriff or justice may make the order if satisfied, in relation to any cash to be further detained, that either of the following conditions is met

(5) The first condition is that there are reasonable grounds for suspecting that the cash is recoverable property and that either—

    (*a*)   its continued detention is justified while its derivation is further investigated or consideration is given to bringing (in the United Kingdom or elsewhere) proceedings against any person for an offence with which the cash is connected, or

    (*b*)   proceedings against any person for an offence with which the cash is connected have been started and have not been concluded.

(6) The second condition is that there are reasonable grounds for suspecting that the cash is intended to be used in unlawful conduct and that either—

    (*a*)   its continued detention is justified while its intended use is further investigated or consideration is given to bringing (in the United Kingdom or elsewhere) proceedings against any person for an offence with which the cash is connected, or

    (*b*)   proceedings against any person for an offence with which the cash is connected have been started and have not been concluded.

(7) An application for an order under subsection (2) may also be made in respect of any cash seized under section 294(2), and the court, sheriff or justice may make the order if satisfied that—

    (*a*)   the condition in subsection (5) or (6) is met in respect of part of the cash, and

    (*b*)   it is not reasonably practicable to detain only that part.

(8) An order under subsection (2) must provide for notice to be given to persons affected by it.

Amendments
1   Substituted by the Serious Crime Act 2007, s 79, Sch 11, paras 1, 7.
2   Inserted by the Serious Organised Crime and Police Act 2005, s 100(1), (2).
3   Substituted by the Policing and Crime Act 2009, s 64.

296 Interest

(1)   If cash is detained under section 295 for more than 48 hours [(calculated in accordance with section 295(1B))]¹, it is at the first opportunity to be paid into an interest-bearing account and held there; and the interest accruing on it is to be added to it on its forfeiture or release.

(2)   In the case of cash detained under section 295 which was seized under section 294(2), the customs officer[, constable or accredited financial investigator]² must, on paying it into the account, release the part of the cash to which the suspicion does not relate.

(3)   Subsection (1) does not apply if the cash or, as the case may be, the part to which the suspicion relates is required as evidence of an offence or evidence in proceedings under this Chapter.

Amendments
1   Inserted by the Serious Organised Crime and Police Act 2005, s 100(1), (3).
2   Substituted by the Serious Crime Act 2007, s 79, Sch 11, paras 1, 8.

297 Release of detained cash

(1)   This section applies while any cash is detained under section 295.

(2)   A magistrates' court or (in Scotland) the sheriff may direct the release of the whole or any part of the cash if the following condition is met.

(3)   The condition is that the court or sheriff is satisfied, on an application by the person from whom the cash was seized, that the conditions in section 295 for the detention of the cash are no longer met in relation to the cash to be released.

(4)   A customs officer, constable [or accredited financial investigator]¹ or (in Scotland) procurator fiscal may, after notifying the magistrates' court, sheriff or justice under whose order cash is being detained, release the whole or any part of it if satisfied that the detention of the cash to be released is no longer justified.

Amendments
1   Inserted by the Serious Crime Act 2007, s 79, Sch 11, paras 1, 9.

Forfeiture

298 Forfeiture

(1)   While cash is detained under section 295, an application for the forfeiture of the whole or any part of it may be made—

(*a*)   to a magistrates' court by the Commissioners of Customs and Excise[, an accredited financial investigator]¹ or a constable,

(*b*)   (in Scotland) to the sheriff by the Scottish Ministers.

(2)   The court or sheriff may order the forfeiture of the cash or any part of it if satisfied that the cash or part—

(a) is recoverable property, or

(b) is intended by any person for use in unlawful conduct.

(3) But in the case of recoverable property which belongs to joint tenants, one of whom is an excepted joint owner, the order may not apply to so much of it as the court thinks is attributable to the excepted joint owner's share.

(4) Where an application for the forfeiture of any cash is made under this section, the cash is to be detained (and may not be released under any power conferred by this Chapter) until any proceedings in pursuance of the application (including any proceedings on appeal) are concluded.

Amendments
1   Inserted by the Serious Crime Act 2007, s 79, Sch 11, paras 1, 10.

[299   Appeal against decision under section 298

(1) Any party to proceedings for an order for the forfeiture of cash under section 298 who is aggrieved by an order under that section or by the decision of the court not to make such an order may appeal—

(a) in relation to England and Wales, to the Crown Court,

(b) in relation to Scotland, to the Sheriff Principal,

(c) in relation to Northern Ireland, to a county court.

(2) An appeal under subsection (1) must be made before the end of the period of 30 days starting with the day on which the court makes the order or decision.

(3) The court hearing the appeal may make any order it thinks appropriate.

(4) If the court upholds the appeal against an order forfeiting the cash, it may order the release of the cash.][1]

Amendments
1   Substituted by the Serious Organised Crime and Police Act 2005, s 101(1).

300   Application of forfeited cash

(1) Cash forfeited under this Chapter, and any accrued interest on it—

(a) if forfeited by a magistrates' court in England and Wales or Northern Ireland, is to be paid into the Consolidated Fund,

(b) if forfeited by the sheriff, is to be paid into the Scottish Consolidated Fund.

(2) But it is not to be paid in—

(a) before the end of the period within which an appeal under section 299 may be made, or

(b) if a person appeals under that section, before the appeal is determined or otherwise disposed of.

Supplementary

301   Victims and other owners

(1)   A person who claims that any cash detained under this Chapter, or any part of it, belongs to him may apply to a magistrates' court or (in Scotland) the sheriff for the cash or part to be released to him.

(2)   The application may be made in the course of proceedings under section 295 or 298 or at any other time.

(3)   If it appears to the court or sheriff concerned that—

(*a*)   the applicant was deprived of the cash to which the application relates, or of property which it represents, by unlawful conduct,

(*b*)   the property he was deprived of was not, immediately before he was deprived of it, recoverable property, and

(*c*)   that cash belongs to him,

the court or sheriff may order the cash to which the application relates to be released to the applicant

(4)   If—

(*a*)   the applicant is not the person from whom the cash to which the application relates was seized,

(*b*)   it appears to the court or sheriff that that cash belongs to the applicant,

(*c*)   the court or sheriff is satisfied that the conditions in section 295 for the detention of that cash are no longer met or, if an application has been made under section 298, the court or sheriff decides not to make an order under that section in relation to that cash, and

(*d*)   no objection to the making of an order under this subsection has been made by the person from whom that cash was seized,

the court or sheriff may order the cash to which the application relates to be released to the applicant or to the person from whom it was seized

302   Compensation

(1)   If no forfeiture order is made in respect of any cash detained under this Chapter, the person to whom the cash belongs or from whom it was seized may make an application to the magistrates' court or (in Scotland) the sheriff for compensation.

(2)   If, for any period beginning with the first opportunity to place the cash in an interest-bearing account after the initial detention of the cash for 48 hours [(calculated in accordance with section 295(1B))][1], the cash was not held in an interest-bearing account while detained, the court or sheriff may order an amount of compensation to be paid to the applicant.

(3)   The amount of compensation to be paid under subsection (2) is the amount the court or sheriff thinks would have been earned in interest in the period in question if the cash had been held in an interest-bearing account.

(4)   If the court or sheriff is satisfied that, taking account of any interest to be paid under section 296 or any amount to be paid under subsection (2), the applicant has suffered loss as a result of the detention of the cash and that the circumstances are exceptional, the court or sheriff may order compensation (or additional compensation) to be paid to him.

(5)   The amount of compensation to be paid under subsection (4) is the amount the court or sheriff thinks reasonable, having regard to the loss suffered and any other relevant circumstances.

(6)   If the cash was seized by a customs officer, the compensation is to be paid by the Commissioners of Customs and Excise.

(7)   If the cash was seized by a constable, the compensation is to be paid as follows—

(*a*)   in the case of a constable of a police force in England and Wales, it is to be paid out of the police fund from which the expenses of the police force are met,

(*b*)   in the case of a constable of a police force in Scotland, it is to be paid by the police authority or joint police board for the police area for which that force is maintained,

(*c*)   in the case of a police officer within the meaning of the Police (Northern Ireland) Act 2000 (c. 32), it is to be paid out of money provided by the Chief Constable.

[(7A) If the cash was seized by an accredited financial investigator who was not an officer of Revenue and Customs or a constable, the compensation is to be paid as follows–

(*a*)   in the case of an investigator–

(i)   who was employed by a police authority in England and Wales under section 15 of the Police Act 1996 (c. 16) and was under the direction and control of the chief officer of police of the police force maintained by the authority, or

(ii)   who was a member of staff of the City of London police force,
it is to be paid out of the police fund from which the expenses of the police force are met,

(*b*)   in the case of an investigator who was a member of staff of the Police Service of Northern Ireland, it is to be paid out of money provided by the Chief Constable,

(*c*)   in the case of an investigator who was a member of staff of a department of the Government of the United Kingdom, it is to be paid by the Minister of the Crown in charge of the department or by the department,

(*d*)   in the case of an investigator who was a member of staff of a Northern Ireland department, it is to be paid by the department,

(*e*)   in any other case, it is to be paid by the employer of the investigator.

(7B)   The Secretary of State may by order amend subsection (7A).][2]

(8)   If a forfeiture order is made in respect only of a part of any cash detained under this Chapter, this section has effect in relation to the other part.

Amendments
1   Inserted by the Serious Organised Crime and Police Act 2005, s 100(1), (3).
2   Inserted by the Serious Crime Act 2007, s 79, Sch 11, paras 1, 11.

[302A   Powers for prosecutors to appear in proceedings

(1)   The Director of Public Prosecutions or the Director of Public Prosecutions for Northern Ireland may appear for a constable [or an accredited financial investigator][1] in proceedings under this Chapter if the Director–

(*a*)   is asked by, or on behalf of, a constable [or (as the case may be) an accredited financial investigator]¹ to do so, and

(*b*)   considers it appropriate to do so.

(2)   The Director of Revenue and Customs Prosecutions may appear for the Commissioners for Her Majesty's Revenue and Customs or an officer of Revenue and Customs in proceedings under this Chapter if the Director–

(*a*)   is asked by, or on behalf of, the Commissioners for Her Majesty's Revenue and Customs or (as the case may be) an officer of Revenue and Customs to do so, and

(*b*)   considers it appropriate to do so.

(3)   The Directors may charge fees for the provision of services under this section.

[(4)   The references in subsection (1) to an accredited financial investigator do not include an accredited financial investigator who is an officer of Revenue and Customs but the references in subsection (2) to an officer of Revenue and Customs do include an accredited financial investigator who is an officer of Revenue and Customs.]¹]¹

Amendments

1   Inserted by the Serious Crime Act 2007, ss 79, 84(1), Sch 11, paras 1, 12.

303 'The minimum amount'

(1)   In this Chapter, the minimum amount is the amount in sterling specified in an order made by the Secretary of State after consultation with the Scottish Ministers.

(2)   For that purpose the amount of any cash held in a currency other than sterling must be taken to be its sterling equivalent, calculated in accordance with the prevailing rate of exchange.

[303A Financial investigators

(1)   In this Chapter (apart from this section) any reference in a provision to an accredited financial investigator is a reference to an accredited financial investigator who falls within a description specified in an order made for the purposes of that provision by the Secretary of State under section 453.

(2)   Subsection (1) does not apply to the second reference to an accredited financial investigator in section 290(4)(*c*).

(3)   Where an accredited financial investigator of a particular description–

(*a*)   applies for an order under section 295,

(*b*)   applies for forfeiture under section 298, or

(*c*)   brings an appeal under, or relating to, this Chapter,

any subsequent step in the application or appeal, or any further application or appeal relating to the same matter, may be taken, made or brought by a different accredited financial investigator of the same description.]¹

Amendments

1   Inserted by the Serious Crime Act 2007, s 79, Sch 11, paras 1, 13.

CHAPTER 4
GENERAL

Recoverable property

304 Property obtained through unlawful conduct

(1) Property obtained through unlawful conduct is recoverable property.

(2) But if property obtained through unlawful conduct has been disposed of (since it was so obtained), it is recoverable property only if it is held by a person into whose hands it may be followed.

(3) Recoverable property obtained through unlawful conduct may be followed into the hands of a person obtaining it on a disposal by—

    (*a*) the person who through the conduct obtained the property, or

    (*b*) a person into whose hands it may (by virtue of this subsection) be followed.

305 Tracing property, etc.

(1) Where property obtained through unlawful conduct ('the original property') is or has been recoverable, property which represents the original property is also recoverable property.

(2) If a person enters into a transaction by which—

    (*a*) he disposes of recoverable property, whether the original property or property which (by virtue of this Chapter) represents the original property, and

    (*b*) he obtains other property in place of it,

    the other property represents the original property

(3) If a person disposes of recoverable property which represents the original property, the property may be followed into the hands of the person who obtains it (and it continues to represent the original property).

306 Mixing property

(1) Subsection (2) applies if a person's recoverable property is mixed with other property (whether his property or another's).

(2) The portion of the mixed property which is attributable to the recoverable property represents the property obtained through unlawful conduct.

(3) Recoverable property is mixed with other property if (for example) it is used—

    (*a*) to increase funds held in a bank account,

    (*b*) in part payment for the acquisition of an asset,

    (*c*) for the restoration or improvement of land,

    (*d*) by a person holding a leasehold interest in the property to acquire the freehold.

307 Recoverable property: accruing profits

(1) This section applies where a person who has recoverable property obtains further property consisting of profits accruing in respect of the recoverable property.

(2)   The further property is to be treated as representing the property obtained through unlawful conduct.

308   General exceptions

(1)   If—

(*a*)   a person disposes of recoverable property, and

(*b*)   the person who obtains it on the disposal does so in good faith, for value and without notice that it was recoverable property,

the property may not be followed into that person's hands and, accordingly, it ceases to be recoverable

(2)   If recoverable property is vested, forfeited or otherwise disposed of in pursuance of powers conferred by virtue of this Part, it ceases to be recoverable.

(3)   If—

(*a*)   in pursuance of a judgment in civil proceedings (whether in the United Kingdom or elsewhere), the defendant makes a payment to the claimant or the claimant otherwise obtains property from the defendant,

(*b*)   the claimant's claim is based on the defendant's unlawful conduct, and

(*c*)   apart from this subsection, the sum received, or the property obtained, by the claimant would be recoverable property,

the property ceases to be recoverable

In relation to Scotland, 'claimant' and 'defendant' are to be read as 'pursuer' and 'defender'

(4)   If—

(*a*)   a payment is made to a person in pursuance of a compensation order under Article 14 of the Criminal Justice (Northern Ireland) Order 1994 (S.I. 1994/2795 (N.I. 15)), section 249 of the Criminal Procedure (Scotland) Act 1995 (c. 46) or section 130 of the Powers of Criminal Courts (Sentencing) Act 2000 (c. 6) [or in pursuance of a service compensation order under the Armed Forces Act 2006][1], and

(*b*)   apart from this subsection, the sum received would be recoverable property,

the property ceases to be recoverable

(5)   If—

(*a*)   a payment is made to a person in pursuance of a restitution order under section 27 of the Theft Act (Northern Ireland) 1969 (c. 16 (N.I.)) or section 148(2) of the Powers of Criminal Courts (Sentencing) Act 2000 or a person otherwise obtains any property in pursuance of such an order, and

(*b*)   apart from this subsection, the sum received, or the property obtained, would be recoverable property,

the property ceases to be recoverable

(6)   If—

(a)   in pursuance of an order made by the court under section 382(3) or 383(5) of the Financial Services and Markets Act 2000 (c. 8) (restitution orders), an amount is paid to or distributed among any persons in accordance with the court's directions, and

(b)   apart from this subsection, the sum received by them would be recoverable property,

the property ceases to be recoverable

(7)   If—

(a)   in pursuance of a requirement of the Financial Services Authority under section 384(5) of the Financial Services and Markets Act 2000 (power of authority to require restitution), an amount is paid to or distributed among any persons, and

(b)   apart from this subsection, the sum received by them would be recoverable property,

the property ceases to be recoverable

(8)   Property is not recoverable while a restraint order applies to it, that is—

(a)   an order under section 41, 120 or 190, or

(b)   an order under any corresponding provision of an enactment mentioned in section 8(7)(a) to (g).

(9)   Property is not recoverable if it has been taken into account in deciding the amount of a person's benefit from criminal conduct for the purpose of making a confiscation order, that is—

(a)   an order under section 6, 92 or 156, or

(b)   an order under a corresponding provision of an enactment mentioned in section 8(7)(a) to (g),

and, in relation to an order mentioned in paragraph (b), the reference to the amount of a person's benefit from criminal conduct is to be read as a reference to the corresponding amount under the enactment in question

(10)   Where—

(a)   a person enters into a transaction to which section 305(2) applies, and

(b)   the disposal is one to which subsection (1) or (2) applies,

this section does not affect the recoverability (by virtue of section 305(2)) of any property obtained on the transaction in place of the property disposed of

Amendments

1   Inserted by the Armed Forces Act 2006, s 378(1), Sch 16, para 197.

309   Other exemptions

(1)   An order may provide that property is not recoverable or (as the case may be) associated property if—

(a)   it is prescribed property, or

(*b*)   it is disposed of in pursuance of a prescribed enactment or an enactment of a prescribed description.

(2)   An order may provide that if property is disposed of in pursuance of a prescribed enactment or an enactment of a prescribed description, it is to be treated for the purposes of section 278 as if it had been disposed of in pursuance of a recovery order.

(3)   An order under this section may be made so as to apply to property, or a disposal of property, only in prescribed circumstances; and the circumstances may relate to the property or disposal itself or to a person who holds or has held the property or to any other matter.

(4)   In this section, an order means an order made by the Secretary of State after consultation with the Scottish Ministers, and prescribed means prescribed by the order.

310 Granting interests

(1)   If a person grants an interest in his recoverable property, the question whether the interest is also recoverable is to be determined in the same manner as it is on any other disposal of recoverable property.

(2)   Accordingly, on his granting an interest in the property ('the property in question')—

(*a*)   where the property in question is property obtained through unlawful conduct, the interest is also to be treated as obtained through that conduct,

(*b*)   where the property in question represents in his hands property obtained through unlawful conduct, the interest is also to be treated as representing in his hands the property so obtained.

Insolvency

311 Insolvency

(1)   Proceedings for a recovery order may not be taken or continued in respect of property to which subsection (3) applies unless the appropriate court gives leave and the proceedings are taken or (as the case may be) continued in accordance with any terms imposed by that court.

(2)   An application for an order for the further detention of any cash to which subsection (3) applies may not be made under section 295 unless the appropriate court gives leave.

(3)   This subsection applies to recoverable property, or property associated with it, if—

(*a*)   it is an asset of a company being wound up in pursuance of a resolution for voluntary winding up,

(*b*)   it is an asset of a company and a voluntary arrangement under Part 1 of the 1986 Act, or Part 2 of the 1989 Order, has effect in relation to the company,

(*c*)   an order under section 2 of the 1985 Act, section 286 of the 1986 Act or Article 259 of the 1989 Order (appointment of interim trustee or interim receiver) has effect in relation to the property,

(*d*)   it is an asset comprised in the estate of an individual who has been adjudged bankrupt or, in relation to Scotland, of a person whose estate has been sequestrated,

(e)   it is an asset of an individual and a voluntary arrangement under Part 8 of the 1986 Act, or Part 8 of the 1989 Order, has effect in relation to him, or

(f)   in relation to Scotland, it is property comprised in the estate of a person who has granted a trust deed within the meaning of the 1985 Act.

(4)   An application under this section, or under any provision of the 1986 Act or the 1989 Order, for leave to take proceedings for a recovery order may be made without notice to any person.

(5)   Subsection (4) does not affect any requirement for notice of an application to be given to any person acting as an insolvency practitioner or to the official receiver (whether or not acting as an insolvency practitioner).

(6)   References to the provisions of the 1986 Act in sections 420 and 421 of that Act, or to the provisions of the 1989 Order in Articles 364 or 365 of that Order, (insolvent partnerships and estates of deceased persons) include subsections (1) to (3) above.

(7)   In this section—

(a)   the 1985 Act means the Bankruptcy (Scotland) Act 1985 (c. 66),

(b)   the 1986 Act means the Insolvency Act 1986 (c. 45),

(c)   the 1989 Order means the Insolvency (Northern Ireland) Order 1989 (S.I. 1989/2405 (N.I. 19)),

and in subsection (8) 'the applicable enactment' means whichever enactment mentioned in paragraphs (a) to (c) is relevant to the resolution, arrangement, order or trust deed mentioned in subsection (3)

(8)   In this section—

(a)   an asset means any property within the meaning of the applicable enactment or, where the 1985 Act is the applicable enactment, any property comprised in an estate to which the 1985 Act applies,

(b)   the appropriate court means the court which, in relation to the resolution, arrangement, order or trust deed mentioned in subsection (3), is the court for the purposes of the applicable enactment or, in relation to Northern Ireland, the High Court,

(c)   acting as an insolvency practitioner has the same meaning as in section 433,

(d)   other expressions used in this section and in the applicable enactment have the same meaning as in that enactment.

Delegation of enforcement functions

312 Performance of functions of Scottish Ministers by constables in Scotland

(1)   In Scotland, a constable engaged in temporary service with the Scottish Ministers in connection with their functions under this Part may perform functions, other than those specified in subsection (2), on behalf of the Scottish Ministers.

(2)   The specified functions are the functions conferred on the Scottish Ministers by –

(a)   sections 244(1) and (2) and 256(1) and (7) (proceedings in the Court of Session),

(b)   section 267(2) (trustee for civil recovery),

(*c*)   sections 271(3) and (4) and 272(5) (agreements about associated and joint property),

(*d*)   section 275(3) (pension schemes),

(*e*)   section 282(1) (exemptions),

(*f*)   section 283(5) and (8) (compensation),

(*g*)   section 287(2) (financial threshold),

(*h*)   section 293(1) (code of practice),

(*i*)   section 298(1) (forfeiture),

(*j*)   section 303(1) (minimum amount).

313 ...[1]

[1] ...

Amendments

1   Repealed by the Serious Crime Act 2007, ss 74(2)(*b*), 92, Sch 8, Pt 2, paras 85, 90, Sch 14.

Interpretation

314 Obtaining and disposing of property

(1)   References to a person disposing of his property include a reference—

(*a*)   to his disposing of a part of it, or

(*b*)   to his granting an interest in it,

(or to both); and references to the property disposed of are to any property obtained on the disposal

(2)   A person who makes a payment to another is to be treated as making a disposal of his property to the other, whatever form the payment takes.

(3)   Where a person's property passes to another under a will or intestacy or by operation of law, it is to be treated as disposed of by him to the other.

(4)   A person is only to be treated as having obtained his property for value in a case where he gave unexecuted consideration if the consideration has become executed consideration.

[*Sections 315 only applies to Northern Ireland so is not reproduced in this title.*]

316 General interpretation

(1)   In this Part—

'associated property' has the meaning given by section 245,

'cash' has the meaning given by section 289(6) or (7),

'constable', in relation to Northern Ireland, means a police officer within the meaning of the Police (Northern Ireland) Act 2000 (c. 32),

'country' includes territory,

'the court' (except in sections 253(2) and (3) and 262(2) and (3) and Chapter 3) means the High Court or (in relation to proceedings in Scotland) the Court of Session,

'dealing' with property includes disposing of it, taking possession of it or removing it from the United Kingdom,

'enforcement authority'—

[(*a*)   in relation to England and Wales, means SOCA, the Director of Public Prosecutions, the Director of Revenue and Customs Prosecutions or the Director of the Serious Fraud Office,]¹

(*b*)   in relation to Scotland, means the Scottish Ministers,

[(*c*)   in relation to Northern Ireland, means SOCA, the Director of the Serious Fraud Office or the Director of Public Prosecutions for Northern Ireland,]²

'excepted joint owner' has the meaning given by section 270(4),

'interest', in relation to land—

(*a*)   in the case of land in England and Wales or Northern Ireland, means any legal estate and any equitable interest or power,

(*b*)   in the case of land in Scotland, means any estate, interest, servitude or other heritable right in or over land, including a heritable security,

'interest', in relation to property other than land, includes any right (including a right to possession of the property),

'interim administration order' has the meaning given by section 256(2),

'interim receiving order' has the meaning given by section 246(2),

'the minimum amount' (in Chapter 3) has the meaning given by section 303,

'part', in relation to property, includes a portion,

'premises' has the same meaning as in the Police and Criminal Evidence Act 1984 (c. 60),

['prohibitory property order' has the meaning given by section 255A(2);

'property freezing order' has the meaning given by section 245A(2);]³

'property obtained through unlawful conduct' has the meaning given by section 242,

'recoverable property' is to be read in accordance with sections 304 to 310,

'recovery order' means an order made under section 266,

'respondent' means—

(*a*)   where proceedings are brought by the enforcement authority by virtue of Chapter 2, the person against whom the proceedings are brought,

(*b*)   where no such proceedings have been brought but the enforcement authority has applied for [a property freezing order, an interim receiving order, a prohibitory property order or an]⁴ interim administration order, the person against whom he intends to bring such proceedings,

'share', in relation to an excepted joint owner, has the meaning given by section 270(4),

'unlawful conduct' has the meaning given by section 241,

'value' means market value

(2)   The following provisions apply for the purposes of this Part.

(3)   For the purpose of deciding whether or not property was recoverable at any time (including times before commencement), it is to be assumed that this Part was in force at that and any other relevant time.

(4)   Property is all property wherever situated and includes—

   (*a*)   money,

   (*b*)   all forms of property, real or personal, heritable or moveable,

   (*c*)   things in action and other intangible or incorporeal property.

(5)   Any reference to a person's property (whether expressed as a reference to the property he holds or otherwise) is to be read as follows.

(6)   In relation to land, it is a reference to any interest which he holds in the land.

(7)   In relation to property other than land, it is a reference—

   (*a*)   to the property (if it belongs to him), or

   (*b*)   to any other interest which he holds in the property.

(8)   References to the satisfaction of the enforcement authority's right to recover property obtained through unlawful conduct are to be read in accordance with section 279.

[(8A)   In relation to an order in England and Wales or Northern Ireland which is a recovery order, a property freezing order, an interim receiving order or an order under section 276, references to the enforcement authority are, unless the context otherwise requires, references to the enforcement authority which is seeking, or (as the case may be) has obtained, the order.][2]

(9)   Proceedings against any person for an offence are concluded when—

   (*a*)   the person is convicted or acquitted,

   (*b*)   the prosecution is discontinued or, in Scotland, the trial diet is deserted simpliciter, or

   (*c*)   the jury is discharged without a finding [otherwise than in circumstances where the proceedings are continued without a jury][5].

Amendments

1   Substituted by the Serious Crime Act 2007, s 74(2)(*b*), Sch 8, Pt 2, paras 85, 91(1), (2)(*a*).
2   Inserted by the Serious Crime Act 2007, s 74(2)(*b*), Sch 8, Pt 2, paras 85, 91(1), (2)(*b*), (3).
3   Inserted by the Serious Organised Crime and Police Act 2005, s 109, Sch 6, paras 4, 22(1), (2).
4   Substituted by the Serious Organised Crime and Police Act 2005, s 109, Sch 6, paras 4, 22(1), (3).
5   Inserted by the Criminal Justice Act 2003, s 331, Sch 36, Pt 4, para 78.

PART 6
REVENUE FUNCTIONS

General functions

317   [SOCA's][1] general Revenue functions

(1)   For the purposes of this section the qualifying condition is that [SOCA][1] has reasonable grounds to suspect that—

(*a*)   income arising or a gain accruing to a person in respect of a chargeable period is chargeable to income tax or is a chargeable gain (as the case may be) and arises or accrues as a result of the person's or another's criminal conduct (whether wholly or partly and whether directly or indirectly), or

(*b*)   a company is chargeable to corporation tax on its profits arising in respect of a chargeable period and the profits arise as a result of the company's or another person's criminal conduct (whether wholly or partly and whether directly or indirectly).

(2)   If the qualifying condition is satisfied [SOCA][1] may serve on the Commissioners of Inland Revenue (the Board) a notice which—

(*a*)   specifies the person or the company (as the case may be) and the period, and

(*b*)   states that [SOCA][1] intends to carry out, in relation to the person or the company (as the case may be) and in respect of the period, such of the general Revenue functions as are specified in the notice.

(3)   Service of a notice under subsection (2) vests in [SOCA][1], in relation to the person or the company (as the case may be) and in respect of the period, such of the general Revenue functions as are specified in the notice; but this is subject to section 318.

(4)   [SOCA][1]—

(*a*)   may at any time serve on the Board a notice of withdrawal of the notice under subsection (2);

(*b*)   must serve such a notice of withdrawal on the Board if the qualifying condition ceases to be satisfied.

(5)   A notice under subsection (2) and a notice of withdrawal under subsection (4) may be in respect of one or more periods.

(6)   Service of a notice under subsection (4) divests [SOCA][1] of the functions concerned in relation to the person or the company (as the case may be) and in respect of the period or periods specified in the notice.

(7)   The vesting of a function in [SOCA][1] under this section does not divest the Board or an officer of the Board of the function.

(8)   If—

(*a*)   apart from this section the Board's authorisation would be required for the exercise of a function, and

(*b*)   the function is vested in [SOCA][1] under this section,

the authorisation is not required in relation to the function as so vested

(9)   It is immaterial whether a chargeable period or any part of it falls before or after the passing of this Act.

Amendments

1   Substituted by the Serious Crime Act 2007, s 74(2)(*c*), Sch 8, Pt 3, paras 92, 93.

318   Revenue functions regarding employment

(1)   Subsection (2) applies if—

(*a*)   [SOCA]¹ serves a notice or notices under section 317(2) in relation to a company and in respect of a period or periods, and

(*b*)   the company is an employer.

(2)   The general Revenue functions vested in [SOCA]¹ do not include functions relating to any requirement which—

(*a*)   is imposed on the company in its capacity as employer, and

(*b*)   relates to a year of assessment which does not fall wholly within the period or periods.

(3)   Subsection (4) applies if—

(*a*)   [SOCA]¹ serves a notice or notices under section 317(2) in relation to an individual and in respect of a year or years of assessment, and

(*b*)   the individual is a self-employed earner.

(4)   The general Revenue functions vested in [SOCA]¹ do not include functions relating to any liability to pay Class 2 contributions in respect of a period which does not fall wholly within the year or years of assessment.

(5)   In this section in its application to Great Britain—

(*a*)   'self-employed earner' has the meaning given by section 2(1)(*b*) of the Social Security Contributions and Benefits Act 1992 (c. 4);

(*b*)   'Class 2 contributions' must be construed in accordance with section 1(2)(*c*) of that Act.

(6)   In this section in its application to Northern Ireland—

(*a*)   'self-employed earner' has the meaning given by section 2(1)(*b*) of the Social Security Contributions and Benefits (Northern Ireland) Act 1992 (c. 7);

(*b*)   'Class 2 contributions' must be construed in accordance with section 1(2)(*c*) of that Act.

Amendments

1   Substituted by the Serious Crime Act 2007, s 74(2)(*c*), Sch 8, Pt 3, paras 92, 94.

319   Source of income

(1)   For the purpose of the exercise by [SOCA]¹ of any function vested in [it]¹ by virtue of this Part it is immaterial that [SOCA]¹ cannot identify a source for any income.

(2)   An assessment made by [SOCA]¹ under section 29 of the Taxes Management Act 1970 (c. 9) (assessment where loss of tax discovered) in respect of income charged to tax under [Chapter 8 of Part 5 of the Income Tax (Trading and Other Income) Act 2005]² must not be reduced or quashed only because it does not specify (to any extent) the source of the income.

(3)   If [SOCA]¹ serves on the Board a notice of withdrawal under section 317(4), any assessment made by [it]¹ under section 29 of the Taxes Management Act 1970 is invalid to the extent that it does not specify a source for the income.

(4)   Subsections (2) and (3) apply in respect of years of assessment whenever occurring.

Amendments
1   Substituted by the Serious Crime Act 2007, s 74(2)(*c*), Sch 8, Pt 3, paras 92, 95.
2   Substituted by the Income Tax (Trading and Other Income) Act 2005, s 882(1), Sch 1, Pt 2, paras 581, 582.

320   ...[1]

...[1]

Amendments
1   Repealed by the Transfer of Tribunal Functions and Revenue and Customs Appeals Order 2009, SI 2009/56, art 3(1), Sch 1, para 333.

Inheritance tax functions

321   [SOCA's][1] functions: transfers of value

(1)   For the purposes of this section the qualifying condition is that [SOCA][1] has reasonable grounds to suspect that—

    (*a*)   there has been a transfer of value within the meaning of the Inheritance Tax Act 1984 (c. 51), and

    (*b*)   the value transferred by [the transfer of value][1] is attributable (in whole or part) to criminal property.

(2)   If the qualifying condition is satisfied [SOCA][1] may serve on the Board a notice which—

    (*a*)   specifies the transfer of value, and

    (*b*)   states that [SOCA][1] intends to carry out the Revenue inheritance tax functions in relation to the transfer.

(3)   Service of a notice under subsection (2) vests in [SOCA][1] the Revenue inheritance tax functions in relation to the transfer.

(4)   [SOCA][1]—

    (*a*)   may at any time serve on the Board a notice of withdrawal of the notice under subsection (2);

    (*b*)   must serve such a notice of withdrawal on the Board if the qualifying condition ceases to be satisfied.

(5)   Service of a notice under subsection (4) divests [SOCA][1] of the Revenue inheritance tax functions in relation to the transfer.

(6)   The vesting of a function in [SOCA][1] under this section does not divest the Board or an officer of the Board of the function.

(7)   It is immaterial whether a transfer of value is suspected to have occurred before or after the passing of this Act.

Amendments
1   Substituted by the Serious Crime Act 2007, s 74(2)(*c*), Sch 8, Pt 3, paras 92, 97.

322 [SOCA's][1] functions: certain settlements

(1)   For the purposes of this section the qualifying condition is that [SOCA][1] has reasonable grounds to suspect that—

   (*a*)   all or part of the property comprised in a settlement is relevant property for the purposes of Chapter 3 of Part 3 of the Inheritance Tax Act 1984 (settlements without interest in possession), and

   (*b*)   the relevant property is (in whole or part) criminal property.

(2)   If the qualifying condition is satisfied [SOCA][1] may serve on the Board a notice which—

   (*a*)   specifies the settlement concerned,

   (*b*)   states that [SOCA][1] intends to carry out the Revenue inheritance tax functions in relation to the settlement, and

   (*c*)   states the period for which [SOCA][1] intends to carry them out.

(3)   Service of a notice under subsection (2) vests in [SOCA][1] the Revenue inheritance tax functions in relation to the settlement for the period.

(4)   [SOCA][1]—

   (*a*)   may at any time serve on the Board a notice of withdrawal of the notice under subsection (2);

   (*b*)   must serve such a notice of withdrawal on the Board if the qualifying condition ceases to be satisfied.

(5)   Service of a notice under subsection (4) divests [SOCA][1] of the Revenue inheritance tax functions in relation to the settlement for the period.

(6)   The vesting of a function in [SOCA][1] under this section does not divest the Board or an officer of the Board of the function.

(7)   It is immaterial whether the settlement is commenced or a charge to tax arises or a period or any part of it falls before or after the passing of this Act.

Amendments

1   Substituted by the Serious Crime Act 2007, s 74(2)(*c*), Sch 8, Pt 3, paras 92, 98.

General

323 Functions

(1)   The general Revenue functions are such of the functions vested in the Board or in an officer of the Board as relate to any of the following matters—

   (*a*)   income tax;

   (*b*)   capital gains tax;

   (*c*)   corporation tax;

   (*d*)   national insurance contributions;

   (*e*)   statutory sick pay;

   (*f*)   statutory maternity pay;

[(*g*)   ordinary statutory paternity pay;]¹

[(*ga*) additional statutory paternity pay;]²

(*h*)   statutory adoption pay;

(*i*)   student loans.

(2)   The Revenue inheritance tax functions are such functions vested in the Board or in an officer of the Board as relate to inheritance tax. ,

(3)   But the general Revenue functions and the Revenue inheritance tax functions do not include any of the following functions—

(*a*)   functions relating to the making of subordinate legislation (within the meaning given by section 21(1) of the Interpretation Act 1978 (c. 30));

(*b*)   the function of the prosecution of offences;

(*c*)   the function of authorising an officer for the purposes of section 20BA of the Taxes Management Act 1970 (c. 9) (orders for delivery of documents);

(*d*)   the function of giving information under that section;

(*e*)   ...³

(*f*)   ...³

(4)   For the purposes of this section in its application to Great Britain—

(*a*)   national insurance contributions are contributions payable under Part 1 of the Social Security Contributions and Benefits Act 1992 (c. 4);

(*b*)   'statutory sick pay' must be construed in accordance with section 151(1) of that Act;

(*c*)   'statutory maternity pay' must be construed in accordance with section 164(1) of that Act;

[(*d*)   'ordinary statutory paternity pay' must be construed in accordance with sections 171ZA and 171ZB of that Act;]¹

[(*da*) 'additional statutory paternity pay' must be construed in accordance with sections 171ZEA and 171ZEB of that Act;]²

(*e*)   'statutory adoption pay' must be construed in accordance with section 171ZL of that Act;

(*f*)   'student loans' must be construed in accordance with the Education (Student Loans) (Repayment) Regulations 2000 (S.I. 2000/944).

(5)   For the purposes of this section in its application to Northern Ireland—

(*a*)   national insurance contributions are contributions payable under Part 1 of the Social Security Contributions and Benefits (Northern Ireland) Act 1992 (c. 7);

(*b*)   'statutory sick pay' must be construed in accordance with section 147(1) of that Act;

(*c*)   'statutory maternity pay' must be construed in accordance with section 160(1) of that Act;

(*d*) ['ordinary statutory paternity pay' and 'additional statutory paternity pay']¹ must be construed in accordance with any Northern Ireland legislation which corresponds to Part 12ZA of the Social Security Contributions and Benefits Act 1992;

(*e*) 'statutory adoption pay' must be construed in accordance with any Northern Ireland legislation which corresponds to Part 12ZB of that Act;

(*f*) 'student loans' must be construed in accordance with the Education (Student Loans) (Repayment) Regulations (Northern Ireland) 2000 (S.R. 2000/121).

Amendments
1   Substituted by the Work and Families Act 2006, s 11(1), Sch 1, para 59.
2   Inserted by the Work and Families Act 2006, s 11(1), Sch 1, para 59(1), (2), (3).
3   Repealed by the Finance Act 2007, s 114, Sch 27, Pt 5(1).

324   Exercise of Revenue functions

(1)   This section applies in relation to the exercise by [SOCA]¹ of—

(*a*)   general Revenue functions;

(*b*)   Revenue inheritance tax functions.

(2)   [Section 2B(2)]¹ does not apply.

(3)   [SOCA]¹ must apply—

(*a*)   any interpretation of the law which has been published by the Board;

(*b*)   any concession which has been published by the Board and which is available generally to any person falling within its terms.

(4)   [SOCA]¹ must also take account of any material published by the Board which does not fall within subsection (3).

(5)   [SOCA]¹ must provide the Board with such documents and information as [the Board]¹ consider appropriate.

(6)   'Concession' includes any practice, interpretation or other statement in the nature of a concession.

Amendments
1   Substituted by the Serious Crime Act 2007, s 74(2)(*c*), Sch 8, Pt 3, paras 92, 99.

325   Declarations

(1)   ...¹

[(2)   Every member of SOCA's staff who is assigned to carry out any of SOCA's functions under this Part must, as soon as practicable after being so assigned, make a declaration in the form set out in Schedule 8 before a person nominated by the Director General of SOCA for the purpose.]²

Amendments
1   Repealed by the Serious Crime Act 2007, ss 74(2)(*c*), 92, Sch 8, Pt 3, paras 92, 100(1), (2), Sch 14.
2   Substituted by the Serious Crime Act 2007, s 74(2)(*c*), Sch 8, Pt 3, paras 92, 100(1), (3).

326 Interpretation

(1)   Criminal conduct is conduct which—

    (*a*)   constitutes an offence in any part of the United Kingdom, or

    (*b*)   would constitute an offence in any part of the United Kingdom if it occurred there.

(2)   But criminal conduct does not include conduct constituting an offence relating to a matter under the care and management of the Board.

(3)   In applying subsection (1) it is immaterial whether conduct occurred before or after the passing of this Act.

(4)   Property is criminal property if it constitutes a person's benefit from criminal conduct or it represents such a benefit (in whole or part and whether directly or indirectly); and it is immaterial—

    (*a*)   who carried out the conduct;

    (*b*)   who benefited from it.

(5)   A person benefits from conduct if he obtains property as a result of or in connection with the conduct.

(6)   If a person obtains a pecuniary advantage as a result of or in connection with conduct, he is to be taken to obtain as a result of or in connection with the conduct a sum of money equal to the value of the pecuniary advantage.

(7)   References to property or a pecuniary advantage obtained in connection with conduct include references to property or a pecuniary advantage obtained in both that connection and some other.

(8)   If a person benefits from conduct his benefit is the property obtained as a result of or in connection with the conduct.

(9)   Property is all property wherever situated and includes—

    (*a*)   money;

    (*b*)   all forms of property, real or personal, heritable or moveable;

    (*c*)   things in action and other intangible or incorporeal property.

(10)   The following rules apply in relation to property—

    (*a*)   property is obtained by a person if he obtains an interest in it;

    (*b*)   references to an interest, in relation to land in England and Wales or Northern Ireland, are to any legal estate or equitable interest or power;

    (*c*)   references to an interest, in relation to land in Scotland, are to any estate, interest, servitude or other heritable right in or over land, including a heritable security;

    (*d*)   references to an interest, in relation to property other than land, include references to a right (including a right to possession).

(11)   Any reference to an officer of the Board includes a reference to—

    (*a*)   a collector of taxes;

    (*b*)   an inspector of taxes.

(12)   Expressions used in this Part and in the Taxes Acts have the same meaning as in the Taxes Acts (within the meaning given by section 118 of the Taxes Management Act 1970 (c. 9)).

(13)   This section applies for the purposes of this Part.

PART 7
MONEY LAUNDERING

Offences

327   Concealing etc

(1)   A person commits an offence if he—

(*a*)   conceals criminal property;

(*b*)   disguises criminal property;

(*c*)   converts criminal property;

(*d*)   transfers criminal property;

(*e*)   removes criminal property from England and Wales or from Scotland or from Northern Ireland.

(2)   But a person does not commit such an offence if—

(*a*)   he makes an authorised disclosure under section 338 and (if the disclosure is made before he does the act mentioned in subsection (1)) he has the appropriate consent;

(*b*)   he intended to make such a disclosure but had a reasonable excuse for not doing so;

(*c*)   the act he does is done in carrying out a function he has relating to the enforcement of any provision of this Act or of any other enactment relating to criminal conduct or benefit from criminal conduct.

[(2A)   Nor does a person commit an offence under subsection (1) if—

(*a*)   he knows, or believes on reasonable grounds, that the relevant criminal conduct occurred in a particular country or territory outside the United Kingdom, and

(*b*)   the relevant criminal conduct—

(i)   was not, at the time it occurred, unlawful under the criminal law then applying in that country or territory, and

(ii)   is not of a description prescribed by an order made by the Secretary of State.

(2B)   In subsection (2A) 'the relevant criminal conduct' is the criminal conduct by reference to which the property concerned is criminal property.

(2C)   A deposit-taking body that does an act mentioned in paragraph (c) or (d) of subsection (1) does not commit an offence under that subsection if—

(*a*)   it does the act in operating an account maintained with it, and (*b*) the value of the criminal property concerned is less than the threshold amount determined under section 339A for the act.]¹

(3) Concealing or disguising criminal property includes concealing or disguising its nature, source, location, disposition, movement or ownership or any rights with respect to it.

Amendments

1   Inserted by the Serious Organised Crime and Police Act 2005, ss 102(1), (2), 103(1), (2).

328 Arrangements

(1) A person commits an offence if he enters into or becomes concerned in an arrangement which he knows or suspects facilitates (by whatever means) the acquisition, retention, use or control of criminal property by or on behalf of another person.

(2) But a person does not commit such an offence if—

(*a*) he makes an authorised disclosure under section 338 and (if the disclosure is made before he does the act mentioned in subsection (1)) he has the appropriate consent;

(*b*) he intended to make such a disclosure but had a reasonable excuse for not doing so;

(*c*) the act he does is done in carrying out a function he has relating to the enforcement of any provision of this Act or of any other enactment relating to criminal conduct or benefit from criminal conduct.

[(3) Nor does a person commit an offence under subsection (1) if—

(*a*) he knows, or believes on reasonable grounds, that the relevant criminal conduct occurred in a particular country or territory outside the United Kingdom, and

(*b*) the relevant criminal conduct—

(i) was not, at the time it occurred, unlawful under the criminal law then applying in that country or territory, and

(ii) is not of a description prescribed by an order made by the Secretary of State.

(4) In subsection (3) 'the relevant criminal conduct' is the criminal conduct by reference to which the property concerned is criminal property.

(5) A deposit-taking body that does an act mentioned in subsection (1) does not commit an offence under that subsection if—

(*a*) it does the act in operating an account maintained with it, and

(*b*) the arrangement facilitates the acquisition, retention, use or control of criminal property of a value that is less than the threshold amount determined under section 339A for the act.]¹

Amendments

1   Inserted by the Serious Organised Crime and Police Act 2005, ss 102(1), (3), 103(1), (3).

329   Acquisition, use and possession

(1)   A person commits an offence if he—

(a)   acquires criminal property;

(b)   uses criminal property;

(c)   has possession of criminal property.

(2)   But a person does not commit such an offence if—

(a)   he makes an authorised disclosure under section 338 and (if the disclosure is made before he does the act mentioned in subsection (1)) he has the appropriate consent;

(b)   he intended to make such a disclosure but had a reasonable excuse for not doing so;

(c)   he acquired or used or had possession of the property for adequate consideration;

(d)   the act he does is done in carrying out a function he has relating to the enforcement of any provision of this Act or of any other enactment relating to criminal conduct or benefit from criminal conduct.

[(2A)   Nor does a person commit an offence under subsection (1) if—

(a)   he knows, or believes on reasonable grounds, that the relevant criminal conduct occurred in a particular country or territory outside the United Kingdom, and

(b)   the relevant criminal conduct—

(i)   was not, at the time it occurred, unlawful under the criminal law then applying in that country or territory, and

(ii)   is not of a description prescribed by an order made by the Secretary of State.

(2B)   In subsection (2A) 'the relevant criminal conduct' is the criminal conduct by reference to which the property concerned is criminal property.

(2C)   A deposit-taking body that does an act mentioned in subsection (1) does not commit an offence under that subsection if—

(a)   it does the act in operating an account maintained with it, and

(b)   the value of the criminal property concerned is less than the threshold amount determined under section 339A for the act.]¹

(3)   For the purposes of this section—

(a)   a person acquires property for inadequate consideration if the value of the consideration is significantly less than the value of the property;

(b)   a person uses or has possession of property for inadequate consideration if the value of the consideration is significantly less than the value of the use or possession;

(c)   the provision by a person of goods or services which he knows or suspects may help another to carry out criminal conduct is not consideration.

Amendments

1   Inserted by the Serious Organised Crime and Police Act 2005, ss 102(1), (4), 103(1), (4).

330 Failure to disclose: regulated sector

(1) A person commits an offence if [the conditions in subsections (2) to (4) are satisfied]¹.

(2) The first condition is that he—

(*a*) knows or suspects, or

(*b*) has reasonable grounds for knowing or suspecting,

that another person is engaged in money laundering

(3) The second condition is that the information or other matter—

(*a*) on which his knowledge or suspicion is based, or

(*b*) which gives reasonable grounds for such knowledge or suspicion,

came to him in the course of a business in the regulated sector

[(3A) The third condition is—

(*a*) that he can identify the other person mentioned in subsection (2) or the whereabouts of any of the laundered property, or

(*b*) that he believes, or it is reasonable to expect him to believe, that the information or other matter mentioned in subsection (3) will or may assist in identifying that other person or the whereabouts of any of the laundered property.]²

[(4) The fourth condition is that he does not make the required disclosure to—

(*a*) a nominated officer, or

(*b*) a person authorised for the purposes of this Part by the Director General of [SOCA]³,

as soon as is practicable after the information or other matter mentioned in subsection (3) comes to him.

(5) The required disclosure is a disclosure of—

(*a*) the identity of the other person mentioned in subsection (2), if he knows it,

(*b*) the whereabouts of the laundered property, so far as he knows it, and

(*c*) the information or other matter mentioned in subsection (3).]¹

[(5A) The laundered property is the property forming the subject-matter of the money laundering that he knows or suspects, or has reasonable grounds for knowing or suspecting, that other person to be engaged in.]²

(6) But he does not commit an offence under this section if—

(*a*) he has a reasonable excuse for not making the required disclosure,

(*b*) he is a professional legal adviser [or ...⁴ relevant professional adviser]⁵ and—

(i) if he knows either of the things mentioned in subsection (5)(a) and (b), he knows the thing because of information or other matter that came to him in privileged circumstances, or

(ii) the information or other matter mentioned in subsection (3) came to him in privileged circumstances, or

(*c*) subsection (7) [or (7B)]⁵ applies to him.]¹

(7) This subsection applies to a person if—

245

(a)   he does not know or suspect that another person is engaged in money laundering, and

(b)   he has not been provided by his employer with such training as is specified by the Secretary of State by order for the purposes of this section.

[(7A) Nor does a person commit an offence under this section if—

(a)   he knows, or believes on reasonable grounds, that the money laundering is occurring in a particular country or territory outside the United Kingdom, and

(b)   the money laundering—

(i)   is not unlawful under the criminal law applying in that country or territory, and

(ii)   is not of a description prescribed in an order made by the Secretary of State.]²

[(7B) This subsection applies to a person if—

(a)   he is employed by, or is in partnership with, a professional legal adviser or a relevant professional adviser to provide the adviser with assistance or support,

(b)   the information or other matter mentioned in subsection (3) comes to the person in connection with the provision of such assistance or support, and

(c)   the information or other matter came to the adviser in privileged circumstances.]⁵

(8)   In deciding whether a person committed an offence under this section the court must consider whether he followed any relevant guidance which was at the time concerned—

(a)   issued by a supervisory authority or any other appropriate body,

(b)   approved by the Treasury, and

(c)   published in a manner it approved as appropriate in its opinion to bring the guidance to the attention of persons likely to be affected by it.

(9)   A disclosure to a nominated officer is a disclosure which—

(a)   is made to a person nominated by the alleged offender's employer to receive disclosures under this section, and

(b)   is made in the course of the alleged offender's employment …⁶.

[(9A) But a disclosure which satisfies paragraphs (a) and (b) of subsection (9) is not to be taken as a disclosure to a nominated officer if the person making the disclosure—

(a)   is a professional legal adviser [or …⁴ relevant professional adviser]⁵,

(b)   makes it for the purpose of obtaining advice about making a disclosure under this section, and

(c)   does not intend it to be a disclosure under this section.]²

(10)   Information or other matter comes to a professional legal adviser [or …⁴ relevant professional adviser]⁵ in privileged circumstances if it is communicated or given to him—

(a)   by (or by a representative of) a client of his in connection with the giving by the adviser of legal advice to the client,

(b)   by (or by a representative of) a person seeking legal advice from the adviser, or (*c*)   by a person in connection with legal proceedings or contemplated legal proceedings.

(11)   But subsection (10) does not apply to information or other matter which is communicated or given with the intention of furthering a criminal purpose.

(12)   Schedule 9 has effect for the purpose of determining what is—

(*a*)   a business in the regulated sector;

(*b*)   a supervisory authority.

(13)   An appropriate body is any body which regulates or is representative of any trade, profession, business or employment carried on by the alleged offender.

[(14)   A relevant professional adviser is an accountant, auditor or tax adviser who is a member of a professional body which is established for accountants, auditors or tax advisers (as the case may be) and which makes provision for—

(*a*)   testing the competence of those seeking admission to membership of such a body as a condition for such admission; and

(*b*)   imposing and maintaining professional and ethical standards for its members, as well as imposing sanctions for non-compliance with those standards.][5]

Amendments

1   Substituted by the Serious Organised Crime and Police Act 2005, s 104(1), (2), (3).
2   Inserted by the Serious Organised Crime and Police Act 2005, ss 102(1), (5), 104(1), (3), 106(1), (2).
3   Substituted by the Serious Crime Act 2007, s 74(2)(*f*), Sch 8, Pt 6, paras 121, 126.
4   Repealed by the Terrorism Act 2000 and Proceeds of Crime Act 2002 (Amendment) Regulations 2007, SI 2007/3398, reg 3, Sch 2, paras 1, 2.
5   Inserted by the Proceeds of Crime Act 2002 and Money Laundering Regulations 2003 (Amendment) Order 2006, SI 2006/308, art 2.
6   Repealed by the Serious Organised Crime and Police Act 2005, ss 105(1), (2), 174(2), Sch 17, Pt 2 (as amended by the Serious Organised Crime and Police Act 2005 (Amendment) Order 2005, SI 2005/3496, art 5).

331   Failure to disclose: nominated officers in the regulated sector

(1)   A person nominated to receive disclosures under section 330 commits an offence if the conditions in subsections (2) to (4) are satisfied.

(2)   The first condition is that he—

(*a*)   knows or suspects, or

(*b*)   has reasonable grounds for knowing or suspecting,

that another person is engaged in money laundering

(3)   The second condition is that the information or other matter—

(*a*)   on which his knowledge or suspicion is based, or

(*b*)   which gives reasonable grounds for such knowledge or suspicion,

came to him in consequence of a disclosure made under section 330

[(3A)   The third condition is—

(*a*)   that he knows the identity of the other person mentioned in subsection (2), or the whereabouts of any of the laundered property, in consequence of a disclosure made under section 330,

(b)   that that other person, or the whereabouts of any of the laundered property, can be identified from the information or other matter mentioned in subsection (3), or

(c)   that he believes, or it is reasonable to expect him to believe, that the information or other matter will or may assist in identifying that other person or the whereabouts of any of the laundered property.]¹

[(4)   The fourth condition is that he does not make the required disclosure to a person authorised for the purposes of this Part by the Director General of [SOCA]² as soon as is practicable after the information or other matter mentioned in subsection (3) comes to him.

(5)   The required disclosure is a disclosure of—

(a)   the identity of the other person mentioned in subsection (2), if disclosed to him under section 330,

(b)   the whereabouts of the laundered property, so far as disclosed to him under section 330, and

(c)   the information or other matter mentioned in subsection (3).]³

[(5A) The laundered property is the property forming the subject-matter of the money laundering that he knows or suspects, or has reasonable grounds for knowing or suspecting, that other person to be engaged in.]¹

[(6)   But he does not commit an offence under this section if he has a reasonable excuse for not making the required disclosure.]³

[(6A) Nor does a person commit an offence under this section if—

(a)   he knows, or believes on reasonable grounds, that the money laundering is occurring in a particular country or territory outside the United Kingdom, and

(b)   the money laundering—

(i)   is not unlawful under the criminal law applying in that country or territory, and

(ii)   is not of a description prescribed in an order made by the Secretary of State.]¹

(7)   In deciding whether a person committed an offence under this section the court must consider whether he followed any relevant guidance which was at the time concerned—

(a)   issued by a supervisory authority or any other appropriate body,

(b)   approved by the Treasury, and

(c)   published in a manner it approved as appropriate in its opinion to bring the guidance to the attention of persons likely to be affected by it.

(8)   Schedule 9 has effect for the purpose of determining what is a supervisory authority.

(9)   An appropriate body is a body which regulates or is representative of a trade, profession, business or employment.

Amendments

1   Inserted by the Serious Organised Crime and Police Act 2005, ss 102(1), (6), 104(1), (4).
2   Substituted by the Serious Crime Act 2007, s 74(2)(f), Sch 8, Pt 6, paras 121, 127.
3   Substituted by the Serious Organised Crime and Police Act 2005, s 104(1), (4).

332 Failure to disclose: other nominated officers

(1) A person nominated to receive disclosures under section 337 or 338 commits an offence if the conditions in subsections (2) to (4) are satisfied.

(2) The first condition is that he knows or suspects that another person is engaged in money laundering.

(3) The second condition is that the information or other matter on which his knowledge or suspicion is based came to him in consequence of a disclosure made under [the applicable section][1].

[(3A) The third condition is—

    (*a*) that he knows the identity of the other person mentioned in subsection (2), or the whereabouts of any of the laundered property, in consequence of a disclosure made under the applicable section,

    (*b*) that that other person, or the whereabouts of any of the laundered property, can be identified from the information or other matter mentioned in subsection (3), or

    (*c*) that he believes, or it is reasonable to expect him to believe, that the information or other matter will or may assist in identifying that other person or the whereabouts of any of the laundered property.][2]

[(4) The fourth condition is that he does not make the required disclosure to a person authorised for the purposes of this Part by the Director General of [SOCA][3] as soon as is practicable after the information or other matter mentioned in subsection (3) comes to him.

(5) The required disclosure is a disclosure of—

    (*a*) the identity of the other person mentioned in subsection (2), if disclosed to him under the applicable section,

    (*b*) the whereabouts of the laundered property, so far as disclosed to him under the applicable section, and

    (*c*) the information or other matter mentioned in subsection (3).][1]

[(5A) The laundered property is the property forming the subject-matter of the money laundering that he knows or suspects that other person to be engaged in.

(5B) The applicable section is section 337 or, as the case may be, section 338.][2]

[(6) But he does not commit an offence under this section if he has a reasonable excuse for not making the required disclosure.][1]

[(7) Nor does a person commit an offence under this section if—

    (*a*) he knows, or believes on reasonable grounds, that the money laundering is occurring in a particular country or territory outside the United Kingdom, and

    (*b*) the money laundering—

        (i) is not unlawful under the criminal law applying in that country or territory, and

        (ii) is not of a description prescribed in an order made by the Secretary of State.][3]

Amendments

1   Substituted by the Serious Organised Crime and Police Act 2005, s 104(1), (5), (6).
2   Inserted by the Serious Organised Crime and Police Act 2005, ss 102(1), (7), 104(1), (6).
3   Substituted by the Serious Crime Act 2007, s 74(2)(*f*), Sch 8, Pt 6, paras 121, 128.

333 ...[1]

   ...[1]

Amendments

1   Repealed by the Terrorism Act 2000 and Proceeds of Crime Act 2002 (Amendment) Regulations 2007, SI 2007/3398, reg 3, Sch 2, paras 1, 3.

[333A   Tipping off: regulated sector

(1)   A person commits an offence if—

(*a*)   the person discloses any matter within subsection (2);

(*b*)   the disclosure is likely to prejudice any investigation that might be conducted following the disclosure referred to in that subsection; and

(*c*)   the information on which the disclosure is based came to the person in the course of a business in the regulated sector.

(2)   The matters are that the person or another person has made a disclosure under this Part—

(*a*)   to a constable,

(*b*)   to an officer of Revenue and Customs,

(*c*)   to a nominated officer, or

(*d*)   to a member of staff of the Serious Organised Crime Agency authorised for the purposes of this Part by the Director General of that Agency,

of information that came to that person in the course of a business in the regulated sector.

(3)   A person commits an offence if—

(*a*)   the person discloses that an investigation into allegations that an offence under this Part has been committed is being contemplated or is being carried out;

(*b*)   the disclosure is likely to prejudice that investigation; and

(*c*)   the information on which the disclosure is based came to the person in the course of a business in the regulated sector.

(4)   A person guilty of an offence under this section is liable—

(*a*)   on summary conviction to imprisonment for a term not exceeding three months, or to a fine not exceeding level 5 on the standard scale, or to both;

(*b*)   on conviction on indictment to imprisonment for a term not exceeding two years, or to a fine, or to both.

(5)   This section is subject to—

(*a*)   section 333B (disclosures within an undertaking or group etc),

(*b*)   section 333C (other permitted disclosures between institutions etc), and (*c*)   section 333D (other permitted disclosures etc).]¹

Amendments

1   Inserted by the Terrorism Act 2000 and Proceeds of Crime Act 2002 (Amendment) Regulations 2007, SI 2007/3398, reg 3, Sch 2, paras 1, 4.

[333B   Disclosures within an undertaking or group etc

(1)   An employee, officer or partner of an undertaking does not commit an offence under section 333A if the disclosure is to an employee, officer or partner of the same undertaking.

(2)   A person does not commit an offence under section 333A in respect of a disclosure by a credit institution or a financial institution if—

(*a*)   the disclosure is to a credit institution or a financial institution,

(*b*)   the institution to whom the disclosure is made is situated in an EEA State or in a country or territory imposing equivalent money laundering requirements, and

(*c*)   both the institution making the disclosure and the institution to whom it is made belong to the same group.

(3)   In subsection (2) 'group' has the same meaning as in Directive 2002/87/EC of the European Parliament and of the Council of 16th December 2002 on the supplementary supervision of credit institutions, insurance undertakings and investment firms in a financial conglomerate.

(4)   A professional legal adviser or a relevant professional adviser does not commit an offence under section 333A if—

(*a*)   the disclosure is to professional legal adviser or a relevant professional adviser,

(*b*)   both the person making the disclosure and the person to whom it is made carry on business in an EEA State or in a country or territory imposing equivalent money laundering requirements, and

(*c*)   those persons perform their professional activities within different undertakings that share common ownership, management or control.]¹

Amendments

1   Inserted by the Terrorism Act 2000 and Proceeds of Crime Act 2002 (Amendment) Regulations 2007, SI 2007/3398, reg 3, Sch 2, paras 1, 4.

[333C   Other permitted disclosures between institutions etc

(1)   This section applies to a disclosure—

(*a*)   by a credit institution to another credit institution,

(*b*)   by a financial institution to another financial institution,

(*c*)   by a professional legal adviser to another professional legal adviser, or

(*d*)   by a relevant professional adviser of a particular kind to another relevant professional adviser of the same kind.

(2)   A person does not commit an offence under section 333A in respect of a disclosure to which this section applies if—

(*a*)   the disclosure relates to—

    (i)   a client or former client of the institution or adviser making the disclosure and the institution or adviser to whom it is made,

    (ii)   a transaction involving them both, or

    (iii)   the provision of a service involving them both;

(*b*)   the disclosure is for the purpose only of preventing an offence under this Part of this Act;

(*c*)   the institution or adviser to whom the disclosure is made is situated in an EEA State or in a country or territory imposing equivalent money laundering requirements; and

(*d*)   the institution or adviser making the disclosure and the institution or adviser to whom it is made are subject to equivalent duties of professional confidentiality and the protection of personal data (within the meaning of section 1 of the Data Protection Act 1998).][1]

Amendments

1   Inserted by the Terrorism Act 2000 and Proceeds of Crime Act 2002 (Amendment) Regulations 2007, SI 2007/3398, reg 3, Sch 2, paras 1, 4.

[333D Other permitted disclosures etc

(1)   A person does not commit an offence under section 333A if the disclosure is—

(*a*)   to the authority that is the supervisory authority for that person by virtue of the Money Laundering Regulations 2007 (S.I. 2007/2157); or

(*b*)   for the purpose of—

    (i)   the detection, investigation or prosecution of a criminal offence (whether in the United Kingdom or elsewhere),

    (ii)   an investigation under this Act, or

    (iii)   the enforcement of any order of a court under this Act.

(2)   A professional legal adviser or a relevant professional adviser does not commit an offence under section 333A if the disclosure—

(*a*)   is to the adviser's client, and

(*b*)   is made for the purpose of dissuading the client from engaging in conduct amounting to an offence.

(3)   A person does not commit an offence under section 333A(1) if the person does not know or suspect that the disclosure is likely to have the effect mentioned in section 333A(1)(*b*).

(4)   A person does not commit an offence under section 333A(3) if the person does not know or suspect that the disclosure is likely to have the effect mentioned in section 333A(3)(*b*).][1]

Amendments

1   Inserted by the Terrorism Act 2000 and Proceeds of Crime Act 2002 (Amendment) Regulations 2007, SI 2007/3398, reg 3, Sch 2, paras 1, 4.

[333E   Interpretation of sections 333A to 333D

(1)   For the purposes of sections 333A to 333D, Schedule 9 has effect for determining—

(*a*)   what is a business in the regulated sector, and

(*b*)   what is a supervisory authority.

(2)   In those sections—

'credit institution' has the same meaning as in Schedule 9;

'financial institution' means an undertaking that carries on a business in the regulated sector by virtue of any of paragraphs (*b*) to (*i*) of paragraph 1(1) of that Schedule.

(3)   References in those sections to a disclosure by or to a credit institution or a financial institution include disclosure by or to an employee, officer or partner of the institution acting on its behalf.

(4)   For the purposes of those sections a country or territory imposes 'equivalent money laundering requirements' if it imposes requirements equivalent to those laid down in Directive 2005/60/EC of the European Parliament and of the Council of 26th October 2005 on the prevention of the use of the financial system for the purpose of money laundering and terrorist financing.

(5)   In those sections 'relevant professional adviser' means an accountant, auditor or tax adviser who is a member of a professional body which is established for accountants, auditors or tax advisers (as the case may be) and which makes provision for—

(*a*)   testing the competence of those seeking admission to membership of such a body as a condition for such admission; and

(*b*)   imposing and maintaining professional and ethical standards for its members, as well as imposing sanctions for non-compliance with those standards.][1]

Amendments

1   Inserted by the Terrorism Act 2000 and Proceeds of Crime Act 2002 (Amendment) Regulations 2007, SI 2007/3398, reg 3, Sch 2, paras 1, 4.

334   Penalties

(1)   A person guilty of an offence under section 327, 328 or 329 is liable—

(*a*)   on summary conviction, to imprisonment for a term not exceeding six months or to a fine not exceeding the statutory maximum or to both, or

(*b*)   on conviction on indictment, to imprisonment for a term not exceeding 14 years or to a fine or to both.

(2)   A person guilty of an offence under section 330, 331 [or 332][1] is liable—

(*a*)   on summary conviction, to imprisonment for a term not exceeding six months or to a fine not exceeding the statutory maximum or to both, or

(*b*)   on conviction on indictment, to imprisonment for a term not exceeding five years or to a fine or to both.

[(3)   A person guilty of an offence under section 339(1A) is liable on summary conviction to a fine not exceeding level 5 on the standard scale.][2]

Amendments

1   Substituted by the Terrorism Act 2000 and Proceeds of Crime Act 2002 (Amendment) Regula-
     tions 2007, SI 2007/3398, reg 3, Sch 2, paras 1, 5.
2   Inserted by the Serious Organised Crime and Police Act 2005, s 105(1), (3).

Consent

335   Appropriate consent

(1)   The apropriate consent is—

    (*a*)   the consent of a nominated officer to do a prohibited act if an authorised
        disclosure is made to the nominated officer;

    (*b*)   the consent of a constable to do a prohibited act if an authorised disclosure is
        made to a constable;

    (*c*)   the consent of a customs officer to do a prohibited act if an authorised disclosure
        is made to a customs officer.

(2)   A person must be treated as having the appropriate consent if—

    (*a*)   he makes an authorised disclosure to a constable or a customs officer, and

    (*b*)   the condition in subsection (3) or the condition in subsection (4) is satisfied.

(3)   The condition is that before the end of the notice period he does not receive notice from
a constable or customs officer that consent to the doing of the act is refused.

(4)   The condition is that—

    (*a*)   before the end of the notice period he receives notice from a constable or customs
        officer that consent to the doing of the act is refused, and

    (*b*)   the moratorium period has expired.

(5)   The notice period is the period of seven working days starting with the first working day
after the person makes the disclosure.

(6)   The moratorium period is the period of 31 days starting with the day on which the
person receives notice that consent to the doing of the act is refused.

(7)   A working day is a day other than a Saturday, a Sunday, Christmas Day, Good Friday or
a day which is a bank holiday under the Banking and Financial Dealings Act 1971 (c. 80)
in the part of the United Kingdom in which the person is when he makes the disclosure.

(8)   References to a prohibited act are to an act mentioned in section 327(1), 328(1) or 329(1)
(as the case may be).

(9)   A nominated officer is a person nominated to receive disclosures under section 338.

(10)   Subsections (1) to (4) apply for the purposes of this Part.

336   Nominated officer: consent

(1)   A nominated officer must not give the appropriate consent to the doing of a prohibited
act unless the condition in subsection (2), the condition in subsection (3) or the
condition in subsection (4) is satisfied.

(2)   The condition is that—

    (*a*)   he makes a disclosure that property is criminal property to a person authorised
        for the purposes of this Part by [the Director General of [SOCA][1]][2], and

(b) such a person gives consent to the doing of the act.

(3) The condition is that—

(a) he makes a disclosure that property is criminal property to a person authorised for the purposes of this Part by [the Director General of [SOCA]^1]^2, and

(b) before the end of the notice period he does not receive notice from such a person that consent to the doing of the act is refused.

(4) The condition is that—

(a) he makes a disclosure that property is criminal property to a person authorised for the purposes of this Part by [the Director General of [SOCA]^1]^2,

(b) before the end of the notice period he receives notice from such a person that consent to the doing of the act is refused, and

(c) the moratorium period has expired.

(5) A person who is a nominated officer commits an offence if—

(a) he gives consent to a prohibited act in circumstances where none of the conditions in subsections (2), (3) and (4) is satisfied, and

(b) he knows or suspects that the act is a prohibited act.

(6) A person guilty of such an offence is liable—

(a) on summary conviction, to imprisonment for a term not exceeding six months or to a fine not exceeding the statutory maximum or to both, or

(b) on conviction on indictment, to imprisonment for a term not exceeding five years or to a fine or to both.

(7) The notice period is the period of seven working days starting with the first working day after the nominated officer makes the disclosure.

(8) The moratorium period is the period of 31 days starting with the day on which the nominated officer is given notice that consent to the doing of the act is refused.

(9) A working day is a day other than a Saturday, a Sunday, Christmas Day, Good Friday or a day which is a bank holiday under the Banking and Financial Dealings Act 1971 (c. 80) in the part of the United Kingdom in which the nominated officer is when he gives the appropriate consent.

(10) References to a prohibited act are to an act mentioned in section 327(1), 328(1) or 329(1) (as the case may be).

(11) A nominated officer is a person nominated to receive disclosures under section 338.

Amendments
1   Substituted by the Serious Crime Act 2007, s 74(2)(f), Sch 8, Pt 6, paras 121, 129.
2   Substituted by the Serious Organised Crime and Police Act 2005, s 59, Sch 4, paras 168, 173.

Disclosures

337 Protected disclosures

(1) A disclosure which satisfies the following three conditions is not to be taken to breach any restriction on the disclosure of information (however imposed).

(2)   The first condition is that the information or other matter disclosed came to the person making the disclosure (the discloser) in the course of his trade, profession, business or employment.

(3)   The second condition is that the information or other matter—

    (*a*)   causes the discloser to know or suspect, or

    (*b*)   gives him reasonable grounds for knowing or suspecting,

    that another person is engaged in money laundering

(4)   The third condition is that the disclosure is made to a constable, a customs officer or a nominated officer as soon as is practicable after the information or other matter comes to the discloser.

[(4A)   Where a disclosure consists of a disclosure protected under subsection (1) and a disclosure of either or both of—

    (*a*)   the identity of the other person mentioned in subsection (3), and

    (*b*)   the whereabouts of property forming the subject-matter of the money laundering that the discloser knows or suspects, or has reasonable grounds for knowing or suspecting, that other person to be engaged in,

    the disclosure of the thing mentioned in paragraph (*a*) or (*b*) (as well as the disclosure protected under subsection (1)) is not to be taken to breach any restriction on the disclosure of information (however imposed).][1]

(5)   A disclosure to a nominated officer is a disclosure which—

    (*a*)   is made to a person nominated by the discloser's employer to receive disclosures under [section 330 or][1] this section, and

    (*b*)   is made in the course of the discloser's employment ...[2].

Amendments

1   Inserted by the Serious Organised Crime and Police Act 2005, ss 104(1), (7), 106(1), (3).
2   Repealed by the Serious Organised Crime and Police Act 2005, s 105(1), (2), 174(2), Sch 17, Pt 2.

338   Authorised disclosures

(1)   For the purposes of this Part a disclosure is authorised if—

    (*a*)   it is a disclosure to a constable, a customs officer or a nominated officer by the alleged offender that property is criminal property,

    (*b*)   ...[1] and

    (*c*)   the first[, second or third][2] condition set out below is satisfied.

(2)   The first condition is that the disclosure is made before the alleged offender does the prohibited act.

[(2A)   The second condition is that—

    (*a*)   the disclosure is made while the alleged offender is doing the prohibited act,

    (*b*)   he began to do the act at a time when, because he did not then know or suspect that the property constituted or represented a person's benefit from criminal conduct, the act was not a prohibited act, and

(c)   the disclosure is made on his own initiative and as soon as is practicable after he first knows or suspects that the property constitutes or represents a person's benefit from criminal conduct.]³

(3)   The [third]² condition is that—

(a)   the disclosure is made after the alleged offender does the prohibited act,

(b)   [he has a good excuse]⁴ for his failure to make the disclosure before he did the act, and

(c)   the disclosure is made on his own initiative and as soon as it is practicable for him to make it.

(4)   An authorised disclosure is not to be taken to breach any restriction on the disclosure of information (however imposed).

(5)   A disclosure to a nominated officer is a disclosure which—

(a)   is made to a person nominated by the alleged offender's employer to receive authorised disclosures, and

(b)   ...¹.

(6)   References to the prohibited act are to an act mentioned in section 327(1), 328(1) or 329(1) (as the case may be).

Amendments

1   Repealed by the Serious Organised Crime and Police Act 2005, ss 105(1), (2), (4), 174(2), Sch 17, Pt 2.
2   Substituted by the Serious Organised Crime and Police Act 2005, s 106(1), (4), (6).
3   Inserted by the Serious Organised Crime and Police Act 2005, s 106(1), (5).
4   Substituted by the Terrorism Act 2000 and Proceeds of Crime Act 2002 (Amendment) Regulations 2007, SI 2007/3398, reg 3, Sch 2, paras 1, 6.

339 Form and manner of disclosures

(1)   The Secretary of State may by order prescribe the form and manner in which a disclosure under section 330, 331, 332 or 338 must be made.

[(1A) A person commits an offence if he makes a disclosure under section 330, 331, 332 or 338 otherwise than in the form prescribed under subsection (1) or otherwise than in the manner so prescribed.

(1B) But a person does not commit an offence under subsection (1A) if he has a reasonable excuse for making the disclosure otherwise than in the form prescribed under subsection (1) or (as the case may be) otherwise than in the manner so prescribed.]¹

[(2)   The power under subsection (1) to prescribe the form in which a disclosure must be made includes power to provide for the form to include a request to a person making a disclosure that the person provide information specified or described in the form if he has not provided it in making the disclosure.

(3)   Where under subsection (2) a request is included in a form prescribed under subsection (1), the form must—

(a)   state that there is no obligation to comply with the request, and

(b)   explain the protection conferred by subsection (4) on a person who complies with the request.]²

(4)   A disclosure made in pursuance of a request under subsection (2) is not to be taken to breach any restriction on the disclosure of information (however imposed).

(5)   ...³

(6)   ...³

(7)   Subsection (2) does not apply to a disclosure made to a nominated officer.

Amendments

1   Inserted by the Serious Organised Crime and Police Act 2005, s 105(1), (5).
2   Substituted by the Serious Organised Crime and Police Act 2005, s 105(1), (5).
3   Revoked by the Serious Organised Crime and Police Act 2005, s 174(2), Sch 17, Pt 2.

[339ZA   Disclosures to SOCA

Where a disclosure is made under this Part to a constable or an officer of Revenue and Customs, the constable or officer of Revenue and Customs must disclose it in full to a person authorised for the purposes of this Part by the Director General of the Serious Organised Crime Agency as soon as practicable after it has been made.]¹

Amendments

1   Inserted by the Terrorism Act 2000 and Proceeds of Crime Act 2002 (Amendment) Regulations 2007, SI 2007/3398, reg 3, Sch 2, paras 1, 7.

[Threshold amounts

339A   Threshold amounts

(1)   This section applies for the purposes of sections 327(2C), 328(5) and 329(2C).

(2)   The threshold amount for acts done by a deposit-taking body in operating an account is £250 unless a higher amount is specified under the following provisions of this section (in which event it is that higher amount).

(3)   An officer of Revenue and Customs, or a constable, may specify the threshold amount for acts done by a deposit-taking body in operating an account—

   (*a*)   when he gives consent, or gives notice refusing consent, to the deposit-taking body's doing of an act mentioned in section 327(1), 328(1) or 329(1) in opening, or operating, the account or a related account, or

   (*b*)   on a request from the deposit-taking body.

(4)   Where the threshold amount for acts done in operating an account is specified under subsection (3) or this subsection, an officer of Revenue and Customs, or a constable, may vary the amount (whether on a request from the deposit-taking body or otherwise) by specifying a different amount.

(5)   Different threshold amounts may be specified under subsections (3) and (4) for different acts done in operating the same account.

(6)   The amount specified under subsection (3) or (4) as the threshold amount for acts done in operating an account must, when specified, not be less than the amount specified in subsection (2).

(7)   The Secretary of State may by order vary the amount for the time being specified in subsection (2).

(8)   For the purposes of this section, an account is related to another if each is maintained with the same deposit-taking body and there is a person who, in relation to each account, is the person or one of the persons entitled to instruct the body as respects the operation of the account.][1]

Amendments

1   Inserted by the Serious Organised Crime and Police Act 2005, s 103(1), (5).

Interpretation

340   Interpretation

(1)   This section applies for the purposes of this Part.

(2)   Criminal conduct is conduct which—

   (a)   constitutes an offence in any part of the United Kingdom, or

   (b)   would constitute an offence in any part of the United Kingdom if it occurred there.

(3)   Property is criminal property if—

   (a)   it constitutes a person's benefit from criminal conduct or it represents such a benefit (in whole or part and whether directly or indirectly), and

   (b)   the alleged offender knows or suspects that it constitutes or represents such a benefit.

(4)   It is immaterial—

   (a)   who carried out the conduct;

   (b)   who benefited from it;

   (c)   whether the conduct occurred before or after the passing of this Act.

(5)   A person benefits from conduct if he obtains property as a result of or in connection with the conduct.

(6)   If a person obtains a pecuniary advantage as a result of or in connection with conduct, he is to be taken to obtain as a result of or in connection with the conduct a sum of money equal to the value of the pecuniary advantage.

(7)   References to property or a pecuniary advantage obtained in connection with conduct include references to property or a pecuniary advantage obtained in both that connection and some other.

(8)   If a person benefits from conduct his benefit is the property obtained as a result of or in connection with the conduct.

(9)   Property is all property wherever situated and includes—

   (a)   money;

   (b)   all forms of property, real or personal, heritable or moveable;

   (c)   things in action and other intangible or incorporeal property.

(10)   The following rules apply in relation to property—

   (a)   property is obtained by a person if he obtains an interest in it;

(*b*)   references to an interest, in relation to land in England and Wales or Northern Ireland, are to any legal estate or equitable interest or power;

(*c*)   references to an interest, in relation to land in Scotland, are to any estate, interest, servitude or other heritable right in or over land, including a heritable security;

(*d*)   references to an interest, in relation to property other than land, include references to a right (including a right to possession).

(11)   Money laundering is an act which—

(*a*)   constitutes an offence under section 327, 328 or 329,

(*b*)   constitutes an attempt, conspiracy or incitement to commit an offence specified in paragraph (*a*),

(*c*)   constitutes aiding, abetting, counselling or procuring the commission of an offence specified in paragraph (*a*), or

(*d*)   would constitute an offence specified in paragraph (*a*), (*b*) or (*c*) if done in the United Kingdom.

(12)   For the purposes of a disclosure to a nominated officer—

(*a*)   references to a person's employer include any body, association or organisation (including a voluntary organisation) in connection with whose activities the person exercises a function (whether or not for gain or reward), and

(*b*)   references to employment must be construed accordingly.

(13)   References to a constable include references to a person authorised for the purposes of this Part by [the Director General of [SOCA][1]][2].

[(14)   'Deposit-taking body' means—

(*a*)   a business which engages in the activity of accepting deposits, or

(*b*)   the National Savings Bank.][3]

Amendments

1   Substituted by the Serious Crime Act 2007, s 74(2)(*f*), Sch 8, Pt 6, paras 121, 130.
2   Substituted by the Serious Organised Crime and Police Act 2005, s 59, Sch 4, paras 168, 174.
3   Inserted by the Serious Organised Crime and Police Act 2005, s 103(1), (6).

PART 8
INVESTIGATIONS

CHAPTER 1
INTRODUCTION

341 Investigations

(1)   For the purposes of this Part a confiscation investigation is an investigation into—

(*a*)   whether a person has benefited from his criminal conduct, or

(*b*)   the extent or whereabouts of his benefit from his criminal conduct.

(2) For the purposes of this Part a civil recovery investigation is an investigation into—

    (*a*) whether property is recoverable property or associated property,

    (*b*) who holds the property, or

    (*c*) its extent or whereabouts.

(3) But an investigation is not a civil recovery investigation if—

    (*a*) proceedings for a recovery order have been started in respect of the property in question,

    (*b*) an interim receiving order applies to the property in question,

    (*c*) an interim administration order applies to the property in question, or

    (*d*) the property in question is detained under section 295.

[(3A) For the purposes of this Part a detained cash investigation is–

    (*a*) an investigation for the purposes of Chapter 3 of Part 5 into the derivation of cash detained under section 295 or a part of such cash, or

    (*b*) an investigation for the purposes of Chapter 3 of Part 5 into whether cash detained under section 295, or a part of such cash, is intended by any person to be used in unlawful conduct.][1]

(4) For the purposes of this Part a money laundering investigation is an investigation into whether a person has committed a money laundering offence.

[(5) For the purposes of this Part an exploitation proceeds investigation is an investigation for the purposes of Part 7 of the Coroners and Justice Act 2009 (criminal memoirs etc) into—

    (*a*) whether a person is a qualifying offender,

    (*b*) whether a person has obtained exploitation proceeds from a relevant offence,

    (*c*) the value of any benefits derived by a person from a relevant offence, or

    (*d*) the available amount in respect of a person.

Paragraphs (*a*) to (*d*) are to be construed in accordance with that Part of that Act.][2]

Amendments

1   Inserted by the Serious Crime Act 2007, s 75(1).

2   Inserted by the Coroners and Justice Act 2009, s 169, Sch 19, paras 1, 2.

342 Offences of prejudicing investigation

(1) This section applies if a person knows or suspects that an appropriate officer or (in Scotland) a proper person is acting (or proposing to act) in connection with a confiscation investigation, a civil recovery investigation[, a detained cash investigation][1][, an exploitation proceeds investigation][2] or a money laundering investigation which is being or is about to be conducted.

(2) The person commits an offence if—

    (*a*) he makes a disclosure which is likely to prejudice the investigation, or (*b*)   he falsifies, conceals, destroys or otherwise disposes of, or causes or permits the falsification, concealment, destruction or disposal of, documents which are relevant to the investigation.

(3)   A person does not commit an offence under subsection (2)(*a*) if—

(*a*)   he does not know or suspect that the disclosure is likely to prejudice the investigation,

(*b*)   the disclosure is made in the exercise of a function under this Act or any other enactment relating to criminal conduct or benefit from criminal conduct or in compliance with a requirement imposed under or by virtue of this Act, or

[(*ba*)   the disclosure is of a matter within section 33A(2) or (3)(*a*) (money laundering: tipping off) and the information on which the disclosure is based came to the person in the course of a business in the regulated sector,][3]

[(*bb*)   the disclosure is made in the exercise of a function under Part 7 of the Coroners and Justice Act 2009 (criminal memoirs etc) or in compliance with a requirement imposed under or by virtue of that Act,][2]

(*c*)   he is a professional legal adviser and the disclosure falls within subsection (4).

(4)   A disclosure falls within this subsection if it is a disclosure—

(*a*)   to (or to a representative of) a client of the professional legal adviser in connection with the giving by the adviser of legal advice to the client, or

(*b*)   to any person in connection with legal proceedings or contemplated legal proceedings.

(5)   But a disclosure does not fall within subsection (4) if it is made with the intention of furthering a criminal purpose.

(6)   A person does not commit an offence under subsection (2)(*b*) if—

(*a*)   he does not know or suspect that the documents are relevant to the investigation, or

(*b*)   he does not intend to conceal any facts disclosed by the documents from any appropriate officer or (in Scotland) proper person carrying out the investigation.

(7)   A person guilty of an offence under subsection (2) is liable—

(*a*)   on summary conviction, to imprisonment for a term not exceeding six months or to a fine not exceeding the statutory maximum or to both, or

(*b*)   on conviction on indictment, to imprisonment for a term not exceeding five years or to a fine or to both.

(8)   For the purposes of this section—

(*a*)   'appropriate officer' must be construed in accordance with section 378;

(*b*)   'proper person' must be construed in accordance with section 412;

[(*c*)   Schedule 9 has effect for determining what is a business in the regulated sector.][3]

Amendments

1   Inserted by the Serious Crime Act 2007, s 77, Sch 10, paras 1, 2.
2   Inserted by the Coroners and Justice Act 2009, s 169, Sch 19, paras 1, 3.

3   Inserted by the Terrorism Act 2000 and Proceeds of Crime Act 2002 (Amendment) Regulations 2007, SI 2007/3398, reg 3, Sch 2, paras 1, 8.

CHAPTER 2
ENGLAND AND WALES AND NORTHERN IRELAND

Judges and courts

343 Judges

(1)   In this Chapter references to a judge in relation to an application must be construed in accordance with this section.

(2)   In relation to an application for the purposes of a confiscation investigation or a money laundering investigation a judge is—

(*a*)   in England and Wales, a judge entitled to exercise the jurisdiction of the Crown Court;

(*b*)   in Northern Ireland, a Crown Court judge.

(3)   In relation to an application for the purposes of a civil recovery investigation [or an exploitation proceeds investigation][1] [or a detained cash investigation][2] a judge is a judge of the High Court.

Amendments
1   Inserted by the Coroners and Justice Act 2009, s 169, Sch 19, paras 1, 4.
2   Inserted by the Serious Crime Act 2007, s 77, Sch 10, paras 1, 3.

344   Courts

In this Chapter references to the court are to—

(*a*)   the Crown Court, in relation to an order for the purposes of a confiscation investigation or a money laundering investigation;

(*b*)   the High Court, in relation to an order for the purposes of a civil recovery investigation [or an exploitation proceeds investigation][1] [or a detained cash investigation][2].

Amendments
1   Inserted by the Coroners and Justice Act 2009, s 169, Sch 19, paras 1, 5.
2   Inserted by the Serious Crime Act 2007, s 77, Sch 10, paras 1, 4.

Production orders

345   Production orders

(1)   A judge may, on an application made to him by an appropriate officer, make a production order if he is satisfied that each of the requirements for the making of the order is fulfilled.

(2)   The application for a production order must state that—

(*a*)   a person specified in the application is subject to a confiscation investigation[, an exploitation proceeds investigation]¹ or a money laundering investigation, or

(*b*)   property specified in the application is subject to a civil recovery investigation [or a detained cash investigation]².

(3)   The application must also state that—

(*a*)   the order is sought for the purposes of the investigation;

(*b*)   the order is sought in relation to material, or material of a description, specified in the application;

(*c*)   a person specified in the application appears to be in possession or control of the material.

(4)   A production order is an order either—

(*a*)   requiring the person the application for the order specifies as appearing to be in possession or control of material to produce it to an appropriate officer for him to take away, or

(*b*)   requiring that person to give an appropriate officer access to the material,

within the period stated in the order

(5)   The period stated in a production order must be a period of seven days beginning with the day on which the order is made, unless it appears to the judge by whom the order is made that a longer or shorter period would be appropriate in the particular circumstances.

Amendments

1   Inserted by the Coroners and Justice Act 2009, s 169, Sch 19, paras 1, 6.
2   Inserted by the Serious Crime Act 2007, s 75(2).

346 Requirements for making of production order

(1)   These are the requirements for the making of a production order.

(2)   There must be reasonable grounds for suspecting that—

(*a*)   in the case of a confiscation investigation, the person the application for the order specifies as being subject to the investigation has benefited from his criminal conduct;

(*b*)   in the case of a civil recovery investigation, the property the application for the order specifies as being subject to the investigation is recoverable property or associated property;

[(*ba*) in the case of a detained cash investigation into the derivation of cash, the property the application for the order specifies as being subject to the investigation, or a part of it, is recoverable property;

(*bb*) in the case of a detained cash investigation into the intended use of cash, the property the application for the order specifies as being subject to the investigation, or a part of it, is intended by any person to be used in unlawful conduct;]¹

(*c*)   in the case of a money laundering investigation, the person the application for the order specifies as being subject to the investigation has committed a money laundering offence;

[(*d*)   in the case of an exploitation proceeds investigation, the person the application for the order specifies as being subject to the investigation is within subsection (2A).]²

[(2A)   A person is within this subsection if, for the purposes of Part 7 of the Coroners and Justice Act 2009 (criminal memoirs etc), exploitation proceeds have been obtained by the person from a relevant offence by reason of any benefit derived by the person.

This subsection is to be construed in accordance with that Part.]²

(3)   There must be reasonable grounds for believing that the person the application specifies as appearing to be in possession or control of the material so specified is in possession or control of it.

(4)   There must be reasonable grounds for believing that the material is likely to be of substantial value (whether or not by itself) to the investigation for the purposes of which the order is sought.

(5)   There must be reasonable grounds for believing that it is in the public interest for the material to be produced or for access to it to be given, having regard to—

      (*a*)   the benefit likely to accrue to the investigation if the material is obtained;

      (*b*)   the circumstances under which the person the application specifies as appearing to be in possession or control of the material holds it.

Amendments
1   Inserted by the Serious Crime Act 2007, s 75(3).
2   Inserted by the Coroners and Justice Act 2009, s 169, Sch 19, paras 1, 7.

347   Order to grant entry

(1)   This section applies if a judge makes a production order requiring a person to give an appropriate officer access to material on any premises.

(2)   The judge may, on an application made to him by an appropriate officer and specifying the premises, make an order to grant entry in relation to the premises.

(3)   An order to grant entry is an order requiring any person who appears to an appropriate officer to be entitled to grant entry to the premises to allow him to enter the premises to obtain access to the material.

348   Further provisions

(1)   A production order does not require a person to produce, or give access to, privileged material.

(2)   Privileged material is any material which the person would be entitled to refuse to produce on grounds of legal professional privilege in proceedings in the High Court.

(3)   A production order does not require a person to produce, or give access to, excluded material.

(4)   A production order has effect in spite of any restriction on the disclosure of information (however imposed).

(5)   An appropriate officer may take copies of any material which is produced, or to which access is given, in compliance with a production order.

(6)   Material produced in compliance with a production order may be retained for so long as it is necessary to retain it (as opposed to copies of it) in connection with the investigation for the purposes of which the order was made.

(7)   But if an appropriate officer has reasonable grounds for believing that—

(a)   the material may need to be produced for the purposes of any legal proceedings, and

(b)   it might otherwise be unavailable for those purposes,

it may be retained until the proceedings are concluded

349   Computer information

(1)   This section applies if any of the material specified in an application for a production order consists of information contained in a computer.

(2)   If the order is an order requiring a person to produce the material to an appropriate officer for him to take away, it has effect as an order to produce the material in a form in which it can be taken away by him and in which it is visible and legible.

(3)   If the order is an order requiring a person to give an appropriate officer access to the material, it has effect as an order to give him access to the material in a form in which it is visible and legible.

350   Government departments

(1)   A production order may be made in relation to material in the possession or control of an authorised government department.

(2)   An order so made may require any officer of the department (whether named in the order or not) who may for the time being be in possession or control of the material to comply with it.

(3)   An order containing such a requirement must be served as if the proceedings were civil proceedings against the department.

(4)   If an order contains such a requirement—

(a)   the person on whom it is served must take all reasonable steps to bring it to the attention of the officer concerned;

(b)   any other officer of the department who is in receipt of the order must also take all reasonable steps to bring it to the attention of the officer concerned.

(5)   If the order is not brought to the attention of the officer concerned within the period stated in the order (in pursuance of section 345(4)) the person on whom it is served must report the reasons for the failure to—

(a)   a judge entitled to exercise the jurisdiction of the Crown Court or (in Northern Ireland) a Crown Court judge, in the case of an order made for the purposes of a confiscation investigation or a money laundering investigation;

(b)   a High Court judge, in the case of an order made for the purposes of a civil recovery investigation [or an exploitation proceeds investigation][1] [or a detained cash investigation][2].

(6)   An authorised government department is a government department, or a Northern Ireland department, which is an authorised department for the purposes of the Crown Proceedings Act 1947 (c. 44).

266

Amendments
1   Inserted by the Coroners and Justice Act 2009, s 169, Sch 19, paras 1, 8.
2   Inserted by the Serious Crime Act 2007, s 77, Sch 10, paras 1, 5.

351   Supplementary

(1)   An application for a production order or an order to grant entry may be made ex parte to a judge in chambers.

(2)   Rules of court may make provision as to the practice and procedure to be followed in connection with proceedings relating to production orders and orders to grant entry.

(3)   An application to discharge or vary a production order or an order to grant entry may be made to the court by—

   (*a*)   the person who applied for the order;

   (*b*)   any person affected by the order.

(4)   The court—

   (*a*)   may discharge the order;

   (*b*)   may vary the order.

(5)   If an accredited financial investigator, [a member of SOCA's staff,]¹ a constable or a customs officer applies for a production order or an order to grant entry, an application to discharge or vary the order need not be by the same accredited financial investigator, [member of SOCA's staff,]¹ constable or customs officer.

(6)   References to a person who applied for a production order or an order to grant entry must be construed accordingly.

(7)   Production orders and orders to grant entry have effect as if they were orders of the court.

(8)   Subsections (2) to (7) do not apply to orders made in England and Wales for the purposes of a civil recovery investigation [or an exploitation proceeds investigation]² [or a detained cash investigation]³.

Amendments
1   Inserted by the Serious Crime Act 2007, s 74(2)(*d*), Sch 8, Pt 4, paras 103, 104.
2   Inserted by the Coroners and Justice Act 2009, s 169, Sch 19, paras 1, 9.
3   Inserted by the Serious Crime Act 2007, s 77, Sch 10, paras 1, 6.

Search and seizure warrants

352   Search and seizure warrants

(1)   A judge may, on an application made to him by an appropriate officer, issue a search and seizure warrant if he is satisfied that either of the requirements for the issuing of the warrant is fulfilled.

(2)   The application for a search and seizure warrant must state that—

   (*a*)   a person specified in the application is subject to a confiscation investigation[, an exploitation proceeds investigation]¹ or a money laundering investigation, or

   (*b*)   property specified in the application is subject to a civil recovery investigation [or a detained cash investigation]².

(3)   The application must also state—

    (*a*)   that the warrant is sought for the purposes of the investigation;

    (*b*)   that the warrant is sought in relation to the premises specified in the application;

    (*c*)   that the warrant is sought in relation to material specified in the application, or that there are reasonable grounds for believing that there is material falling within section 353(6), (7)[, (7A), (7B)]^2 or (8) on the premises.

(4)   A search and seizure warrant is a warrant authorising an appropriate person—

    (*a*)   to enter and search the premises specified in the application for the warrant, and

    (*b*)   to seize and retain any material found there which is likely to be of substantial value (whether or not by itself) to the investigation for the purposes of which the application is made.

(5)   An appropriate person is—

    (*a*)   a constable[, an accredited financial investigator]^2 or a customs officer, if the warrant is sought for the purposes of a confiscation investigation or a money laundering investigation;

    (*b*)   a [member of SOCA's staff or of the staff of the relevant Director]^3, if the warrant is sought for the purposes of a civil recovery investigation;

    [(*c*)   a constable[, an accredited financial investigator]^2 or an officer of Revenue and Customs, if the warrant is sought for the purposes of a detained cash investigation;]^2

    [(*d*)   a member of SOCA's staff, if the warrant is sought for the purposes of an exploitation proceeds investigation.]^1

[(5A) In this Part 'relevant Director'–

    (*a*)   in relation to England and Wales, means the Director of Public Prosecutions, the Director of Revenue and Customs Prosecutions or the Director of the Serious Fraud Office; and

    (*b*)   in relation to Northern Ireland, means the Director of the Serious Fraud Office or the Director of Public Prosecutions for Northern Ireland.]^2

(6)   The requirements for the issue of a search and seizure warrant are—

    (*a*)   that a production order made in relation to material has not been complied with and there are reasonable grounds for believing that the material is on the premises specified in the application for the warrant, or

    (*b*)   that section 353 is satisfied in relation to the warrant.

[(7)   The reference in paragraph (*a*) or (*c*) of subsection (5) to an accredited financial investigator is a reference to an accredited financial investigator who falls within a description specified in an order made for the purposes of that paragraph by the Secretary of State under section 453.]^2

Amendments

1   Inserted by the Coroners and Justice Act 2009, s 169, Sch 19, paras 1, 10.
2   Inserted by the Serious Crime Act 2007, ss 74(2)(*d*), 76(1), 77, 80(1), (2), Sch 8, Pt 4, paras 103, 105(1), (3), Sch 10, paras 1, 7.
3   Substituted by the Serious Crime Act 2007, s 74(2)(*d*), Sch 8, Pt 4, paras 103, 105(1), (2).

353 Requirements where production order not available

(1) This section is satisfied in relation to a search and seizure warrant if—

    (*a*) subsection (2) applies, and

    (*b*) either the first or the second set of conditions is complied with.

(2) This subsection applies if there are reasonable grounds for suspecting that—

    (*a*) in the case of a confiscation investigation, the person specified in the application for the warrant has benefited from his criminal conduct;

    (*b*) in the case of a civil recovery investigation, the property specified in the application for the warrant is recoverable property or associated property;

    [(*ba*) in the case of a detained cash investigation into the derivation of cash, the property specified in the application for the warrant, or a part of it, is recoverable property;

    (*bb*) in the case of a detained cash investigation into the intended use of cash, the property specified in the application for the warrant, or a part of it, is intended by any person to be used in unlawful conduct;][1]

    (*c*) in the case of a money laundering investigation, the person specified in the application for the warrant has committed a money laundering offence;

    [(*d*) in the case of an exploitation proceeds investigation, the person specified in the application for the warrant is within section 346(2A).][2]

(3) The first set of conditions is that there are reasonable grounds for believing that—

    (*a*) any material on the premises specified in the application for the warrant is likely to be of substantial value (whether or not by itself) to the investigation for the purposes of which the warrant is sought,

    (*b*) it is in the public interest for the material to be obtained, having regard to the benefit likely to accrue to the investigation if the material is obtained, and

    (*c*) it would not be appropriate to make a production order for any one or more of the reasons in subsection (4).

(4) The reasons are—

    (*a*) that it is not practicable to communicate with any person against whom the production order could be made;

    (*b*) that it is not practicable to communicate with any person who would be required to comply with an order to grant entry to the premises;

    (*c*) that the investigation might be seriously prejudiced unless an appropriate person is able to secure immediate access to the material.

(5) The second set of conditions is that—

    (*a*) there are reasonable grounds for believing that there is material on the premises specified in the application for the warrant and that the material falls within subsection (6), (7)[, (7A), (7B)][1][, (8) or (8A)][3],

    (*b*) there are reasonable grounds for believing that it is in the public interest for the material to be obtained, having regard to the benefit likely to accrue to the investigation if the material is obtained, and (*c*)   any one or more of the requirements in subsection (9) is met.

(6)   In the case of a confiscation investigation, material falls within this subsection if it cannot be identified at the time of the application but it—

(*a*)   relates to the person specified in the application, the question whether he has benefited from his criminal conduct or any question as to the extent or whereabouts of his benefit from his criminal conduct, and

(*b*)   is likely to be of substantial value (whether or not by itself) to the investigation for the purposes of which the warrant is sought.

(7)   In the case of a civil recovery investigation, material falls within this subsection if it cannot be identified at the time of the application but it—

(*a*)   relates to the property specified in the application, the question whether it is recoverable property or associated property, the question as to who holds any such property, any question as to whether the person who appears to hold any such property holds other property which is recoverable property, or any question as to the extent or whereabouts of any property mentioned in this paragraph, and

(*b*)   is likely to be of substantial value (whether or not by itself) to the investigation for the purposes of which the warrant is sought.

[(7A) In the case of a detained cash investigation into the derivation of cash, material falls within this subsection if it cannot be identified at the time of the application but it–

(*a*)   relates to the property specified in the application, the question whether the property, or a part of it, is recoverable property or any other question as to its derivation, and

(*b*)   is likely to be of substantial value (whether or not by itself) to the investigation for the purposes of which the warrant is sought.

(7B)   In the case of a detained cash investigation into the intended use of cash, material falls within this subsection if it cannot be identified at the time of the application but it–

(*a*)   relates to the property specified in the application or the question whether the property, or a part of it, is intended by any person to be used in unlawful conduct, and

(*b*)   is likely to be of substantial value (whether or not by itself) to the investigation for the purposes of which the warrant is sought.][1]

(8)   In the case of a money laundering investigation, material falls within this subsection if it cannot be identified at the time of the application but it—

(*a*)   relates to the person specified in the application or the question whether he has committed a money laundering offence, and

(*b*)   is likely to be of substantial value (whether or not by itself) to the investigation for the purposes of which the warrant is sought.

[(8A) In the case of an exploitation proceeds investigation, material falls within this subsection if it cannot be identified at the time of the application but it—

(*a*)   relates to the person specified in the application, the question whether exploitation proceeds have been obtained from a relevant offence in relation to that person, any question as to the extent or whereabouts of any benefit as a result of which exploitation proceeds are obtained or any question about the person's available amount, and

(b)   is likely to be of substantial value (whether or not by itself) to the investigation for the purposes of which the warrant is sought.

This subsection is to be construed in accordance with Part 7 of the Coroners and Justice Act 2009 (criminal memoirs etc).]²

(9)   The requirements are—

(a)   that it is not practicable to communicate with any person entitled to grant entry to the premises;

(b)   that entry to the premises will not be granted unless a warrant is produced;

(c)   that the investigation might be seriously prejudiced unless an appropriate person arriving at the premises is able to secure immediate entry to them.

(10)   An appropriate person is—

(a)   a constable[, an accredited financial investigator]¹ or a customs officer, if the warrant is sought for the purposes of a confiscation investigation or a money laundering investigation;

(b)   a member of [SOCA's staff or of the staff of the relevant Director]⁴, if the warrant is sought for the purposes of a civil recovery investigation;

[(c)   a constable[, an accredited financial investigator]¹ or an officer of Revenue and Customs, if the warrant is sought for the purposes of a detained cash investigation;]¹

[(d)   a member of SOCA's staff, if the warrant is sought for the purposes of an exploitation proceeds investigation.]²

[(11)   The reference in paragraph (a) or (c) of subsection (10) to an accredited financial investigator is a reference to an accredited financial investigator who falls within a description specified in an order made for the purposes of that paragraph by the Secretary of State under section 453.]¹

Amendments
1   Inserted by the Serious Crime Act 2007, ss 76(2), (3), 77, 80(3), (4), Sch 10, paras 1, 8.
2   Inserted by the Coroners and Justice Act 2009, s 169, Sch 19, paras 1, 11(a), (c), (d).
3   Substituted by the Coroners and Justice Act 2009, s 169, Sch 19, paras 1, 11(b).
4   Substituted by the Serious Crime Act 2007, s 74(2)(d), Sch 8, Pt 4, paras 103, 106.

354   Further provisions: general

(1)   A search and seizure warrant does not confer the right to seize privileged material.

(2)   Privileged material is any material which a person would be entitled to refuse to produce on grounds of legal professional privilege in proceedings in the High Court.

(3)   A search and seizure warrant does not confer the right to seize excluded material.

355   Further provisions: confiscation and money laundering

(1)   This section applies to—

(a)   search and seizure warrants sought for the purposes of a confiscation investigation or a money laundering investigation, and

(b)   powers of seizure under them.

(2)   In relation to such warrants and powers, the Secretary of State may make an order
which applies the provisions to which subsections (3) and (4) apply subject to any
specified modifications.

(3)   This subsection applies to the following provisions of the Police and Criminal Evidence
Act 1984 (c. 60)—

(a)   section 15 (search warrants -safeguards);

(b)   section 16 (execution of warrants);

(c)   section 21 (access and copying);

(d)   section 22 (retention).

(4)   This subsection applies to the following provisions of the Police and Criminal Evidence
(Northern Ireland) Order 1989 (S.I. 1989/1341 (N.I. 12))—

(a)   Article 17 (search warrants -safeguards);

(b)   Article 18 (execution of warrants);

(c)   Article 23 (access and copying);

(d)   Article 24 (retention).

356   Further provisions: civil recovery [and detained cash][1]

(1)   This section applies to search and seizure warrants sought for the purposes of civil
recovery investigations [or exploitation proceeds investigations][2] [or detained cash
investigations][1].

(2)   An application for a warrant may be made ex parte to a judge in chambers.

(3)   A warrant may be issued subject to conditions.

(4)   A warrant continues in force until the end of the period of one month starting with the
day on which it is issued.

(5)   A warrant authorises the person it names to require any information which is held in a
computer and is accessible from the premises specified in the application for the
warrant, and which the named person believes relates to any matter relevant to the
investigation, to be produced in a form—

(a)   in which it can be taken away, and

(b)   in which it is visible and legible.

(6)   ...[3]

(7)   A warrant may include provision authorising a person who is exercising powers under it
to do other things which—

(a)   are specified in the warrant, and

(b)   need to be done in order to give effect to it.

(8)   Copies may be taken of any material seized under a warrant.

(9)   Material seized under a warrant may be retained for so long as it is necessary to retain it (as opposed to copies of it) in connection with the investigation for the purposes of which the warrant was issued.

(10)   But [if the appropriate person has reasonable]⁴ grounds for believing that—

    (*a*)   the material may need to be produced for the purposes of any legal proceedings, and

    (*b*)   it might otherwise be unavailable for those purposes,

it may be retained until the proceedings are concluded.

[(11)   The appropriate person is–

    (*a*)   [an appropriate officer]⁴, if the warrant was issued for the purposes of a civil recovery investigation;

    (*b*)   a constable[, an accredited financial investigator]¹ or an officer of Revenue and Customs, if the warrant was issued for the purposes of a detained cash investigation.]¹

[(12)   The reference in paragraph (*b*) of subsection (11) to an accredited financial investigator is a reference to an accredited financial investigator who falls within a description specified in an order made for the purposes of that paragraph by the Secretary of State under section 453.]¹

Amendments
1   Inserted by the Serious Crime Act 2007, ss 77, 80(5), (6), Sch 10, paras 1, 9(1), (2), (3), (6).
2   Inserted by the Coroners and Justice Act 2009, s 169, Sch 19, paras 1, 12.
3   Repealed by the Serious Crime Act 2007, ss 74(2)(*d*), 92, Sch 8, Pt 4, paras 103, 107(1), (2), Sch 14.
4   Substituted by the Serious Crime Act 2007, ss 74(2)(*d*), 77, Sch 8, Pt 4, paras 103, 107(1), (3), Sch 10, paras 1, 9(1), (5).

Disclosure orders

357   Disclosure orders

(1)   A judge may, on an application made to him by [the relevant authority]¹, make a disclosure order if he is satisfied that each of the requirements for the making of the order is fulfilled.

(2)   No application for a disclosure order may be made in relation to a [detained cash investigation or a]² money laundering investigation.

[(2A)   The relevant authority may only make an application for a disclosure order in relation to a confiscation investigation if the relevant authority is in receipt of a request to do so from an appropriate officer.]²

(3)   The application for a disclosure order must state that—

    (*a*)   a person specified in the application is subject to a confiscation investigation which is being carried out by [an appropriate officer]¹ and the order is sought for the purposes of the investigation, or

    (*b*)   property specified in the application is subject to a civil recovery investigation and the order is sought for the purposes of the investigation[, or

    (*c*)   a person specified in the application is subject to an exploitation proceeds investigation and the order is sought for the purposes of the investigation.]³

(4)   A disclosure order is an order authorising [an appropriate officer]¹ to give to any person [the appropriate officer]¹ considers has relevant information notice in writing requiring him to do, with respect to any matter relevant to the investigation for the purposes of which the order is sought, any or all of the following—

    (*a*)   answer questions, either at a time specified in the notice or at once, at a place so specified;

    (*b*)   provide information specified in the notice, by a time and in a manner so specified;

    (*c*)   produce documents, or documents of a description, specified in the notice, either at or by a time so specified or at once, and in a manner so specified.

(5)   Relevant information is information (whether or not contained in a document) which [the appropriate officer concerned]¹ considers to be relevant to the investigation.

(6)   A person is not bound to comply with a requirement imposed by a notice given under a disclosure order unless evidence of authority to give the notice is produced to him.

[(7)   In this Part 'relevant authority' means–

    (*a*)   in relation to a confiscation investigation, a prosecutor; and

    (*b*)   in relation to a civil recovery investigation, a member of SOCA's staff or the relevant Director[; and

    (*c*)   in relation to an exploitation proceeds investigation, a member of SOCA's staff.]³

(8)   For the purposes of subsection (7)(*a*) a prosecutor is–

    (*a*)   in relation to a confiscation investigation carried out by a member of SOCA's staff, the relevant Director or any specified person;

    (*b*)   in relation to a confiscation investigation carried out by an accredited financial investigator, the Director of Public Prosecutions, the Director of Public Prosecutions for Northern Ireland or any specified person;

    (*c*)   in relation to a confiscation investigation carried out by a constable, the Director of Public Prosecutions, the Director of Public Prosecutions for Northern Ireland, the Director of the Serious Fraud Office or any specified person; and

    (*d*)   in relation to a confiscation investigation carried out by an officer of Revenue and Customs, the Director of Revenue and Customs Prosecutions, the Director of Public Prosecutions for Northern Ireland or any specified person.

(9)   In subsection (8) 'specified person' means any person specified, or falling within a description specified, by an order of the Secretary of State.]²

Amendments

1   Substituted by the Serious Crime Act 2007, s 74(2)(*d*), Sch 8, Pt 4, paras 103, 108(1), (2), (4), (5), (6).

2   Inserted by the Serious Crime Act 2007, ss 74(2)(*d*), 77, Sch 8, Pt 4, paras 103, 108(1), (3), (7), Sch 10, paras 1, 10.

3   Inserted by the Coroners and Justice Act 2009, s 169, Sch 19, paras 1, 13.

358   Requirements for making of disclosure order

(1)   These are the requirements for the making of a disclosure order.

(2)   There must be reasonable grounds for suspecting that—

(*a*)   in the case of a confiscation investigation, the person specified in the application for the order has benefited from his criminal conduct;

(*b*)   in the case of a civil recovery investigation, the property specified in the application for the order is recoverable property or associated property;

[(*c*)   in the case of an exploitation proceeds investigation, the person specified in the application for the order is a person within section 346(2A).]¹

(3)   There must be reasonable grounds for believing that information which may be provided in compliance with a requirement imposed under the order is likely to be of substantial value (whether or not by itself) to the investigation for the purposes of which the order is sought.

(4)   There must be reasonable grounds for believing that it is in the public interest for the information to be provided, having regard to the benefit likely to accrue to the investigation if the information is obtained.

Amendments

1   Inserted by the Coroners and Justice Act 2009, s 169, Sch 19, paras 1, 14.

359 Offences

(1)   A person commits an offence if without reasonable excuse he fails to comply with a requirement imposed on him under a disclosure order.

(2)   A person guilty of an offence under subsection (1) is liable on summary conviction to—

(*a*)   imprisonment for a term not exceeding six months,

(*b*)   a fine not exceeding level 5 on the standard scale, or

(*c*)   both.

(3)   A person commits an offence if, in purported compliance with a requirement imposed on him under a disclosure order, he—

(*a*)   makes a statement which he knows to be false or misleading in a material particular, or

(*b*)   recklessly makes a statement which is false or misleading in a material particular.

(4)   A person guilty of an offence under subsection (3) is liable—

(*a*)   on summary conviction, to imprisonment for a term not exceeding six months or to a fine not exceeding the statutory maximum or to both, or

(*b*)   on conviction on indictment, to imprisonment for a term not exceeding two years or to a fine or to both.

360 Statements

(1)   A statement made by a person in response to a requirement imposed on him under a disclosure order may not be used in evidence against him in criminal proceedings.

(2)   But subsection (1) does not apply—

(*a*)   in the case of proceedings under Part 2 or 4,

(*b*)   on a prosecution for an offence under section 359(1) or (3),

(c)   on a prosecution for an offence under section 5 of the Perjury Act 1911 (c. 6) or Article 10 of the Perjury (Northern Ireland) Order 1979 (S.I. 1979/1714 (N.I. 19)) (false statements), or

(d)   on a prosecution for some other offence where, in giving evidence, the person makes a statement inconsistent with the statement mentioned in subsection (1).

(3)   A statement may not be used by virtue of subsection (2)(d) against a person unless—

(a)   evidence relating to it is adduced, or

(b)   a question relating to it is asked,

by him or on his behalf in the proceedings arising out of the prosecution

361 Further provisions

(1)   A disclosure order does not confer the right to require a person to answer any privileged question, provide any privileged information or produce any privileged document, except that a lawyer may be required to provide the name and address of a client of his.

(2)   A privileged question is a question which the person would be entitled to refuse to answer on grounds of legal professional privilege in proceedings in the High Court.

(3)   Privileged information is any information which the person would be entitled to refuse to provide on grounds of legal professional privilege in proceedings in the High Court.

(4)   Privileged material is any material which the person would be entitled to refuse to produce on grounds of legal professional privilege in proceedings in the High Court.

(5)   A disclosure order does not confer the right to require a person to produce excluded material.

(6)   A disclosure order has effect in spite of any restriction on the disclosure of information (however imposed).

(7)   [An appropriate officer][1] may take copies of any documents produced in compliance with a requirement to produce them which is imposed under a disclosure order.

(8)   Documents so produced may be retained for so long as it is necessary to retain them (as opposed to a copy of them) in connection with the investigation for the purposes of which the order was made.

(9)   But if [an appropriate officer][1] has reasonable grounds for believing that—

(a)   the documents may need to be produced for the purposes of any legal proceedings, and

(b)   they might otherwise be unavailable for those purposes,

they may be retained until the proceedings are concluded

Amendments
1   Substituted by the Serious Crime Act 2007, s 74(2)(d), Sch 8, Pt 4, paras 103, 109.

362 Supplementary

(1)   An application for a disclosure order may be made ex parte to a judge in chambers.

(2)   Rules of court may make provision as to the practice and procedure to be followed in connection with proceedings relating to disclosure orders.

(3)   An application to discharge or vary a disclosure order may be made to the court by—

(*a*)   the [person who applied for the order]¹;

(*b*)   any person affected by the order.

(4)   The court—

    (*a*)   may discharge the order;

    (*b*)   may vary the order.

[(4A)   If a member of SOCA's staff or a person falling within a description of persons specified by virtue of section 357(9) applies for a disclosure order, an application to discharge or vary the order need not be by the same member of SOCA's staff or (as the case may be) the same person falling within that description.

(4B)   References to a person who applied for a disclosure order must be construed accordingly.]²

(5)   Subsections (2) to [(4B)]¹ do not apply to orders made in England and Wales for the purposes of a civil recovery investigation [or an exploitation proceeds investigation]³.

Amendments

1   Substituted by the Serious Crime Act 2007, s 74(2)(*d*), Sch 8, Pt 4, paras 103, 110(1), (2), (4).
2   Inserted by the Serious Crime Act 2007, s 74(2)(*d*), Sch 8, Pt 4, paras 103, 110(1), (3).
3   Inserted by the Coroners and Justice Act 2009, s 169, Sch 19, paras 1, 15.

Customer information orders

363   Customer information orders

(1)   A judge may, on an application made to him by an appropriate officer, make a customer information order if he is satisfied that each of the requirements for the making of the order is fulfilled.

[(1A)   No application for a customer information order may be made in relation to a detained cash investigation.]¹

(2)   The application for a customer information order must state that—

    (*a*)   a person specified in the application is subject to a confiscation investigation[, an exploitation proceeds investigation]² or a money laundering investigation, or

    (*b*)   property specified in the application is subject to a civil recovery investigation and a person specified in the application appears to hold the property.

(3)   The application must also state that—

    (*a*)   the order is sought for the purposes of the investigation;

    (*b*)   the order is sought against the financial institution or financial institutions specified in the application.

(4)   An application for a customer information order may specify—

    (*a*)   all financial institutions,

    (*b*)   a particular description, or particular descriptions, of financial institutions, or

    (*c*)   a particular financial institution or particular financial institutions.

(5) A customer information order is an order that a financial institution covered by the application for the order must, on being required to do so by notice in writing given by an appropriate officer, provide any such customer information as it has relating to the person specified in the application.

(6) A financial institution which is required to provide information under a customer information order must provide the information to an appropriate officer in such manner, and at or by such time, as an appropriate officer requires.

(7) If a financial institution on which a requirement is imposed by a notice given under a customer information order requires the production of evidence of authority to give the notice, it is not bound to comply with the requirement unless evidence of the authority has been produced to it.

Amendments
1   Inserted by the Serious Crime Act 2007, s 77, Sch 10, paras 1, 11.
2   Inserted by the Coroners and Justice Act 2009, s 169, Sch 19, paras 1, 16.

364 Meaning of customer information

(1) 'Customer information', in relation to a person and a financial institution, is information whether the person holds, or has held, an account or accounts at the financial institution (whether solely or jointly with another) and (if so) information as to—

(a) the matters specified in subsection (2) if the person is an individual;

(b) the matters specified in subsection (3) if the person is a company or limited liability partnership or a similar body incorporated or otherwise established outside the United Kingdom.

(2) The matters referred to in subsection (1)(a) are—

(a) the account number or numbers;

(b) the person's full name;

(c) his date of birth;

(d) his most recent address and any previous addresses;

(e) the date or dates on which he began to hold the account or accounts and, if he has ceased to hold the account or any of the accounts, the date or dates on which he did so;

(f) such evidence of his identity as was obtained by the financial institution under or for the purposes of any legislation relating to money laundering;

(g) the full name, date of birth and most recent address, and any previous addresses, of any person who holds, or has held, an account at the financial institution jointly with him;

(h) the account number or numbers of any other account or accounts held at the financial institution to which he is a signatory and details of the person holding the other account or accounts.

(3) The matters referred to in subsection (1)(b) are—

(a) the account number or numbers;

(b) the person's full name;

(c)   a description of any business which the person carries on;

(d)   the country or territory in which it is incorporated or otherwise established and any number allocated to it under [the Companies Act 2006][1] or corresponding legislation of any country or territory outside the United Kingdom;

(e)   any number assigned to it for the purposes of value added tax in the United Kingdom;

(f)   its registered office, and any previous registered offices, under [the Companies Act 2006 (or corresponding earlier legislation)][1] or anything similar under corresponding legislation of any country or territory outside the United Kingdom;

(g)   its registered office, and any previous registered offices, under the Limited Liability Partnerships Act 2000 (c. 12) or anything similar under corresponding legislation of any country or territory outside Great Britain;

(h)   the date or dates on which it began to hold the account or accounts and, if it has ceased to hold the account or any of the accounts, the date or dates on which it did so;

(i)   such evidence of its identity as was obtained by the financial institution under or for the purposes of any legislation relating to money laundering;

(j)   the full name, date of birth and most recent address and any previous addresses of any person who is a signatory to the account or any of the accounts.

(4)   The Secretary of State may by order provide for information of a description specified in the order—

(a)   to be customer information, or

(b)   no longer to be customer information.

(5)   Money laundering is an act which—

(a)   constitutes an offence under section 327, 328 or 329 of this Act or section 18 of the Terrorism Act 2000 (c. 11), or

[(aa)   constitutes an offence specified in section 415(1A) of this Act,][7]

(b)   would constitute an offence specified in paragraph (a) [or (aa)][2] if done in the United Kingdom.

Amendments

1   Substituted by the Companies Act 2006 (Consequential Amendments, Transitional Provisions and Savings) Order 2009, SI 2009/1941, s 2(1), Sch 1, para 196(1), (2).

2   Inserted by the Serious Organised Crime and Police Act 2005, s 107(1), (2).

365 Requirements for making of customer information order

(1)   These are the requirements for the making of a customer information order.

(2)   In the case of a confiscation investigation, there must be reasonable grounds for suspecting that the person specified in the application for the order has benefited from his criminal conduct.

(3)   In the case of a civil recovery investigation, there must be reasonable grounds for suspecting that—

(*a*)   the property specified in the application for the order is recoverable property or associated property;

(*b*)   the person specified in the application holds all or some of the property.

(4)   In the case of a money laundering investigation, there must be reasonable grounds for suspecting that the person specified in the application for the order has committed a money laundering offence.

(5)   In the case of any investigation, there must be reasonable grounds for believing that customer information which may be provided in compliance with the order is likely to be of substantial value (whether or not by itself) to the investigation for the purposes of which the order is sought.

(6)   In the case of any investigation, there must be reasonable grounds for believing that it is in the public interest for the customer information to be provided, having regard to the benefit likely to accrue to the investigation if the information is obtained.

366 Offences

(1)   A financial institution commits an offence if without reasonable excuse it fails to comply with a requirement imposed on it under a customer information order.

(2)   A financial institution guilty of an offence under subsection (1) is liable on summary conviction to a fine not exceeding level 5 on the standard scale.

(3)   A financial institution commits an offence if, in purported compliance with a customer information order, it—

(*a*)   makes a statement which it knows to be false or misleading in a material particular, or

(*b*)   recklessly makes a statement which is false or misleading in a material particular.

(4)   A financial institution guilty of an offence under subsection (3) is liable—

(*a*)   on summary conviction, to a fine not exceeding the statutory maximum, or

(*b*)   on conviction on indictment, to a fine.

367 Statements

(1)   A statement made by a financial institution in response to a customer information order may not be used in evidence against it in criminal proceedings.

(2)   But subsection (1) does not apply—

(*a*)   in the case of proceedings under Part 2 or 4,

(*b*)   on a prosecution for an offence under section 366(1) or (3), or

(*c*)   on a prosecution for some other offence where, in giving evidence, the financial institution makes a statement inconsistent with the statement mentioned in subsection (1).

(3)   A statement may not be used by virtue of subsection (2)(*c*) against a financial institution unless—

(*a*)   evidence relating to it is adduced, or

(*b*)   a question relating to it is asked,

by or on behalf of the financial institution in the proceedings arising out of the prosecution

368   Disclosure of information

A customer information order has effect in spite of any restriction on the disclosure of information (however imposed)

369   Supplementary

(1)   An application for a customer information order may be made ex parte to a judge in chambers.

(2)   Rules of court may make provision as to the practice and procedure to be followed in connection with proceedings relating to customer information orders.

(3)   An application to discharge or vary a customer information order may be made to the court by—

(*a*)   the person who applied for the order;

(*b*)   any person affected by the order.

(4)   The court—

(*a*)   may discharge the order;

(*b*)   may vary the order.

(5)   If an accredited financial investigator, [a member of SOCA's staff,]¹ a constable or a customs officer applies for a customer information order, an application to discharge or vary the order need not be by the same accredited financial investigator, [member of SOCA's staff,]¹ constable or customs officer.

(6)   References to a person who applied for a customer information order must be construed accordingly.

(7)   An accredited financial investigator, [a member of SOCA's staff,]¹ a constable or a customs officer may not make an application for a customer information order or an application to vary such an order unless he is a senior appropriate officer or he is authorised to do so by a senior appropriate officer.

(8)   Subsections (2) to (6) do not apply to orders made in England and Wales for the purposes of a civil recovery investigation.

Amendments
1   Inserted by the Serious Crime Act 2007, s 74(2)(*d*), Sch 8, Pt 4, paras 103, 111.

Account monitoring orders

370   Account monitoring orders

(1)   A judge may, on an application made to him by an appropriate officer, make an account monitoring order if he is satisfied that each of the requirements for the making of the order is fulfilled.

[(1A)   No application for an account monitoring order may be made in relation to a detained cash investigation.]¹

(2)   The application for an account monitoring order must state that—

(*a*)   a person specified in the application is subject to a confiscation investigation[, an exploitation proceeds investigation]² or a money laundering investigation, or (*b*)   property specified in the application is subject to a civil recovery investigation and a person specified in the application appears to hold the property.

(3)   The application must also state that—

(*a*)   the order is sought for the purposes of the investigation;

(*b*)   the order is sought against the financial institution specified in the application in relation to account information of the description so specified.

(4)   Account information is information relating to an account or accounts held at the financial institution specified in the application by the person so specified (whether solely or jointly with another).

(5)   The application for an account monitoring order may specify information relating to—

(*a*)   all accounts held by the person specified in the application for the order at the financial institution so specified,

(*b*)   a particular description, or particular descriptions, of accounts so held, or

(*c*)   a particular account, or particular accounts, so held.

(6)   An account monitoring order is an order that the financial institution specified in the application for the order must, for the period stated in the order, provide account information of the description specified in the order to an appropriate officer in the manner, and at or by the time or times, stated in the order.

(7)   The period stated in an account monitoring order must not exceed the period of 90 days beginning with the day on which the order is made.

Amendments
1   Inserted by the Serious Crime Act 2007, s 77, Sch 10, paras 1, 12.
2   Inserted by the Coroners and Justice Act 2009, s 169, Sch 19, paras 1, 17.

371   Requirements for making of account monitoring order

(1)   These are the requirements for the making of an account monitoring order.

(2)   In the case of a confiscation investigation, there must be reasonable grounds for suspecting that the person specified in the application for the order has benefited from his criminal conduct.

(3)   In the case of a civil recovery investigation, there must be reasonable grounds for suspecting that—

(*a*)   the property specified in the application for the order is recoverable property or associated property;

(*b*)   the person specified in the application holds all or some of the property.

(4)   In the case of a money laundering investigation, there must be reasonable grounds for suspecting that the person specified in the application for the order has committed a money laundering offence.

(5)   In the case of any investigation, there must be reasonable grounds for believing that account information which may be provided in compliance with the order is likely to be of substantial value (whether or not by itself) to the investigation for the purposes of which the order is sought.

(6) In the case of any investigation, there must be reasonable grounds for believing that it is in the public interest for the account information to be provided, having regard to the benefit likely to accrue to the investigation if the information is obtained.

372 Statements

(1) A statement made by a financial institution in response to an account monitoring order may not be used in evidence against it in criminal proceedings.

(2) But subsection (1) does not apply—

(*a*) in the case of proceedings under Part 2 or 4,

(*b*) in the case of proceedings for contempt of court, or

(*c*) on a prosecution for an offence where, in giving evidence, the financial institution makes a statement inconsistent with the statement mentioned in subsection (1).

(3) A statement may not be used by virtue of subsection (2)(*c*) against a financial institution unless—

(*a*) evidence relating to it is adduced, or

(*b*) a question relating to it is asked,

by or on behalf of the financial institution in the proceedings arising out of the prosecution

373 Applications

An application for an account monitoring order may be made ex parte to a judge in chambers

374 Disclosure of information

An account monitoring order has effect in spite of any restriction on the disclosure of information (however imposed)

375 Supplementary

(1) Rules of court may make provision as to the practice and procedure to be followed in connection with proceedings relating to account monitoring orders.

(2) An application to discharge or vary an account monitoring order may be made to the court by—

(*a*) the person who applied for the order;

(*b*) any person affected by the order.

(3) The court—

(*a*) may discharge the order;

(*b*) may vary the order.

(4) If an accredited financial investigator, [a member of SOCA's staff,][1] a constable or a customs officer applies for an account monitoring order, an application to discharge or vary the order need not be by the same accredited financial investigator, [member of SOCA's staff,][1] constable or customs officer.

(5) References to a person who applied for an account monitoring order must be construed accordingly.

(6)   Account monitoring orders have effect as if they were orders of the court.

(7)   This section does not apply to orders made in England and Wales for the purposes of a civil recovery investigation.

Amendments

1   Inserted by the Serious Crime Act 2007, s 74(2)(*d*), Sch 8, Pt 4, paras 103, 112.

... [1]

376 ... [1]

... [1]

Amendments

1   Repealed by the Serious Crime Act 2007, ss 74(2)(*d*), 92, Sch 8, Pt 4, paras 103, 113, Sch 14.

Code of practice

377 Code of practice [of Secretary of State etc.][1]

(1)   The Secretary of State must prepare a code of practice as to the exercise by all of the following of functions they have under this Chapter—

   (*a*)   [the Director General of SOCA][2];

   (*b*)   [other members of SOCA's staff][2];

   (*c*)   accredited financial investigators;

   (*d*)   constables;

   (*e*)   customs officers.

(2)   After preparing a draft of the code the Secretary of State—

   (*a*)   must publish the draft;

   (*b*)   must consider any representations made to him about the draft;

   (*c*)   may amend the draft accordingly.

(3)   After the Secretary of State has proceeded under subsection (2) he must lay the code before Parliament.

(4)   When he has done so the Secretary of State may bring the code into operation on such day as he may appoint by order.

(5)   A person specified in subsection (1)(*a*) to (*e*) must comply with a code of practice which is in operation under this section in the exercise of any function he has under this Chapter.

(6)   If such a person fails to comply with any provision of such a code of practice he is not by reason only of that failure liable in any criminal or civil proceedings.

(7)   But the code of practice is admissible in evidence in such proceedings and a court may take account of any failure to comply with its provisions in determining any question in the proceedings.

(8)   The Secretary of State may from time to time revise a code previously brought into operation under this section; and the preceding provisions of this section apply to a revised code as they apply to the code as first prepared.

(9)   The following provisions do not apply to an appropriate officer [or the relevant authority]¹ in the exercise of any function [either]² has under this Chapter—

(*a*)   section 67(9) of the Police and Criminal Evidence Act 1984 (c. 60) (application of codes of practice under that Act to persons other than police officers);

(*b*)   Article 66(8) of the Police and Criminal Evidence (Northern Ireland) Order 1989 (S.I. 1989/1341 (N.I. 12)) (which makes similar provision for Northern Ireland).

Amendments
1   Inserted by the Serious Crime Act 2007, s 74(2)(*d*), Sch 8, Pt 4, paras 103, 114(1), (2), (4)(*a*).
2   Substituted by the Serious Crime Act 2007, s 74(2)(*d*), Sch 8, Pt 4, paras 103, 114(1), (3), (4)(*b*).

[377A   Code of practice of Attorney General or Advocate General for Northern Ireland

(1)   The Attorney General must prepare a code of practice as to–

(*a*)   the exercise by the Director of Public Prosecutions, the Director of Revenue and Customs Prosecutions and the Director of the Serious Fraud Office of functions they have under this Chapter; and

(*b*)   the exercise by any other person, who is the relevant authority by virtue of section 357(9) in relation to a confiscation investigation, of functions he has under this Chapter in relation to England and Wales as the relevant authority.

(2)   The Advocate General for Northern Ireland must prepare a code of practice as to–

(*a*)   the exercise by the Director of Public Prosecutions for Northern Ireland of functions he has under this Chapter; and

(*b*)   the exercise by any other person, who is the relevant authority by virtue of section 357(9) in relation to a confiscation investigation, of functions he has under this Chapter in relation to Northern Ireland as the relevant authority.

(3)   After preparing a draft of the code the Attorney General or (as the case may be) the Advocate General for Northern Ireland–

(*a*)   must publish the draft;

(*b*)   must consider any representations made to him about the draft;

(*c*)   may amend the draft accordingly.

(4)   After the Attorney General or the Advocate General for Northern Ireland has proceeded under subsection (3) he must lay the code before Parliament.

(5)   When the code has been so laid the Attorney General or (as the case may be) the Advocate General for Northern Ireland may bring the code into operation on such day as he may appoint by order.

(6)   A person specified in subsection (1)(*a*) or (*b*) or (2)(*a*) or (*b*) must comply with a code of practice which is in operation under this section in the exercise of any function he has under this Chapter to which the code relates.

(7)   If such a person fails to comply with any provision of such a code of practice the person is not by reason only of that failure liable in any criminal or civil proceedings.

(8) But the code of practice is admissible in evidence in such proceedings and a court may take account of any failure to comply with its provisions in determining any question in the proceedings.

(9) The Attorney General or (as the case may be) the Advocate General for Northern Ireland may from time to time revise a code previously brought into operation under this section; and the preceding provisions of this section apply to a revised code as they apply to the code as first prepared.

(10) In this section references to the Advocate General for Northern Ireland are to be read, before the coming into force of section 27(1) of the Justice (Northern Ireland) Act 2002 (c. 26), as references to the Attorney General for Northern Ireland.][1]

Amendments
1   Inserted by the Serious Crime Act 2007, s 74(2)(*d*), Sch 8, Pt 4, paras 103, 115.

Interpretation

378   Officers

(1) In relation to a confiscation investigation these are appropriate officers—

   (*a*)   [a member of SOCA's staff][1];

   (*b*)   an accredited financial investigator;

   (*c*)   a constable;

   (*d*)   a customs officer.

(2) In relation to a confiscation investigation these are senior appropriate officers—

   (*a*)   [a senior member of SOCA's staff][1];

   (*b*)   a police officer who is not below the rank of superintendent;

   (*c*)   a customs officer who is not below such grade as is designated by the Commissioners of Customs and Excise as equivalent to that rank;

   (*d*)   an accredited financial investigator who falls within a description specified in an order made for the purposes of this paragraph by the Secretary of State under section 453.

(3) In relation to a civil recovery investigation[—

   (*a*)   a member of SOCA's staff or the relevant Director is an appropriate officer;

   (*b*)   a senior member of SOCA's staff is a senior appropriate officer.][1]

[(3A) In relation to a detained cash investigation these are appropriate officers–

   (*a*)   a constable;

   [(*ab*) an accredited financial investigator;][2]

   (*b*)   an officer of Revenue and Customs.][2]

[(3B) The reference in paragraph (*ab*) of subsection (3A) to an accredited financial investigator is a reference to an accredited financial investigator who falls within a description specified in an order made for the purposes of that paragraph by the Secretary of State under section 453.][2]

(4)   In relation to a money laundering investigation these are appropriate officers—

    (*a*)   an accredited financial investigator;

    (*b*)   a constable;

    (*c*)   a customs officer.

(5)   For the purposes of section 342, in relation to a money laundering investigation a person authorised for the purposes of money laundering investigations by [the Director General of [SOCA]¹]³ is also an appropriate officer.

(6)   In relation to a money laundering investigation these are senior appropriate officers—

    (*a*)   a police officer who is not below the rank of superintendent;

    (*b*)   a customs officer who is not below such grade as is designated by the Commissioners of Customs and Excise as equivalent to that rank;

    (*c*)   an accredited financial investigator who falls within a description specified in an order made for the purposes of this paragraph by the Secretary of State under section 453.

[(6A) In relation to an exploitation proceeds investigation, a member of SOCA's staff is an appropriate officer.]⁴

(7)   ...⁵

[(8)   For the purposes of this Part a senior member of SOCA's staff is–

    (*a*)   the Director General of SOCA; or

    (*b*)   any member of SOCA's staff authorised by the Director General (whether generally or specifically) for this purpose.]²

Amendments

1   Substituted by the Serious Crime Act 2007, s 74(2)(*d*), Sch 8, Pt 4, paras 103, 116(1), (2), (3), (4), (5).
2   Inserted by the Serious Crime Act 2007, ss 74(2)(*d*), 77, 80(7), (8), Sch 8, Pt 4, paras 103, 116(1), (7), Sch 10, paras 1, 13.
3   Substituted by the Serious Organised Crime and Police Act 2005, s 59, Sch 4, paras 168, 175.
4   Inserted by the Coroners and Justice Act 2009, s 169, Sch 19, paras 1, 18.
5   Repealed by the Serious Crime Act 2007, ss 74(2)(*d*), 92, Sch 8, Pt 4, paras 103, 116(1), (6), Sch 14.

379   Miscellaneous

'Document', 'excluded material' and 'premises' have the same meanings as in the Police and Criminal Evidence Act 1984 (c. 60) or (in relation to Northern Ireland) the Police and Criminal Evidence (Northern Ireland) Order 1989 (S.I. 1989/1341 (N.I. 12))

[*Sections 380 to 412 only apply to Scotland so are not reproduced in this title.*]

CHAPTER 4
INTERPRETATION

413   Criminal conduct

(1)   Criminal conduct is conduct which—

    (*a*)   constitutes an offence in any part of the United Kingdom, or (*b*)   would constitute an offence in any part of the United Kingdom if it occurred there.

(2)   A person benefits from conduct if he obtains property or a pecuniary advantage as a result of or in connection with the conduct.

(3)   References to property or a pecuniary advantage obtained in connection with conduct include references to property or a pecuniary advantage obtained in both that connection and some other.

(4)   If a person benefits from conduct his benefit is the property or pecuniary advantage obtained as a result of or in connection with the conduct.

(5)   It is immaterial—

(*a*)   whether conduct occurred before or after the passing of this Act, and

(*b*)   whether property or a pecuniary advantage constituting a benefit from conduct was obtained before or after the passing of this Act.

414 Property

(1)   Property is all property wherever situated and includes—

(*a*)   money;

(*b*)   all forms of property, real or personal, heritable or moveable;

(*c*)   things in action and other intangible or incorporeal property.

(2)   'Recoverable property' and 'associated property' have the same meanings as in Part 5.

(3)   The following rules apply in relation to property—

(*a*)   property is obtained by a person if he obtains an interest in it;

(*b*)   references to an interest, in relation to land in England and Wales or Northern Ireland, are to any legal estate or equitable interest or power;

(*c*)   references to an interest, in relation to land in Scotland, are to any estate, interest, servitude or other heritable right in or over land, including a heritable security;

(*d*)   references to an interest, in relation to property other than land, include references to a right (including a right to possession).

415 Money laundering offences

(1)   An offence under section 327, 328 or 329 is a money laundering offence.

[(1A) Each of the following is a money laundering offence—

(*a*)   an offence under section 93A, 93B or 93C of the Criminal Justice Act 1988;

(*b*)   an offence under section 49, 50 or 51 of the Drug Trafficking Act 1994;

(*c*)   an offence under section 37 or 38 of the Criminal Law (Consolidation) (Scotland) Act 1995;

(*d*)   an offence under article 45, 46 or 47 of the Proceeds of Crime (Northern Ireland) Order 1996.][1]

(2)   Each of the following is a money laundering offence—

(*a*)   an attempt, conspiracy or incitement to commit an offence specified in subsection (1);

(*b*)   aiding, abetting, counselling or procuring the commission of an offence specified in subsection (1).

Amendments

1   Inserted by the Serious Organised Crime and Police Act 2005, s 107(1), (4).

416   Other interpretative provisions

(1)   These expressions are to be construed in accordance with these provisions of this Part—

civil recovery investigation: section 341(2) and (3)

confiscation investigation: section 341(1)

[detained cash investigation: section 341(3A)][1]

money laundering investigation: section 341(4)

(2)   In the application of this Part to England and Wales and Northern Ireland, these expressions are to be construed in accordance with these provisions of this Part—

account information: section 370(4)

account monitoring order: section 370(6)

appropriate officer: section 378

customer information: section 364

customer information order: section 363(5)

disclosure order: section 357(4)

document: section 379

order to grant entry: section 347(3)

production order: section 345(4)

[relevant authority: section 357(7) to (9)

relevant Director: section 352(5A)][1]

search and seizure warrant: section 352(4)

senior appropriate officer: section 378

[senior member of SOCA's staff: section 378(8).][1]

(3)   In the application of this Part to Scotland, these expressions are to be construed in accordance with these provisions of this Part—

account information: section 404(5)

account monitoring order: section 404(7)

customer information: section 398

customer information order: section 397(6)

disclosure order: section 391(4)

production order: section 380(5)

proper person: section 412

search warrant: section 387(4)

(4)   'Financial institution' means a person carrying on a business in the regulated sector.

(5)   But a person who ceases to carry on a business in the regulated sector (whether by virtue of paragraph 5 of Schedule 9 or otherwise) is to continue to be treated as a financial institution for the purposes of any requirement under—

(a)   a customer information order, or

(b)   an account monitoring order,

to provide information which relates to a time when the person was a financial institution

(6)   References to a business in the regulated sector must be construed in accordance with Schedule 9.

(7)   'Recovery order', 'interim receiving order' and 'interim administration order' have the same meanings as in Part 5.

[(7A) 'Unlawful conduct' has the meaning given by section 241.]¹

(8)   References to notice in writing include references to notice given by electronic means.

(9)   This section and sections 413 to 415 apply for the purposes of this Part.

Amendments

1   Inserted by the Serious Crime Act 2007, ss 74(2)(*d*), 77, Sch 8, Pt 4, paras 103, 117, Sch 10, paras 1, 24.

PART 9
INSOLVENCY ETC

Bankruptcy in England and Wales

417   Modifications of the 1986 Act

(1)   This section applies if a person is adjudged bankrupt in England and Wales.

(2)   The following property is excluded from his estate for the purposes of Part 9 of the 1986 Act—

(a)   property for the time being subject to a restraint order which was made under section 41, 120 or 190 before the order adjudging him bankrupt;

(b)   any property in respect of which an order under section 50 ...¹ is in force;

(c)   any property in respect of which an order under section 128(3) is in force;

(d)   any property in respect of which an order under section 198 ...¹ is in force.

(3)   Subsection (2)(*a*) applies to heritable property in Scotland only if the restraint order is recorded in the General Register of Sasines or registered in the Land Register of Scotland before the order adjudging the person bankrupt.

(4)   If in the case of a debtor an interim receiver stands at any time appointed under section 286 of the 1986 Act and any property of the debtor is then subject to a restraint order made under section 41, 120 or 190 the powers conferred on the receiver by virtue of that Act do not apply to property then subject to the restraint order.

Amendments
1   Repealed by the Serious Crime Act 2007, ss 74(2)(*a*), 92Sch 8, Pt 1, paras 1, 69, Sch 14.

418   Restriction of powers

(1)   If a person is adjudged bankrupt in England and Wales the powers referred to in subsection (2) must not be exercised in relation to the property referred to in subsection (3).

(2)   These are the powers—

   (*a*)   the powers conferred on a court by sections 41 to 67 and the powers of a receiver appointed under section 48 [or 50][1];

   (*b*)   the powers conferred on a court by sections 120 to 136 and Schedule 3 and the powers of an administrator appointed under section 125 or 128(3);

   (*c*)   the powers conferred on a court by sections 190 to 215 and the powers of a receiver appointed under section 196 [or 198][1].

(3)   This is the property—

   (*a*)   property which is for the time being comprised in the bankrupt's estate for the purposes of Part 9 of the 1986 Act;

   (*b*)   property in respect of which his trustee in bankruptcy may (without leave of the court) serve a notice under section 307, 308 or 308A of the 1986 Act (after-acquired property, tools, tenancies etc);

   (*c*)   property which is to be applied for the benefit of creditors of the bankrupt by virtue of a condition imposed under section 280(2)(*c*) of the 1986 Act;

   (*d*)   in a case where a confiscation order has been made under section 6 or 156 of this Act, any sums remaining in the hands of a receiver appointed under section 50[or 198][1] of this Act after the amount required to be paid under the confiscation order has been fully paid;

   (*e*)   in a case where a confiscation order has been made under section 92 of this Act, any sums remaining in the hands of an administrator appointed under section 128 of this Act after the amount required to be paid under the confiscation order has been fully paid.

(4)   But nothing in the 1986 Act must be taken to restrict (or enable the restriction of) the powers referred to in subsection (2).

(5)   In a case where a petition in bankruptcy was presented or a receiving order or adjudication in bankruptcy was made before 29 December 1986 (when the 1986 Act came into force) this section has effect with these modifications—

   (*a*)   for the reference in subsection (3)(*a*) to the bankrupt's estate for the purposes of Part 9 of that Act substitute a reference to the property of the bankrupt for the purposes of the 1914 Act;

   (*b*)   omit subsection (3)(*b*);

   (*c*)   for the reference in subsection (3)(*c*) to section 280(2)(*c*) of the 1986 Act substitute a reference to section 26(2) of the 1914 Act;

   (*d*)   for the reference in subsection (4) to the 1986 Act substitute a reference to the 1914 Act.

Amendments

1   Substituted by the Serious Crime Act 2007, s 74(2)(*a*), Sch 8, Pt 1, paras 1, 70.

419 Tainted gifts

(1)   This section applies if a person who is adjudged bankrupt in England and Wales has made a tainted gift (whether directly or indirectly).

(2)   No order may be made under section 339, 340 or 423 of the 1986 Act (avoidance of certain transactions) in respect of the making of the gift at any time when—

    (*a*)   any property of the recipient of the tainted gift is subject to a restraint order under section 41, 120 or 190, or

    (*b*)   there is in force in respect of such property an order under section 50, ...[1] 128(3) [or 198][2].

(3)   Any order made under section 339, 340 or 423 of the 1986 Act after an order mentioned in subsection (2)(*a*) or (*b*) is discharged must take into account any realisation under Part 2, 3 or 4 of this Act of property held by the recipient of the tainted gift.

(4)   A person makes a tainted gift for the purposes of this section if he makes a tainted gift within the meaning of Part 2, 3 or 4.

(5)   In a case where a petition in bankruptcy was presented or a receiving order or adjudication in bankruptcy was made before 29 December 1986 (when the 1986 Act came into force) this section has effect with the substitution for a reference to section 339, 340 or 423 of the 1986 Act of a reference to section 27, 42 or 44 of the 1914 Act.

Amendments

1   Repealed by the Serious Crime Act 2007, ss 74(2)(*a*), 92, Sch 8, Pt 1, paras 1, 71(*a*), Sch 14.
2   Substituted by the Serious Crime Act 2007, s 74(2)(*a*), Sch 8, Pt 1, paras 1, 71(*b*).

[*Sections 420 to 422 only apply to Scotland so are not reproduced in this title.*]

[*Sections 423 to 425 only apply to Northern Ireland so are not reproduced in this title.*]

Winding up in England and Wales and Scotland

426 Winding up under the 1986 Act

(1)   In this section 'company' means any company which may be wound up under the 1986 Act.

(2)   If an order for the winding up of a company is made or it passes a resolution for its voluntary winding up, the functions of the liquidator (or any provisional liquidator) are not exercisable in relation to the following property—

    (*a*)   property for the time being subject to a restraint order which was made under section 41, 120 or 190 before the relevant time;

    (*b*)   any property in respect of which an order under section 50 ...[1] is in force;

    (*c*)   any property in respect of which an order under section 128(3) is in force;

    (*d*)   any property in respect of which an order under section 198 ...[1] is in force.

(3)   Subsection (2)(*a*) applies to heritable property in Scotland only if the restraint order is recorded in the General Register of Sasines or registered in the Land Register of Scotland before the relevant time.

(4)   If an order for the winding up of a company is made or it passes a resolution for its voluntary winding up the powers referred to in subsection (5) must not be exercised in the way mentioned in subsection (6) in relation to any property—

    (*a*)   which is held by the company, and

    (*b*)   in relation to which the functions of the liquidator are exercisable.

(5)   These are the powers—

    (*a*)   the powers conferred on a court by sections 41 to 67 and the powers of a receiver appointed under section 48 [or 50]^2;

    (*b*)   the powers conferred on a court by sections 120 to 136 and Schedule 3 and the powers of an administrator appointed under section 125 or 128(3);

    (*c*)   the powers conferred on a court by sections 190 to 215 and the powers of a receiver appointed under section 196 [or 198]^2.

(6)   The powers must not be exercised—

    (*a*)   so as to inhibit the liquidator from exercising his functions for the purpose of distributing property to the company's creditors;

    (*b*)   so as to prevent the payment out of any property of expenses (including the remuneration of the liquidator or any provisional liquidator) properly incurred in the winding up in respect of the property.

(7)   But nothing in the 1986 Act must be taken to restrict (or enable the restriction of) the exercise of the powers referred to in subsection (5).

(8)   For the purposes of the application of Parts 4 and 5 of the 1986 Act (winding up) to a company which the Court of Session has jurisdiction to wind up, a person is not a creditor in so far as any sum due to him by the company is due in respect of a confiscation order made under section 6, 92 or 156.

(9)   The relevant time is—

    (*a*)   if no order for the winding up of the company has been made, the time of the passing of the resolution for voluntary winding up;

    (*b*)   if such an order has been made, but before the presentation of the petition for the winding up of the company by the court such a resolution has been passed by the company, the time of the passing of the resolution;

    (*c*)   if such an order has been made, but paragraph (*b*) does not apply, the time of the making of the order.

(10)   In a case where a winding up of a company commenced or is treated as having commenced before 29 December 1986, this section has effect with the following modifications—

    (*a*)   in subsections (1) and (7) for 'the 1986 Act' substitute 'the Companies Act 1985';

    (*b*)   in subsection (8) for 'Parts 4 and 5 of the 1986 Act' substitute 'Parts 20 and 21 of the Companies Act 1985'.

Amendments
1   Repealed by the Serious Crime Act 2007, ss 74(2)(*a*), 92, Sch 8, Pt 1, paras 1, 78(1), (2), Sch 14.
2   Substituted by the Serious Crime Act 2007, s 74(2)(*a*), Sch 8, Pt 1, paras 1, 78(1), (3).

427   Tainted gifts

(1)   In this section 'company' means any company which may be wound up under the 1986 Act.

(2)   This section applies if—

    (*a*)   an order for the winding up of a company is made or it passes a resolution for its voluntary winding up, and

    (*b*)   it has made a tainted gift (whether directly or indirectly).

(3)   No order may be made under section 238, 239 or 423 of the 1986 Act (avoidance of certain transactions) and no decree may be granted under section 242 or 243 of that Act (gratuitous alienations and unfair preferences), or otherwise, in respect of the making of the gift at any time when—

    (*a*)   any property of the recipient of the tainted gift is subject to a restraint order under section 41, 120 or 190, or

    (*b*)   there is in force in respect of such property an order under section 50, ...[1] 128(3) [or 198][2].

(4)   Any order made under section 238, 239 or 423 of the 1986 Act or decree granted under section 242 or 243 of that Act, or otherwise, after an order mentioned in subsection (3)(*a*) or (*b*) is discharged must take into account any realisation under Part 2, 3 or 4 of this Act of property held by the recipient of the tainted gift.

(5)   A person makes a tainted gift for the purposes of this section if he makes a tainted gift within the meaning of Part 2, 3 or 4.

(6)   In a case where the winding up of a company commenced or is treated as having commenced before 29 December 1986 this section has effect with the substitution—

    (*a*)   for references to section 239 of the 1986 Act of references to section 615 of the Companies Act 1985 (c. 6);

    (*b*)   for references to section 242 of the 1986 Act of references to section 615A of the Companies Act 1985;

    (*c*)   for references to section 243 of the 1986 Act of references to section 615B of the Companies Act 1985.

Amendments
1   Repealed by the Serious Crime Act 2007, ss 74(2)(*a*), 92, Sch 8, Pt 1, paras 1, 79(*a*), Sch 14.
2   Substituted by the Serious Crime Act 2007, s 74(2)(*a*), Sch 8, Pt 1, paras 1, 79(*b*).

[*Sections 428 and 429 only apply to Northern Ireland so are not reproduced in this title.*]

Floating charges

430   Floating charges

(1)   In this section 'company' means a company which may be wound up under

    (*a*)   the 1986 Act, or

(*b*)   the 1989 Order.

(2)   If a company holds property which is subject to a floating charge, and a receiver has been appointed by or on the application of the holder of the charge, the functions of the receiver are not exercisable in relation to the following property—

    (*a*)   property for the time being subject to a restraint order which was made under section 41, 120 or 190 before the appointment of the receiver;

    (*b*)   any property in respect of which an order under section 50 ...[1] is in force;

    (*c*)   any property in respect of which an order under section 128(3) is in force;

    (*d*)   any property in respect of which an order under section 198 ...[1] is in force.

(3)   Subsection (2)(*a*) applies to heritable property in Scotland only if the restraint order is recorded in the General Register of Sasines or registered in the Land Register of Scotland before the appointment of the receiver.

(4)   If a company holds property which is subject to a floating charge, and a receiver has been appointed by or on the application of the holder of the charge, the powers referred to in subsection (5) must not be exercised in the way mentioned in subsection (6) in relation to any property—

    (*a*)   which is held by the company, and

    (*b*)   in relation to which the functions of the receiver are exercisable.

(5)   These are the powers—

    (*a*)   the powers conferred on a court by sections 41 to 67 and the powers of a receiver appointed under section 48 [or 50][2];

    (*b*)   the powers conferred on a court by sections 120 to 136 and Schedule 3 and the powers of an administrator appointed under section 125 or 128(3);

    (*c*)   the powers conferred on a court by sections 190 to 215 and the powers of a receiver appointed under section 196 [or 198][2].

(6)   The powers must not be exercised—

    (*a*)   so as to inhibit the receiver from exercising his functions for the purpose of distributing property to the company's creditors;

    (*b*)   so as to prevent the payment out of any property of expenses (including the remuneration of the receiver) properly incurred in the exercise of his functions in respect of the property.

(7)   But nothing in the 1986 Act or the 1989 Order must be taken to restrict (or enable the restriction of) the exercise of the powers referred to in subsection (5).

(8)   In this section 'floating charge' includes a floating charge within the meaning of section 462 of the Companies Act 1985 (c. 6).

Amendments

1   Repealed by the Serious Crime Act 2007, ss 74(2)(*a*), 92, Sch 8, Pt 1, paras 1, 82(1), (2), Sch 14.

2   Substituted by the Serious Crime Act 2007, s 74(2)(*a*), Sch 8, Pt 1, paras 1, 82(1), (3).

Limited liability partnerships

431 Limited liability partnerships

(1) In sections 426, 427 and 430 'company' includes a limited liability partnership which may be wound up under the 1986 Act.

(2) A reference in those sections to a company passing a resolution for its voluntary winding up is to be construed in relation to a limited liability partnership as a reference to the partnership making a determination for its voluntary winding up.

Insolvency practitioners

432 Insolvency practitioners

(1) Subsections (2) and (3) apply if a person acting as an insolvency practitioner seizes or disposes of any property in relation to which his functions are not exercisable because—

   (*a*) it is for the time being subject to a restraint order made under section 41, 120 or 190, or

   (*b*) it is for the time being subject to [a property freezing order made under section 245A, an interim receiving order made under section 246, a prohibitory property order made under section 255A][1] or an interim administration order made under section 256,

and at the time of the seizure or disposal he believes on reasonable grounds that he is entitled (whether in pursuance of an order of a court or otherwise) to seize or dispose of the property

(2) He is not liable to any person in respect of any loss or damage resulting from the seizure or disposal, except so far as the loss or damage is caused by his negligence.

(3) He has a lien on the property or the proceeds of its sale—

   (*a*) for such of his expenses as were incurred in connection with the liquidation, bankruptcy, sequestration or other proceedings in relation to which he purported to make the seizure or disposal, and

   (*b*) for so much of his remuneration as may reasonably be assigned to his acting in connection with those proceedings.

(4) Subsection (2) does not prejudice the generality of any provision of the 1985 Act, the 1986 Act, the 1989 Order or any other Act or Order which confers protection from liability on him.

(5) Subsection (7) applies if—

   (*a*) property is subject to a restraint order made under section 41, 120 or 190,

   (*b*) a person acting as an insolvency practitioner incurs expenses in respect of property subject to the restraint order, and

   (*c*) he does not know (and has no reasonable grounds to believe) that the property is subject to the restraint order.

(6) Subsection (7) also applies if—

   (*a*) property is subject to a restraint order made under section 41, 120 or 190,

(b)   a person acting as an insolvency practitioner incurs expenses which are not ones in respect of property subject to the restraint order, and

(c)   the expenses are ones which (but for the effect of the restraint order) might have been met by taking possession of and realising property subject to it.

(7)   Whether or not he has seized or disposed of any property, he is entitled to payment of the expenses under—

(a)   section 54(2) [or, 55(3)]^2 if the restraint order was made under section 41;

(b)   section 130(3) or 131(3) if the restraint order was made under section 120;

(c)   section 202(2) [or 203(3)]^2 if the restraint order was made under section 190.

(8)   Subsection (10) applies if—

(a)   property is subject to [a property freezing order made under section 245A, an interim receiving order made under section 246, a prohibitory property order made under section 255A]^1 or an interim administration order made under section 256,

(b)   a person acting as an insolvency practitioner incurs expenses in respect of property subject to the order, and

(c)   he does not know (and has no reasonable grounds to believe) that the property is subject to the order.

(9)   Subsection (10) also applies if—

(a)   property is subject to [a property freezing order made under section 245A, an interim receiving order made under section 246, a prohibitory property order made under section 255A]^1 or an interim administration order made under section 256,

(b)   a person acting as an insolvency practitioner incurs expenses which are not ones in respect of property subject to the order, and

(c)   the expenses are ones which (but for the effect of the order) might have been met by taking possession of and realising property subject to it.

(10)   Whether or not he has seized or disposed of any property, he is entitled to payment of the expenses under section 280.

Amendments
1   Substituted by the Serious Organised Crime and Police Act 2005, s 109, Sch 6, paras 4, 23.
2   Substituted by the Serious Crime Act 2007, s 74(2)(a), Sch 8, Pt 1, paras 1, 83.

433 Meaning of insolvency practitioner

(1)   This section applies for the purposes of section 432.

(2)   A person acts as an insolvency practitioner if he so acts within the meaning given by section 388 of the 1986 Act or Article 3 of the 1989 Order; but this is subject to subsections (3) to (5).

(3)   The expression 'person acting as an insolvency practitioner' includes the official receiver acting as receiver or manager of the property concerned.

(4)   In applying section 388 of the 1986 Act under subsection (2) above—

(*a*) the reference in section 388(2)(*a*) to a permanent or interim trustee in sequestration must be taken to include a reference to a trustee in sequestration;

(*b*) section 388(5) (which includes provision that nothing in the section applies to
anything done by the official receiver or the Accountant in Bankruptcy) must be
ignored.

(5) In applying Article 3 of the 1989 Order under subsection (2) above, paragraph (5)
(which includes provision that nothing in the Article applies to anything done by the
official receiver) must be ignored.

Interpretation

434 Interpretation

(1) The following paragraphs apply to references to Acts or Orders—

(*a*) the 1913 Act is the Bankruptcy (Scotland) Act 1913 (c. 20);

(*b*) the 1914 Act is the Bankruptcy Act 1914 (c. 59);

(*c*) the 1985 Act is the Bankruptcy (Scotland) Act 1985 (c. 66);

(*d*) the 1986 Act is the Insolvency Act 1986 (c. 45);

(*e*) the 1989 Order is the Insolvency (Northern Ireland) Order 1989 (S.I. 1989/2405
(N.I. 19)).

(2) An award of sequestration is made on the date of sequestration within the meaning of
section 12(4) of the 1985 Act.

(3) This section applies for the purposes of this Part.

PART 10
INFORMATION

England and Wales and Northern Ireland

[435 Use of information by certain Directors

(1) Information obtained by or on behalf of the Director in connection with the exercise of
any of his functions under, or in relation to, Part 5 or 8 may be used by him in
connection with his exercise of any of his other functions (whether under, or in relation
to, either Part, another Part of this Act or otherwise).

(2) Information obtained by or on behalf of the Director in connection with the exercise of
any of his functions (whether under, or in relation to, this Act or otherwise) which are
not functions under, or in relation to, Part 5 or 8 may be used by him in connection with
his exercise of any of his functions under, or in relation to, Part 5 or 8.

(3) This section applies to information obtained before the coming into force of the section
as well as to information obtained after the coming into force of the section.

(4) In this section 'the Director' means–

(*a*) the Director of Public Prosecutions;

(*b*) the Director of the Serious Fraud Office; or

(*c*) the Director of Public Prosecutions for Northern Ireland.][1]

Amendments

1   Substituted by the Serious Crime Act 2007, s 74(2)(*f*), Sch 8, Pt 6, paras 121, 131.

436   Disclosure of information to [certain Directors]¹

(1)   Information which is held by or on behalf of a permitted person (whether it was obtained before or after the coming into force of [subsection (10)]¹) may be disclosed to the Director for the purpose of the exercise by the Director of his functions [under, or in relation to, Part 5 or 8]².

(2)   A disclosure under this section is not to be taken to breach any restriction on the disclosure of information (however imposed).

(3)   But nothing in this section authorises the making of a disclosure—

(*a*)   which contravenes the Data Protection Act 1998 (c. 29);

(*b*)   which is prohibited by Part 1 of the Regulation of Investigatory Powers Act 2000 (c. 23).

(4)   This section does not affect a power to disclose which exists apart from this section.

(5)   These are permitted persons—

(*a*)   a constable;

[(*b*)   ...³]⁴

(*c*)   ...⁵

(*d*)   the Director of the Serious Fraud Office;

(*e*)   the Commissioners of Inland Revenue;

(*f*)   the Commissioners of Customs and Excise;

(*g*)   the Director of Public Prosecutions;

[(*ga*)   ...³]⁶

(*h*)   the Director of Public Prosecutions for Northern Ireland.

(6)   The Secretary of State may by order designate as permitted persons other persons who exercise functions which he believes are of a public nature.

(7)   But an order under subsection (6) must specify the functions in respect of which the designation is made.

(8)   Information must not be disclosed under this section on behalf of the Commissioners of Inland Revenue or on behalf of the Commissioners of Customs and Excise unless the Commissioners concerned authorise the disclosure.

(9)   The power to authorise a disclosure under subsection (8) may be delegated (either generally or for a specified purpose)—

(*a*)   in the case of the Commissioners of Inland Revenue, to an officer of the Board of Inland Revenue;

(*b*)   in the case of the Commissioners of Customs and Excise, to a customs officer.

[(10)   In this section 'the Director' has the same meaning as in section 435.]²

Amendments
1   Substituted by the Serious Crime Act 2007, s 74(2)(*f*), Sch 8, Pt 6, paras 121, 132(1), (2), (3)(*a*).
2   Inserted by the Serious Crime Act 2007, s 74(2)(*f*), Sch 8, Pt 6, paras 121, 132(1), (3)(*b*), (5).
3   Repealed by the Serious Crime Act 2007, ss 74(2)(*f*), 92, Sch 8, Pt 6, paras 121, 132(1), (4), Sch 14.
4   Substituted by the Serious Organised Crime and Police Act 2005, s 59, Sch 4, paras 168, 176.
5   Repealed by the Serious Organised Crime and Police Act 2005, s 59, Sch 4, paras 168, 176.
6   Inserted by the Commissioners for Revenue and Customs Act 2005, s 50(6), Sch 4, para 98.

437   Further disclosure

(1)   Subsection (2) applies to information obtained under section 436 from the Commissioners of Inland Revenue or from the Commissioners of Customs and Excise or from a person acting on behalf of either of them.

(2)   Such information must not be further disclosed except—

(*a*)   for a purpose connected with the exercise of the Director's functions [under, or in relation to, Part 5 or 8]¹, and

(*b*)   with the consent of the Commissioners concerned.

(3)   Consent under subsection (2) may be given—

(*a*)   in relation to a particular disclosure;

(*b*)   in relation to disclosures made in circumstances specified or described in the consent.

(4)   The power to consent to further disclosure under subsection (2)(*b*) may be delegated (either generally or for a specified purpose)—

(*a*)   in the case of the Commissioners of Inland Revenue, to an officer of the Board of Inland Revenue;

(*b*)   in the case of the Commissioners of Customs and Excise, to a customs officer.

(5)   Subsection (6) applies to information obtained under section 436 from a permitted person other than the Commissioners of Inland Revenue or the Commissioners of Customs and Excise or a person acting on behalf of either of them.

(6)   A permitted person who discloses such information to the Director may make the disclosure subject to such conditions as to further disclosure by the Director as the permitted person thinks appropriate; and the information must not be further disclosed in contravention of the conditions.

[(7)   In this section 'the Director' has the same meaning as in section 435.]¹

Amendments
1   Inserted by the Serious Crime Act 2007, s 74(2)(*f*), Sch 8, Pt 6, paras 121, 133.

438   Disclosure of information by [certain Directors]¹

(1)   Information obtained by or on behalf of the Director in connection with the exercise of any of his functions [under, or in relation to, Part 5 or 8]² may be disclosed by him if the disclosure is for the purposes of any of the following—

(*a*)   any criminal investigation which is being or may be carried out, whether in the United Kingdom or elsewhere;

(*b*)   any criminal proceedings which have been or may be started, whether in the United Kingdom or elsewhere;

(c)   the exercise of the Director's functions [under, or in relation to, Part 5 or 8]^2;

(d)   the exercise by the prosecutor of functions under Parts 2, 3 and 4;

(e)   the exercise by the Scottish Ministers of their functions under Part 5;

(f)   the exercise by a customs officer[, an accredited financial investigator]^3 or a constable of his functions under Chapter 3 of Part 5;

[(fa)   the exercise of any functions of SOCA, another Director or the Director of Revenue and Customs Prosecutions under, or in relation to, Part 5 or 8;]^2

(g)   safeguarding national security;

(h)   investigations or proceedings outside the United Kingdom which have led or may lead to the making of an external order within the meaning of section 447;

(i)   the exercise of a designated function.

(2)   ...^{4}

(3)   ...^{4}

(4)   ...^{4}

(5)   If the Director makes a disclosure of information for a purpose specified in subsection (1) he may make any further disclosure of the information by the person to whom he discloses it subject to such conditions as he thinks fit.

(6)   Such a person must not further disclose the information in contravention of the conditions.

(7)   A disclosure under this section is not to be taken to breach any restriction on the disclosure of information (however imposed).

(8)   But nothing in this section authorises the making of a disclosure—

(a)   which contravenes the Data Protection Act 1998 (c. 29);

(b)   which is prohibited by Part 1 of the Regulation of Investigatory Powers Act 2000 (c. 23).

[(8A)   This section does not affect a power to disclose which exists apart from this section.

(8B)   This section applies to information obtained before the coming into force of subsection (10) as well as to information obtained after the coming into force of that subsection.]^2

(9)   A designated function is a function which the Secretary of State thinks is a function of a public nature and which he designates by order.

[(10)   In this section 'the Director' has the same meaning as in section 435.]^2

Amendments

1   Substituted by the Serious Crime Act 2007, s 74(2)(*f*), Sch 8, Pt 6, paras 121, 134(1), (2).

2   Inserted by the Serious Crime Act 2007, s 74(2)(*f*), Sch 8, Pt 6, paras 121, 134(1), (3), (5), (6).

3   Inserted by the Serious Crime Act 2007, s 79, Sch 11, paras 1, 14.

4   Repealed by the Serious Crime Act 2007, ss 74(2)(*f*), 92, Sch 8, Pt 6, paras 121, 134(1), (4), Sch 14.

[*Sections 439 to 441 only apply to Scotland so are not reproduced in this title.*]

Overseas purposes

442 Restriction on disclosure for overseas purposes

(1) Section 18 of the Anti-terrorism, Crime and Security Act 2001 (c. 24) (restrictions on disclosure of information for overseas purposes) applies to a disclosure of information authorised by section 438(1)(*a*) or (*b*) or 441(2)(*a*) or (*b*).

(2) In the application of section 18 of the Anti-terrorism, Crime and Security Act 2001 by virtue of subsection (1) section 20 of that Act must be ignored and the following subsection is substituted for subsection (2) of section 18 of that Act—

'(2) In subsection (1) the reference, in relation to a direction, to a relevant disclosure is a reference to a disclosure which—

   (*a*) is made for a purpose authorised by section 438(1)(*a*) or (*b*) or 441(2)(*a*) or (*b*) of the Proceeds of Crime Act 2002, and

   (*b*) is of any such information as is described in the direction.'.

PART 11
CO-OPERATION

443 Enforcement in different parts of the United Kingdom

(1) Her Majesty may by Order in Council make provision—

   (*a*) for an order made by a court under Part 2 to be enforced in Scotland or Northern Ireland;

   (*b*) for an order made by a court under Part 3 to be enforced in England and Wales or Northern Ireland;

   (*c*) for an order made by a court under Part 4 to be enforced in England and Wales or Scotland;

   (*d*) for an order made under Part 8 in one part of the United Kingdom to be enforced in another part;

   (*e*) for a warrant issued under Part 8 in one part of the United Kingdom to be executed in another part.

(2) Her Majesty may by Order in Council make provision—

   (*a*) for a function of a receiver appointed in pursuance of Part 2 to be exercisable in Scotland or Northern Ireland;

   (*b*) for a function of an administrator appointed in pursuance of Part 3 to be exercisable in England and Wales or Northern Ireland;

   (*c*) for a function of a receiver appointed in pursuance of Part 4 to be exercisable in England and Wales or Scotland.

(3) An Order under this section may include—

   (*a*) provision conferring and imposing functions on the prosecutor[, SOCA and the relevant Director][1];

   (*b*) provision about the registration of orders and warrants;

(c)   provision allowing directions to be given in one part of the United Kingdom about the enforcement there of an order made or warrant issued in another part;

(d)   provision about the authentication in one part of the United Kingdom of an order made or warrant issued in another part.

(4)   An Order under this section may—

(a)   amend an enactment;

(b)   apply an enactment (with or without modifications).

[(5)   In this section 'relevant Director' has the meaning given by section 352(5A).]²

Amendments

1   Substituted by the Serious Crime Act 2007, s 74(2)(*f*), Sch 8, Pt 6, paras 121, 137(1), (2).
2   Inserted by the Serious Crime Act 2007, s 74(2)(*f*), Sch 8, Pt 6, paras 121, 137(1), (3).

444   External requests and orders

(1)   Her Majesty may by Order in Council—

(a)   make provision for a prohibition on dealing with property which is the subject of an external request;

(b)   make provision for the realisation of property for the purpose of giving effect to an external order.

(2)   An Order under this section may include provision which (subject to any specified modifications) corresponds to any provision of Part 2, 3 or 4 or Part 5 except Chapter 3.

(3)   An Order under this section may include—

[(a)   provision about the functions of any of the listed persons in relation to external requests and orders;]¹

(b)   provision about the registration of external orders;

(c)   provision about the authentication of any judgment or order of an overseas court, and of any other document connected with such a judgment or order or any proceedings relating to it;

(d)   provision about evidence (including evidence required to establish whether proceedings have been started or are likely to be started in an overseas court);

(e)   provision to secure that any person affected by the implementation of an external request or the enforcement of an external order has an opportunity to make representations to a court in the part of the United Kingdom where the request is being implemented or the order is being enforced.

[(4)   For the purposes of subsection (3)(*a*) 'the listed persons' are—

(a)   the Secretary of State;

(b)   the Lord Advocate;

(c)   the Scottish Ministers;

(d)   [SOCA]²;

(e)   the Director of Public Prosecutions;

(f)   the Director of Public Prosecutions for Northern Ireland;

(*g*)   the Director of the Serious Fraud Office; and

(*h*)   the Director of Revenue and Customs Prosecutions.]³

Amendments
1   Substituted by the Serious Organised Crime and Police Act 2005, s 108(1), (2).
2   Inserted by the Serious Crime Act 2007, s 74(2)(*f*), Sch 8, Pt 6, paras 121, 138.
3   Inserted by the Serious Organised Crime and Police Act 2005, s 108(1), (3).

445   External investigations

(1)   Her Majesty may by Order in Council make—

(*a*)   provision to enable orders equivalent to those under Part 8 to be made, and warrants equivalent to those under Part 8 to be issued, for the purposes of an external investigation;

(*b*)   provision creating offences in relation to external investigations which are equivalent to offences created by Part 8.

(2)   An Order under this section may include—

(*a*)   provision corresponding to any provision of Part 8 (subject to any specified modifications);

(*b*)   provision about the functions of the Secretary of State, the Lord Advocate, the Scottish Ministers, [SOCA, the Director of Public Prosecutions, the Director of Public Prosecutions for Northern Ireland, the Director of Revenue and Customs Prosecutions]¹, the Director of the Serious Fraud Office, constables and customs officers;

(*c*)   provision about evidence (including evidence required to establish whether an investigation is being carried out in a country or territory outside the United Kingdom).

(3)   But an Order under this section must not provide for a disclosure order to be made for the purposes of an external investigation into whether a money laundering offence has been committed.

Amendments
1   Substituted by the Serious Crime Act 2007, s 74(2)(*f*), Sch 8, Pt 6, paras 121, 139.

446   Rules of court

Rules of court may make such provision as is necessary or expedient to give effect to an Order in Council made under this Part (including provision about the exercise of functions of a judge conferred or imposed by the Order)

447   Interpretation

(1)   An external request is a request by an overseas authority to prohibit dealing with relevant property which is identified in the request.

(2)   An external order is an order which—

(*a*)   is made by an overseas court where property is found or believed to have been obtained as a result of or in connection with criminal conduct, and

(b)   is for the recovery of specified property or a specified sum of money.

(3)   An external investigation is an investigation by an overseas authority into—

    (a)   whether property has been obtained as a result of or in connection with criminal conduct, ...[1]

    [(aa)   the extent or whereabouts of property obtained as a result of or in connection with criminal conduct, or][2]

    (b)   whether a money laundering offence has been committed.

(4)   Property is all property wherever situated and includes—

    (a)   money;

    (b)   all forms of property, real or personal, heritable or moveable;

    (c)   things in action and other intangible or incorporeal property.

(5)   Property is obtained by a person if he obtains an interest in it.

(6)   References to an interest, in relation to property other than land, include references to a right (including a right to possession).

(7)   Property is relevant property if there are reasonable grounds to believe that it may be needed to satisfy an external order which has been or which may be made.

(8)   Criminal conduct is conduct which—

    (a)   constitutes an offence in any part of the United Kingdom, or

    (b)   would constitute an offence in any part of the United Kingdom if it occurred there.

(9)   A money laundering offence is conduct carried out in a country or territory outside the United Kingdom and which if carried out in the United Kingdom would constitute any of the following offences—

    (a)   an offence under section 327, 328 or 329;

    (b)   an attempt, conspiracy or incitement to commit an offence specified in paragraph (a);

    (c)   aiding, abetting, counselling or procuring the commission of an offence specified in paragraph (a).

(10)   An overseas court is a court of a country or territory outside the United Kingdom.

(11)   An overseas authority is an authority which has responsibility in a country or territory outside the United Kingdom—

    (a)   for making a request to an authority in another country or territory (including the United Kingdom) to prohibit dealing with relevant property,

    (b)   for carrying out an investigation into whether property has been obtained as a result of or in connection with criminal conduct, or

    (c)   for carrying out an investigation into whether a money laundering offence has been committed.

(12)   This section applies for the purposes of this Part.

1   Repealed by the Serious Organised Crime and Police Act 2005, s 174(2), Sch 17, Pt 2.
2   Inserted by the Serious Organised Crime and Police Act 2005, s 108(1), (4).

PART 12
MISCELLANEOUS AND GENERAL

Miscellaneous

448   Tax

Schedule 10 contains provisions about tax

449   [SOCA's]¹ staff: pseudonyms

(1)   This section applies to a member of [SOCA's staff]¹ if—

   (*a*)   he is [assigned by SOCA]¹ to do anything for the purposes of this Act, and

   (*b*)   it is necessary or expedient for the purpose of doing the thing for the member of the staff of the Agency to identify himself by name.

(2)   [An authorised person]¹ may direct that such a member of [SOCA's staff]¹ may for that purpose identify himself by means of a pseudonym.

(3)   For the purposes of any proceedings or application under this Act a certificate signed by [an authorised person]¹ which sufficiently identifies the member of [SOCA's staff]¹ by reference to the pseudonym is conclusive evidence that that member of the staff of the Agency is authorised to use the pseudonym.

(4)   In any proceedings or application under this Act a member of [SOCA's staff]¹ in respect of whom a direction under this section is in force must not be asked (and if asked is not required to answer) any question which is likely to reveal his true identity.

(5)   ...²

[(6)   In this section 'authorised person' means a member of SOCA's staff authorised by SOCA for the purposes of this section.]³

1   Substituted by the Serious Crime Act 2007, s 74(2)(*f*), Sch 8, Pt 6, paras 121, 140(1), (2), (3), (4), (5), (6).
2   Repealed by the Serious Crime Act 2007, ss 74(2)(*f*), 92, Sch 8, Pt 6, paras 121, 140(1), (7), Sch 14.
3   Inserted by the Serious Crime Act 2007, s 74(2)(*f*), Sch 8, Pt 6, paras 121, 140(1), (7).

[449A   Staff of relevant Directors: pseudonyms

(1)   This section applies to a member of the staff of the relevant Director if–

   (*a*)   the member is to exercise a function as a member of that staff under, or in relation to, Part 5 or 8; and

   (*b*)   it is necessary or expedient for the purpose of exercising that function for the member of staff to identify himself by name.

(2)   The relevant Director may direct that such a member of staff may for that purpose identify himself by means of a pseudonym.

(3)   For the purposes of any proceedings or application under this Act, a certificate signed by the relevant Director which sufficiently identifies the member of staff by reference to the pseudonym is conclusive evidence that that member of staff is authorised to use the pseudonym.

(4)   In any proceedings or application under this Act a member of the staff of the relevant Director in respect of whom a direction under this section is in force must not be asked (and if asked is not required to answer) any question which is likely to reveal his true identity.

(5)   The relevant Director may not delegate the exercise of his functions under this section or otherwise authorise another person to exercise those functions on his behalf.

(6)   In this section 'relevant Director' has the meaning given by section 352(5A).][1]

Amendments

1   Inserted by the Serious Crime Act 2007, s 74(2)(*d*), Sch 8, Pt 4, paras 103, 118.

[*Section 450 only applies to Scotland so is not reproduced in this title.*]

451   [Revenue and Customs prosecutions][1]

(1)   Proceedings for a specified offence may be started [by the Director of Revenue and Customs Prosecutions or by order of the Commissioners for Her Majesty's Revenue and Customs][1] (the Commissioners).

[(2)   Where proceedings under subsection (1) are instituted by the Commissioners, the proceedings must be brought in the name of an officer of Revenue and Customs.][1]

(3)   ...[2]

(4)   If the Commissioners investigate, or propose to investigate, any matter to help them to decide—

    (*a*)   whether there are grounds for believing that a specified offence has been committed, or

    (*b*)   whether a person is to be prosecuted for such an offence,

    the matter must be treated as an assigned matter within the meaning of the Customs and Excise Management Act 1979 (c. 2)

(5)   This section—

    (*a*)   does not prevent any person (including a [officer of Revenue and Customs][2]) who has power to arrest, detain or prosecute a person for a specified offence from doing so;

    (*b*)   does not prevent a court from dealing with a person brought before it following his arrest by a [officer of Revenue and Customs][2] for a specified offence, even if the proceedings were not started by an order under subsection (1).

(6)   The following are specified offences—

    (*a*)   an offence under Part 7;

    (*b*)   an offence under section 342;

    (*c*)   an attempt, conspiracy or incitement to commit an offence specified in paragraph (*a*) or (*b*);

(*d*)   aiding, abetting, counselling or procuring the commission of an offence specified in paragraph (*a*) or (*b*).

(7)   This section does not apply to proceedings on indictment in Scotland.

Amendments
1   Substituted by the Commissioners for Revenue and Customs Act 2005, s 50(6), Sch 4, para 99(*a*), (*b*), (*d*), (*e*).
2   Repealed by the Commissioners for Revenue and Customs Act 2005, ss 50(6), 52(2), Sch 4, para 99(*c*), Sch 5.

452   Crown servants

(1)   The Secretary of State may by regulations provide that any of the following provisions apply to persons in the public service of the Crown.

(2)   The provisions are—

(*a*)   the provisions of Part 7;

(*b*)   section 342.

453   References to financial investigators

(1)   The Secretary of State may by order provide that a specified reference in this Act to an accredited financial investigator is a reference to such an investigator who falls within a specified description.

(2)   A description may[, in particular,]¹ be framed by reference to a grade designated by a specified person [or by reference to particular types of training undertaken]¹.

Amendments
1   Inserted by the Serious Crime Act 2007, s 81(1).

[453A   Certain offences in relation to financial investigators

(1)   A person commits an offence if he assaults an accredited financial investigator who is acting in the exercise of a relevant power.

(2)   A person commits an offence if he resists or wilfully obstructs an accredited financial investigator who is acting in the exercise of a relevant power.

(3)   A person guilty of an offence under subsection (1) is liable on summary conviction–

(*a*)   to imprisonment for a term not exceeding 51 weeks; or

(*b*)   to a fine not exceeding level 5 on the standard scale;

or to both.

(4)   A person guilty of an offence under subsection (2) is liable on summary conviction–

(*a*)   to imprisonment for a term not exceeding 51 weeks; or

(*b*)   to a fine not exceeding level 3 on the standard scale; or to both.

(5)   In this section 'relevant power' means a power exercisable under–

(*a*)   section 45 or 194 (powers to seize property to which restraint orders apply);

(*b*)   section 289 (powers to search for cash);

(*c*)   section 294 (powers to seize cash);

(*d*)   section 295(1) (power to detain seized cash); or

(*e*)   a search and seizure warrant issued under section 352.

(6)   In the application of this section to England and Wales in relation to an offence committed before the commencement of section 281(5) of the Criminal Justice Act 2003 (c. 44) (alteration of penalties for summary offences), and in the application of this section to Northern Ireland–

(*a*)   the reference to 51 weeks in subsection (3)(*a*) is to be read as a reference to 6 months; and

(*b*)   the reference to 51 weeks in subsection (4)(*a*) is to be read as a reference to 1 month.]¹

Amendments

1   Inserted by the Serious Crime Act 2007, s 81(2).

454   Customs officers

For the purposes of this Act a customs officer is a person commissioned by the Commissioners of Customs and Excise under section 6(3) of the Customs and Excise Management Act 1979 (c. 2)

455   Enactment

In this Act (except in section 460(1)) a reference to an enactment includes a reference to—

(*a*)   an Act of the Scottish Parliament;

(*b*)   Northern Ireland legislation.

General

456   Amendments

Schedule 11 contains miscellaneous and consequential amendments

457   Repeals and revocations

Schedule 12 contains repeals and revocations

458   Commencement

(1)   The preceding provisions of this Act (except the provisions specified in subsection (3)) come into force in accordance with provision made by the Secretary of State by order.

(2)   But no order may be made which includes provision for the commencement of Part 5, 8 or 10 unless the Secretary of State has consulted the Scottish Ministers.

(3)   The following provisions come into force in accordance with provision made by the Scottish Ministers by order after consultation with the Secretary of State—

(*a*)   Part 3;

(*b*)   this Part, to the extent that it relates to Part 3.

459 Orders and regulations

(1) References in this section to subordinate legislation are to—

    (*a*)   any Order in Council under this Act;

    (*b*)   any order under this Act (other than one falling to be made by a court);

    (*c*)   any regulations under this Act.

(2) Subordinate legislation—

    (*a*)   may make different provision for different purposes;

    (*b*)   may include supplementary, incidental, saving or transitional provisions.

(3) Any power to make subordinate legislation is exercisable by statutory instrument [(other than the power of the Advocate General for Northern Ireland to make an order under section 377A(5) which is exercisable by statutory rule for the purposes of the Statutory Rules (Northern Ireland) Order 1979 (S.I. 1979/1573 (N.I.12)))][1].

(4) A statutory instrument is subject to annulment in pursuance of a resolution of either House of Parliament if it contains subordinate legislation other than—

    (*a*)   an order under section 75(7) or (8), 223(7) or (8), 282, 292(4), [302(7B),][1] 309, [339A(7),][2] 364(4), 377(4)[, 377A(5)][1], 436(6), 438(9) or 458;

    (*b*)   subordinate legislation made by the Scottish Ministers;

    (*c*)   an Order in Council made under section 443 which makes provision only in relation to Scotland.

(5) A statutory instrument is subject to annulment in pursuance of a resolution of the Scottish Parliament if it contains—

    (*a*)   subordinate legislation made by the Scottish Ministers other than an order under section 142(6) or (7), 293(4), 398(4), 410(4), 439(6), 441(9) or 458;

    (*b*)   an Order in Council made under section 443 which makes provision only in relation to Scotland.

(6) No order may be made—

    (*a*)   by the Secretary of State under section 75(7) or (8), 223(7) or (8), 282, 292(4), [302(7B),][1] 309, [339A(7),][2] 364(4), 377(4), 436(6) or 438(9) unless a draft of the order has been laid before Parliament and approved by a resolution of each House;

    [(*aa*)   by the Attorney General or the Advocate General for Northern Ireland under section 377A(5) unless a draft of the order has been laid before Parliament and approved by a resolution of each House;][1]

    (*b*)   by the Scottish Ministers under section 142(6) or (7), 293(4), 398(4), 410(4), 439(6) or 441(9) unless a draft of the order has been laid before and approved by a resolution of the Scottish Parliament.

[(6A) If a draft of an order under section 302(7B) would, apart from this subsection, be treated as a hybrid instrument for the purposes of the standing orders of either House of Parliament, it shall proceed in that House as if it were not a hybrid instrument.][1]

(7) The Scottish Ministers must lay before the Scottish Parliament a copy of every statutory instrument containing an Order in Council made under section 444 or 445.

[(8)   In this section references to the Advocate General for Northern Ireland are to be read, before the coming into force of section 27(1) of the Justice (Northern Ireland) Act 2002 (c. 26), as references to the Attorney General for Northern Ireland.]¹

Amendments

1   Inserted by the Serious Crime Act 2007, ss 74(2)(*d*), 79, Sch 8, Pt 4, paras 103, 119, Sch 11, paras 1, 15.
2   Inserted by the Serious Organised Crime and Police Act 2005, s 103(1), (7).

460   Finance

(1)   The following are to be paid out of money provided by Parliament—

    (*a*)   any expenditure incurred by any Minister of the Crown under this Act;

    (*b*)   any increase attributable to this Act in the sums payable out of money so provided under any other enactment.

(2)   Any sums received by the Secretary of State in consequence of this Act are to be paid into the Consolidated Fund.

[(3)   Subject to anything in this Act–

    (*a*)   any sums received by the Director of Public Prosecutions, the Director of Revenue and Customs Prosecutions or the Director of the Serious Fraud Office in consequence of this Act are to be paid into the Consolidated Fund; and

    (*b*)   any sums received by the Director of Public Prosecutions for Northern Ireland in consequence of this Act are to be paid to the Secretary of State.]¹

Amendments

1   Inserted by the Serious Crime Act 2007, s 74(2)(*f*), Sch 8, Pt 6, paras 121, 141.

461   Extent

(1)   Part 2 extends to England and Wales only.

(2)   In Part 8, Chapter 2 extends to England and Wales and Northern Ireland only.

(3)   These provisions extend to Scotland only—

    (*a*)   Part 3;

    (*b*)   in Part 8, Chapter 3.

(4)   Part 4 extends to Northern Ireland only.

(5)   The amendments in Schedule 11 have the same extent as the provisions amended.

(6)   The repeals and revocations in Schedule 12 have the same extent as the provisions repealed or revoked.

462   Short title

This Act may be cited as the Proceeds of Crime Act 2002

Schedule 1

...¹

...¹

Amendments

1   Repealed by the Serious Crime Act 2007, ss 74(2)(*f*), 92, Sch 8, Pt 6, paras 121, 142, Sch 14.

Schedule 2
Lifestyle offences: England and Wales

Section 75

Drug trafficking

1

(1)   An offence under any of the following provisions of the Misuse of Drugs Act 1971 (c. 38)—

   (*a*)   section 4(2) or (3) (unlawful production or supply of controlled drugs);

   (*b*)   section 5(3) (possession of controlled drug with intent to supply);

   (*c*)   section 8 (permitting certain activities relating to controlled drugs);

   (*d*)   section 20 (assisting in or inducing the commission outside the UK of an offence punishable under a corresponding law).

(2)   An offence under any of the following provisions of the Customs and Excise Management Act 1979 (c. 2) if it is committed in connection with a prohibition or restriction on importation or exportation which has effect by virtue of section 3 of the Misuse of Drugs Act 1971—

   (*a*)   section 50(2) or (3) (improper importation of goods);

   (*b*)   section 68(2) (exploration of prohibited or restricted goods);

   (*c*)   section 170 (fraudulent evasion).

(3)   An offence under either of the following provisions of the Criminal Justice (International Co-operation) Act 1990 (c. 5)—

   (*a*)   section 12 (manufacture or supply of a substance for the time being specified in Schedule 2 to that Act);

   (*b*)   section 19 (using a ship for illicit traffic in controlled drugs).

Money laundering

2

An offence under either of the following provisions of this Act—

   (*a*)   section 327 (concealing etc criminal property);

   (*b*)   section 328 (assisting another to retain criminal property).

Directing terrorism

3

An offence under section 56 of the Terrorism Act 2000 (c. 11) (directing the activities of a terrorist organisation).

312

People trafficking

[4

(1)   An offence under section 25, 25A or 25B of the Immigration Act 1971 (c. 77) (assisting unlawful immigration etc).

[(2)   An offence under any of sections 57 to 59 of the Sexual Offences Act 2003 (trafficking for sexual exploitation).]¹

[(3)   An offence under section 4 of the Asylum and Immigration (Treatment of Claimants, etc.) Act 2004 (exploitation).]²]³

Amendments

1   Substituted by the Sexual Offences Act 2003, s 139, Sch 6, para 46(1), (2).
2   Inserted by the Asylum and Immigration (Treatment of Claimants, etc.) Act 2004, s 5(7).
3   Substituted by the Nationality, Immigration and Asylum Act 2002, s 114(3), Sch 7, para 31.

Arms trafficking

5

(1)   An offence under either of the following provisions of the Customs and Excise Management Act 1979 if it is committed in connection with a firearm or ammunition—

(*a*)   section 68(2) (exportation of prohibited goods);

(*b*)   section 170 (fraudulent evasion).

(2)   An offence under section 3(1) of the Firearms Act 1968 (c. 27) (dealing in firearms or ammunition by way of trade or business).

(3)   In this paragraph 'firearm' and 'ammunition' have the same meanings as in section 57 of the Firearms Act 1968 (c. 27).

Counterfeiting

6

An offence under any of the following provisions of the Forgery and Counterfeiting Act 1981 (c. 45)—

(*a*)   section 14 (making counterfeit notes or coins);

(*b*)   section 15 (passing etc counterfeit notes or coins);

(*c*)   section 16 (having counterfeit notes or coins);

(*d*)   section 17 (making or possessing materials or equipment for counterfeiting).

Intellectual property

7

(1)   An offence under any of the following provisions of the Copyright, Designs and Patents Act 1988 (c. 48)—

(*a*)   section 107(1) (making or dealing in an article which infringes copyright);

(*b*)   section 107(2) (making or possessing an article designed or adapted for making a copy of a copyright work);

(*c*)   section 198(1) (making or dealing in an illicit recording);

(*d*)   section 297A (making or dealing in unauthorised decoders).

(2)   An offence under section 92(1), (2) or (3) of the Trade Marks Act 1994 (c. 26) (unauthorised use etc of trade mark).

[Prostitution and child sex

8

(1)   An offence under section 33 or 34 of the Sexual Offences Act 1956 (keeping or letting premises for use as a brothel).

(2)   An offence under any of the following provisions of the Sexual Offences Act 2003–

(*a*)   section 14 (arranging or facilitating commission of a child sex offence);

(*b*)   section 48 (causing or inciting child prostitution or pornography);

(*c*)   section 49 (controlling a child prostitute or a child involved in pornography);

(*d*)   section 50 (arranging or facilitating child prostitution or pornography);

(*e*)   section 52 (causing or inciting prostitution for gain);

(*f*)   section 53 (controlling prostitution for gain).]¹

Amendments
1   Substituted by the Sexual Offences Act 2003, s 139, Sch 6, para 46(1), (3).

Blackmail

9

An offence under section 21 of the Theft Act 1968 (c. 60) (blackmail).

[9A

An offence under section 12(1) or (2) of the Gangmasters (Licensing) Act 2004 (acting as a gangmaster other than under the authority of a licence, possession of false documents etc).]¹

Amendments
1   Inserted by the Gangmasters (Licensing) Act 2004, s 14(4).

Inchoate offences

10

(1)   An offence of attempting, conspiring or inciting the commission of an offence specified in this Schedule.

[(1A) An offence under section 44 of the Serious Crime Act 2007 of doing an act capable of encouraging or assisting the commission of an offence specified in this Schedule.]¹

(2)   An offence of aiding, abetting, counselling or procuring the commission of such an offence.

Amendments
1   Inserted by the Serious Crime Act 2007, s 63(2), Sch 6, Pt 2, para 62.

Schedule 3
Administrators: further provision

Section 137

General

1

In this Schedule, unless otherwise expressly provided—

(*a*)   references to an administrator are to an administrator appointed under section 125 or 128(3);

(*b*)   references to realisable property are to the realisable property in respect of which the administrator is appointed.

Appointment etc

2

(1)   If the office of administrator is vacant, for whatever reason, the court must appoint a new administrator.

(2)   Any property vested in the previous administrator by virtue of paragraph 5(4) vests in the new administrator.

(3)   Any order under section 125 or 128(7) in relation to the previous administrator applies in relation to the new administrator when he gives written notice of his appointment to the person subject to the order.

(4)   The administration of property by an administrator must be treated as continuous despite any temporary vacancy in that office.

(5)   The appointment of an administrator is subject to such conditions as to caution as the accountant of court may impose.

(6)   The premium of any bond of caution or other security required by such conditions must be treated as part of the administrator's expenses in the exercise of his functions.

Functions

3

(1)   An administrator—

(*a*)   may, if appointed under section 125, and

(*b*)   must, if appointed under section 128(3),

as soon as practicable take possession of the realisable property and of the documents mentioned in sub-paragraph (2)

(2)   Those documents are any document which—

(*a*)   is in the possession or control of the person ('A') in whom the property is vested (or would be vested but for an order made under paragraph 5(4)), and

315

(*b*)   relates to the property or to A's assets, business or financial affairs.

(3)   An administrator is entitled to have access to, and to copy, any document relating to the property or to A's assets, business or financial affairs and not falling within sub-paragraph (2)(*a*).

(4)   An administrator may bring, defend or continue any legal proceedings relating to the property.

(5)   An administrator may borrow money so far as it is necessary to do so to safeguard the property and may for the purposes of such borrowing create a security over any part of the property.

(6)   An administrator may, if he considers that it would be beneficial for the management or realisation of the property—

(*a*)   carry on any business of A;

(*b*)   exercise any right of A as holder of securities in a company;

(*c*)   grant a lease of the property or take on lease any other property;

(*d*)   enter into any contract, or execute any deed, as regards the property or as regards A's business.

(7)   An administrator may, where any right, option or other power forms part of A's estate, make payments or incur liabilities with a view to—

(*a*)   obtaining property which is the subject of, or

(*b*)   maintaining,

the right, option or power

(8)   An administrator may effect or maintain insurance policies as regards the property on A's business.

(9)   An administrator may, if appointed under section 128(3), complete any uncompleted title which A has to any heritable estate; but completion of title in A's name does not validate by accretion any unperfected right in favour of any person other than the administrator.

(10)   An administrator may sell, purchase or exchange property or discharge any security for an obligation due to A; but it is incompetent for the administrator or an associate of his (within the meaning of section 74 of the Bankruptcy (Scotland) Act 1985 (c. 66)) to purchase any of A's property in pursuance of this sub-paragraph.

(11)   An administrator may claim, vote and draw dividends in the sequestration of the estate (or bankruptcy or liquidation) of a debtor of A and may accede to a voluntary trust deed for creditors of such a debtor.

(12)   An administrator may discharge any of his functions through agents or employees, but is personally liable to meet the fees and expenses of any such agent or employee out of such remuneration as is payable to the administrator on a determination by the accountant of court.

(13)   An administrator may take such professional advice as he considers necessary in connection with the exercise of his functions.

(14)   An administrator may at any time apply to the court for directions as regards the exercise of his functions.

(15)   An administrator may exercise any power specifically conferred on him by the court, whether conferred on his appointment or subsequently.

(16)   An administrator may—

(*a*)   enter any premises;

(*b*)   search for or inspect anything authorised by the court;

(*c*)   make or obtain a copy, photograph or other record of anything so authorised;

(*d*)   remove anything which the administrator is required or authorised to take possession of in pursuance of an order of the court.

(17)   An administrator may do anything incidental to the powers and duties listed in the previous provisions of this paragraph.

Consent of accountant of court

4

An administrator proposing to exercise any power conferred by paragraph 3(4) to (17) must first obtain the consent of the accountant of court.

Dealings in good faith with administrator

5

(1)   A person dealing with an administrator in good faith and for value is not concerned to enquire whether the administrator is acting within the powers mentioned in paragraph 3.

(2)   Sub-paragraph (1) does not apply where the administrator or an associate purchases property in contravention of paragraph 3(10).

(3)   The validity of any title is not challengeable by reason only of the administrator having acted outwith the powers mentioned in paragraph 3.

(4)   The exercise of a power mentioned in paragraph 3(4) to (11) must be in A's name except where and in so far as an order made by the court under this sub-paragraph vests the property in the administrator (or in a previous administrator).

(5)   The court may make an order under sub-paragraph (4) on the application of the administrator or on its own motion.

Money received by administrator

6

(1)   All money received by an administrator in the exercise of his functions must be deposited by him, in the name (unless vested in the administrator by virtue of paragraph 5(4)) of the holder of the property realised, in an appropriate bank or institution.

(2)   But the administrator may at any time retain in his hands a sum not exceeding £200 or such other sum as may be prescribed by the Scottish Ministers by regulations.

(3)   In sub-paragraph (1), 'appropriate bank or institution' means a bank or institution mentioned in section 3(1) of the Banking Act 1987 (c. 22) or for the time being specified in Schedule 2 to that Act.

Effect of appointment of administrator on diligence

7

(1)   An arrestment or [poinding] of realisable property executed on or after the appointment of an administrator does not create a preference for the arrester or poinder.

(2)   Any realisable property so arrested or poinded, or (if the property has been sold) the proceeds of sale, must be handed over to the administrator.

(3)   A poinding of the ground in respect of realisable property on or after such appointment is ineffectual in a question with the administrator except for the interest mentioned in sub-paragraph (4).

(4)   That interest is—

(*a*)   interest on the debt of a secured creditor for the current half-yearly term, and

(*b*)   arrears of interest on that debt for one year immediately before the commencement of that term.

(5)   On and after such appointment no other person may raise or insist in an adjudication against realisable property or be confirmed as executor-creditor on that property.

(6)   An inhibition on realisable property which takes effect on or after such appointment does not create a preference for the inhibitor in a question with the administrator.

(7)   This paragraph is without prejudice to sections 123 and 124.

(8)   In this paragraph, the reference to an administrator is to an administrator appointed under section 128(3).

Supervision

8

(1)   If the accountant of court reports to the court that an administrator has failed to perform any duty imposed on him, the court may, after giving the administrator an opportunity to be heard as regards the matter—

(*a*)   remove him from office,

(*b*)   censure him, or

(*c*)   make such other order as it thinks fit.

(2)   Section 6 of the Judicial Factors (Scotland) Act 1889 (c. 39) (supervision of judicial factors) does not apply in relation to an administrator.

Accounts and remuneration

9

(1)   Not later than two weeks after the issuing of any determination by the accountant of court as to the remuneration and expenses payable to the administrator, the administrator or the Lord Advocate may appeal against it to the court.

(2)   The amount of remuneration payable to the administrator must be determined on the basis of the value of the work reasonably undertaken by him, regard being had to the extent of the responsibilities involved.

(3) The accountant of court may authorise the administrator to pay without taxation an account in respect of legal services incurred by the administrator.

Discharge of administrator

10

(1) After an administrator has lodged his final accounts under paragraph 9(1), he may apply to the accountant of court to be discharged from office.

(2) A discharge, if granted, frees the administrator from all liability (other than liability arising from fraud) in respect of any act or omission of his in exercising his functions as administrator.

[*Schedule 4 only applies to Scotland so is not reproduced in this title.*]

[*Schedule 5 only applies to Northern Ireland so is not reproduced in this title.*]

Schedule 6
Powers of interim receiver or administrator

Sections 247 and 257

Seizure

1

Power to seize property to which the order applies.

Information

2

(1) Power to obtain information or to require a person to answer any question.

(2) A requirement imposed in the exercise of the power has effect in spite of any restriction on the disclosure of information (however imposed)

(3) An answer given by a person in pursuance of such a requirement may not be used in evidence against him in criminal proceedings.

(4) Sub-paragraph (3) does not apply—

(*a*) on a prosecution for an offence under section 5 of the Perjury Act 1911, section 44(2) of the Criminal Law (Consolidation) (Scotland) Act 1995 or Article 10 of the Perjury (Northern Ireland) Order 1979 (false statements), or

(*b*) on a prosecution for some other offence where, in giving evidence, he makes a statement inconsistent with it.

(5) But an answer may not be used by virtue of sub-paragraph (4)(*b*) against a person unless—

(*a*) evidence relating to it is adduced, or

(*b*) a question relating to it is asked,

by him or on his behalf in the proceedings arising out of the prosecution

Entry, search, etc.

3

(1)   Power to—

    (*a*)   enter any premises in the United Kingdom to which the interim order applies, and

    (*b*)   take any of the following steps.

(2)   Those steps are—

    (*a*)   to carry out a search for or inspection of anything described in the order,

    (*b*)   to make or obtain a copy, photograph or other record of anything so described,

    (*c*)   to remove anything which he is required to take possession of in pursuance of the order or which may be required as evidence in the proceedings under Chapter 2 of Part 5.

(3)   The order may describe anything generally, whether by reference to a class or otherwise.

Supplementary

4

(1)   An order making any provision under paragraph 2 or 3 must make provision in respect of legal professional privilege (in Scotland, legal privilege within the meaning of Chapter 3 of Part 8).

(2)   An order making any provision under paragraph 3 may require any person—

    (*a*)   to give the interim receiver or administrator access to any premises which he may enter in pursuance of paragraph 3,

    (*b*)   to give the interim receiver or administrator any assistance he may require for taking the steps mentioned in that paragraph.

Management

5

(1)   Power to manage any property to which the order applies.

(2)   Managing property includes—

    (*a*)   selling or otherwise disposing of assets comprised in the property which are perishable or which ought to be disposed of before their value diminishes,

    (*b*)   where the property comprises assets of a trade or business, carrying on, or arranging for another to carry on, the trade or business,

    (*c*)   incurring capital expenditure in respect of the property.

Schedule 7
Powers of trustee for civil recovery

Section 267

Sale

1

Power to sell the property or any part of it or interest in it.

Expenditure

2

Power to incur expenditure for the purpose of—

(*a*) acquiring any part of the property, or any interest in it, which is not vested in him,

(*b*) discharging any liabilities, or extinguishing any rights, to which the property is subject.

Management

3

(1) Power to manage property.

(2) Managing property includes doing anything mentioned in paragraph 5(2) of Schedule 6.

Legal proceedings

4

Power to start, carry on or defend any legal proceedings in respect of the property.

Compromise

5

Power to make any compromise or other arrangement in connection with any claim relating to the property.

Supplementary

6

(1) For the purposes of, or in connection with, the exercise of any of his powers—

(*a*) power by his official name to do any of the things mentioned in sub-paragraph (2),

(*b*) power to do any other act which is necessary or expedient.

(2) Those things are—

(*a*) holding property,

(*b*)   entering into contracts,

(*c*)   suing and being sued,

(*d*)   employing agents,

(*e*)   executing a power of attorney, deed or other instrument.

Schedule 8
Forms of declarations

Section 325

. . .¹

. . .¹

Amendments
1   Repealed by the Serious Crime Act 2007, ss 74(2)(*c*), 92, Sch 8, Pt 3, paras 92, 101(1), (2), Sch 14.

Members of [SOCA's staff]¹

'I, A.B., do solemnly declare that I will not disclose any information received by me in carrying out the functions under Part 6 of the Proceeds of Crime Act 2002 which I may from time to time be [assigned by SOCA]¹ to carry out except for the purposes of those functions, or [to SOCA]¹ or in accordance with [its]¹ instructions, or for the purposes of any prosecution for [an offence relating to a former Inland Revenue matter (being a matter listed in Schedule 1 to the Commissioners for Revenue and Customs Act 2005 except for paragraphs 2, 10, 13, 14, 15, 17, 19, 28, 29 and 30),]² or in such other cases as may be required or permitted by law.'

Amendments
1   Substituted by the Serious Crime Act 2007, s 74(2)(*c*), Sch 8, Pt 3, paras 92, 101(1), (3), (4), (5), (6).
2   Substituted by the Commissioners for Revenue and Customs Act 2005, s 50(6), Sch 4, para 100.

Schedule 9
Regulated sector and supervisory authorities

Section 330

[PART 1
REGULATED SECTOR

Business in the regulated sector

1

(1)   A business is in the regulated sector to the extent that it consists of—

(*a*)   the acceptance by a credit institution of deposits or other repayable funds from the public, or the granting by a credit institution of credits for its own account;

(*b*)   the carrying on of one or more of the activities listed in points 2 to 12[, 14 and 15]^1 of Annex 1 to the Banking Consolidation Directive by an undertaking other than—

    (i)   a credit institution; or

    (ii)   an undertaking whose only listed activity is trading for own account in one or more of the products listed in point 7 of Annex 1 to the Banking Consolidation Directive and which does not act on behalf of a customer (that is, a third party which is not a member of the same group as the undertaking);

(*c*)   the carrying on of activities covered by the Life Assurance Consolidation Directive by an insurance company authorised in accordance with that Directive;

(*d*)   the provision of investment services or the performance of investment activities by a person (other than a person falling within Article 2 of the Markets in Financial Instruments Directive) whose regular occupation or business is the provision to other persons of an investment service or the performance of an investment activity on a professional basis;

(*e*)   the marketing or other offering of units or shares by a collective investment undertaking;

(*f*)   the activities of an insurance intermediary as defined in Article 2(5) of the Insurance Mediation Directive, other than a tied insurance intermediary as mentioned in Article 2(7) of that Directive, in respect of contracts of long-term insurance within the meaning given by article 3(1) of, and Part II of Schedule 1 to, the Financial Services and Markets Act 2000 (Regulated Activities) Order 2001;

(*g*)   the carrying on of any of the activities mentioned in paragraphs (*b*) to (*f*) by a branch located in an EEA State of a person referred to in those paragraphs (or of an equivalent person in any other State), wherever its head office is located;

(*h*)   the activities of the National Savings Bank;

(*i*)   any activity carried on for the purpose of raising money authorised to be raised under the National Loans Act 1968 under the auspices of the Director of Savings;

(*j*)   the carrying on of statutory audit work within the meaning of section 1210 of the Companies Act 2006 (meaning of 'statutory auditor' etc) by any firm or individual who is a statutory auditor within the meaning of Part 42 of that Act (statutory auditors);

(*k*)   the activities of a person appointed to act as an insolvency practitioner within the meaning of section 388 of the Insolvency Act 1986 (meaning of 'act as insolvency practitioner')or article 3 of the Insolvency (Northern Ireland) Order 1989;

(*l*)   the provision to other persons of accountancy services by a firm or sole practitioner who by way of business provides such services to other persons;

(*m*)   the provision of advice about the tax affairs of other persons by a firm or sole practitioner who by way of business provides advice about the tax affairs of other persons;

(*n*)   the participation in financial or real property transactions concerning—

(i)   the buying and selling of real property (or, in Scotland, heritable property) or business entities;

(ii)   the managing of client money, securities or other assets;

(iii)   the opening or management of bank, savings or securities accounts;

(iv)   the organisation of contributions necessary for the creation, operation or management of companies; or

(v)   the creation, operation or management of trusts, companies or similar structures,

by a firm or sole practitioner who by way of business provides legal or notarial services to other persons;

(*o*)   the provision to other persons by way of business by a firm or sole practitioner of any of the services mentioned in sub-paragraph (4);

(*p*)   the carrying on of estate agency work (within the meaning given by section 1 of the Estate Agents Act 1979 (estate agency work)) by a firm or a sole practitioner who carries on, or whose employees carry on, such work;

(*q*)   the trading in goods (including dealing as an auctioneer) whenever a transaction involves the receipt of a payment or payments in cash of at least 15,000 euros in total, whether the transaction is executed in a single operation or in several operations which appear to be linked, by a firm or sole trader who by way of business trades in goods;

(*r*)   operating a casino under a casino operating licence (within the meaning given by section 65(2) of the Gambling Act 2005 (nature of licence)).

(2)   For the purposes of sub-paragraph (1)(*a*) and (*b*) 'credit institution' means—

(*a*)   a credit institution as defined in [Article 4(1)][1] of the Banking Consolidation Directive; or

(*b*)   a branch (within the meaning of Article 4(3) of that Directive) located in an EEA state of an institution falling within paragraph (*a*) (or of an equivalent institution in any other State) wherever its head office is located.

(3)   For the purposes of sub-paragraph (1)(*n*) a person participates in a transaction by assisting in the planning or execution of the transaction or otherwise acting for or on behalf of a client in the transaction.

(4)   The services referred to in sub-paragraph (1)(*o*) are—

(*a*)   forming companies or other legal persons;

(*b*)   acting, or arranging for another person to act—

(i)   as a director or secretary of a company;

(ii)   as a partner of a partnership; or

(iii)   in a similar position in relation to other legal persons;

(*c*)   providing a registered office, business address, correspondence or administrative address or other related services for a company, partnership or any other legal person or arrangement;

(*d*)   acting, or arranging for another person to act, as—

      (i)   a trustee of an express trust or similar legal arrangement; or

      (ii)   a nominee shareholder for a person other than a company whose securities are listed on a regulated market.

(5)   For the purposes of sub-paragraph (4)(*d*) 'regulated market'—

    (*a*)   in relation to any EEA State, has the meaning given by point 14 of Article 4(1) of the Markets in Financial Instruments Directive; and

    (*b*)   in relation to any other State, means a regulated financial market which subjects companies whose securities are admitted to trading to disclosure obligations which are contained in international standards and are equivalent to the specified disclosure obligations.

(6)   For the purposes of sub-paragraph (5) 'the specified disclosure obligations' means disclosure requirements consistent with—

    (*a*)   Article 6(1) to (4) of Directive 2003/6/EC of the European Parliament and of the Council of 28th January 2003 on insider dealing and market manipulation;

    (*b*)   Articles 3, 5, 7, 8, 10, 14 and 16 of Directive 2003/71/EC of the European Parliament and of the Council of 4th November 2003 on the prospectuses to be published when securities are offered to the public or admitted to trading;

    (*c*)   Articles 4 to 6, 14, 16 to 19 and 30 of Directive 2004/109/EC of the European Parliament and of the Council of 15th December 2004 relating to the harmonisation of transparency requirements in relation to information about issuers whose securities are admitted to trading on a regulated market; or

    (*d*)   Community legislation made under the provisions mentioned in paragraphs (*a*) to (*c*).

(7)   For the purposes of sub-paragraph (1)(*j*) and (*l*) to (*q*) 'firm' means any entity, whether or not a legal person, that is not an individual and includes a body corporate and a partnership or other unincorporated association.

(8)   For the purposes of sub-paragraph (1)(*q*) 'cash' means notes, coins or travellers' cheques in any currency.][2]

Amendments

1   Substituted by the Electronic Money Regulations 2011, SI 2011/99, reg 79, Sch 4, Pt 1, para 4(*a*), (*b*).

2   Substituted by the Proceeds of Crime Act 2002 (Business in the Regulated Sector and Supervisory Authorities) Order 2007, SI 2007/3287, art 2.

[Excluded activities

2

(1)   A business is not in the regulated sector to the extent that it consists of—

    (*a*)   the issuing of withdrawable share capital within the limit set by section 6 of the Industrial and Provident Societies Act 1965 (maximum shareholding in society), or the acceptance of deposits from the public within the limit set by section 7(3) of that Act (carrying on of banking by societies), by a society registered under that Act;

(*b*)   the issuing of withdrawable share capital within the limit set by section 6 of the Industrial and Provident Societies Act (Northern Ireland) 1969 (maximum shareholding in society), or the acceptance of deposits from the public within the limit set by section 7(3) of that Act (carrying on of banking by societies), by a society registered under that Act;

(*c*)   the carrying on of any activity in respect of which a person who is (or falls within a class of persons) specified in any of paragraphs 2 to 23, 25 to 38 or 40 to 49 of the Schedule to the Financial Services and Markets Act 2000 (Exemption) Order 2001 is exempt;

(*d*)   the exercise of the functions specified in section 45 of the Financial Services Act 1986 (miscellaneous exemptions) by a person who was an exempted person for the purposes of that section immediately before its repeal;

(*e*)   the engaging in financial activity which fulfils all of the conditions set out in paragraphs (*a*) to (*g*) of sub-paragraph (3) of this paragraph by a person whose main activity is that of a high value dealer; or

(*f*)   the preparation of a home information pack (within the meaning of Part 5 of the Housing Act 2004 (home information packs)) or a document or information for inclusion in a home information pack.

(2)   For the purposes of sub-paragraph (1)(*e*) a 'high value dealer' means a person mentioned in paragraph 1(1)(*q*) when carrying on the activities mentioned in that paragraph.

(3)   A business is not in the regulated sector to the extent that it consists of financial activity if—

(*a*)   the person's total annual turnover in respect of the financial activity does not exceed £64,000;

(*b*)   the financial activity is limited in relation to any customer to no more than one transaction exceeding 1,000 euros, whether the transaction is carried out in a single operation, or a series of operations which appear to be linked;

(*c*)   the financial activity does not exceed 5% of the person's total annual turnover;

(*d*)   the financial activity is ancillary to the person's main activity and directly related to that activity;

(*e*)   the financial activity is not the transmission or remittance of money (or any representation of monetary value) by any means;

(*f*)   the main activity of the person carrying on the financial activity is not an activity mentioned in paragraph 1(1)(*a*) to (*p*) or (*r*); and

(*g*)   the financial activity is provided only to customers of the person's main activity and is not offered to the public.

(4)   A business is not in the regulated sector if it is carried on by—

(*a*)   the Auditor General for Scotland;

(*b*)   the Auditor General for Wales;

(*c*)   the Bank of England;

(*d*)   the Comptroller and Auditor General;

(e)   the Comptroller and Auditor General for Northern Ireland;

(f)   the Official Solicitor to the Supreme Court, when acting as trustee in his official capacity; or

(g)   the Treasury Solicitor.]¹

Amendments
1   Substituted by the Proceeds of Crime Act 2002 (Business in the Regulated Sector and Supervisory Authorities) Order 2007, SI 2007/3287, art 2.

[Interpretation

3

(1)   In this Part—

'the Banking Consolidation Directive' means directive 2006/48/EC of the European Parliament and of the Council of 14th June 2006 relating to the taking up and pursuit of the business of credit institutions [as last amended by Directive 2009/111/EC]¹;

'the Insurance Mediation Directive' means directive 2002/92/EC of the European Parliament and of the Council of 9th December 2002 on insurance mediation;

'the Life Assurance Consolidation Directive' means directive 2002/83/EC of the European Parliament and of the Council of 5th November 2002 concerning life assurance; and

'the Markets in Financial Instruments Directive' means directive 2004/39/EC of the European Parliament and of the Council of 12th April 2004 on markets in financial instruments.

(2)   In this Part references to amounts in euros include references to equivalent amounts in another currency.

(3)   Terms used in this Part and in the Banking Consolidation Directive or the Markets in Financial Instruments Directive have the same meaning in this Part as in those Directives.]²

Amendments
1   Substituted by the Electronic Money Regulations 2011, SI 2011/99, reg 79, Sch 4, Pt 1, para 4(c).
2   Substituted by the Proceeds of Crime Act 2002 (Business in the Regulated Sector and Supervisory Authorities) Order 2007, SI 2007/3287, art 2.

[PART 2
SUPERVISORY AUTHORITIES

4

(1)   The following bodies are supervisory authorities—

(a)   the Commissioners for Her Majesty's Revenue and Customs;

(b)   the Department of Enterprise, Trade and Investment in Northern Ireland;

(c)   the Financial Services Authority;

(d)   the Gambling Commission;

(*e*)   the Office of Fair Trading;

(*f*)   the Secretary of State; and

(*g*)   the professional bodies listed in sub-paragraph (2).

(2)   The professional bodies referred to in sub-paragraph (1)(*g*) are—

(*a*)   the Association of Accounting Technicians;

(*b*)   the Association of Chartered Certified Accountants;

(*c*)   the Association of International Accountants;

(*d*)   the Association of Taxation Technicians;

(*e*)   the Chartered Institute of Management Accountants;

(*f*)   the Chartered Institute of Public Finance and Accountancy;

(*g*)   the Chartered Institute of Taxation;

(*h*)   the Council for Licensed Conveyancers;

(*i*)   the Faculty of Advocates;

(*j*)   the Faculty Office of the Archbishop of Canterbury;

(*k*)   the General Council of the Bar;

(*l*)   the General Council of the Bar of Northern Ireland;

(*m*)   the Insolvency Practitioners Association;

(*n*)   the Institute of Certified Bookkeepers;

(*o*)   the Institute of Chartered Accountants in England and Wales;

(*p*)   the Institute of Chartered Accountants in Ireland;

(*q*)   the Institute of Chartered Accountants of Scotland;

(*r*)   the Institute of Financial Accountants;

(*s*)   the International Association of Book-keepers;

(*t*)   the Law Society;

(*u*)   the Law Society for Northern Ireland; and

(*v*)   the Law Society of Scotland.][1]

Amendments

1   Substituted by the Proceeds of Crime Act 2002 (Business in the Regulated Sector and Supervisory Authorities) Order 2007, SI 2007/3287, art 2.

PART 3
POWER TO AMEND

5

The Treasury may by order amend Part 1 or 2 of this Schedule.

Schedule 10
Tax

Section 448

PART 1
GENERAL

1

Sections 75 and 77 of the Taxes Management Act 1970 (c. 9) (receivers: income tax and capital gains tax) shall not apply in relation to—

(*a*)   a receiver appointed under section 48 [or 50][1];

(*b*)   an administrator appointed under section 125 or 128;

(*c*)   a receiver appointed under section 196 [or 198][1];

[(*ca*)   a receiver appointed under section 245E;][2]

(*d*)   an interim receiver appointed under section 246;

(*e*)   an interim administrator appointed under section 256.

Amendments

1   Substituted by the Serious Crime Act 2007, s 74(2)(*a*), Sch 8, Pt 1, paras 1, 84.
2   Inserted by the Serious Crime Act 2007, s 83(3).

PART 2
PROVISIONS RELATING TO PART 5

INTRODUCTORY

2

(1)   The vesting of property in the trustee for civil recovery or any other person by a recovery order or in pursuance of an order under section 276 is referred to as a Part 5 transfer.

(2)   The person who holds the property immediately before the vesting is referred to as the transferor; and the person in whom the property is vested is referred to as the transferee.

(3)   Any amount paid in respect of the transfer by the trustee for civil recovery, or another, to a person who holds the property immediately before the vesting is referred to (in relation to that person) as a compensating payment.

(4)   If the recovery order provides or (as the case may be) the terms on which the order under section 276 is made provide for the creation of any interest in favour of a person who holds the property immediately before the vesting, he is to be treated instead as receiving (in addition to any payment referred to in sub-paragraph (3)) a compensating payment of an amount equal to the value of the interest.

(5)   Where the property belongs to joint tenants immediately before the vesting and a compensating payment is made to one or more (but not both or all) of the joint tenants, this Part has effect separately in relation to each joint tenant.

(6)   Expressions used in this paragraph have the same meaning as in Part 5 of this Act.

(7)   'The Taxes Act 1988' means the Income and Corporation Taxes Act 1988 (c. 1), and 'the Allowances Act 2001' means the Capital Allowances Act 2001 (c. 2)[, and 'ITTOIA 2005' means the Income Tax (Trading and Other Income) Act 2005][1].

(8)   This paragraph applies for the purposes of this Part.

Amendments

1   Inserted by the Income Tax (Trading and Other Income) Act 2005, s 882(1), Sch 1, Pt 2, paras 581, 583(1), (2).

CAPITAL GAINS TAX

3

(1)   If a gain attributable to a Part 5 transfer accrues to the transferor, it is not a chargeable gain.

(2)   But if a compensating payment is made to the transferor—

        (*a*)   sub-paragraph (1) does not apply, and

        (*b*)   the consideration for the transfer is the amount of the compensating payment.

(3)   If a gain attributable to the forfeiture under section 298 of property consisting of—

        (*a*)   notes or coins in any currency other than sterling,

        (*b*)   anything mentioned in section 289(6)(*b*) to (*d*), if expressed in any currency other than sterling, or

        (*c*)   bearer bonds or bearer shares,

        accrues to the person who holds the property immediately before the forfeiture, it is not a chargeable gain

(4)   This paragraph has effect as if it were included in Chapter 1 of Part 2 of the Taxation of Chargeable Gains Act 1992 (c. 12).

INCOME TAX AND CORPORATION TAX

Accrued income scheme

4

If a Part 5 transfer is a transfer of securities within the meaning of [Chapter 2 of Part 12 of the Income Tax Act 2007, that Part does not apply to the transfer][1].

Amendments
1   Substituted by the Income Tax Act 2007, s 1027, Sch 1, Pt 2, para 424.

Discounted securities

5

In the case of a Part 5 transfer of property consisting of a [deeply]¹ discounted security (within the meaning of [Chapter 8 of Part 4 of ITTOIA 2005]¹), it is not to be treated as a transfer for the purposes of [that Chapter]¹.

Amendments
1   Substituted by the Income Tax (Trading and Other Income) Act 2005, s 882(1), Sch 1, Pt 2, paras 581, 583(1), (3).

Rights to receive amounts stated in certificates of deposit etc.

6

In the case of a Part 5 transfer of property consisting of a right to which section 56(2) of the Taxes Act 1988 applies, or a right mentioned in section 56A(1) of that Act, (rights stated in certificates of deposit etc.)[, or a right falling within the definition of 'deposit rights' in section 552(1) of ITTOIA 2005]¹ it is not to be treated as a disposal of the right for the purposes of section 56(2) [of the Taxes Act 1988 or Chapter 11 of Part 4 of ITTOIA 2005]².

Amendments
1   Inserted by the Income Tax (Trading and Other Income) Act 2005, s 882(1), Sch 1, Pt 2, paras 581, 583(1), (4)(*a*).
2   Substituted by the Income Tax (Trading and Other Income) Act 2005, s 882(1), Sch 1, Pt 2, paras 581, 583(1), (4)(*b*).

Non-qualifying offshore funds

7

In the case of a Part 5 transfer of property consisting of an asset mentioned in section 757(1)(*a*) or (*b*) of the Taxes Act 1988 (interests in non-qualifying offshore funds etc.), it is not to be treated as a disposal for the purposes of that section.

Futures and options

8

In the case of a Part 5 transfer of property consisting of futures or options (within the meaning of [section 562 of ITTOIA 2005]¹), it is not to be treated as a disposal of the futures or options for the purposes of [Chapter 12 of Part 4 of that Act]¹.

Amendments
1   Substituted by the Income Tax (Trading and Other Income) Act 2005, s 882(1), Sch 1, Pt 2, paras 581, 583(1), (5).

Loan relationships

9

(1)   Sub-paragraph (2) applies if, apart from this paragraph, a Part 5 transfer would be a related transaction for the purposes of [Part 5 of the Corporation Tax Act 2009 (loan relationships)][1].

(2)   The Part 5 transfer is to be disregarded for the purposes of [that Part][1], except for the purpose of identifying any person in whose case any debit or credit not relating to the transaction is to be brought into account.

Amendments
1   Substituted by the Corporation Tax Act 2009, s 1322, Sch 1, Pt 2, paras 546, 547(1), (2).

Exception from paragraphs 4 to 9

10

Paragraphs 4 to 9 do not apply if a compensating payment is made to the transferor.

Trading stock

11

(1)   Sub-paragraph (2) applies, in the case of a Part 5 transfer of property consisting of the trading stock of a trade, for the purpose of computing any profits of the trade for tax purposes.

(2)   If, because of the transfer, the trading stock is to be treated for that purpose as if it had been sold in the course of the trade, the amount realised on the sale is to be treated for that purpose as equal to its acquisition cost.

(3)   Sub-paragraph (2) has effect in spite of anything in [section 173 of ITTOIA 2005 or section 162 of the Corporation Tax Act 2009 (valuation of trading stock on cessation)][1].

(4)   In this paragraph, trading stock and trade have the same meaning as in [section 174 of ITTOIA 2005 or (as the case may be) section 163 of the Corporation Tax Act 2009][1].

Amendments
1   Substituted by the Corporation Tax Act 2009, s 1322, Sch 1, Pt 2, paras 546, 547(1), (3).

CAPITAL ALLOWANCES

Plant and machinery

12

(1)   If there is a Part 5 transfer of plant or machinery, Part 2 of the Allowances Act 2001 is to have effect as if a transferor who has incurred qualifying expenditure were required to bring the disposal value of the plant or machinery into account in accordance with section 61 of that Act for the chargeable period in which the transfer occurs.

(2)   But the Part 5 transfer is not to be treated as a disposal event for the purposes of Part 2 of that Act other than by virtue of sub-paragraph (1).

13

(1)   If a compensating payment is made to the transferor, the disposal value to be brought into account is the amount of the payment.

(2)   Otherwise, the disposal value to be brought into account is the amount which would give rise neither to a balancing allowance nor to a balancing charge.

14

(1)   Paragraph 13(2) does not apply if the qualifying expenditure has been allocated to the main pool or a class pool.

(2)   Instead, the disposal value to be brought into account is the notional written-down value of the qualifying expenditure incurred by the transferor on the provision of the plant or machinery.

(3)   The notional written-down value is—

$QE - A$

where—

QE is the qualifying expenditure incurred by the transferor on the provision of the plant or machinery,

A is the total of all allowances which could have been made to the transferor in respect of the expenditure if—

(a)   that expenditure had been the only expenditure that had ever been taken into account in determining his available qualifying expenditure, and

(b)   all allowances had been made in full

(4)   But if—

(a)   the Part 5 transfer of the plant or machinery occurs in the same chargeable period as that in which the qualifying expenditure is incurred, and

(b)   a first-year allowance is made in respect of an amount of the expenditure,

the disposal value to be brought into account is that which is equal to the balance left after deducting the first year allowance

15

(1)   Paragraph 13 does not apply if—

(a)   a qualifying activity is carried on in partnership,

(b)   the Part 5 transfer is a transfer of plant or machinery which is partnership property, and

(c)   compensating payments are made to one or more, but not both or all, of the partners.

(2)   Instead, the disposal value to be brought into account is the sum of—

(a)   any compensating payments made to any of the partners, and

(b)   in the case of each partner to whom a compensating payment has not been made, his share of the tax-neutral amount.

(3)   A partner's share of the tax-neutral amount is to be determined according to the profit-sharing arrangements for the twelve months ending immediately before the date of the Part 5 transfer.

16

(1)   Paragraph 13 does not apply if—

(*a*)   a qualifying activity is carried on in partnership,

(*b*)   the Part 5 transfer is a transfer of plant or machinery which is not partnership property but is owned by two or more of the partners ('the owners'),

(*c*)   the plant or machinery is used for the purposes of the qualifying activity, and

(*d*)   compensating payments are made to one or more, but not both or all, of the owners.

(2)   Instead, the disposal value to be brought into account is the sum of—

(*a*)   any compensating payments made to any of the owners, and

(*b*)   in the case of each owner to whom a compensating payment has not been made, his share of the tax-neutral amount.

(3)   An owner's share of the tax-neutral amount is to be determined in proportion to the value of his interest in the plant or machinery.

17

(1)   Paragraphs 12 to 16 have effect as if they were included in section 61 of the Allowances Act 2001.

(2)   In paragraphs 15 and 16, the tax-neutral amount is the amount that would be brought into account as the disposal value under paragraph 13(2) or (as the case may be) 14 if the provision in question were not disapplied.

...[1]

18

...[1]

Amendments

1   Repealed by the Finance Act 2008, s 84(5), Sch 27, Pt 1, para 24.

19

...[1]

Amendments

1   Repealed by the Finance Act 2008, s 84(5), Sch 27, Pt 1, para 24.

20

...[1]

Amendments

1   Repealed by the Finance Act 2008, s 84(5), Sch 27, Pt 1, para 24.

21

...¹

Amendments
1   Repealed by the Finance Act 2008, s 84(5), Sch 27, Pt 1, para 24.

Flat conversion

22

(1)   If there is a Part 5 transfer of a relevant interest in a flat, Part 4A of the Allowances Act 2001 is to have effect as if the transfer were a balancing event within section 393N of that Act.

(2)   But the Part 5 transfer is not to be treated as a balancing event for the purposes of Part 4A of that Act other than by virtue of sub-paragraph (1).

23

(1)   If a compensating payment is made to the transferor, the proceeds from the balancing event are the amount of the payment.

(2)   Otherwise, the proceeds from the balancing event are the amount which is equal to the residue of qualifying expenditure immediately before the transfer.

24

(1)   Paragraph 23 does not apply to determine the proceeds from the balancing event if—

(*a*)   the relevant interest in the flat is partnership property, and

(*b*)   compensating payments are made to one or more, but not both or all, of the partners.

(2)   Instead, the proceeds from the balancing event are the sum of—

(*a*)   any compensating payments made to any of the partners, and

(*b*)   in the case of each partner to whom a compensating payment has not been made, his share of the amount which is equal to the residue of qualifying expenditure immediately before the transfer.

(3)   A partner's share of that amount is to be determined according to the profit-sharing arrangements for the twelve months ending immediately before the date of the transfer.

25

Paragraphs 22 to 24 have effect as if they were included in Part 4A of the Allowances Act 2001.

Research and development

26

If there is a Part 5 transfer of an asset representing qualifying expenditure incurred by a person, the disposal value he is required to bring into account under section 443(1) of the Allowances Act 2001 for any chargeable period is to be determined as follows (and not in accordance with subsection (4) of that section).

27

(1)   If a compensating payment is made to the transferor, the disposal value he is required to bring into account is the amount of the payment.

(2)   Otherwise, the disposal value he is required to bring into account is nil.

28

(1)   Paragraph 27 does not apply to determine the disposal value to be brought into account if—

  (*a*)   the asset is partnership property, and

  (*b*)   compensating payments are made to one or more, but not both or all, of the partners.

(2)   Instead, the disposal value to be brought into account is equal to the sum of any compensating payments.

29

Paragraphs 26 to 28 have effect as if they were included in Part 6 of the Allowances Act 2001.

EMPLOYEE ETC. SHARE SCHEMES

Share options

30

Section 135(6) of the Taxes Act 1988 (gains by directors and employees) does not make any person chargeable to tax in respect of any gain realised by the trustee for civil recovery.

Conditional acquisition of shares

31

Section 140A(4) of the Taxes Act 1988 (disposal etc. of shares) does not make the transferor chargeable to income tax in respect of a Part 5 transfer of shares or an interest in shares.

Shares acquired at an undervalue

32

Section 162(5) of the Taxes Act 1988 (employee shareholdings) does not make the transferor chargeable to income tax in respect of a Part 5 transfer of shares.

Shares in dependent subsidiaries

33

Section 79 of the Finance Act 1988 (c. 39) (charge on increase in value of shares) does not make the transferor chargeable to income tax in respect of a Part 5 transfer of shares or an interest in shares.

[*Schedules 11 and 12 amend other legislation so are not reproduced in this title.*]

Appendix 2

CRIMINAL PROCEDURE RULES 2010

SI 2010/60

[Parts 1 to 55 are not reproduced in this title.]

PART 56
CONFISCATION PROCEEDINGS UNDER THE CRIMINAL JUSTICE ACT 1988 AND THE DRUG TRAFFICKING ACT 1994

56.1 Statements, etc. relevant to making confiscation orders

(1)   Where a prosecutor or defendant—

    (*a*)   tenders to a magistrates' court any statement or other document under section 73 of the Criminal Justice Act 1988 in any proceedings in respect of an offence listed in Schedule 4 to that Act; or

    (*b*)   tenders to the Crown Court any statement or other document under section 11 of the Drug Trafficking Act 1994 or section 73 of the 1988 Act in any proceedings in respect of a drug trafficking offence or in respect of an offence to which Part VI of the 1988 Act applies,

he must serve a copy as soon as practicable on the defendant or the prosecutor, as the case may be.

(2)   Any statement tendered by the prosecutor to the magistrates' court under section 73 of the 1988 Act or to the Crown Court under section 11(1) of the 1994 Act or section 73(1A) of the 1988 Act shall include the following particulars—

    (*a*)   the name of the defendant;

    (*b*)   the name of the person by whom the statement is made and the date on which it was made;

    (*c*)   where the statement is not tendered immediately after the defendant has been convicted, the date on which and the place where the relevant conviction occurred; and

    (*d*)   such information known to the prosecutor as is relevant to the determination as to whether or not the defendant has benefited from drug trafficking or relevant criminal conduct and to the assessment of the value of his proceeds of drug trafficking or, as the case may be, benefit from relevant criminal conduct.

(3)   Where, in accordance with section 11(7) of the 1994 Act or section 73(1C) of the 1988 Act, the defendant indicates the extent to which he accepts any allegation contained within the prosecutor's statement, if he indicates the same in writing to the prosecutor, he must serve a copy of that reply on the court officer.

(4)   Expressions used in this rule shall have the same meanings as in the 1994 Act or, where appropriate, the 1988 Act.

[Note. The relevant provisions of the 1988 and 1994 Acts were repealed on 24th March 2003, but they continue to have effect in respect of proceedings for offences committed before that date.]

56.2   Postponed determinations

(1)   Where an application is made by the defendant or the prosecutor–

  (*a*)   to a magistrates' court under section 72A(5)(*a*) of the Criminal Justice Act 1988 asking the court to exercise its powers under section 72A(4) of that Act; or

  (*b*)   to the Crown Court under section 3(5)(*a*) of the Drug Trafficking Act 1994 asking the Court to exercise its powers under section 3(4) of that Act, or under section 72A(5)(*a*) of the 1988 Act asking the court to exercise its powers under section 72A(4) of the 1988 Act,

  the application must be made in writing and a copy must be served on the prosecutor or the defendant, as the case may be.

(2)   A party served with a copy of an application under paragraph (1) shall, within 28 days of the date of service, notify the applicant and the court officer, in writing, whether or not he proposes to oppose the application, giving his reasons for any opposition.

(3)   After the expiry of the period referred to in paragraph (2), the court shall determine whether an application under paragraph (1) is to be dealt with—

  (*a*)   without a hearing; or

  (*b*)   at a hearing at which the parties may be represented.

[Note. The relevant provisions of the 1988 and 1994 Acts were repealed on 24th March 2003, but they continue to have effect in respect of proceedings for offences committed before that date.]

56.3   Confiscation orders – revised assessments

(1)   Where the prosecutor makes an application under section 13, 14 or 15 of the Drug Trafficking Act 1994 or section 74A, 74B or 74C of the Criminal Justice Act 1988, the application must be in writing and a copy must be served on the defendant.

(2)   The application must include the following particulars—

  (*a*)   the name of the defendant;

  (*b*)   the date on which and the place where any relevant conviction occurred;

  (*c*)   the date on which and the place where any relevant confiscation order was made or, as the case may be, varied;

  (*d*)   the grounds on which the application is made; and

  (*e*)   an indication of the evidence available to support the application.

[Note. The relevant provisions of the 1988 and 1994 Acts were repealed on 24th March 2003, but they continue to have effect in respect of proceedings for offences committed before that date.]

56.4   Application to the Crown Court to discharge or vary order to make material available

(1)   Where an order under section 93H of the Criminal Justice Act 1988 (order to make material available) or section 55 of the Drug Trafficking Act 1994 (order to make material available) has been made by the Crown Court, any person affected by it may apply in writing to the court officer for the order to be discharged or varied, and on hearing such an application a circuit judge may discharge the order or make such variations to it as he thinks fit.

(2)   Subject to paragraph (3), where a person proposes to make an application under paragraph (1) for the discharge or variation of an order, he shall give a copy of the application, not later than 48 hours before the making of the application—

(a)   to a constable at the police station specified in the order; or

(b)   to the office of the appropriate officer who made the application, as specified in the order,

in either case together with a notice indicating the time and place at which the application for discharge or variation is to be made.

(3)   A circuit judge may direct that paragraph (2) need not be complied with if he is satisfied that the person making the application has good reason to seek a discharge or variation of the order as soon as possible and it is not practicable to comply with that paragraph.

(4)   In this rule:

'constable' includes a person commissioned by the Commissioners for Her Majesty's Revenue and Customs;

'police station' includes a place for the time being occupied by Her Majesty's Revenue and Customs.

[Note. The relevant provision of the 1988 Act was repealed on 24th February 2003, but it continues to have effect in respect of proceedings for offences committed before that date.]

56.5   Application to the Crown Court for increase in term of imprisonment in default of payment

(1)   This rule applies to applications made, or that have effect as made, to the Crown Court under section 10 of the Drug Trafficking Act 1994 and section 75A of the Criminal Justice Act 1988 (interest on sums unpaid under confiscation orders).

(2)   Notice of an application to which this rule applies to increase the term of imprisonment or detention fixed in default of payment of a confiscation order by a person ('the defendant') shall be made by the prosecutor in writing to the court officer.

(3)   A notice under paragraph (2) shall—

(a)   state the name and address of the defendant;

(b)   specify the grounds for the application;

(c)   give details of the enforcement measures taken, if any; and

(d)   include a copy of the confiscation order.

(4)   On receiving a notice under paragraph (2), the court officer shall—

(*a*) forthwith send to the defendant and the magistrates' court required to enforce payment of the confiscation order under section 140(1) of the Powers of Criminal Courts (Sentencing) Act 2000, a copy of the said notice; and

(*b*) notify in writing the applicant and the defendant of the date, time and place appointed for the hearing of the application.

(5) Where the Crown Court makes an order pursuant to an application mentioned in paragraph (1) above, the court officer shall send forthwith a copy of the order—

(*a*) to the applicant;

(*b*) to the defendant;

(*c*) where the defendant is at the time of the making of the order in custody, to the person having custody of him; and

(*d*) to the magistrates' court mentioned in paragraph (4)(*a*).

[Note. The relevant provisions of the 1988 and 1994 Acts were repealed on 24th March 2003, but they continue to have effect in respect of proceedings for offences committed before that date.]

56.6 Drug trafficking – compensation on acquittal in the Crown Court

Where a Crown Court cancels a confiscation order under section 22(2) of the Drug Trafficking Act 1994, the court officer shall serve notice to that effect on the High Court and on the magistrates' court which has responsibility for enforcing the order.

[Note. The relevant provision of the 1994 Act was repealed on 24th March 2003, but it continues to have effect in respect of proceedings for offences committed before that date.)

PART 57
PROCEEDS OF CRIME ACT 2002: RULES APPLICABLE TO ALL PRO-CEEDINGS

57.1 Interpretation

In this Part and in Parts 58, 59, 60 and 61:

'business day' means any day other than a Saturday, Sunday, Christmas Day or Good Friday, or a bank holiday under the Banking and Financial Dealings Act 1971, in England and Wales;

'document' means anything in which information of any description is recorded;

'hearsay evidence' means evidence consisting of hearsay within the meaning of section 1(2) of the Civil Evidence Act 1995;

'restraint proceedings' means proceedings under sections 42 and 58(2) and (3) of the Proceeds of Crime Act 2002;

'receivership proceedings' means proceedings under sections 48, 49, 50, 51, 54(4), 59(2) and (3), 62 and 63 of the 2002 Act;

'witness statement' means a written statement signed by a person which contains the evidence, and only that evidence, which that person would be allowed to give orally; and

words and expressions used have the same meaning as in Part 2 of the 2002 Act.

57.2 Calculation of time

(1)   This rule shows how to calculate any period of time for doing any act which is specified by this Part and Parts 58, 59, 60 and 61 for the purposes of any proceedings under Part 2 of the Proceeds of Crime Act 2002 or by an order of the Crown Court in restraint proceedings or receivership proceedings.

(2)   A period of time expressed as a number of days shall be computed as clear days.

(3)   In this rule 'clear days' means that in computing the number of days—

    (*a*)   the day on which the period begins; and

    (*b*)   if the end of the period is defined by reference to an event, the day on which that event occurs,

are not included.

(4)   Where the specified period is five days or less and includes a day which is not a business day that day does not count.

57.3 Court office closed

When the period specified by this Part or Parts 58, 59, 60 and 61, or by an order of the Crown Court under Part 2 of the Proceeds of Crime Act 2002, for doing any act at the court office falls on a day on which the office is closed, that act shall be in time if done on the next day on which the court office is open.

57.4 Application for registration of Scottish or Northern Ireland order

(1)   This rule applies to an application for registration of an order under article 6 of the Proceeds of Crime Act 2002 (Enforcement in different parts of the United Kingdom) Order 2002.

(2)   The application may be made without notice.

(3)   The application must be in writing and may be supported by a witness statement which must—

    (*a*)   exhibit the order or a certified copy of the order; and

    (*b*)   to the best of the witness's ability, give full details of the realisable property located in England and Wales in respect of which the order was made and specify the person holding that realisable property.

(4)   If the court registers the order, the applicant must serve notice of the registration on—

    (*a*)   any person who holds realisable property to which the order applies; and

    (*b*)   any other person whom the applicant knows to be affected by the order.

(5)   The permission of the Crown Court under rule 57.13 is not required to serve the notice outside England and Wales.

57.5 Application to vary or set aside registration

(1)   An application to vary or set aside registration of an order under article 6 of the Proceeds of Crime Act 2002 (Enforcement in different parts of the United Kingdom) Order 2002 may be made to the Crown Court by—

    (*a*)   any person who holds realisable property to which the order applies; and

    (*b*)   any other person affected by the order.

(2)   The application must be in writing and may be supported by a witness statement.

(3)   The application and any witness statement must be lodged with the Crown Court.

(4)   The application must be served on the person who applied for registration at least seven days before the date fixed by the court for hearing the application, unless the Crown Court specifies a shorter period.

(5)   No property in England and Wales may be realised in pursuance of the order before the Crown Court has decided the application.

57.6   Register of orders

(1)   The Crown Court must keep, under the direction of the Lord Chancellor, a register of the orders registered under article 6 of the Proceeds of Crime Act 2002 (Enforcement in different parts of the United Kingdom) Order 2002.

(2)   The register must include details of any variation or setting aside of a registration under rule 57.5 and of any execution issued on a registered order.

(3)   If the person who applied for registration of an order which is subsequently registered notifies the Crown Court that the court which made the order has varied or discharged the order, details of the variation or discharge, as the case may be, must be entered in the register.

57.7   Statements of truth

(1)   Any witness statement required to be served by this Part or by Parts 58, 59, 60 or 61 must be verified by a statement of truth contained in the witness statement.

(2)   A statement of truth is a declaration by the person making the witness statement to the effect that the witness statement is true to the best of his knowledge and belief and that he made the statement knowing that, if it were tendered in evidence, he would be liable to prosecution if he wilfully stated in it anything which he knew to be false or did not believe to be true.

(3)   The statement of truth must be signed by the person making the witness statement.

(4)   If the person making the witness statement fails to verify the witness statement by a statement of truth, the Crown Court may direct that it shall not be admissible as evidence.

57.8   Use of witness statements for other purposes

(1)   Except as provided by this rule, a witness statement served in proceedings under Part 2 of the Proceeds of Crime Act 2002 may be used only for the purpose of the proceedings in which it is served.

(2)   Paragraph (1) does not apply if and to the extent that—

    (*a*)   the witness gives consent in writing to some other use of it;

    (*b*)   the Crown Court gives permission for some other use; or

    (*c*)   the witness statement has been put in evidence at a hearing held in public.

57.9   Expert evidence

(1)   A party to proceedings under Part 2 of the Proceeds of Crime Act 2002 who wishes to adduce expert evidence (whether of fact or opinion) in the proceedings must, as soon as practicable—

(*a*) serve on the other parties a statement in writing of any finding or opinion which he proposes to adduce by way of such evidence; and

(*b*) serve on any party who requests it in writing, a copy of (or if it appears to the party proposing to adduce the evidence to be more practicable, a reasonable opportunity to examine)—

  (i) the record of any observation, test, calculation or other procedure on which the finding or opinion is based, and

  (ii) any document or other thing or substance in respect of which the observation, test, calculation or other procedure mentioned in paragraph (1)(*b*)(i) has been carried out.

(*c*) A party may serve notice in writing waiving his right to be served with any of the matters mentioned in paragraph (1) and, in particular, may agree that the statement mentioned in paragraph (1)(*a*) may be given to him orally and not served in writing.

(*d*) If a party who wishes to adduce expert evidence in proceedings under Part 2 of the 2002 Act fails to comply with this rule he may not adduce that evidence in those proceedings without the leave of the court, except where rule 57.10 applies.

57.10 Exceptions to procedure for expert evidence

(1) If a party has reasonable grounds for believing that the disclosure of any evidence in compliance with rule 57.9 might lead to the intimidation, or attempted intimidation, of any person on whose evidence he intends to rely in the proceedings, or otherwise to the course of justice being interfered with, he shall not be obliged to comply with those requirements in relation to that evidence, unless the Crown Court orders otherwise.

(2) Where, in accordance with paragraph (1), a party considers that he is not obliged to comply with the requirements imposed by rule 57.9 with regard to any evidence in relation to any other party, he must serve notice in writing on that party stating—

(*a*) that the evidence is being withheld; and

(*b*) the reasons for withholding the evidence.

57.11 Service of documents

(1) Part 4 and rule 32.1 (notice required to accompany process served outside the United Kingdom and translations) shall not apply in restraint proceedings and receivership proceedings.

(2) Where this Part or Parts 58, 59, 60 or 61 requires service of a document, then, unless the Crown Court directs otherwise, the document may be served by any of the following methods—

(*a*) in all cases, by delivering the document personally to the party to be served;

(*b*) if no solicitor is acting for the party to be served by delivering the document at, or by sending it by first class post to, his residence or his last-known residence; or

(*c*) if a solicitor is acting for the party to be served—

  (i) by delivering the document at, or sending it by first class post to, the solicitor's business address, or

(ii) where the solicitor's business address includes a numbered box at a document exchange, by leaving the document at that document exchange or at a document exchange which transmits documents on every business day to that document exchange, or

(iii) if the solicitor has indicated that he is willing to accept service by facsimile transmission, by sending a legible copy of the document by facsimile transmission to the solicitor's office.

(3) A document shall, unless the contrary is proved, be deemed to have been served—

(*a*) in the case of service by first class post, on the second business day after posting;

(*b*) in the case of service in accordance with paragraph (2)(*c*)(ii), on the second business day after the day on which it is left at the document exchange; and

(*c*) in the case of service in accordance with paragraph (2)(*c*)(iii), where it is transmitted on a business day before 4 p.m., on that day and in any other case, on the next business day.

(4) An order made in restraint proceedings or receivership proceedings may be enforced against the defendant or any other person affected by it notwithstanding that service of a copy of the order has not been effected in accordance with this rule if the Crown Court is satisfied that the person had notice of the order by being present when the order was made.

57.12 Service by an alternative method

(1) Where it appears to the Crown Court that there is a good reason to authorise service by a method not otherwise permitted by rule 57.11, the court may make an order permitting service by an alternative method.

(2) An application for an order permitting service by an alternative method—

(*a*) must be supported by evidence; and

(*b*) may be made without notice.

(3) An order permitting service by an alternative method must specify—

(*a*) the method of service; and

(*b*) the date when the document will be deemed to be served.

57.13 Service outside the jurisdiction

(1) Where this Part requires a document to be served on someone who is outside England and Wales, it may be served outside England and Wales with the permission of the Crown Court.

(2) Where a document is to be served outside England and Wales it may be served by any method permitted by the law of the country in which it is to be served.

(3) Nothing in this rule or in any court order shall authorise or require any person to do anything in the country where the document is to be served which is against the law of that country.

(4) Where this Part requires a document to be served a certain period of time before the date of a hearing and the recipient does not appear at the hearing, the hearing must not take place unless the Crown Court is satisfied that the document has been duly served.

57.14 Certificates of service

(1) Where this Part requires that the applicant for an order in restraint proceedings or receivership proceedings serve a document on another person, the applicant must lodge a certificate of service with the Crown Court within seven days of service of the document.

(2) The certificate must state—

(*a*) the method of service;

(*b*) the date of service; and

(*c*) if the document is served under rule 57.12, such other information as the court may require when making the order permitting service by an alternative method.

(3) Where a document is to be served by the Crown Court in restraint proceedings and receivership proceedings and the court is unable to serve it, the court must send a notice of non-service stating the method attempted to the party who requested service.

57.15 External requests and orders

(1) The rules in this Part and in Parts 59 to 61 and 71 apply with the necessary modifications to proceedings under The Proceeds of Crime Act 2002 (External Requests and Orders) Order 2005 in the same way that they apply to corresponding proceedings under Part 2 of the Proceeds of Crime Act 2002.

(2) This table shows how provisions of the 2005 Order correspond with provisions of the 2002 Act.

[Article of The Proceeds of Crime Act 2002 (External Requests and Orders) Order 2005	*Section of the Proceeds of Crime Act 2002*
8	41
9	42
10	43
11	44
15	48
16	49
17	58
23	31
27	50
28	51
41	62
42	63
44	65
45	66][1]

Amendments

1   Substituted by the Criminal Procedure (Amendment) Rules 2010, SI 2010/1921, r 19.

PART 58

PROCEEDS OF CRIME ACT 2002: RULES APPLICABLE ONLY TO CONFISCATION PROCEEDINGS

58.1 Statements in connection with confiscation orders

(1) When the prosecutor is required, under section 16 of the Proceeds of Crime Act 2002, to give a statement to the Crown Court, the prosecutor must also, as soon as practicable, serve a copy of the statement on the defendant.

(2) Any statement given to the Crown Court by the prosecutor under section 16 of the 2002 Act must, in addition to the information required by the 2002 Act, include the following information—

   (*a*)   the name of the defendant;

   (*b*)   the name of the person by whom the statement is made and the date on which it is made; and

   (*c*)   where the statement is not given to the Crown Court immediately after the defendant has been convicted, the date on which and the place where the relevant conviction occurred.

(3) Where, under section 17 of the 2002 Act, the Crown Court orders the defendant to indicate the extent to which he accepts each allegation in a statement given by the prosecutor, the defendant must indicate this in writing to the prosecutor and must give a copy to the Crown Court.

(4) Where the Crown Court orders the defendant to give to it any information under section 18 of the 2002 Act, the defendant must provide the information in writing and must, as soon as practicable, serve a copy of it on the prosecutor.

58.2 Postponement of confiscation proceedings

The Crown Court may grant a postponement under section 14(1)(*b*) of the Proceeds of Crime Act 2002 without a hearing.

58.3 Application for reconsideration

(1) This rule applies where the prosecutor makes an application under section 19, 20 or 21 of the Proceeds of Crime Act 2002.

(2) The application must be in writing and give details of—

   (*a*)   the name of the defendant;

   (*b*)   the date on which and the place where any relevant conviction occurred;

   (*c*)   the date on which and the place where any relevant confiscation order was made or varied;

   (*d*)   the grounds for the application; and

   (*e*)   an indication of the evidence available to support the application.

(3) The application must be lodged with the Crown Court.

(4) The application must be served on the defendant at least seven days before the date fixed by the court for hearing the application, unless the Crown Court specifies a shorter period.

58.4 Application for new calculation of available amount

(1) This rule applies where the prosecutor or a receiver makes an application under section 22 of the Proceeds of Crime Act 2002 for a new calculation of the available amount.

(2) The application must be in writing and may be supported by a witness statement.

(3) The application and any witness statement must be lodged with the Crown Court.

(4) The application and any witness statement must be served on—

   (*a*)   the defendant;

   (*b*)   the receiver, if the prosecutor is making the application and a receiver has been appointed under section 50 of the 2002 Act; and

   (*c*)   the prosecutor, if the receiver is making the application,

at least seven days before the date fixed by the court for hearing the application, unless the Crown Court specifies a shorter period.

58.5 Variation of confiscation order due to inadequacy of available amount

(1) This rule applies where the defendant or a receiver makes an application under section 23 of the Proceeds of Crime Act 2002 for the variation of a confiscation order.

(2) The application must be in writing and may be supported by a witness statement.

(3) The application and any witness statement must be lodged with the Crown Court.

(4) The application and any witness statement must be served on—

   (*a*)   the prosecutor;

   (*b*)   the defendant, if the receiver is making the application; and

   (*c*)   the receiver, if the defendant is making the application and a receiver has been appointed under section 50 of the 2002 Act,

at least seven days before the date fixed by the court for hearing the application, unless the Crown Court specifies a shorter period.

58.6 Application by magistrates' court officer to discharge confiscation order

(1) This rule applies where a magistrates' court officer makes an application under section 24 or 25 of the Proceeds of Crime Act 2002 for the discharge of a confiscation order.

(2) The application must be in writing and give details of—

   (*a*)   the confiscation order;

   (*b*)   the amount outstanding under the order; and

   (*c*)   the grounds for the application.

(3) The application must be served on—

   (*a*)   the defendant;

   (*b*)   the prosecutor; and

   (*c*)   any receiver appointed under section 50 of the 2002 Act.

(4)   The Crown Court may determine the application without a hearing unless a person listed in paragraph (3) indicates, within seven days after the application was served on him, that he would like to make representations.

(5)   If the Crown Court makes an order discharging the confiscation order, the court must, at once, send a copy of the order to—

(*a*)   the magistrates' court officer who applied for the order;

(*b*)   the defendant;

(*c*)   the prosecutor; and

(*d*)   any receiver appointed under section 50 of the 2002 Act.

58.7   Application for variation of confiscation order made against an absconder

(1)   This rule applies where the defendant makes an application under section 29 of the Proceeds of Crime Act 2002 for the variation of a confiscation order made against an absconder.

(2)   The application must be in writing and supported by a witness statement which must give details of—

(*a*)   the confiscation order made against an absconder under section 6 of the 2002 Act as applied by section 28 of the 2002 Act;

(*b*)   the circumstances in which the defendant ceased to be an absconder;

(*c*)   the defendant's conviction of the offence or offences concerned; and

(*d*)   the reason why he believes the amount required to be paid under the confiscation order was too large.

(3)   The application and witness statement must be lodged with the Crown Court.

(4)   The application and witness statement must be served on the prosecutor at least seven days before the date fixed by the court for hearing the application, unless the Crown Court specifies a shorter period.

58.8   Application for discharge of confiscation order made against an absconder

(1)   This rule applies if the defendant makes an application under section 30 of the Proceeds of Crime Act 2002 for the discharge of a confiscation order.

(2)   The application must be in writing and supported by a witness statement which must give details of—

(*a*)   the confiscation order made under section 28 of the 2002 Act;

(*b*)   the date on which the defendant ceased to be an absconder;

(*c*)   the acquittal of the defendant if he has been acquitted of the offence concerned; and

(*d*)   if the defendant has not been acquitted of the offence concerned—

(i)   the date on which the defendant ceased to be an absconder,

(ii)   the date on which the proceedings taken against the defendant were instituted and a summary of steps taken in the proceedings since then, and

      (iii)   any indication given by the prosecutor that he does not intend to proceed against the defendant.

(3)   The application and witness statement must be lodged with the Crown Court.

(4)   The application and witness statement must be served on the prosecutor at least seven days before the date fixed by the court for hearing the application, unless the Crown Court specifies a shorter period.

(5)   If the Crown Court orders the discharge of the confiscation order, the court must serve notice on the magistrates' court responsible for enforcing the order.

58.9   Application for increase in term of imprisonment in default

(1)   This rule applies where the prosecutor makes an application under section 39(5) of the Proceeds of Crime Act 2002 to increase the term of imprisonment in default of payment of a confiscation order.

(2)   The application must be made in writing and give details of—

    (a)   the name and address of the defendant;

    (b)   the confiscation order;

    (c)   the grounds for the application; and

    (d)   the enforcement measures taken, if any.

(3)   On receipt of the application, the court must—

    (a)   at once, send to the defendant and the magistrates' court responsible for enforcing the order, a copy of the application; and

    (b)   fix a time, date and place for the hearing and notify the applicant and the defendant of that time, date and place.

(4)   If the Crown Court makes an order increasing the term of imprisonment in default, the court must, at once, send a copy of the order to—

    (a)   the applicant;

    (b)   the defendant;

    (c)   where the defendant is in custody at the time of the making of the order, the person having custody of the defendant; and

    (d)   the magistrates' court responsible for enforcing the order.

58.10   Compensation – general

(1)   This rule applies to an application for compensation under section 72 of the Proceeds of Crime Act 2002.

(2)   The application must be in writing and may be supported by a witness statement.

(3)   The application and any witness statement must be lodged with the Crown Court.

(4)   The application and any witness statement must be served on—

    (a)   the person alleged to be in default; and

(*b*)   the person [or authority][1] by whom the compensation would be payable under section 72(9) [or 302(7A)][1] of the 2002 Act (or if the compensation is payable out of a police fund under section 72(9)(*a*) [or 302(7A)][1], the chief officer of the police force concerned),

at least seven days before the date fixed by the court for hearing the application, unless the Crown Court directs otherwise.

Amendments

1   Inserted by the Criminal Procedure (Amendment) Rules 2010, SI 2010/1921, r 20.

58.11 Compensation – confiscation order made against absconder

(1)   This rule applies to an application for compensation under section 73 of the Proceeds of Crime Act 2002.

(2)   The application must be in writing and supported by a witness statement which must give details of—

    (*a*)   the confiscation order made under section 28 of the 2002 Act;

    (*b*)   the variation or discharge of the confiscation order under section 29 or 30 of the 2002 Act;

    (*c*)   the realisable property to which the application relates; and

    (*d*)   the loss suffered by the applicant as a result of the confiscation order.

(3)   The application and witness statement must be lodged with the Crown Court.

(4)   The application and witness statement must be served on the prosecutor at least seven days before the date fixed by the court for hearing the application, unless the Crown Court specifies a shorter period.

58.12 Payment of money in bank or building society account in satisfaction of confiscation order

(1)   An order under section 67 of the Proceeds of Crime Act 2002 requiring a bank or building society to pay money to a magistrates' court officer ('a payment order') shall—

    (*a*)   be directed to the bank or building society in respect of which the payment order is made;

    (*b*)   name the person against whom the confiscation order has been made;

    (*c*)   state the amount which remains to be paid under the confiscation order;

    (*d*)   state the name and address of the branch at which the account in which the money ordered to be paid is held and the sort code of that branch, if the sort code is known;

    (*e*)   state the name in which the account in which the money ordered to be paid is held and the account number of that account, if the account number is known;

    (*f*)   state the amount which the bank or building society is required to pay to the court officer under the payment order;

    (*g*)   give the name and address of the court officer to whom payment is to be made; and (*h*)   require the bank or building society to make payment within a period of seven days beginning on the day on which the payment order is made, unless it appears to the court that a longer or shorter period would be appropriate in the particular circumstances.

(2)   The payment order shall be served on the bank or building society in respect of which it is made by leaving it at, or sending it by first class post to, the principal office of the bank or building society.

(3)   A payment order which is served by first class post shall, unless the contrary is proved, be deemed to have been served on the second business day after posting.

(4)   In this rule 'confiscation order' has the meaning given to it by section 88(6) of the Proceeds of Crime Act 2002.

PART 59
PROCEEDS OF CRIME ACT 2002: RULES APPLICABLE ONLY TO RESTRAINT PROCEEDINGS

59.1   Application for restraint order

(1)   This rule applies where the prosecutor, or an accredited financial investigator, makes an application for a restraint order under section 42 of the Proceeds of Crime Act 2002.

(2)   The application may be made without notice.

(3)   The application must be in writing and supported by a witness statement which must—

(*a*)   give the grounds for the application;

(*b*)   to the best of the witness's ability, give full details of the realisable property in respect of which the applicant is seeking the order and specify the person holding that realisable property;

(*c*)   give the grounds for, and full details of, any application for an ancillary order under section 41(7) of the 2002 Act for the purposes of ensuring that the restraint order is effective; and

(*d*)   where the application is made by an accredited financial investigator, include a statement that he has been authorised to make the application under section 68 of the 2002 Act.

59.2   Restraint orders

(1)   The Crown Court may make a restraint order subject to exceptions, including, but not limited to, exceptions for reasonable living expenses and reasonable legal expenses, and for the purpose of enabling any person to carry on any trade, business or occupation.

(2)   But the Crown Court must not make an exception for legal expenses where this is prohibited by section 41(4) of the Proceeds of Crime Act 2002.

(3)   An exception to a restraint order may be made subject to conditions.

(4)   The Crown Court must not require the applicant for a restraint order to give any undertaking relating to damages sustained as a result of the restraint order by a person who is prohibited from dealing with realisable property by the restraint order.

(5) The Crown Court may require the applicant for a restraint order to give an undertaking to pay the reasonable expenses of any person, other than a person who is prohibited from dealing with realisable property by the restraint order, which are incurred in complying with the restraint order.

(6) A restraint order must include a statement that disobedience of the order, either by a person to whom the order is addressed, or by another person, may be contempt of court and the order must include details of the possible consequences of being held in contempt of court.

(7) Unless the Crown Court directs otherwise, a restraint order made without notice has effect until the court makes an order varying or discharging the restraint order.

(8) The applicant for a restraint order must—

   (*a*) serve copies of the restraint order and of the witness statement made in support of the application on the defendant and any person who is prohibited from dealing with realisable property by the restraint order; and

   (*b*) notify any person whom the applicant knows to be affected by the restraint order of the terms of the restraint order.

59.3 Application for discharge or variation of restraint order by a person affected by the order

(1) This rule applies where a person affected by a restraint order makes an application to the Crown Court under section 42(3) of the Proceeds of Crime Act 2002 to discharge or vary the restraint order or any ancillary order made under section 41(7) of the Act.

(2) The application must be in writing and may be supported by a witness statement.

(3) The application and any witness statement must be lodged with the Crown Court.

(4) The application and any witness statement must be served on the person who applied for the restraint order and any person who is prohibited from dealing with realisable property by the restraint order (if he is not the person making the application) at least two days before the date fixed by the court for hearing the application, unless the Crown Court specifies a shorter period.

59.4 Application for variation of restraint order by the person who applied for the order

(1) This rule applies where the applicant for a restraint order makes an application under section 42(3) of the Proceeds of Crime Act 2002 to the Crown Court to vary the restraint order or any ancillary order made under section 41(7) of the 2002 Act (including where the court has already made a restraint order and the applicant is seeking to vary the order in order to restrain further realisable property).

(2) The application may be made without notice if the application is urgent or if there are reasonable grounds for believing that giving notice would cause the dissipation of realisable property which is the subject of the application.

(3) The application must be in writing and must be supported by a witness statement which must—

   (*a*) give the grounds for the application;

(b)   where the application is for the inclusion of further realisable property in the order give full details, to the best of the witness's ability, of the realisable property in respect of which the applicant is seeking the order and specify the person holding that realisable property; and

(c)   where the application is made by an accredited financial investigator, include a statement that he has been authorised to make the application under section 68 of the 2002 Act.

(4)   The application and witness statement must be lodged with the Crown Court.

(5)   Except where, under paragraph (2), notice of the application is not required to be served, the application and witness statement must be served on any person who is prohibited from dealing with realisable property by the restraint order at least 2 days before the date fixed by the court for hearing the application, unless the Crown Court specifies a shorter period.

(6)   If the court makes an order for the variation of a restraint order, the applicant must serve copies of the order and of the witness statement made in support of the application on—

(a)   the defendant;

(b)   any person who is prohibited from dealing with realisable property by the restraint order (whether before or after the variation); and

(c)   any other person whom the applicant knows to be affected by the order.

59.5   Application for discharge of a restraint order by the person who applied for the order

(1)   This rule applies where the applicant for a restraint order makes an application under section 42(3) of the Proceeds of Crime Act 2002 to discharge the order or any ancillary order made under section 41(7) of the 2002 Act.

(2)   The application may be made without notice.

(3)   The application must be in writing and must state the grounds for the application.

(4)   If the court makes an order for the discharge of a restraint order, the applicant must serve copies of the order on—

(a)   the defendant;

(b)   any person who is prohibited from dealing with realisable property by the restraint order (whether before or after the discharge); and

(c)   any other person whom the applicant knows to be affected by the order.

59.6   Application to punish for contempt of court

(1)   This rule applies where a person is accused of disobeying a restraint order.

(2)   An applicant who wants the Crown Court to exercise its power to punish that person for contempt of court must comply with the rules in Part 62 (Contempt of court).

[Note. The Crown Court has inherent power to punish for contempt of court a person who disobeys its order: see section 45 of the Senior Courts Act 1981.]

PART 60

PROCEEDS OF CRIME ACT 2002: RULES APPLICABLE ONLY TO RECEIVERSHIP PROCEEDINGS

60.1 Application for appointment of a management or an enforcement receiver

(1) This rule applies to an application for the appointment of a management receiver under section 48(1) of the Proceeds of Crime Act 2002 and an application for the appointment of an enforcement receiver under section 50(1) of the 2002 Act.

(2) The application may be made without notice if—

(*a*) the application is joined with an application for a restraint order under rule 59.1;

(*b*) the application is urgent; or

(*c*) there are reasonable grounds for believing that giving notice would cause the dissipation of realisable property which is the subject of the application.

(3) The application must be in writing and must be supported by a witness statement which must—

(*a*) give the grounds for the application;

(*b*) give full details of the proposed receiver;

(*c*) to the best of the witness' ability, give full details of the realisable property in respect of which the applicant is seeking the order and specify the person holding that realisable property;

(*d*) where the application is made by an accredited financial investigator, include a statement that he has been authorised to make the application under section 68 of the 2002 Act; and

(*e*) if the proposed receiver is not a [person falling within section 55(8) of the 2002 Act][1] and the applicant is asking the court to allow the receiver to act—

(i) without giving security, or

(ii) before he has given security or satisfied the court that he has security in place,
explain the reasons why that is necessary.

(4) Where the application is for the appointment of an enforcement receiver, the applicant must provide the Crown Court with a copy of the confiscation order made against the defendant.

(5) The application and witness statement must be lodged with the Crown Court.

(6) Except where, under paragraph (2), notice of the application is not required to be served, the application and witness statement must be lodged with the Crown Court and served on—

(*a*) the defendant;

(*b*) any person who holds realisable property to which the application relates; and

(*c*) any other person whom the applicant knows to be affected by the application,

at least seven days before the date fixed by the court for hearing the application, unless the Crown Court specifies a shorter period.

(7)   If the court makes an order for the appointment of a receiver, the applicant must serve copies of the order and of the witness statement made in support of the application on—

    (*a*)   the defendant;

    (*b*)   any person who holds realisable property to which the order applies; and

    (*c*)   any other person whom the applicant knows to be affected by the order.

Amendments

1   Substituted by the Criminal Procedure (Amendment) Rules 2010, SI 2010/1921, r 21(*a*).

60.2 Application for conferral of powers on a management receiver or an enforcement receiver

(1)   This rule applies to an application for the conferral of powers on a management receiver under section 49(1) of the Proceeds of Crime Act 2002 or an enforcement receiver under section 51(1) of the 2002 Act.

(2)   The application may be made without notice if the application is to give the receiver power to take possession of property and—

    (*a*)   the application is joined with an application for a restraint order under rule 59.1;

    (*b*)   the application is urgent; or

    (*c*)   there are reasonable grounds for believing that giving notice would cause the dissipation of the property which is the subject of the application.

(3)   The application must be made in writing and supported by a witness statement which must—

    (*a*)   give the grounds for the application;

    (*b*)   give full details of the realisable property in respect of which the applicant is seeking the order and specify the person holding that realisable property; and

    (*c*)   where the application is made by an accredited financial investigator, include a statement that he has been authorised to make the application under section 68 of the 2002 Act.

(4)   Where the application is for the conferral of powers on an enforcement receiver, the applicant must provide the Crown Court with a copy of the confiscation order made against the defendant.

(5)   The application and witness statement must be lodged with the Crown Court.

(6)   Except where, under paragraph (2), notice of the application is not required to be served, the application and witness statement must be served on—

    (*a*)   the defendant;

    (*b*)   any person who holds realisable property in respect of which a receiver has been appointed or in respect of which an application for a receiver has been made;

    (*c*)   any other person whom the applicant knows to be affected by the application; and

    (*d*)   the receiver (if one has already been appointed),

at least seven days before the date fixed by the court for hearing the application, unless the Crown Court specifies a shorter period.

(7)   If the court makes an order for the conferral of powers on a receiver, the applicant must serve copies of the order on—

    (*a*)   the defendant;

    (*b*)   any person who holds realisable property in respect of which the receiver has been appointed; and

    (*c*)   any other person whom the applicant knows to be affected by the order.

60.3   Applications for discharge or variation of receivership orders, and applications for other orders

(1)   This rule applies to applications under section 62(3) of the Proceeds of Crime Act 2002 for orders (by persons affected by the action of receivers) and applications under section 63(1) of the 2002 Act for the discharge or variation of orders relating to receivers.

(2)   The application must be made in writing and lodged with the Crown Court.

(3)   The application must be served on the following persons (except where they are the person making the application)—

    (*a*)   the person who applied for appointment of the receiver;

    (*b*)   the defendant;

    (*c*)   any person who holds realisable property in respect of which the receiver has been appointed;

    (*d*)   the receiver; and

    (*e*)   any other person whom the applicant knows to be affected by the application,

at least seven days before the date fixed by the court for hearing the application, unless the Crown Court specifies a shorter period.

(4)   If the court makes an order for the discharge or variation of an order relating to a receiver under section 63(2) of the 2002 Act, the applicant must serve copies of the order on any persons whom he knows to be affected by the order.

60.4   Sums in the hands of receivers

(1)   This rule applies where the amount payable under a confiscation order has been fully paid and any sums remain in the hands of an enforcement receiver.

(2)   The receiver must make an application to the Crown Court for directions as to the distribution of the sums in his hands.

(3)   The application and any evidence which the receiver intends to rely on in support of the application must be served on—

    (*a*)   the defendant; and

    (*b*)   any other person who held (or holds) interests in any property realised by the receiver,

at least seven days before the date fixed by the court for hearing the application, unless the Crown Court specifies a shorter period.

(4)   If any of the provisions listed in paragraph (5) (provisions as to the vesting of funds in a trustee in bankruptcy) apply, then the Crown Court must make a declaration to that effect.

(5)   These are the provisions—

   (*a*)   section 31B of the Bankruptcy (Scotland) Act 1985;

   (*b*)   section 306B of the Insolvency Act 1986; and

   (*c*)   article 279B of The Insolvency (Northern Ireland) Order 1989.

60.5 Security

(1)   This rule applies where the Crown Court appoints a receiver under section 48 or 50 of the Proceeds of Crime Act 2002 and the receiver is not a [person falling within section 55(8) of the 2002 Act][1] (and it is immaterial whether the receiver is a permanent or temporary [member of staff or on secondment][1] from elsewhere).

(2)   The Crown Court may direct that before the receiver begins to act, or within a specified time, he must either—

   (*a*)   give such security as the Crown Court may determine; or

   (*b*)   file with the Crown Court and serve on all parties to any receivership proceedings evidence that he already has in force sufficient security,

to cover his liability for his acts and omissions as a receiver.

(3)   The Crown Court may terminate the appointment of a receiver if he fails to—

   (*a*)   give the security; or

   (*b*)   satisfy the court as to the security he has in force,

by the date specified.

Amendments

1   Substituted by the Criminal Procedure (Amendment) Rules 2010, SI 2010/1921, r 21.

60.6 Remuneration

(1)   This rule applies where the Crown Court appoints a receiver under section 48 or 50 of the Proceeds of Crime Act 2002 and the receiver is not a [person falling within section 55(8) of the 2002 Act][1] (and it is immaterial whether the receiver is a permanent or temporary [member of staff or on secondment][1] from elsewhere).

(2)   The receiver may only charge for his services if the Crown Court—

   (*a*)   so directs; and

   (*b*)   specifies the basis on which the receiver is to be remunerated.

(3)   Unless the Crown Court orders otherwise, in determining the remuneration of the receiver, the Crown Court shall award such sum as is reasonable and proportionate in all the circumstances and which takes into account—

   (*a*)   the time properly given by him and his staff to the receivership;

   (*b*)   the complexity of the receivership;

   (*c*)   any responsibility of an exceptional kind or degree which falls on the receiver in consequence of the receivership;

   (*d*)   the effectiveness with which the receiver appears to be carrying out, or to have carried out, his duties; and (*e*)   the value and nature of the subject matter of the receivership.

(4)   The Crown Court may refer the determination of a receiver's remuneration to be ascertained by the taxing authority of the Crown Court and rules 76.11 to 76.14 shall have effect as if the taxing authority was ascertaining costs.

(5)   A receiver appointed under section 48 of the 2002 Act is to receive his remuneration by realising property in respect of which he is appointed, in accordance with section 49(2)(*d*) of the 2002 Act.

(6)   A receiver appointed under section 50 of the 2002 Act is to receive his remuneration by applying to the magistrates' court officer for payment under section 55(4)(*b*) of the 2002 Act.

Amendments

1   Substituted by the Criminal Procedure (Amendment) Rules 2010, SI 2010/1921, r 21.

60.7   Accounts

(1)   The Crown Court may order a receiver appointed under section 48 or 50 of the Proceeds of Crime Act 2002 to prepare and serve accounts.

(2)   A party to receivership proceedings served with such accounts may apply for an order permitting him to inspect any document in the possession of the receiver relevant to those accounts.

(3)   Any party to receivership proceedings may, within 14 days of being served with the accounts, serve notice on the receiver—

(*a*)   specifying any item in the accounts to which he objects;

(*b*)   giving the reason for such objection; and

(*c*)   requiring the receiver within 14 days of receipt of the notice, either—

(i)   to notify all the parties who were served with the accounts that he accepts the objection, or

(ii)   if he does not accept the objection, to apply for an examination of the accounts in relation to the contested item.

(4)   When the receiver applies for the examination of the accounts he must at the same time lodge with the Crown Court—

(*a*)   the accounts; and

(*b*)   a copy of the notice served on him under this section of the rule.

(5)   If the receiver fails to comply with paragraph (3)(*c*) of this rule, any party to receivership proceedings may apply to the Crown Court for an examination of the accounts in relation to the contested item.

(6)   At the conclusion of its examination of the accounts the court will certify the result.

60.8   Non-compliance by receiver

(1)   If a receiver appointed under section 48 or 50 of the Proceeds of Crime Act 2002 fails to comply with any rule, practice direction or direction of the Crown Court, the Crown Court may order him to attend a hearing to explain his non-compliance.

(2)   At the hearing, the Crown Court may make any order it considers appropriate, including—

    (*a*)   terminating the appointment of the receiver;

    (*b*)   reducing the receiver's remuneration or disallowing it altogether; and

    (*c*)   ordering the receiver to pay the costs of any party.

PART 61
PROCEEDS OF CRIME ACT 2002: RULES APPLICABLE TO RE-STRAINT AND RECEIVERSHIP PROCEEDINGS

61.1   Distress and forfeiture

(1)   This rule applies to applications under sections 58(2) and (3) and 59(2) and (3) of the Proceeds of Crime Act 2002 for leave of the Crown Court to levy distress against property or exercise a right of forfeiture by peaceable re-entry in relation to a tenancy, in circumstances where the property or tenancy is the subject of a restraint order or a receiver has been appointed in respect of the property or tenancy.

(2)   The application must be made in writing to the Crown Court.

(3)   The application must be served on—

    (*a*)   the person who applied for the restraint order or the order appointing the receiver; and

    (*b*)   any receiver appointed in respect of the property or tenancy,

at least seven days before the date fixed by the court for hearing the application, unless the Crown Court specifies a shorter period.

61.2   Joining of applications

An application for the appointment of a management receiver or enforcement receiver under rule 60.1 may be joined with—

    (*a*)   an application for a restraint order under rule 59.1; and

    (*b*)   an application for the conferral of powers on the receiver under rule 60.2.

61.3   Applications to be dealt with in writing

Applications in restraint proceedings and receivership proceedings are to be dealt with without a hearing, unless the Crown Court orders otherwise.

61.4   Business in chambers

Restraint proceedings and receivership proceedings may be heard in chambers.

61.5   Power of court to control evidence

(1)   When hearing restraint proceedings and receivership proceedings, the Crown Court may control the evidence by giving directions as to—

    (*a*)   the issues on which it requires evidence;

    (*b*)   the nature of the evidence which it requires to decide those issues; and (*c*)   the way in which the evidence is to be placed before the court.

(2)   The court may use its power under this rule to exclude evidence that would otherwise be admissible.

(3)   The court may limit cross-examination in restraint proceedings and receivership proceedings.

61.6 Evidence of witnesses

(1)   The general rule is that, unless the Crown Court orders otherwise, any fact which needs to be proved in restraint proceedings or receivership proceedings by the evidence of a witness is to be proved by their evidence in writing.

(2)   Where evidence is to be given in writing under this rule, any party may apply to the Crown Court for permission to cross-examine the person giving the evidence.

(3)   If the Crown Court gives permission under paragraph (2) but the person in question does not attend as required by the order, his evidence may not be used unless the court gives permission.

61.7 Witness summons

(1)   Any party to restraint proceedings or receivership proceedings may apply to the Crown Court to issue a witness summons requiring a witness to—

(*a*)   attend court to give evidence; or

(*b*)   produce documents to the court.

(2)   Rule 28.3 applies to an application under this rule as it applies to an application under section 2 of the Criminal Procedure (Attendance of Witnesses) Act 1965.

61.8 Hearsay evidence

Section 2(1) of the Civil Evidence Act 1995 (duty to give notice of intention to rely on hearsay evidence) does not apply to evidence in restraint proceedings and receivership proceedings.

61.9 Disclosure and inspection of documents

(1)   This rule applies where, in the course of restraint proceedings or receivership proceedings, an issue arises as to whether property is realisable property.

(2)   The Crown Court may make an order for disclosure of documents.

(3)   Part 31 of the Civil Procedure Rules 1998 as amended from time to time shall have effect as if the proceedings were proceedings in the High Court.

61.10 Court documents

(1)   Any order which the Crown Court issues in restraint proceedings or receivership proceedings must—

(*a*)   state the name and judicial title of the person who made it;

(*b*)   bear the date on which it is made; and

(*c*)   be sealed by the Crown Court.

(2)   The Crown Court may place the seal on the order—

(*a*)   by hand; or

(b)   by printing a facsimile of the seal on the order whether electronically or otherwise.

(3)   A document purporting to bear the court's seal shall be admissible in evidence without further proof.

61.11   Consent orders

(1)   This rule applies where all the parties to restraint proceedings or receivership proceedings agree the terms in which an order should be made.

(2)   Any party may apply for a judgment or order in the terms agreed.

(3)   The Crown Court may deal with an application under paragraph (2) without a hearing.

(4)   Where this rule applies—

(a)   the order which is agreed by the parties must be drawn up in the terms agreed;

(b)   it must be expressed as being 'By Consent'; and

(c)   it must be signed by the legal representative acting for each of the parties to whom the order relates or by the party if he is a litigant in person.

(5)   Where an application is made under this rule, then the requirements of any other rule as to the procedure for making an application do not apply.

61.12   Slips and omissions

(1)   The Crown Court may at any time correct an accidental slip or omission in an order made in restraint proceedings or receivership proceedings.

(2)   A party may apply for a correction without notice.

61.13   Supply of documents from court records

(1)   No document relating to restraint proceedings or receivership proceedings may be supplied from the records of the Crown Court for any person to inspect or copy unless the Crown Court grants permission.

(2)   An application for permission under paragraph (1) must be made on notice to the parties to the proceedings

61.14   Disclosure of documents in criminal proceedings

(1)   This rule applies where—

(a)   proceedings for an offence have been started in the Crown Court and the defendant has not been either convicted or acquitted on all counts; and

(b)   an application for a restraint order under section 42(1) of the Proceeds of Crime Act 2002 has been made.

(2)   The judge presiding at the proceedings for the offence may be supplied from the records of the Crown Court with documents relating to restraint proceedings and any receivership proceedings.

(3)   Such documents must not otherwise be disclosed in the proceedings for the offence.

61.15   Preparation of documents

(1)   Every order in restraint proceedings or receivership proceedings will be drawn up by the Crown Court unless—

(a)   the Crown Court orders a party to draw it up;

(b)   a party, with the permission of the Crown Court, agrees to draw it up; or

(c)   the order is made by consent under rule 61.10.

(2)   The Crown Court may direct that—

(a)   an order drawn up by a party must be checked by the Crown Court before it is sealed; or

(b)   before an order is drawn up by the Crown Court, the parties must lodge an agreed statement of its terms.

(3)   Where an order is to be drawn up by a party—

(a)   he must lodge it with the Crown Court no later than seven days after the date on which the court ordered or permitted him to draw it up so that it can be sealed by the Crown Court; and

(b)   if he fails to lodge it within that period, any other party may draw it up and lodge it.

(4)   Nothing in this rule shall require the Crown Court to accept a document which is illegible, has not been duly authorised, or is unsatisfactory for some other similar reason.

61.16   Change of solicitor

(1)   This rule applies where—

(a)   a party for whom a solicitor is acting in restraint proceedings or receivership proceedings wants to change his solicitor;

(b)   a party, after having represented himself in such proceedings, appoints a solicitor to act on his behalf (except where the solicitor is appointed only to act as an advocate for a hearing); or

(c)   a party, after having been represented by a solicitor in such proceedings, intends to act in person.

(2)   Where this rule applies, the party or his solicitor (where one is acting) must—

(a)   lodge notice of the change at the Crown Court; and

(b)   serve notice of the change on every other party and, where paragraph (1)(a) or (c) applies, on the former solicitor.

(3)   The notice lodged at the Crown Court must state that notice has been served as required by paragraph (2)(b).

(4)   Subject to paragraph (5), where a party has changed his solicitor or intends to act in person, the former solicitor will be considered to be the party's solicitor unless and until—

(a)   notice is served in accordance with paragraph (2); or

(b)   the Crown Court makes an order under rule 61.17 and the order is served as required by paragraph (3) of that rule.

(5)   Where the certificate of a LSC funded client is revoked or discharged—

   (*a*)   the solicitor who acted for that person will cease to be the solicitor acting in the proceedings as soon as his retainer is determined under regulation 4 of The Community Legal Service (Costs) Regulations 2000; and

   (*b*)   if that person wishes to continue, where he appoints a solicitor to act on his behalf paragraph (2) will apply as if he had previously represented himself in the proceedings.

(6)   'Certificate' in paragraph (5) means a certificate issued under the Funding Code (approved under section 9 of the Access to Justice Act 1999) and 'LSC funded client' means an individual who receives services funded by the Legal Services Commission as part of the Community Legal Service within the meaning of Part I of the 1999 Act.

61.17   Application by solicitor for declaration that solicitor has ceased to act

(1)   A solicitor may apply to the Crown Court for an order declaring that he has ceased to be the solicitor acting for a party to restraint proceedings or receivership proceedings.

(2)   Where an application is made under this rule—

   (*a*)   notice of the application must be given to the party for whom the solicitor is acting, unless the Crown Court directs otherwise; and

   (*b*)   the application must be supported by evidence.

(3)   Where the Crown Court makes an order that a solicitor has ceased to act, the solicitor must serve a copy of the order on every party to the proceedings.

61.18   Application by other party for declaration that solicitor has ceased to act

(1)   Where—

   (*a*)   a solicitor who has acted for a party to restraint proceedings or receivership proceedings—

      (i)   has died,

      (ii)   has become bankrupt,

      (iii)   has ceased to practise, or

      (iv)   cannot be found, and

   (*b*)   the party has not given notice of a change of solicitor or notice of intention to act in person as required by rule 61.16,

any other party may apply to the Crown Court for an order declaring that the solicitor has ceased to be the solicitor acting for the other party in the proceedings.

(2)   Where an application is made under this rule, notice of the application must be given to the party to whose solicitor the application relates unless the Crown Court directs otherwise.

(3)   Where the Crown Court makes an order under this rule, the applicant must serve a copy of the order on every other party to the proceedings.

61.19   Order for costs

(1)   This rule applies where the Crown Court is deciding whether to make an order for costs in restraint proceedings or receivership proceedings.

(2)   The court has discretion as to—

    (*a*)   whether costs are payable by one party to another;

    (*b*)   the amount of those costs; and

    (*c*)   when they are to be paid.

(3)   If the court decides to make an order about costs—

    (*a*)   the general rule is that the unsuccessful party will be ordered to pay the costs of the successful party; but

    (*b*)   the court may make a different order.

(4)   In deciding what order (if any) to make about costs, the court must have regard to all of the circumstances, including—

    (*a*)   the conduct of all the parties; and

    (*b*)   whether a party has succeeded on part of an application, even if he has not been wholly successful.

(5)   The orders which the court may make include an order that a party must pay—

    (*a*)   a proportion of another party's costs;

    (*b*)   a stated amount in respect of another party's costs;

    (*c*)   costs from or until a certain date only;

    (*d*)   costs incurred before proceedings have begun;

    (*e*)   costs relating to particular steps taken in the proceedings;

    (*f*)   costs relating only to a distinct part of the proceedings; and

    (*g*)   interest on costs from or until a certain date, including a date before the making of an order.

(6)   Where the court would otherwise consider making an order under paragraph (5)(*f*), it must instead, if practicable, make an order under paragraph (5)(*a*) or (*c*).

(7)   Where the court has ordered a party to pay costs, it may order an amount to be paid on account before the costs are assessed.

[Note. See section 52 of the Senior Courts Act 1981.]

61.20   Assessment of costs

(1)   Where the Crown Court has made an order for costs in restraint proceedings or receivership proceedings it may either—

    (*a*)   make an assessment of the costs itself; or

    (*b*)   order assessment of the costs under rule 76.11.

(2)   In either case, the Crown Court or the assessing authority, as the case may be, must—

    (*a*)   only allow costs which are proportionate to the matters in issue; and

    (*b*)   resolve any doubt which it may have as to whether the costs were reasonably incurred or reasonable and proportionate in favour of the paying party.

(3) The Crown Court or the assessing authority, as the case may be, is to have regard to all the circumstances in deciding whether costs were proportionately or reasonably incurred or proportionate and reasonable in amount.

(4) In particular, the Crown Court or the assessing authority must give effect to any orders which have already been made.

(5) The Crown Court or the assessing authority must also have regard to—

    (*a*) the conduct of all the parties, including in particular, conduct before, as well as during, the proceedings;

    (*b*) the amount or value of the property involved;

    (*c*) the importance of the matter to all the parties;

    (*d*) the particular complexity of the matter or the difficulty or novelty of the questions raised;

    (*e*) the skill, effort, specialised knowledge and responsibility involved;

    (*f*) the time spent on the application; and

    (*g*) the place where and the circumstances in which work or any part of it was done.

61.21 Time for complying with an order for costs

A party to restraint proceedings or receivership proceedings must comply with an order for the payment of costs within 14 days of—

    (*a*) the date of the order if it states the amount of those costs;

    (*b*) if the amount of those costs is decided later under rule 76.11, the date of the assessing authority's decision; or

    (*c*) in either case, such later date as the Crown Court may specify.

61.22 Application of costs rules

Rules 61.19, 61.20 and 61.21 do not apply to the assessment of costs in proceedings to the extent that section 11 of the Access to Justice Act 1999 applies and provisions made under that Act make different provision.

[PART 62
CONTEMPT OF COURT

SECTION 1: GENERAL RULES

62.1 When this Part applies

(1) This Part applies where the court can deal with a person for conduct—

    (*a*) in contempt of court; or

    (*b*) in contravention of the legislation to which rules 62.5 and 62.9 refer.

(2) In this Part, 'respondent' means any such person.

[Note. For the court's powers to punish for contempt of court, see the notes to rules 62.5 and 62.9.]]¹

Amendments
1   Substituted by the Criminal Procedure (Amendment No. 2) Rules 2010, SI 2010/3026, r 9, Sch 2.

[62.2   Exercise of court's power to deal with contempt of court

(1)   The court must determine at a hearing—

    (*a*)   an enquiry under rule 62.8;

    (*b*)   an allegation under rule 62.9.

(2)   The court must not proceed in the respondent's absence unless—

    (*a*)   the respondent's behaviour makes it impracticable to proceed otherwise; or

    (*b*)   the respondent has had at least 14 days' notice of the hearing, or was present when it was arranged.

(3)   If the court hears part of an enquiry or allegation in private, it must announce at a hearing in public—

    (*a*)   the respondent's name;

    (*b*)   in general terms, the nature of any conduct that the respondent admits, or the court finds proved; and

    (*c*)   any punishment imposed.]¹

Amendments
1   Substituted by the Criminal Procedure (Amendment No. 2) Rules 2010, SI 2010/3026, r 9, Sch 2.

[62.3   Notice of suspension of imprisonment by Court of Appeal or Crown Court

(1)   This rule applies where—

    (*a*)   the Court of Appeal or the Crown Court suspends an order of imprisonment for contempt of court; and

    (*b*)   the respondent is absent when the court does so.

(2)   The respondent must be served with notice of the terms of the court's order—

    (*a*)   by any applicant under rule 62.9; or

    (*b*)   by the court officer, in any other case.

[Note. By reason of sections 15 and 45 of the Senior Courts Act 1981 , the Court of Appeal and the Crown Court each has an inherent power to suspend imprisonment for contempt of court, on conditions, or for a period, or both.]]¹

Amendments
1   Substituted by the Criminal Procedure (Amendment No. 2) Rules 2010, SI 2010/3026, r 9, Sch 2.

[62.4   Application to discharge an order for imprisonment

(1)   This rule applies where the court can discharge an order for a respondent's imprisonment for contempt of court.

(2)   A respondent who wants the court to discharge such an order must—

    (*a*)   apply in writing, unless the court otherwise directs, and serve any written application on—

        (i)   the court officer, and

        (ii)   any applicant under rule 62.9 on whose application the respondent was imprisoned;

    (*b*)   in the application—

        (i)   explain why it is appropriate for the order for imprisonment to be discharged, and

        (ii)   give details of any appeal, and its outcome; and

    (*c*)   ask for a hearing, if the respondent wants one.

[Note. By reason of sections 15 and 45 of the Senior Courts Act 1981, the Court of Appeal and the Crown Court each has an inherent power to discharge an order for a respondent's imprisonment for contempt of court in failing to comply with a court order.

Under section 97(4) of the Magistrates' Courts Act 1980, a magistrates' court can discharge an order for imprisonment if the respondent gives evidence.

Under section 12(4) of the Contempt of Court Act 1981, a magistrates' court can discharge an order for imprisonment made under that section.]][1]

Amendments
1   Substituted by the Criminal Procedure (Amendment No. 2) Rules 2010, SI 2010/3026, r 9, Sch 2.

[SECTION 2: CONTEMPT OF COURT BY OBSTRUCTION, DISRUPTION, ETC

62.5   Initial procedure on obstruction, disruption, etc.

(1)   This rule applies where the court observes, or someone reports to the court—

    (*a*)   in the Court of Appeal or the Crown Court, obstructive, disruptive, insulting or intimidating conduct, in the courtroom or in its vicinity, or otherwise immediately affecting the proceedings;

    (*b*)   in the Crown Court, a contravention of—

        (i)   section 3 of the Criminal Procedure (Attendance of Witnesses) Act 1965 (disobeying a witness summons);

        (ii)   section 20 of the Juries Act 1974 (disobeying a jury summons);

        (iii)   section 8 of the Contempt of Court Act 1981 (obtaining details of a jury's deliberations, etc.);

    (*c*)   in a magistrates' court, a contravention of—

        (i)   section 97(4) of the Magistrates' Courts Act 1980 (refusing to give evidence), or

(ii)   section 12 of the Contempt of Court Act 1981 (insulting or interrupting the court, etc.);

(*d*)   a contravention of section 9 of the Contempt of Court Act 1981 (without the court's permission, recording the proceedings, etc.);

(*e*)   any other conduct with which the court can deal as, or as if it were, a criminal contempt of court, except failure to surrender to bail under section 6 of the Bail Act 1976.

(2)   Unless the respondent's behaviour makes it impracticable to do so, the court must—

(*a*)   explain, in terms the respondent can understand (with help, if necessary)—

(i)   the conduct that is in question,

(ii)   that the court can impose imprisonment, or a fine, or both, for such conduct,

(iii)   (where relevant) that the court has power to order the respondent's immediate temporary detention, if in the court's opinion that is required,

(iv)   that the respondent may explain the conduct,

(v)   that the respondent may apologise, if he or she so wishes, and that this may persuade the court to take no further action, and

(vi)   that the respondent may take legal advice; and

(*b*)   allow the respondent a reasonable opportunity to reflect, take advice, explain and, if he or she so wishes, apologise.

(3)   The court may then—

(*a*)   take no further action in respect of that conduct;

(*b*)   enquire into the conduct there and then; or

(*c*)   postpone that enquiry (if a magistrates' court, only until later the same day).

[Note. By reason of sections 15 and 45 of the Senior Courts Act 1981, the Court of Appeal and the Crown Court each has an inherent power to imprison (for a maximum of 2 years), or fine (to an unlimited amount), or both, a respondent for contempt of court for the conduct listed in paragraph (1)(*a*), (*b*), (*d*) or (*e*). See also section 14 of the Contempt of Court Act 1981.

Under section 97(4) of the Magistrates' Courts Act 1980, and under sections 12 and 14 of the Contempt of Court Act 1981, a magistrates' court can imprison (for a maximum of 1 month), or fine (to a maximum of £2,500), or both, a respondent who contravenes a provision listed in paragraph (1)(*c*) or (*d*). Section 12(1) of the 1981 Act allows the court to 'deal with any person who—

(*a*)   wilfully insults the justice or justices, any witness before or officer of the court or any solicitor or counsel having business in the court, during his or their sitting or attendance in court or in going to or returning from the court; or

(*b*)   wilfully interrupts the proceedings of the court or otherwise misbehaves in court.'

Under section 89 of the Powers of Criminal Courts (Sentencing) Act 2000, no respondent who is under 21 may be imprisoned for contempt of court. Under section 108 of that Act, a respondent who is at least 18 but under 21 may be detained if the court is of the opinion that no other method of dealing with him or her is appropriate. Under section 14(2A) of the Contempt of Court Act 1981, a respondent who is under 17 may not be ordered to attend an attendance centre.

Under section 258 of the Criminal Justice Act 2003, a respondent who is imprisoned for contempt of court must be released unconditionally after serving half the term.

Under section 12 of the Access to Justice Act 1999, the respondent may receive advice and representation funded by the Legal Services Commission in 'proceedings for contempt committed, or alleged to have been committed, by an individual in the face of the court'.

By reason of sections 15 and 45 of the Senior Courts Act 1981, the Court of Appeal and the Crown Court each has an inherent power temporarily to detain a respondent, for example to restore order, when dealing with obstructive, disruptive, insulting or intimidating conduct. Under section 12(2) of the Contempt of Court Act 1981, a magistrates' court can temporarily detain a respondent until later the same day on a contravention of that section.

Part 19 contains rules about bail.]][1]

Amendments
1   Substituted by the Criminal Procedure (Amendment No. 2) Rules 2010, SI 2010/3026, r 9, Sch 2.

[62.6   Review after temporary detention

(1)   This rule applies in a case in which the court has ordered the respondent's immediate temporary detention for conduct to which rule 62.5 applies.

(2)   The court must review the case—

(*a*)   if a magistrates' court, later the same day;

(*b*)   in the Court of Appeal or the Crown Court, no later than the next business day.

(3)   On the review, the court must—

(*a*)   unless the respondent is absent, repeat the explanations required by rule 62.5(2)(*a*); and

(*b*)   allow the respondent a reasonable opportunity to reflect, take advice, explain and, if he or she so wishes, apologise.

(4)   The court may then—

(*a*)   take no further action in respect of the conduct;

(*b*)   if a magistrates' court, enquire into the conduct there and then; or

(*c*)   if the Court of Appeal or the Crown Court—

(i)   enquire into the conduct there and then, or

(ii)   postpone the enquiry, and order the respondent's release from such detention in the meantime.][1]

Amendments
1   Substituted by the Criminal Procedure (Amendment No. 2) Rules 2010, SI 2010/3026, r 9, Sch 2.

[62.7   Postponement of enquiry

(1)   This rule applies where the Court of Appeal or the Crown Court postpones the enquiry.

(2)   The court must arrange for the preparation of a written statement containing such particulars of the conduct in question as to make clear what the respondent appears to have done.

(3)   The court officer must serve on the respondent—

   (*a*)   that written statement;

   (*b*)   notice of where and when the postponed enquiry will take place; and

   (*c*)   a notice that—

      (i)   reminds the respondent that the court can impose imprisonment, or a fine, or both, for contempt of court, and

      (ii)   warns the respondent that the court may pursue the postponed enquiry in the respondent's absence, if the respondent does not attend.][1]

Amendments

1   Substituted by the Criminal Procedure (Amendment No. 2) Rules 2010, SI 2010/3026, r 9, Sch 2.

[62.8 Procedure on enquiry

(1)   At an enquiry, the court must—

   (*a*)   ensure that the respondent understands (with help, if necessary) what is alleged, if the enquiry has been postponed from a previous occasion;

   (*b*)   explain what the procedure at the enquiry will be; and

   (*c*)   ask whether the respondent admits the conduct in question.

(2)   If the respondent admits the conduct, the court need not receive evidence.

(3)   If the respondent does not admit the conduct, the court will receive—

   (*a*)   any statement served under rule 62.7;

   (*b*)   any other evidence of the conduct;

   (*c*)   any evidence introduced by the respondent; and

   (*d*)   any representations by the respondent about the conduct.

(4)   If the respondent admits the conduct, or the court finds it proved, the court must—

   (*a*)   before imposing any punishment for contempt of court, give the respondent an opportunity to make representations relevant to punishment;

   (*b*)   explain, in terms the respondent can understand (with help, if necessary)—

      (i)   the reasons for its decision, including its findings of fact, and

      (ii)   the punishment it imposes, and its effect; and

   (*c*)   if a magistrates' court, arrange for the preparation of a written record of those findings.

(5)   The court that conducts an enquiry—

   (*a*)   need not include the same member or members as the court that observed the conduct; but

   (*b*)   may do so, unless that would be unfair to the respondent.][1]

Amendments
1   Substituted by the Criminal Procedure (Amendment No. 2) Rules 2010, SI 2010/3026, r 9, Sch 2.

[SECTION 3: CONTEMPT OF COURT BY FAILURE TO COMPLY WITH COURT ORDER, ETC.

62.9   Initial procedure on failure to comply with court order, etc.

(1)   This rule applies where—

    (*a*)   a party, or other person directly affected, alleges—

        (i)   in the Crown Court, a failure to comply with an order to which rule 6.13 or 6.22 (certain investigation orders), or rule 59.6 (a restraint order), applies,

        (ii)   in the Court of Appeal or the Crown Court, any other conduct with which that court can deal as a civil contempt of court, or

        (iii)   in the Crown Court or a magistrates' court, unauthorised use of disclosed prosecution material under section 17 of the Criminal Procedure and Investigations Act 1996;

    (*b*)   the court deals on its own initiative with conduct to which paragraph (1)(*a*) applies.

(2)   Such a party or person must—

    (*a*)   apply in writing and serve the application on the court officer; and

    (*b*)   serve on the respondent—

        (i)   the application, and

        (ii)   notice of where and when the court will consider the allegation (not less than 14 days after service).

(3)   The application must—

    (*a*)   identify the respondent;

    (*b*)   explain that it is an application for the respondent to be dealt with for contempt of court;

    (*c*)   contain such particulars of the conduct in question as to make clear what is alleged against the respondent; and

    (*d*)   include a notice warning the respondent that the court—

        (i)   can impose imprisonment, or a fine, or both, for contempt of court, and

        (ii)   may deal with the application in the respondent's absence, if the respondent does not attend the hearing.

(4)   A court which acts on its own initiative under paragraph (1)(*b*) must—

    (*a*)   arrange for the preparation of a written statement containing the same information as an application; and

    (*b*)   arrange for the service on the respondent of—

(i)   that written statement, and

(ii)   notice of where and when the court will consider the allegation (not less than 14 days after service).

[Note. By reason of section 45 of the Senior Courts Act 1981, the Crown Court has an inherent power to imprison (for a maximum of 2 years), or fine (to an unlimited amount), or both, a respondent for conduct in contempt of court by failing to comply with a court order or an undertaking given to the court.

Under section 18 of the Criminal Procedure and Investigations Act 1996—

(*a*)   the Crown Court can imprison (for a maximum of 2 years), or fine (to an unlimited amount), or both;

(*b*)   a magistrates' court can imprison (for a maximum of 6 months), or fine (to a maximum of £5,000), or both,

a person who uses disclosed prosecution material in contravention of section 17 of that Act. See also rule 22.8.

Under section 89 of the Powers of Criminal Courts (Sentencing) Act 2000, no respondent who is under 21 may be imprisoned for contempt of court. Under section 108 of that Act, a respondent who is at least 18 but under 21 may be detained if the court is of the opinion that no other method of dealing with him or her is appropriate. Under section 14(2A) of the Contempt of Court Act 1981, a respondent who is under 17 may not be ordered to attend an attendance centre.

Under section 258 of the Criminal Justice Act 2003, a respondent who is imprisoned for contempt of court must be released unconditionally after serving half the term.

The Practice Direction sets out a form of application for use in connection with this rule.

The rules in Part 4 require that an application under this rule must be served by handing it to the person accused of contempt of court unless the court otherwise directs.]][1]

Amendments

1   Substituted by the Criminal Procedure (Amendment No. 2) Rules 2010, SI 2010/3026, r 9, Sch 2.

[62.10   Procedure on hearing

(1)   At the hearing of an allegation under rule 62.9, the court must—

(*a*)   ensure that the respondent understands (with help, if necessary) what is alleged;

(*b*)   explain what the procedure at the hearing will be; and

(*c*)   ask whether the respondent admits the conduct in question.

(2)   If the respondent admits the conduct, the court need not receive evidence.

(3)   If the respondent does not admit the conduct, the court will receive—

(*a*)   the application or written statement served under rule 62.9;

(*b*)   any other evidence of the conduct;

(*c*)   any evidence introduced by the respondent; and

(*d*)   any representations by the respondent about the conduct.

(4)   If the respondent admits the conduct, or the court finds it proved, the court must—

(*a*)   before imposing any punishment for contempt of court, give the respondent an opportunity to make representations relevant to punishment;

(*b*)   explain, in terms the respondent can understand (with help, if necessary)—

(i)   the reasons for its decision, including its findings of fact, and

(ii)   the punishment it imposes, and its effect; and

(*c*)   in a magistrates' court, arrange for the preparation of a written record of those findings.]¹

Amendments

1   Substituted by the Criminal Procedure (Amendment No. 2) Rules 2010, SI 2010/3026, r 9, Sch 2.

[62.11   Introduction of written witness statement or other hearsay

(1)   Where rule 62.9 applies, an applicant or respondent who wants to introduce in evidence the written statement of a witness, or other hearsay, must—

(*a*)   serve a copy of the statement, or notice of other hearsay, on—

(i)   the court officer, and

(ii)   the other party; and

(*b*)   serve the copy or notice—

(i)   when serving the application under rule 62.9, in the case of an applicant, or

(ii)   not more than 7 days after service of that application or of the court's written statement, in the case of the respondent.

(2)   Such service is notice of that party's intention to introduce in evidence that written witness statement, or other hearsay, unless that party otherwise indicates when serving it.

(3)   A party entitled to receive such notice may waive that entitlement.

[Note. On an application under rule 62.9, hearsay evidence is admissible under the Civil Evidence Act 1995. Section 1(2) of the 1995 Act defines hearsay as meaning 'a statement made otherwise than by a person while giving oral evidence in the proceedings which is tendered as evidence of the matters stated'. Section 13 of the Act defines a statement as meaning 'any representation of fact or opinion, however made'.

Under section 2 of the 1995 Act, a party who wants to introduce hearsay in evidence must give reasonable and practicable notice, in accordance with procedure rules, unless the recipient waives that requirement.]]¹

Amendments

1   Substituted by the Criminal Procedure (Amendment No. 2) Rules 2010, SI 2010/3026, r 9, Sch 2.

[62.12   Content of written witness statement

(1)   This rule applies to a written witness statement served under rule 62.11.

(2)   Such a written witness statement must contain a declaration by the person making it that it is true to the best of that person's knowledge and belief.

[Note. By reason of sections 15 and 45 of the Senior Courts Act 1981, the Court of Appeal and the Crown Court each has an inherent power to imprison (for a maximum of 2 years), or fine (to an unlimited amount), or both, for contempt of court a person who, in a written witness statement to which this rule applies, makes, or causes to be made, a false statement without an honest belief in its truth. See also section 14 of the Contempt of Court Act 1981.]][1]

Amendments

1   Substituted by the Criminal Procedure (Amendment No. 2) Rules 2010, SI 2010/3026, r 9, Sch 2.

[62.13 Content of notice of other hearsay

(1)   This rule applies to a notice of hearsay, other than a written witness statement, served under rule 62.11.

(2)   Such a notice must—

    (*a*)   set out the evidence, or attach the document that contains it; and

    (*b*)   identify the person who made the statement that is hearsay.][1]

Amendments

1   Substituted by the Criminal Procedure (Amendment No. 2) Rules 2010, SI 2010/3026, r 9, Sch 2.

[62.14 Cross-examination of maker of written witness statement or other hearsay

(1)   This rule applies where a party wants the court's permission to cross-examine a person who made a statement which another party wants to introduce as hearsay.

(2)   The party who wants to cross-examine that person must—

    (*a*)   apply in writing, with reasons; and

    (*b*)   serve the application on—

        (i)   the court officer, and

        (ii)   the party who served the hearsay.

(3)   A respondent who wants to cross-examine such a person must apply to do so not more than 7 days after service of the hearsay by the applicant.

(4)   An applicant who wants to cross-examine such a person must apply to do so not more than 3 days after service of the hearsay by the respondent.

(5)   The court—

    (*a*)   may decide an application under this rule without a hearing; but

    (*b*)   must not dismiss such an application unless the person making it has had an opportunity to make representations at a hearing.

[Note. See also section 3 of the Civil Evidence Act 1995.]][1]

Amendments

1   Substituted by the Criminal Procedure (Amendment No. 2) Rules 2010, SI 2010/3026, r 9, Sch 2.

[62.15 Credibility and consistency of maker of written witness statement or other hearsay

(1) This rule applies where a party wants to challenge the credibility or consistency of a person who made a statement which another party wants to introduce as hearsay.

(2) The party who wants to challenge the credibility or consistency of that person must—

   (*a*)   serve a written notice of intention to do so on—

      (i)   the court officer, and

      (ii)   the party who served the hearsay; and

   (*b*)   in it, identify any statement or other material on which that party relies.

(3) A respondent who wants to challenge such a person's credibility or consistency must serve such a notice not more than 7 days after service of the hearsay by the applicant.

(4) An applicant who wants to challenge such a person's credibility or consistency must serve such a notice not more than 3 days after service of the hearsay by the respondent.

(5) The party who served the hearsay—

   (*a*)   may call that person to give oral evidence instead; and

   (*b*)   if so, must serve a notice of intention to do so on—

      (i)   the court officer, and

      (ii)   the other party
      as soon as practicable after service of the notice under paragraph (2).

[Note. Section 5(2) of the Civil Evidence Act 1995 describes the procedure for challenging the credibility of the maker of a statement of which hearsay evidence is introduced.

See also section 6 of that Act. The 1995 Act does not allow the introduction of evidence of a previous inconsistent statement otherwise than in accordance with sections 5, 6 and 7 of the Criminal Procedure Act 1865.]][1]

Amendments
1   Substituted by the Criminal Procedure (Amendment No. 2) Rules 2010, SI 2010/3026, r 9, Sch 2.

[62.16   Magistrates' courts' powers to adjourn, etc.

(1) This rule applies where a magistrates' court deals with unauthorised disclosure of prosecution material under sections 17 and 18 of the Criminal Procedure and Investigations Act 1996.

(2) The sections of the Magistrates' Courts Act 1980 listed in paragraph (3) apply as if in those sections—

   (*a*)   'complaint' and 'summons' each referred to an application or written statement under rule 62.9;

   (*b*)   'complainant' meant an applicant; and

   (*c*)   'defendant' meant the respondent.

(3) Those sections are—

   (*a*)   section 51 (issue of summons on complaint);

   (*b*)   section 54 (adjournment);

    (*c*)   section 55 (non-appearance of defendant);

    (*d*)   section 97(1) (summons to witness);

    (*e*)   section 121(1) (constitution and place of sitting of court);

    (*f*)   section 123 (defect in process).

(4)   Section 127 of the 1980 Act (limitation of time) does not apply.

[Note. Under section 19(3) of the Criminal Procedure and Investigations Act 1996, Criminal Procedure Rules may contain provisions equivalent to those contained in Schedule 3 to the Contempt of Court Act 1981 (which allows magistrates' courts in cases of contempt of court to use certain powers such courts possess in other cases).]][1]

Amendments
1   Substituted by the Criminal Procedure (Amendment No. 2) Rules 2010, SI 2010/3026, r 9, Sch 2.

[62.17 Court's power to vary requirements under Section 3

(1)   The court may shorten or extend (even after it has expired) a time limit under rule 62.11, 62.14 or 62.15.

(2)   A person who wants an extension of time must—

    (*a*)   apply when serving the statement, notice or application for which it is needed; and

    (*b*)   explain the delay.][1]

Amendments
1   Substituted by the Criminal Procedure (Amendment No. 2) Rules 2010, SI 2010/3026, r 9, Sch 2.

[Parts 63 to 70 are not reproduced in this title.]

PART 71
APPEAL TO THE COURT OF APPEAL UNDER THE PROCEEDS OF CRIME ACT 2002: GENERAL RULES

71.1 Extension of time

(1)   An application to extend the time limit for giving notice of application for leave to appeal under Part 2 of the Proceeds of Crime Act 2002 must—

    (*a*)   be included in the notice of appeal; and

    (*b*)   state the grounds for the application.

(2)   The parties may not agree to extend any date or time limit set by this Part, Part 72 or Part 73, or by The Proceeds of Crime Act 2002 (Appeals under Part 2) Order 2003.

71.2 Other applications

Rule 68.3(2)(*h*) (form of appeal notice) applies in relation to an application—

(*a*)   by a party to an appeal under Part 2 of the Proceeds of Crime Act 2002 that, under article 7 of The Proceeds of Crime Act 2002 (Appeals under Part 2) Order 2003, a witness be ordered to attend or that the evidence of a witness be received by the Court of Appeal; or

(*b*)   by the defendant to be given leave by the court to be present at proceedings for which leave is required under article 6 of the 2003 Order,

as it applies in relation to applications under Part I of the Criminal Appeal Act 1968 and the form in which rule 68.3 requires notice to be given may be modified as necessary.

71.3   Examination of witness by court

Rule 65.7 (notice of hearings and decisions) applies in relation to an order of the court under article 7 of the Proceeds of Crime Act 2002 (Appeals under Part 2) Order 2003 to require a person to attend for examination as it applies in relation to such an order of the court under Part I of the Criminal Appeal Act 1968.

71.4   Supply of documentary and other exhibits

Rule 65.11 (Registrar's duty to provide copy documents for appeal or reference) applies in relation to an appellant or respondent under Part 2 of the Proceeds of Crime Act 2002 as it applies in relation to an appellant and respondent under Part I of the Criminal Appeal Act 1968.

71.5   Registrar's power to require information from court of trial

The Registrar may require the Crown Court to provide the Court of Appeal with any assistance or information which they may require for the purposes of exercising their jurisdiction under Part 2 of the Proceeds of Crime Act 2002, The Proceeds of Crime Act 2002 (Appeals under Part 2) Order 2003, this Part or Parts 72 and 73.

71.6   Hearing by single judge

Rule 65.6(5) (hearings) applies in relation to a judge exercising any of the powers referred to in article 8 of The Proceeds of Crime Act 2002 (Appeals under Part 2) Order 2003 or the powers in rules 72.2(3) and (4) (respondent's notice), 73.2(2) (notice of appeal) and 73.3(6) (respondent's notice), as it applies in relation to a judge exercising the powers referred to in section 31(2) of the Criminal Appeal Act 1968.

71.7   Determination by full court

Rule 65.5 (renewing an application refused by a judge or the registrar) shall apply where a single judge has refused an application by a party to exercise in his favour any of the powers listed in article 8 of The Proceeds of Crime Act 2002 (Appeals under Part 2) Order 2003, or the power in rule 72.2(3) or (4) as it applies where the judge has refused to exercise the powers referred to in section 31(2) of the Criminal Appeal Act 1968.

71.8   Notice of determination

(1)   This rule applies where a single judge or the Court of Appeal has determined an application or appeal under The Proceeds of Crime Act 2002 (Appeals under Part 2) Order 2003 or under Part 2 of the Proceeds of Crime Act 2002.

(2)   The Registrar must, as soon as practicable, serve notice of the determination on all of the parties to the proceedings.

(3)   Where a single judge or the Court of Appeal has disposed of an application for leave to appeal or an appeal under section 31 of the 2002 Act, the registrar must also, as soon as practicable, serve the order on a court officer of the court of trial and any magistrates' court responsible for enforcing any confiscation order which the Crown Court has made.

71.9   Record of proceedings and transcripts

Rule 65.8(2)(*a*) and (*b*) (duty of Crown Court officer – arranging recording of proceedings in Crown Court and arranging transcription) and rule 65.9 (duty of person transcribing proceedings in the Crown Court) apply in relation to proceedings in respect of which an appeal lies to the Court of Appeal under Part 2 of the Proceeds of Crime Act 2002 as they apply in relation to proceedings in respect of which an appeal lies to the Court of Appeal under Part I of the Criminal Appeal Act 1968.

71.10   Appeal to the Supreme Court

(1)   An application to the Court of Appeal for leave to appeal to the Supreme Court under Part 2 of the Proceeds of Crime Act 2002 must be made—

    (*a*)   orally after the decision of the Court of Appeal from which an appeal lies to the Supreme Court; or

    (*b*)   in the form set out in the Practice Direction, in accordance with article 12 of The Proceeds of Crime Act 2002 (Appeals under Part 2) Order 2003 and served on the Registrar.

(2)   The application may be abandoned at any time before it is heard by the Court of Appeal by serving notice in writing on the Registrar.

(3)   Rule 65.6(5) (hearings) applies in relation to a single judge exercising any of the powers referred to in article 15 of the 2003 Order, as it applies in relation to a single judge exercising the powers referred to in section 31(2) of the Criminal Appeal Act 1968.

(4)   Rule 65.5 (renewing an application refused by a judge or the Registrar) applies where a single judge has refused an application by a party to exercise in his favour any of the powers listed in article 15 of the 2003 Order as they apply where the judge has refused to exercise the powers referred to in section 31(2) of the 1968 Act.

(5)   The form in which rule 65.5(2) requires an application to be made may be modified as necessary.

PART 72
APPEAL TO THE COURT OF APPEAL UNDER THE PROCEEDS OF CRIME ACT 2002: PROSECUTOR'S APPEAL REGARDING CONFISCATION

72.1   Notice of appeal

(1)   Where an appellant wishes to apply to the Court of Appeal for leave to appeal under section 31 of the Proceeds of Crime Act 2002, he must serve a notice of appeal in the form set out in the Practice Direction on—

    (*a*)   the Crown Court officer; and

(*b*)   the defendant.

(2)   When the notice of the appeal is served on the defendant, it must be accompanied by a respondent's notice in the form set out in the Practice Direction for the defendant to complete and a notice which—

  (*a*)   informs the defendant that the result of an appeal could be that the Court of Appeal would increase a confiscation order already imposed on him, make a confiscation order itself or direct the Crown Court to hold another confiscation hearing;

  (*b*)   informs the defendant of any right he has under article 6 of the Proceeds of Crime Act 2002 (Appeals under Part 2) Order 2003 to be present at the hearing of the appeal, although he may be in custody;

  (*c*)   invites the defendant to serve notice on the registrar if he wishes—

    (i)   to apply to the Court of Appeal for leave to be present at proceedings for which leave is required under article 6 of the 2003 Order, or

    (ii)   to present any argument to the Court of Appeal on the hearing of the application or, if leave is given, the appeal, and whether he wishes to present it in person or by means of a legal representative;

  (*d*)   draws to the defendant's attention the effect of rule 71.4 (supply of documentary and other exhibits); and

  (*e*)   advises the defendant to consult a solicitor as soon as possible.

(3)   The appellant must provide a Crown Court officer with a certificate of service stating that he has served the notice of appeal on the defendant in accordance with paragraph (1) or explaining why he has been unable to effect service.

72.2 Respondent's notice

(1)   This rule applies where a defendant is served with a notice of appeal under rule 72.1.

(2)   If the defendant wishes to oppose the application for leave to appeal, he must, not later than 14 days after the date on which he received the notice of appeal, serve on the Registrar and on the appellant a notice in the form set out in the Practice Direction—

  (*a*)   stating the date on which he received the notice of appeal;

  (*b*)   summarising his response to the arguments of the appellant; and

  (*c*)   specifying the authorities which he intends to cite.

(3)   The time for giving notice under this rule may be extended by the Registrar, a single judge or by the Court of Appeal.

(4)   Where the Registrar refuses an application under paragraph (3) for the extension of time, the defendant shall be entitled to have his application determined by a single judge.

(5)   Where a single judge refuses an application under paragraph (3) or (4) for the extension of time, the defendant shall be entitled to have his application determined by the Court of Appeal.

72.3 Amendment and abandonment of appeal

(1)   The appellant may amend a notice of appeal served under rule 72.1 or abandon an appeal under section 31 of the Proceeds of Crime Act 2002—

(a) without the permission of the Court at any time before the Court of Appeal have begun hearing the appeal; and

(b) with the permission of the Court after the Court of Appeal have begun hearing the appeal,

by serving notice in writing on the Registrar.

(2) Where the appellant serves a notice abandoning an appeal under paragraph (1), he must send a copy of it to—

(a) the defendant;

(b) a court officer of the court of trial; and

(c) the magistrates' court responsible for enforcing any confiscation order which the Crown Court has made.

(3) Where the appellant serves a notice amending a notice of appeal under paragraph (1), he must send a copy of it to the defendant.

(4) Where an appeal is abandoned under paragraph (1), the application for leave to appeal or appeal shall be treated, for the purposes of section 85 of the 2002 Act (conclusion of proceedings), as having been refused or dismissed by the Court of Appeal.

PART 73
APPEAL TO THE COURT OF APPEAL UNDER THE PROCEEDS OF CRIME ACT 2002: RESTRAINT OR RECEIVERSHIP ORDERS

73.1 Leave to appeal

(1) Leave to appeal to the Court of Appeal under section 43 or section 65 of the Proceeds of Crime Act 2002 will only be given where—

(a) the Court of Appeal considers that the appeal would have a real prospect of success; or

(b) there is some other compelling reason why the appeal should be heard.

(2) An order giving leave may limit the issues to be heard and be made subject to conditions.

73.2 Notice of appeal

(1) Where an appellant wishes to apply to the Court of Appeal for leave to appeal under section 43 or 65 of the Proceeds of Crime Act 2002 Act, he must serve a notice of appeal in the form set out in the Practice Direction on the Crown Court officer.

(2) Unless the Registrar, a single judge or the Court of Appeal directs otherwise, the appellant must serve the notice of appeal, accompanied by a respondent's notice in the form set out in the Practice Direction for the respondent to complete, on—

(a) each respondent;

(b) any person who holds realisable property to which the appeal relates; and

(c) any other person affected by the appeal,

as soon as practicable and in any event not later than 7 days after the notice of appeal is served on a Crown Court officer.

(3) The appellant must serve the following documents with his notice of appeal—

(*a*)   four additional copies of the notice of appeal for the Court of Appeal;

(*b*)   four copies of any skeleton argument;

(*c*)   one sealed copy and four unsealed copies of any order being appealed;

(*d*)   four copies of any witness statement or affidavit in support of the application for leave to appeal;

(*e*)   four copies of a suitable record of the reasons for judgment of the Crown Court; and

(*f*)   four copies of the bundle of documents used in the Crown Court proceedings from which the appeal lies.

(4)   Where it is not possible to serve all of the documents referred to in paragraph (3), the appellant must indicate which documents have not yet been served and the reasons why they are not currently available.

(5)   The appellant must provide a Crown Court officer with a certificate of service stating that he has served the notice of appeal on each respondent in accordance with paragraph (2) and including full details of each respondent or explaining why he has been unable to effect service.

73.3   Respondent's notice

(1)   This rule applies to an appeal under section 43 or 65 of the Proceeds of Crime Act 2002.

(2)   A respondent may serve a respondent's notice on the Registrar.

(3)   A respondent who—

(*a*)   is seeking leave to appeal from the Court of Appeal; or

(*b*)   wishes to ask the Court of Appeal to uphold the decision of the Crown Court for reasons different from or additional to those given by the Crown Court,

must serve a respondent's notice on the Registrar.

(4)   A respondent's notice must be in the form set out in the Practice Direction and where the respondent seeks leave to appeal to the Court of Appeal it must be requested in the respondent's notice.

(5)   A respondent's notice must be served on the Registrar not later than 14 days after—

(*a*)   the date the respondent is served with notification that the Court of Appeal has given the appellant leave to appeal; or

(*b*)   the date the respondent is served with notification that the application for leave to appeal and the appeal itself are to be heard together.

(6)   Unless the Registrar, a single judge or the Court of Appeal directs otherwise, the respondent serving a respondent's notice must serve the notice on the appellant and any other respondent—

(*a*)   as soon as practicable; and

(*b*)   in any event not later than seven days,

after it is served on the Registrar.

73.4   Amendment and abandonment of appeal

(1)   The appellant may amend a notice of appeal served under rule 73.2 or abandon an appeal under section 43 or 65 of the Proceeds of Crime Act 2002—

   (*a*)   without the permission of the Court at any time before the Court of Appeal have begun hearing the appeal; and

   (*b*)   with the permission of the Court after the Court of Appeal have begun hearing the appeal,

   by serving notice in writing on the Registrar.

(2)   Where the appellant serves a notice under paragraph (1), he must send a copy of it to each respondent.

73.5   Stay

Unless the Court of Appeal or the Crown Court orders otherwise, an appeal under section 43 or 65 of the Proceeds of Crime Act 2002 shall not operate as a stay of any order or decision of the Crown Court.

73.6   Striking out appeal notices and setting aside or imposing conditions on leave to appeal

(1)   The Court of Appeal may—

   (*a*)   strike out the whole or part of a notice of appeal served under rule 73.2; or

   (*b*)   impose or vary conditions upon which an appeal under section 43 or 65 of the Proceeds of Crime Act 2002 may be brought.

(2)   The Court of Appeal will only exercise its powers under paragraph (1) where there is a compelling reason for doing so.

(3)   Where a party is present at the hearing at which leave to appeal was given, he may not subsequently apply for an order that the Court of Appeal exercise its powers under paragraph (1)(*b*).

73.7   Hearing of appeals

(1)   This rule applies to appeals under section 43 or 65 of the Proceeds of Crime Act 2002.

(2)   Every appeal will be limited to a review of the decision of the Crown Court unless the Court of Appeal considers that in the circumstances of an individual appeal it would be in the interests of justice to hold a re-hearing.

(3)   The Court of Appeal will allow an appeal where the decision of the Crown Court was—

   (*a*)   wrong; or

   (*b*)   unjust because of a serious procedural or other irregularity in the proceedings in the Crown Court.

(4)   The Court of Appeal may draw any inference of fact which it considers justified on the evidence.

(5)   At the hearing of the appeal a party may not rely on a matter not contained in his notice of appeal unless the Court of Appeal gives permission.

[Parts 74 to 76 are not reproduced in this title.]

Appendix 3

MAGISTRATES' COURT (DETENTION AND FORFEITURE OF CASH) RULES 2002

SI 2002/2998

1 Citation and commencement

These Rules may be cited as the Magistrates' Courts (Detention and Forfeiture of Cash) Rules 2002 and shall come into force on 30th December 2002.

2 Interpretation

In these Rules—

(a) 'the Act' means the Proceeds of Crime Act 2002;

(b) 'justices' clerk' means the justices' clerk for the justices who are to hear or have heard an application;

(c) words and expressions used have the same meaning as in Chapter 3 of Part 5 of the Act;

(d) a reference to a form is a reference to a form set out in the Schedule to these Rules or a form with the same effect.

3 Prior approval of searches for cash

(1) An application to a justice of the peace under section 290(1) of the Act for prior approval of a search for cash under section 289 of the Act may be made without notice.

(2) A justice of the peace may grant such an application without a hearing and may conduct any hearing in private.

4 First application for the continued detention of seized cash

(1) The first application under section 295(4) of the Act for an order under section 295(2) of the Act for the continued detention of cash seized under section 294 of the Act [may]¹ be made in form A and [may]¹ be sent to the [designated officer for the local justice area]² of the court before which the applicant wishes to make the application.

(2) But where the reasonable grounds for suspicion which led to the seizure of cash to which an application under section 295(4) of the Act relates are connected to the reasonable grounds for suspicion which led to the seizure of other cash to which a previous order made under section 295(2) of the Act relates, then the application may be sent to the [designated officer for the local justice area]² of the court which made the previous order.

(3) Except where paragraph (4) or paragraph (7) applies, a copy of the written application and notification of the hearing of the application shall be given by the applicant to the person from whom the cash was seized.

(4)   Where seized cash is found in a means of unattended dispatch, such as an unattended letter, parcel or container, copies of the written application and notification of the hearing of the application shall be sent by the applicant to the sender and intended recipient of the means of unattended dispatch.

(5)   But where paragraph (4) applies the applicant is not required to send copies of the written application and notification of the hearing to a sender or intended recipient who cannot be identified.

(6)   Where paragraph (4) applies, the court shall not decline to hear an application solely on the ground that it has not been proved that the sender and intended recipient have been given a copy of the written application and notification of the hearing.

(7)   Where unattended cash is seized (other than where the cash is found in a means of unattended dispatch) the applicant need not give a copy of the written application and notification of the hearing to any person.

(8)   ...³

(9)   The [designated officer]² shall give—

    (*a*)   notice of the order ...³, and

    (*b*)   a copy of the order,

to the person from whom the cash was seized and to any other person known to be affected by the order.

Amendments

1   Substituted by the Magistrates' Courts (Miscellaneous Amendments) Rules 2003, SI 2003/1236, rr 91, 92(1).

2   Substituted by the Courts Act 2003 (Consequential Provisions) (No. 2) Order 2005, SI 2005/617, art 2, Schedule, paras 204, 205.

3   Repealed by the Magistrates' Courts (Miscellaneous Amendments) Rules 2003, SI 2003/1236, rr 91, 92(2), (3).

5   Further applications for the continued detention of seized cash

(1)   An application under section 295(4) of the Act for a further order under section 295(2) of the Act for the continued detention of cash [may]¹ be made in Form A and [may]¹ be sent to the [designated officer]² to whom the first application under section 295(4) of the Act was sent.

(2)   The applicant shall send a copy of the application to every person to whom notice of previous related orders made under section 295(2) of the Act has been given.

(3)   The justices' clerk shall fix a date for the hearing of the application, which, unless he directs otherwise, shall not be earlier than seven days from the date on which it is fixed, and the [designated officer]² shall notify that date to the applicant and every person to whom notice of the previous orders has been given.

(4)   ...³

(5)   The [designated officer]² shall give a copy of the order to every person to whom notice of the previous related orders has been given.

(6)   The [designated officer]² shall also give—

    (*a*)   notice of the order ...³, and

    (*b*)   a copy of the order,

to any person other than one referred to in paragraph (5) known to be affected by the order.

Amendments

1   Substituted by the Magistrates' Courts (Miscellaneous Amendments) Rules 2003, SI 2003/1236, rr 91, 93(1).

2   Substituted by the Courts Act 2003 (Consequential Provisions) (No. 2) Order 2005, SI 2005/617, art 2, Schedule, para 205.

3   Repealed by the Magistrates' Courts (Miscellaneous Amendments) Rules 2003, SI 2003/1236, rr 91, 93(2), (3).

6 Applications for the release of detained cash

(1)   An application under section 297(3) or 301(1) of the Act for the release of detained cash shall be made in writing and sent to the [designated officer for the local justice area][1] of the court before which the applicant wishes to make the application.

(2)   But if the applicant has been given notice of an order under section 295(2) of the Act in respect of the detained cash, then the application shall be sent to the [designated officer][1] who sent him that notice.

(3)   The [designated officer][1] shall send a copy of the application to—

      (*a*)   the Commissioners of Customs and Excise, if the cash which is the subject of the application was seized by a customs officer;

      [(*ab*)   the Director General of the Serious Organised Crime Agency if the cash which is the subject of the application was seized by a member of the staff of that Agency who is designated under section 43 of the Serious Organised Crime and Police Act 2005;][2]

      (*b*)   the chief officer of the police force to which the constable belongs ...[3], if the cash which is the subject of the application was seized by a constable; and

      (*c*)   every person to whom notice of the order made under section 295(2) of the Act has been given.

(4)   The justices' clerk shall fix a date for the hearing of the application, which, unless he directs otherwise, shall not be earlier than seven days from the date on which it is fixed, and the [designated officer][1] shall notify that date to the applicant and to every person to whom a copy of the application is required to be sent under paragraph (3).

(5)   At the hearing of an application under section 301(1) of the Act, the court may, if it thinks fit, order that the applicant shall be joined as a party to all the proceedings in relation to the detained cash.

(6)   ...[4]

(7)   A direction under section 297(2) of the Act and an order under section 301(3) or (4) of the Act shall provide for the release of the cash within seven days of the date of the making of the order or direction, or such longer period as, with the agreement of the applicant, may be specified, except that cash shall not be released whilst section 298(4) of the Act applies.

Amendments

1   Substituted by the Courts Act 2003 (Consequential Provisions) (No. 2) Order 2005, SI 2005/617, art 2, Schedule, paras 204, 205.

2   Inserted by the Serious Organised Crime and Police Act 2005 (Consequential and Supplementary Amendments to Secondary Legislation) Order 2006, SI 2006/594, art 2, Schedule, para 31(1), (3).

3   Repealed by the Serious Organised Crime and Police Act 2005 (Consequential and Supplementary Amendments to Secondary Legislation) Order 2006, SI 2006/594, art 2, Schedule, para 31(1), (2).

4   Repealed by the Magistrates' Courts (Miscellaneous Amendments) Rules 2003, SI 2003/1236, rr 91, 94.

7   Application for forfeiture of detained cash

(1)   An application under section 298(1) of the Act for the forfeiture of detained cash [may][1] be in Form G and [may][1] be sent to the [designated officer][1] to whom applications for the continued detention of the cash under section 295(4) of the Act have been sent.

(2)   Where no applications in respect of the cash have been made under section 295(4) of the Act, the application shall be sent to—

   (a)   the [designated officer for the local justice area][2] of the court before which the applicant wishes to make the application; or

   (b)   where the reasonable grounds for suspicion which led to the seizure of cash to which the application for forfeiture relates are connected to the reasonable grounds for suspicion which led to the seizure of cash to which an order made under section 295(2) of the Act relates, to the [designated officer for the local justice area][2] of the court which made the order under section 295(2).

(3)   The applicant shall send a copy of the application to every person to whom notice of an order made under section 295(2) of the Act in respect of the detained cash has been given and to any other person identified by the court as being affected by the application.

(4)   The justices' clerk shall set a date for a directions hearing, which, unless he directs otherwise, shall not be earlier than seven days from the date on which it is fixed, and the [designated officer][1] shall notify that date to the applicant and to every person to whom a copy of the application is required to be sent under paragraph (3).

(5)   At the directions hearing, the court may give directions relating to the management of the proceedings, including directions as to the date for the hearing of the application.

(6)   If neither the person from whom the cash was seized, nor any other person who is affected by the detention of the cash, seeks to contest the application, the court may decide the application at the directions hearing.

(7)   An order for the forfeiture of detained cash under section 298(2) of the Act ...[3] and a copy of the order shall be given by the [designated officer][1] to every person to whom notice of an order made under section 295(2) of the Act in respect of the detained cash has been given and to any other person known to be affected by the order.

Amendments
1   Substituted by the Magistrates' Courts (Miscellaneous Amendments) Rules 2003, SI 2003/1236, rr 91, 95(1).
2   Substituted by the Courts Act 2003 (Consequential Provisions) (No. 2) Order 2005, SI 2005/617, art 2, Schedule, paras 204, 205.
3   Repealed by the Magistrates' Courts (Miscellaneous Amendments) Rules 2003, SI 2003/1236, rr 91, 95(2).

8   Application for compensation

(1)   An application under section 302(1) for compensation shall be made in writing and sent to the [designated officer for the local justice area][1] of the court before which the applicant wishes to make the application.

(2)   But if the applicant has been given notice of an order under section 295(2) of the Act in respect of the cash which is the subject of the application, then the application shall be sent to the [designated officer][1] who sent him that notice.

(3)   The [designated officer][1] shall send a copy of the application to—

(*a*)   the Commissioners of Customs and Excise, if the cash which is the subject of the application was seized by a customs officer;

[(*ab*)   the Director General of the Serious Organised Crime Agency if the cash which is the subject of the application was seized by a member of the staff of that Agency who is designated under section 43 of the Serious Organised Crime and Police Act 2005;][2]

(*b*)   the chief officer of the police force to which the constable belongs ...[3], if the cash which is the subject of the application was seized by a constable.

The justices' clerk shall fix a date for the hearing of the application, which, unless he directs otherwise, shall not be earlier than seven days from the date on which it is fixed, and the [designated officer][1] shall notify the applicant and the person referred to in paragraph (3) of that date.

Amendments

1   Substituted by the Courts Act 2003 (Consequential Provisions) (No. 2) Order 2005, SI 2005/617, art 2, Schedule, paras 204, 205.
2   Inserted by the Serious Organised Crime and Police Act 2005 (Consequential and Supplementary Amendments to Secondary Legislation) Order 2006, SI 2006/594, art 2, Schedule, para 31(1), (3).
3   Repealed by the Serious Organised Crime and Police Act 2005 (Consequential and Supplementary Amendments to Secondary Legislation) Order 2006, SI 2006/594, art 2, Schedule, para 31(1), (2).

9   Notice

Any notification or document required to be given or sent to any person under these Rules may be given by post or by facsimile to his last known address, or to any other address given by that person for the purpose of service of documents under these Rules.

10   Transfer of proceedings

(1)   Any person who is a party to, or affected by, proceedings under Chapter 3 of Part 5 of the Act may, at any time, make an application to the court dealing with the matter for the proceedings to be transferred to a different [local justice area][1].

(2)   Any such application shall be made in writing and sent to the [designated officer for the local justice area][1] in which the proceedings are being dealt with and shall specify the grounds on which it is made.

(3)   The [designated officer][1] shall send a copy of the application to the parties to the proceedings and any other person affected by the proceedings.

(4)   The justices' clerk shall fix a date for the hearing of the application, which, unless he directs otherwise, shall not be earlier than seven days from the date on which it is fixed, and the [designated officer][1] shall notify the date to the applicant and every person to whom a copy of the application is required to be sent under paragraph (3).

(5)   The court may grant the application if it is satisfied that it would be more convenient or fairer for proceedings to be transferred to a different [local justice area][1].

(6)   If the application is granted—

(*a*)   the [designated officer]¹ shall give a copy of the order to the parties to the proceedings and any other person affected by the proceedings;

(*b*)   the [designated officer]¹ shall send all relevant papers to the [designated officer for the local justice area]¹ to which proceedings are transferred;

(*c*)   any further proceedings under Chapter 3 of Part 5 of the Act in respect of the cash to which the proceedings relate shall be dealt with in the [local justice area]¹ to which proceedings are transferred;

(*d*)   any requirement under these Rules to make an application to a [designated officer]¹ shall be read as a requirement to make an application to the [designated officer for the local justice area]¹ to which proceedings are transferred.

Amendments

1   Substituted by the Courts Act 2003 (Consequential Provisions) (No. 2) Order 2005, SI 2005/617, art 2, Schedule, paras 204, 205, 206.

11 Procedure at hearings

(1)   At the hearing of an application under Chapter 3 of Part 5 of the Act, any person to whom notice of the application has been given may attend and be heard on the question of whether the application should be granted, but the fact that any such person does not attend shall not prevent the court from hearing the application.

(2)   Subject to the foregoing provisions of these Rules, proceedings on such an application shall be regulated in the same manner as proceedings on a complaint, and accordingly for the purposes of these Rules, the application shall be deemed to be a complaint, the applicant a complainant, the respondents to be defendants and any notice given by the [designated officer]¹ under rules 5(3), 6(4), 7(4), 8(4) or 10(4) to be a summons: but nothing in this rule shall be construed as enabling a warrant of arrest to be issued for failure to appear in answer to any such notice.

(3)   At the hearing of an application under Chapter 3 of Part 5 of the Act, the court shall require the matters contained in the application to be sworn by the applicant under oath, may require the applicant to answer any questions under oath and may require any response from the respondent to the application to be made under oath.

(4)   The court shall record or cause to be recorded the substance of any statements made under oath which are not already recorded in the written application.

Amendments

1   Substituted by the Courts Act 2003 (Consequential Provisions) (No. 2) Order 2005, SI 2005/617, art 2, Schedule, para 205.

[12 ...¹

... ¹]²

Amendments

1   Repealed by the Courts Act 2003 (Consequential Provisions) (No. 2) Order 2005, SI 2005/617, art 2, Schedule, para 207.

2   Inserted by the Magistrates' Courts (Detention and Forfeiture of Cash) (Amendment) Rules 2003, SI 2003/638, r 2.

Schedule

Rules 4(1) and 5(1) and Rule 2

FORM A
FIRST/FURTHER** APPLICATION FOR CONTINUED DETENTION OF SEIZED CASH

(Section 295(4) Proceeds of Crime Act 2002; MC (Detention and Forfeiture of Cash) Rules 2002 rr 4(1), 5(1))

Magistrates' Court

(Code)

Date

Name of person from whom cash seized

Address*

Names and addresses of any other persons likely to be affected by an order for detention of the cash (if known)

Amount seized/Estimated amount seized (only in the case of a first application for continued detention)**

Amount to which reasonable grounds of suspicion apply/Estimated amount to which reasonable grounds for suspicion apply (only in the case of a first application for continued detention)** where it is not reasonably practicable to detain only that part

Date of seizure

Time of seizure

Place of seizure

Date of latest order for continued detention of seized cash (if any)

Amount detained under latest order for continued detention (if any)

Amounts released since the latest order for continued detention (if any)

I,

of

(official address and position of applicant)

Constable/Customs Officer**, apply for an order under section 295(2) of the Proceeds of Crime Act 2002 authorising the continued detention of cash in the sum of .... and will state upon oath that one of the two grounds below is satisfied in relation to all of the cash/the sum of .... but it is not reasonably practicable to detain only that part of the cash**;

1. There are reasonable grounds for suspecting that the cash is recoverable property and that either—

    (*a*) its continued detention is justified while its derivation is further investigated or consideration is given to bringing (in the United Kingdom or elsewhere) proceedings against any person for an offence with which the cash is connected, or

    (*b*) proceedings against any person for an offence with which the cash is connected have been started and have not been concluded.

2.   There are reasonable grounds for suspecting that the cash is intended to be used in unlawful conduct and that either—

    (*a*)   its continued detention is justified while its intended use is further investigated or consideration is given to bringing (in the United Kingdom or elsewhere) proceedings against any person for an offence with which the cash is connected, or

    (*b*)   proceedings against any person for an offence with which the cash is connected have been started and have not been concluded.
    (state grounds)

Signed

To: The [Designated Officer][1]

Magistrates' Court

Notes to the Applicant—

First Application—You must give a copy of this application and notification of the hearing of it to the person from whom the cash was seized***.

Further Application—This application must wherever possible be submitted to the [designated officer][1] at least seven days before the expiry of the last period of detention that was ordered by the court. You must give a copy of this application to the person from whom the cash was seized and any other person specified in any order made under section 295(2) of the Proceeds of Crime Act 2002***.

* In the case of a means of unattended dispatch such as a letter, parcel or container, insert names and addresses, if known, of sender and intended recipient. In the case of any other unattended cash, state that you believe the cash was unattended and explain your grounds for believing that the cash was unattended.

** Delete as appropriate

*** In the case of a means of unattended dispatch such as a letter, parcel or container, the copy application and, if applicable, notification of hearing should be given to the sender and intended recipient (if known), rather than the person from whom the cash was seized. In the case of any other unattended cash, there is no requirement to give the copy application and, if applicable, notification of hearing to the person from whom the cash was seized.

Amendments

1   Substituted by the Courts Act 2003 (Consequential Provisions) (No. 2) Order 2005, SI 2005/617, art 2, Schedule, paras 205, 208.

FORM B

…[1]

…[1]

Amendments

1   Repealed by the Magistrates' Courts (Miscellaneous Amendments) Rules 2003, SI 2003/1236, rr 91, 96.

FORM C
...

...¹

Amendments

1   Repealed by the Magistrates' Courts (Miscellaneous Amendments) Rules 2003, SI 2003/1236, rr 91, 96.

FORM D
...¹

...¹

Amendments

1   Repealed by the Magistrates' Courts (Miscellaneous Amendments) Rules 2003, SI 2003/1236, rr 91, 96.

FORM E
...¹

...¹

Amendments

1   Repealed by the Magistrates' Courts (Miscellaneous Amendments) Rules 2003, SI 2003/1236, rr 91, 96.

FORM F
...¹

...¹

Amendments

1   Repealed by the Magistrates' Courts (Miscellaneous Amendments) Rules 2003, SI 2003/1236, rr 91, 96.

Rule 7(1)

FORM G
APPLICATION FOR FORFEITURE OF DETAINED CASH

(Section 298(1) of the Proceeds of Crime Act 2002; MC (Detention and Forfeiture of Cash) Rules 2002 r 7(1))

Magistrates' Court

(Code)

Date

Name of person from whom cash seized*

Address*

Names and addresses of any other persons identified by the court as being affected by this application

Amount seized

Date of seizure

Time of seizure

Place of seizure

Date of latest order for continued detention of seized cash (if any)

Amount detained under latest order for continued detention (if any)

Amounts released since the latest order for continued detention (if any)

I,

of

(official address and position of applicant)

Constable/Customs Officer**, apply for an order under section 298(2) of the Proceeds of Crime Act 2002 for the forfeiture of cash in the sum of .... together with any interest accruing thereon pursuant to section 296(1) of that Act, on the grounds that the cash is recoverable property or is intended by any person for use in unlawful conduct.

(state grounds)

To: The [Designated Officer][1]

Magistrates' Court

Note to the Applicant—You must send a copy of this application to the person from whom the cash was seized and any other person specified in any order made under section 295(2) of the Proceeds of Crime Act 2002***.

* In the case of a means of unattended dispatch such as a letter, parcel or container, insert names and addresses, if known, of sender and intended recipient. In the case of any other unattended cash, state that you believe the cash was unattended and explain your grounds for believing that the cash was unattended.

** Delete as appropriate

*** In the case of a means of unattended dispatch such as a letter, parcel or container, the copy application and, if applicable, notification of hearing should be given to the sender and intended recipient (if known), rather than the person from whom the cash was seized. In the case of any other unattended cash, there is no requirement to give the copy application and, if applicable, notification of hearing to the person from whom the cash was seized.

Amendments
1   Substituted by the Courts Act 2003 (Consequential Provisions) (No. 2) Order 2005, SI 2005/617, art 2, Schedule, para 208.

FORM H
.. [1]

.. [1]

Amendments
1   Repealed by the Magistrates' Courts (Miscellaneous Amendments) Rules 2003, SI 2003/1236, rr 91, 96.

Appendix 4 Attorney General guidance to prosecuting bodies on their asset recovery powers under the Proceeds of Crime Act 2002

Issued 5 November 2009

Proceeds Of Crime Act 2002
Section 2A (Contribution to the reduction of crime)
Joint guidance given by the Secretary of State and
Her Majesty's Attorney General

This guidance is given by the Secretary of State to the Serious Organised Crime Agency (SOCA), and by the Attorney General to the Director of Public Prosecutions, the Director of Revenue and Customs Prosecutions, the Director of the Serious Fraud Office and the Director of Public Prosecutions for Northern Ireland, in accordance with section 2A of the Proceeds of Crime Act 2002. In the case of the Director of Public Prosecutions for Northern Ireland, the guidance is given by the Attorney General in her capacity as Attorney General for Northern Ireland. In this guidance, as in section 2A, SOCA and the Directors are referred to as 'relevant authorities'.

1. The reduction of crime is in general best secured by means of criminal investigations and criminal proceedings. However, the non-conviction based asset recovery powers available under the Act can also make an important contribution to the reduction of crime where (i) it is not feasible to secure a conviction, (ii) a conviction is obtained but a confiscation order is not made, or (iii) a relevant authority is of the view that the public interest will be better served by using those powers rather than by seeking a criminal disposal.

2. In any case where proceeds of crime have been identified but it is not feasible to secure a conviction, or a conviction has been secured but no confiscation order made, relevant authorities should consider using the non conviction-based powers available under the Act.

3. In any case where it appears that a conviction might be secured, relevant authorities will consider whether or not it is in the public interest to conduct a criminal investigation and (at a later stage, if sufficient evidence is obtained) a prosecution. In these circumstances relevant authorities may also consider whether or not the public interest might be better served by using the non conviction-based powers available under the Act, applying the principle that a criminal disposal will generally make the best contribution to the reduction of crime.

4.   Any assessment of where the public interest lies should include consideration of all relevant factors. The Code for Crown Prosecutors (in Northern Ireland, the Code for Prosecutors) lists some of the factors that might be relevant in deciding whether or not a prosecution is in the public interest. The same factors might also be relevant in considering, at any stage, whether or not the non conviction-based powers should be used. A vital underlying consideration is the need to retain public confidence in the criminal justice system as a whole, and in the fair and proper use of the non conviction-based powers. In particular, care must be taken not to allow an individual or body corporate to avoid a criminal investigation and prosecution by consenting to the making of a civil recovery order, in circumstances where a criminal disposal would be justified under the overriding principle that the reduction of crime is generally best served by that route, and in accordance with the public interest factors in the relevant prosecutors' Code.

5.   For illustrative purposes only, the following is a non-exhaustive list of circumstances in which use of the non-conviction based powers might be appropriate because it is not feasible to secure a conviction:

   a.   The only known criminality is overseas, and there is no extra-territorial jurisdiction to pursue a criminal case in the courts of England & Wales or Northern Ireland.

   b.   There is no identifiable living suspect who is within the jurisdiction or realistically capable of being brought within the jurisdiction.

   c.   Proceeds of crime can be identified but cannot be linked to any individual suspect or offence.

   d.   A law enforcement authority considers that an investigation could not generate sufficient evidence to create a realistic prospect of conviction.

   e.   A criminal investigation has been conducted but the prosecuting authority considers that there is insufficient evidence to create a realistic prospect of conviction.

   f.   A prosecution has been conducted but has not resulted in a conviction.

6.   Again for illustrative purposes only, the following is a non-exhaustive list of circumstances in which a conviction is feasible, but use of the non conviction-based powers might better serve the overall public interest:

   a.   Using non-conviction based powers better meets an urgent need to take action to prevent or stop offending which is causing immediate harm to the public, even though this might limit the availability of evidence for a future prosecution.

   b.   It is not practicable to investigate all of those with a peripheral involvement in the criminality, and a strategic approach must be taken in order to achieve a manageable and successful prosecution.

    c.   Civil recovery represents a better deployment of resources to target someone with significant property which cannot be explained by legitimate income.

    d.   The offender is being prosecuted in another jurisdiction and is expected to receive a sentence that reflects the totality of the offending, so the public interest does not require a prosecution in this country.

7.   These are examples, and are not intended to include all of the circumstances in which the non conviction-based powers may be used. Every case is different, and must be decided by the relevant authority on its own facts. SOCA is able to seek advice from the relevant prosecuting authority before making a decision, where necessary.

8.   In using the non conviction-based powers, relevant authorities must have regard to, and seek to minimise, any potential prejudice to a related or potential criminal investigation or criminal proceedings. So far as it is practicable to do so, the relevant authority should:

    a.   Liaise with any relevant law enforcement and/or prosecuting authorities before exercising any of its operational functions (other than the seizure of cash), in order to enquire whether doing so would prejudice a criminal investigation or criminal proceedings, and give due weight to any advice so received;

    b.   Keep under review the extent to which taking, continuing or refraining from any course of action has a potential to prejudice a criminal investigation or criminal proceedings and avoid such prejudice where possible; and

    c.   Ensure where possible that information relevant to a criminal investigation or criminal proceedings is disclosed to the relevant law enforcement or prosecution authority at the earliest practical opportunity.

9.   This guidance does not prohibit a criminal investigation by a law enforcement authority being carried out at the same time as a civil recovery and/or tax investigation. Nor does it prevent civil recovery and/or tax proceedings being instituted where a criminal investigation by a law enforcement authority is being carried out at the same time into unrelated criminality, subject to the duty on relevant authorities to seek to minimise prejudice to criminal investigations and proceedings. Similarly this guidance does not prohibit criminal proceedings being instituted or carried on by a prosecuting authority at the same time as a civil recovery and/or tax investigation is carried out.

10.   In no circumstances may criminal and civil/tax proceedings be carried on at the same time in relation to the same criminality. Where criminal proceedings have been stayed by a court, or cannot progress for example because the defendant has absconded, they are not being carried on for the purposes of this prohibition.

11. A relevant authority may agree to accept a reduced sum in satisfaction of a civil recovery claim if satisfied that:

  a.   The sum is reasonable, having regard to all relevant circumstances including the chances of recovering the full amount claimed and the time and public funds likely to be expended in attempting to do so; and

  b.   Accepting the reduced sum would not damage public confidence.

Appendix 5   Guidance for Prosecutors on the Discretion to Instigate Confiscation Proceedings

Introduction

This document provides guidance to prosecutors in order to assist them in deciding whether or not to instigate confiscation proceedings against a defendant. Although following a request by a prosecutor, the courts no longer hold a discretion whether or not to make a confiscation order against a defendant who falls within the statutory regime, the courts retain a jurisdiction to stay confiscation proceedings as an abuse of process. This jurisdiction may be invoked in order to halt proceedings which ought not to have been instigated by the prosecutor. The jurisdiction will only be exercised with "considerable caution" and is ordinarily confined to cases of "true oppression" (*R v Shabir* [2008] EWCA Crim 1809). It is important to note that if the prosecutor correctly identifies the relevant statutory regime and has properly addressed the three questions posed by the House of Lords in *R v May* [2008] 1 AC 1028, as set out in the guidance below, the question of abuse of process will rarely, if ever, arise. The guidance is divided into four sections:

(i)   The principles to be applied when determining whether a defendant's case properly falls within the relevant statutory regime for confiscation.

(ii)   Two examples of how the principles apply to particular sets of facts.

(iii)   The exercise of the prosecutor's discretion.

(iv)   Some examples of when it may be inappropriate for prosecutors to decide to instigate confiscation proceedings.

The principles to be applied when determining whether a defendant's case properly falls within the relevant statutory regime for confiscation.

The possibility of an application for a confiscation order being made should be considered at the earliest opportunity, so that appropriate court orders (such as restraint orders) can be obtained and evidence gathered by financial investigators.

397

Before deciding whether to instigate confiscation proceedings, prosecutors should first examine the facts of the case closely in order to determine the correct statutory regime and to assess whether the statutory preconditions for the making of a confiscation order are met.

In making this assessment in a particular benefit case, prosecutors should consider the three questions posed by the House of Lords in the case of *May*:

   (i)   Has the defendant (D) benefited from relevant criminal conduct?

   (ii)   If so, what is the value of the benefit D has so obtained?

   (iii)   What sum is recoverable from D?

Prosecutors should pay particular attention to the endnote to the case, which provides guidance to the court as to the approach to be taken in confiscation proceedings:

> '(1) The legislation is intended to deprive defendants of the benefit they have gained from relevant criminal conduct, whether or not they have retained such benefit, within the limits of their available means. It does not provide for confiscation in the sense understood by schoolchildren and others, but nor does it operate by way of fine. The benefit gained is the total value of the property or advantage obtained, not the defendant's net profit after deduction of expenses or any amounts payable to co-conspirators.

> (2) The court should proceed by asking the three questions posed above: (i) Has the defendant (D) benefited from relevant criminal conduct? (ii) If so, what is the value of the benefit D has so obtained? (iii) What sum is recoverable from D? Where issues of criminal lifestyle arise the questions must be modified. These are separate questions calling for separate answers, and the questions and answers must not be elided.

> (3) In addressing these questions the court must first establish the facts as best it can on the material available, relying as appropriate on the statutory assumptions. In very many cases the factual findings made will be decisive.

> (4) In addressing the questions the court should focus very closely on the language of the statutory provision in question in the context of the statute and in the light of any statutory definition. The language used is not arcane or obscure and any judicial gloss or exegesis should be viewed with caution. Guidance should ordinarily be sought in the statutory language rather than in the proliferating case law.

> (5) In determining, under the 2002 Act, whether D has obtained property or a pecuniary advantage and, if so, the value of any property or advantage so obtained, the court should (subject to any relevant statutory definition) apply ordinary common law principles to the facts as found. The exercise of this jurisdiction involves no departure from familiar rules governing entitlement and ownership. While the answering of the third question calls for inquiry into

the financial resources of D at the date of the determination, the answering of the first two questions plainly calls for a historical inquiry into past transactions.

(6) D ordinarily obtains property if in law he owns it, whether alone or jointly, which will ordinarily connote a power of disposition or control, as where a person directs a payment or conveyance of property to someone else. He ordinarily obtains a pecuniary advantage if (among other things) he evades a liability to which he is personally subject. Mere couriers or custodians or other very minor contributors to an offence, rewarded by a specific fee and having no interest in the property or the proceeds of sale, are unlikely to be found to have obtained that property. It may be otherwise with money launderers.'

Further consideration of the three statutory questions is set out in the following paragraphs.

Has the defendant (D) benefited from relevant criminal conduct?

The first question for prosecutors to ask is whether the defendant has "benefited" from his criminal conduct within the meaning of the relevant Act. In considering the answer to this question, prosecutors should focus on the language of the relevant statutory provisions. So, for example, when dealing with the Proceeds of Crime Act 2002, "*a person benefits from conduct if he obtains property as a result of or in connection with the conduct*": section 76(4).

There can be no substitute for direct reference to the relevant statutory provisions and to the judgments of the House of Lords in *May* (in particular, on this question, paragraphs 10–19), *Jennings* and *Green* (and subsequent Court of Appeal cases). However, three important statements of principle emerge from these House of Lords decisions and subsequent Court of Appeal decisions:

(i) For confiscation purposes, a defendant will generally only obtain property if in law he has an interest in the property and will only benefit from a pecuniary advantage, if he evades a liability to which he is personally subject. So a defendant convicted of being knowingly concerned in the fraudulent evasion of an excise duty for his role in assisting in the distribution of smuggled cigarettes on which no duty had been paid did not obtain a pecuniary advantage, because the relevant excise duty regulations did not extend liability to those in the defendant's position (*R v Chambers* [2008] EWCA Crim 2467).

(ii) Where a defendant is a member of a long-standing conspiracy to defraud, but only joined the conspiracy on the day on which the police brought it to an end (on which day the conspiracy did not benefit from its criminal conduct), the defendant has not benefited (*R v Olubitan* [2004] 3 Cr App R (S) 70). The provisions relating to "benefit" in the Criminal Justice Act 1988, as amended, are "*not to be construed so that a person may be held to have obtained property or derived a pecuniary advantage when a proper view of the evidence demonstrates that he has not in fact done so*" per May LJ, paragraph 25). These comments apply equally to the Proceeds of Crime Act 2002.

(iii) The mere fact that a defendant is more than a "minor contributor" to an offence in which property is obtained is not sufficient to establish that the defendant himself obtained the property. As the House of Lords said in *CPS v Jennings* (at paragraph 14):

> 'A person's acts may contribute significantly to property (as defined in the Act) being obtained without his obtaining it. But under section 71(4) a person benefits from an offence if he obtains property as a result of or in connection with its commission, and his benefit is the value of the property so obtained, which must be read as meaning "obtained by him".'

If so, what is the value of the benefit D has so obtained?

If the prosecutor concludes that a particular defendant has benefited from conduct, the next question to consider is the value of that benefit. Again, there is no substitute for direct reference to the relevant statutory provisions, and to the judgments of the House of Lords in *May* (in particular, on this question, to paragraphs 20–34), *Jennings* and *Green* (and subsequent Court of Appeal cases). However, four important statements of principle emerge from these House of Lords decisions.

(i) Section 71(4) of the Criminal Justice Act 1988 (and section 76 of the Proceeds of Crime Act 2002) calls for an essentially factual enquiry: what is the value of the property obtained? Where a defendant applies £10,000 of tainted money as a down-payment on a £250,000 house, legitimately borrowing the remainder, "*it cannot plausibly be said that he has obtained the house as a result of or in connection with the commission of his offence*" (see *May*, paragraph 26).

(ii) A defendant who obtains a pecuniary advantage (or property) by deception and then uses some of the proceeds of his crime to pay an accomplice benefits to the total value of pecuniary advantage (or property) obtained. The value of his benefit is unaffected by the payments made to the accomplice, because what matters is what the defendant obtains, not what he retains (*R v Patel* [2000] 2 Cr App R (S) 10). This is consistent with the approach to be taken in drug trafficking cases where no account is taken of the defendant's costs: a defendant's benefit is his gross rather than net profit.

(iii) Where more than one defendant has been convicted for his role in a criminal enterprise, the court will have to consider the benefit attributable to each defendant. In deciding this, the court must consider the capacity in which each defendant receives the proceeds of crime. Where the proceeds of crime are received jointly by more than one defendant, the benefit to each defendant is the full amount of the proceeds received: apportionment in a case of joint receipt is not permitted by statute. Where there is no evidence one way or the other whether the proceeds were obtained jointly by the defendants, the court is entitled to divide the proceeds by the number of conspirators, and declare the benefit figure in that sum (*R v Gibbons* [2003] 2 Cr App R (S) 169).

(iv)   Where defendants have not jointly obtained benefit, but there has been a disposal by one member of a criminal enterprise to another who knowingly receives it, each is treated as the recipient of a benefit to the extent of the value of the property which has come into the possession of each of them. The amount of the benefit a defendant obtains is not affected by the amount which might be obtained by others to whom he transfers any part of the benefit (*R v Sharma* [2006] Cr App R (S) 416).

What sum is recoverable from D?

This is an important stage in the court's decision making, but the answer to the question will be determined by the facts, so that the problems which arise are not, in the main, questions of principle. The relevance of the question to the prosecutor's decision is however apparent. If it appears that a defendant has no assets with which to pay any confiscation order, prosecutors will have to consider whether it would be in the public interest to seek a confiscation order against that defendant.

In order that the above three questions can be properly considered, it is imperative that those responsible for the criminal investigation should be made aware of the importance of establishing the role of a particular defendant in a criminal enterprise, so that the case for confiscation can be presented as clearly as possible.

It is equally important that any basis of plea sets out the defendant's role and that the prosecutor makes clear to the Court whether there are any assertions made by the defendant, which it cannot dispute for the purposes of sentence, but that may be contradicted by information that subsequently becomes available in the confiscation proceedings.

If there is a trial, prosecutors should ensure that, so far as possible, the evidence establishes the precise role of each defendant in the criminal enterprise. As the evidence from the criminal investigation, the financial investigation and the evidence from any trial is revealed, prosecutors should keep under review whether confiscation is appropriate in a particular case. By the end of a trial, evidence which originally provided a firm basis for a decision to instigate proceedings may have been shown to be unreliable. Equally, evidence which originally suggested that a confiscation order ought not to be sought may have been superseded by evidence which leads to the opposite conclusion.

Two examples of how the principles apply to particular sets of facts.

The Court of Appeal has applied the principles found in *May*, *Jennings* and *Green* in a number of recent cases. Two of these cases are particularly helpful as illustrations of the application of the principles: *R v Sivaraman* [2009] 1 Cr App R (S) 80 and *R v Allpress* [2009] EWCA Crim 8.

R v Sivaraman

In *Sivaraman*, the defendant, an employee in a fuel outlet, had pleaded guilty to a conspiracy to evade excise duty. The defendant and the proprietor of the fuel outlet had conspired to buy "red" diesel, to remove the dye, and to sell it on as if it were "normal" diesel. By this means the proprietor obtained a pecuniary advantage arising out of the fact that "red" diesel attracted a lower level of duty than "normal" diesel. The defendant's part in the conspiracy was to accept deliveries of "red" diesel in the course of his employment: he was clearly more than a "*very minor contributor*" to the conspiracy. The total pecuniary advantage obtained in the course of the conspiracy was £128,520 but the defendant had received payments of £15,000 for the part he played. The benefit figure attributable to the defendant was found by the Crown Court to be £128,520.

Applying the principles found in *May*, *Green* and *Jennings* to the facts in *Sivaraman* the Court of Appeal held that the Crown Court had erred and that the correct value of the defendant's benefit was £15,000, because (per Toulson LJ, paragraph 15):

> "the proposition that a person acting purely in the capacity of employee, who receives a consignment of illicit fuel on behalf of his employer, and who, as a reward for doing so, received only an enhanced wage or cash payment, must necessarily as a matter of law be taken to profit to the same extent as his employer does from the purchase and sale of the consignment is unsound."

The reason for this conclusion was that the question whether or not a defendant had obtained property was not determined simply by considering whether the defendant was "*more than a very minor contributor to the offence*". On the contrary, applying the principles of *May*, *Green* and *Jennings*, since the defendant was not a joint purchaser, but rather was an employee, he did not obtain a benefit to the total value of pecuniary advantage obtained, as he had incurred no liability under the relevant regulations. The defendant's benefit was restricted to the property that he had obtained, namely the value of the payment he received for his part in the conspiracy, which was £15,000.

The Court of Appeal stressed the importance of the findings of fact made by the lower courts and of emphasised the need "*to apply the words of the statute in as commonsensical a way as possible*" (paragraph 13). This guidance should be borne in mind by prosecutors.

Prosecutors should also note the comments of the Court in relation to the three issues (i) determining a defendant's criminal liability, (ii) determining a defendant's culpability and therefore the appropriate sentence and (iii) determining the benefit attributable to a defendant are distinct issues which call for different considerations. On this, the court said:

(i) "Conspirators are criminally liable for the acts of their confederates done within the scope of their employment; but, when considering questions of confiscation the focus of the inquiry is on the benefit gained by the relevant defendant, whether individually or jointly" (paragraph 20).

(ii)   Similarly, "the greater the involvement of a defendant in a conspiracy, the greater will be the appropriate level of punishment. But it does not follow that the greater the involvement the greater the resulting benefit to that defendant. Within the statutory definitions contained in the Act, what benefit a defendant gained is a question of fact" (paragraph 19).

R v Allpress, R v Symeou, R v Casal, R v Morris, R v Martin [2009] EWCA Crim 8

In this case the Court of Appeal considered a question which had been left open by the House of Lords in *May*, namely how benefit ought to be calculated where the relevant criminal conduct was money laundering. In reaching its conclusions, the Court of Appeal emphasised the importance of the findings of fact in any particular case.

In *R v Allpress*, the defendant had carried £156,210 of money representing the proceeds of drug trafficking to various destinations in Europe, on behalf of a man named Michael. She was paid £3,600 by way of costs and payments. She pleaded guilty to a money laundering offence, contrary to section 50(1)(a) of the Drug Trafficking Act 1994. The central question for the court was whether the defendant's benefit was the value of the money couriered, or the value of the costs and payments received. The Court of Appeal concluded that the general principles found in *May*, *Green* and *Jennings* were applicable to money launderers. Consequently, the Court said (at paragraph 80) that "*if D's only role in relation to property connected with his criminal conduct, whether in the form of cash or otherwise, was to act as a courier on behalf of another, such property does not amount to property obtained by him within the meaning of POCA 2002 s80(1) or CJA 1988 s71(4) or to "payment or other reward" within in the meaning of DTA 1994 s2(3)*". Consequently the benefit figure for this defendant was £3,600.

In *Symeou* and *Casal* the defendants had also acted as couriers of cash which was the proceeds of drug trafficking. It followed from the Court's analysis of the approach to be taken in relation to cash couriers that in each case the appropriate benefit figure was the sum of money received by way of payments or expenses, rather than the value of the money couriered.

In *Morris*, the defendant had been a solicitor who had laundered the proceeds of a VAT fraud perpetrated by a man named Woolley. The proceeds of the VAT fraud (just short of £8 million) had been paid into the defendant's law firm's bank account over which the defendant had sole operational control. From here the money was transferred by the defendant, for the benefit of Woolley, to various recipients. The defendant was convicted of three money laundering offences, contrary to section 93A(1)(a) of the Criminal Justice Act 1988 and confiscation proceedings were instigated. The judge at first instance had found that the defendant was acting as more than a bare trustee of the funds held in the law firm's account. On the facts, the defendant's control over the money was such that he had obtained the money for the purposes of the Criminal Justice Act 1988. The benefit figure was therefore just short of £8 million. The Court of Appeal upheld the judge's ruling, and considered that the judge's findings of fact were critical. On the facts, the defendant had been more than bare trustee of the money. Since he had control of the account into which the money was paid, the starting point was that he owned the money. His benefit was therefore in the sum of the money laundered.

In *Martin*, the defendant had acted as a custodian for sums of money which derived from his brother's criminal conduct. The defendant pleaded guilty to possession of criminal property contrary to section 329(1)(c) of the Proceeds of Crime Act 2002. The Court of Appeal found that a mere custodian of cash, who had received no direct or indirect personal benefit, ought to be treated in the same way as a courier of cash. It followed that the defendant had not benefited from his criminal conduct.

The exercise of the prosecutor's discretion.

Parliament, by enacting the confiscation legislation in the way that it did, intended to create a scheme to ensure that offenders did not benefit from their offending. A proper application of the statute can produce "draconian results" (per Lord Rodger in *R v Cadman Smith [2002] 1 Cr. App. R. 35, HL*). Furthermore, Parliament's decision to remove the Court's discretion not to make a confiscation order was a deliberate measure designed to strengthen, and not weaken, the legislative framework for confiscation.

Prosecutors have a duty to carry out their functions in accordance with the intention of Parliament, but it is important that they remember that they retain a discretion whether or not to instigate confiscation proceedings. In considering how to exercise their discretion, prosecutors need to consider their role as ministers of justice and should remember the three legitimate aims of confiscation set out in *R v Rezvi, R v Benjafield* [2003] 1 AC 1099, namely to *"punish convicted offenders, to deter the commission of further offences and to reduce the profits available to fund further criminal enterprises"* (per Lord Steyn, paragraph 14).

In general benefit cases, the court is concerned with proceeds arising from offending beyond that for which the defendant has been convicted in the current proceedings and a proper application of the assumptions may result in a confiscation order that is massively greater than the defendant's benefit from particular offending. In particular benefit cases, however, prosecutors must first apply the principles from *May* set out above and answer the three questions and determine that the defendant has benefited from his particular benefit; the approximate amount of that benefit; and how much is likely to be recoverable.

The prosecutor should consider in each case whether the statutory regime would operate in a way that would be oppressive. Examples of when it may be inappropriate for prosecutors to instigate confiscation proceedings are set out below.

Although following a request by a prosecutor, the courts no longer hold a discretion whether or not to make a confiscation order against a defendant who falls within the statutory regime, the courts retain a jurisdiction to stay confiscation proceedings as an abuse of process. This jurisdiction may be invoked in order to halt proceedings which ought not to have been instigated by the prosecutor. The jurisdiction will only be exercised with "considerable caution" and is ordinarily confined to cases of "true oppression" (*R v Shabir [2008] EWCA Crim 1809*). It is important to note that if the guidance set out above is followed, the question of abuse of process will rarely, if ever, arise.

Some examples of when it may be inappropriate for prosecutors to decide to instigate confiscation proceedings.

While the categories of the abuse jurisdiction are not closed, the Court of Appeal has identified three situations in which it is legitimate for proceedings to be stayed.

The first situation is where the Crown has reneged on an earlier agreement not to proceed. As a matter of common sense, it is inappropriate to proceed in such cases.

The second situation is, in a simple benefit case, where the defendant has voluntarily paid full compensation to the victim or victims, or is ready, willing and able immediately to repay all of the victims to the full amount of their losses, and has not otherwise profited from his crime (*R v Morgan* [2009] 1 Cr App R (S) 60). In such cases it may be inappropriate for the prosecutor to instigate confiscation proceeding but this will require an independent judgment on the facts of each case. A decision one way or the other must be properly reasoned and it is advisable to keep a clear and accurate record of the decision.

The third situation calls for the most careful consideration by prosecutors. This situation arises where proper application of the relevant statute to a defendant's case would, if the court were asked to proceed to confiscation, compel the court to find that property obtained in the most part legitimately by the defendant, and to which the defendant would have been entitled but for his criminal conduct, must be treated as benefit. An example of this situation arose in the case of *R v Shabir* [2009] 1 Cr App (S) 84. In that case the defendant was a pharmacist who had submitted false, inflated, claims to the NHS. The total amount obtained by deception was approximately £179,000, but the defendant had been entitled to most of the money claimed, except £464. In that case it was held to be inappropriate to proceed to confiscation, but such examples will be rare and confined to cases of "*true oppression*" (per Hughes LJ, at paragraph 23). In order to establish oppression and thus abuse of process it is clearly not sufficient that the effect of confiscation will be to extract from a defendant a sum greater than his net profit from crime. Moreover, in general benefit cases (where the lifestyle provisions apply), it may be perfectly proper for a confiscation order to be "*massively greater*" than a defendant's benefit from particular offending (*R v Shabir*, per Hughes LJ, at paragraph 27). Any injustice as perceived by the court can, in any event, be overcome by the court declining to apply the lifestyle presumptions (the relevant provision in the Proceeds of Crime Act 2002 is section 10(6)). As in the cases set out above, every case will have to be considered on its own facts, but a decision one way or the other must be properly reasoned and it is advisable to keep a clear and accurate record of the decision.

In addition a fourth situation exists which might be susceptible to a challenge by a defendant to stay confiscation proceedings as an abuse of process, namely where a defendant has obtained paid employment by a false representation to his employer. The defendant's wages may be his benefit (*R v Carter* [2006] EWCA Crim 416), but some cases will arise where the link between the criminality and the receipt of payment from dishonestly obtained employment is too remote, for example, where had the representation been corrected, the employment would have continued, or where after many years of otherwise lawful employment, a relatively minor previous conviction is discovered.

CPS
28 May 2009

Index